Tom Burns, Elcio Cornelsen, Volker Jaeckel, Luiz Gustavo Vieira (eds.)

Revisiting 20th Century Wars

*New readings of modern armed conflicts
in literature and image media*

Tom Burns, Elcio Cornelsen, Volker Jaeckel, Luiz Gustavo Vieira (eds.)

REVISITING 20TH CENTURY WARS

*New readings of modern armed conflicts
in literature and image media*

ibidem-Verlag
Stuttgart

Bibliografische Information der Deutschen Nationalbibliothek
Die Deutsche Nationalbibliothek verzeichnet diese Publikation in der Deutschen Nationalbibliografie; detaillierte bibliografische Daten sind im Internet über http://dnb.d-nb.de abrufbar.

Bibliographic information published by the Deutsche Nationalbibliothek
Die Deutsche Nationalbibliothek lists this publication in the Deutsche Nationalbibliografie; detailed bibliographic data are available in the Internet at http://dnb.d-nb.de.

Cover picture: © icholakov - Fotolia.com

∞

Gedruckt auf alterungsbeständigem, säurefreien Papier
Printed on acid-free paper

ISBN-13: 978-3-8382-0377-5

© *ibidem*-Verlag
Stuttgart 2012

Alle Rechte vorbehalten

Das Werk einschließlich aller seiner Teile ist urheberrechtlich geschützt. Jede Verwertung außerhalb der engen Grenzen des Urheberrechtsgesetzes ist ohne Zustimmung des Verlages unzulässig und strafbar. Dies gilt insbesondere für Vervielfältigungen, Übersetzungen, Mikroverfilmungen und elektronische Speicherformen sowie die Einspeicherung und Verarbeitung in elektronischen Systemen.

All rights reserved. No part of this publication may be reproduced, stored in or introduced into a retrieval system, or transmitted, in any form, or by any means (electronic, mechanical, photocopying, recording or otherwise) without the prior written permission of the publisher. Any person who does any unauthorized act in relation to this publication may be liable to criminal prosecution and civil claims for damages.

Printed in Germany

Contents

Introduction	7
The American Narrative of the Second World War *Thomas LaBorie Burns*	13
Dead on a High Hill: Poetry from the Korean War. *W.D. Ehrhart*	31
The dark song of the night of war. António Lobo Antunes' *Os Cus de Judas*. *Olinda Kleiman*	49
War Imagery. On the First Edition of Ernst Jünger's *Storm of Steel*. *Oliver Lubrich*	71
Through an Enemy Land: On Space and (In)visibility in Euclides da Cunha's *Os sertões*. *Javier Uriarte*	101
Collective Traumas and Common Memories: the Colonial War of Portugal in Africa and European violence of the Twentieth Century. *Roberto Vecchi*	119
Hunters turned into Prey: Predation in Twentieth-Century War Literature *Luiz Gustavo Leitão Vieira*	133
Die finstere Seite des Herzens. Zur Migration von Bildern der religiösen Profanation. *Vicente Sánchez Biosca*	151
Das Eigene und das Fremde im Balkan-Film über den Krieg im ehemaligen Jugoslawien *Elcio Cornelsen*	181
Kampf um Authentizität. Autobiographische Berichte und Sachbücher über den Krieg in Afghanistan *Helmut P. E. Galle*	195

Le vrai problème n'est pas de raconter – Jorge Semprún und das 20. Jahrhundert
Ursula Hennigfeld 213

La Gran Guerra Europea: Germanophobie und Schrecken des Krieges in Romanen von Blasco Ibañez und ihren Verfilmungen
Volker Jaeckel 237

Schuld in Kempowskis Echolot
Valéria Sabrina Pereira 259

Introduction

In 2007, scholars at the Federal University of Minas Gerais, Brazil, long devoted to the analysis of literary representations of war, created a permanent space where students, professors, and any interested party, could gather, discuss, and study the subject. Since then, NEGUE - Núcleo de Estudos de Guerra e Literatura (Center for Studies of War and Literature) has organized several lectures and seminars with Brazilian and foreign scholars; produced, through its permanent members, six master's theses and one PhD dissertation; and published, in addition to scores of papers by its members, one collection of essays entitled *Literatura e Guerra* (Literature and War). With the publication of this volume on twentieth-century war literature, the group intends to cross national frontiers and inaugurate an international dialogue with those also interested in this hardly-defined, urgent, and yet fascinating field we call war literature. Let us begin by clarifying the qualifications just mentioned.

Not only war literature, but war itself is a hardly defined word. Specialists such as anthropologists, sociologists, archeologists, and the like, have had a hard time pinpointing what war really is. If, on one hand, a strict definition, in a single sentence or paragraph, may fail to contemplate and encompass the various and multifaceted aspects armed conflicts have shown throughout history; on the other hand, a broad definition will end up accepting any local feud or rivalry as war. Organized violence is not war. Definitions of war risk being commonplace, lacking specificity or scientific rigor. Perhaps the best way to understand what war is lies in isolating its features, what Robert O'Connell calls a "defining structure"[1]: wars display a) premeditation and planning – war is not a momentary emotional response and requires elements of logistic such as supplies and mobility; b) of collective nature – war deals with societal issues, to be solved through force; c) direction – war is led or conducted by some form of leadership or government; d) willingness – combatants are willing to get engaged in time-consuming actions that imply risks and are willing to kill each other; e) result – war, at least theoretically, must bring about either positive or negative effects, of a certain duration, not only immediate gain. It goes without saying that not all wars in history have displayed all features above. Some wars have been triggered by the whims of dictators who aimed at nothing but their own personal benefit; some men have fought unwillingly, as slaves or conscripts.

However, as a limiting framework, O'Connell's set of characteristics does help us better envisage what we are talking about when we say "war".

The origins of human war may be traced back to seven or eight thousand years ago in the form of what we may call organized theft when two distinct ways of life clashed. As human activities split into two different communities, agricultural and pastoral, certain nomads, devoted to the rearing of cattle, started raiding agricultural settlements. These settlements, in turn, started organizing themselves for protection and raiding other agricultural communities – why not attack weaker parties in search for food, slaves and cattle if this is easier than work, provided you are willing to kill in order to obtain such gains? Thus war is born. The only animal, other than man, that wages war is the ant. Certain species of ants engage themselves in organized, violent confrontations against other creatures in order to acquire long-term benefits. However, the ant's war is inherent, written into their genes – the war of the ants has never been subjected to change. Man's war is utterly different. Human war is a cultural institution, meaning that it has changed over time and space and has been shaped by the cultures that wage them. Eastern cultures, such as China and Japan, favor limited, traditional wars of deception, the ultimate goal being to win without firing a single shot. Ancient cultures of the Americas, such as the Aztecs, and aboriginal peoples, adopt ritualized confrontations aiming at dominance and capturing victims for sacrifices rather than killing the enemy. The model of war we westerners are most familiar with (and tend to view as "fair") is what Victor Davis Hanson has dubbed "the western way of war". The western way of war, conceived in Ancient Greece by the city-states and fought by the hoplites, centers around an open, decisive, short-lived, murderous confrontation that aims at total victory, the total obliteration of the enemy: the battle.

The study and theoretically-grounded analysis of war representation is evidently urgent when we think of how recurrent and encompassing this cultural institution has become. Focusing on the twentieth-century alone, and leaving aside the two most murderous events in human history, i.e. the two world wars, more than 160 armed conflicts have killed over 50,000,000 people since August 1945, that is, *after* the most deadly weapon ever invented was used in Hiroshima and Nagasaki. For more than a hundred years, not a single day has passed without a war going on in one part of the planet. Moreover, the conflicts of the past century were neither the business of a warrior elite nor a restricted affair settled in a matter of hours on a battlefield. Civilians, who were 5% of the casualties in the First World War, responded for 90%

of the victims in the 1990's. Terms such as "front", "rear", "non-combatant", "open city", and the like, have been rendered meaningless in modern technological wars. Engagements such as Verdun or Stalingrad lasted for whole months, claiming tens, sometimes hundreds, of thousands of casualties.

Any study on the subject of war, no matter for what field of human activity, must acknowledge that war is as hideous as it is fascinating. It is naïve and untruthful to deny war's allure over people, which is not the same as advocating in favor of war or viewing it under a positive light. War fascinates because it is an extremely relevant event, affecting millions of lives, shaping the world we live in for millennia; besides, veterans often claim that no other experience in life is as intense as combat, that you never feel as alive as when you risk your life in battle. War, in an apparent contradiction, is as attractive as it is repulsive. War's importance and appeal become evident when we think that the first works of the field we now know as history are about war (Herodotus' *Histories* and Thucydides' *History of the Peloponnesian War*); that some of the world's greatest works of art take war as their subject (Beethoven's symphony "Eroica", Goya's painting "3 de Mayo de 1808", Picasso's huge "Guernica", Coppola's "Apocalypse Now", to name a few); that Freud developed some of his groundbreaking concepts and theory under the influence of, and during, World War I; that medicine sees great development during war, with new medications and practices appearing in response to combat situations; that many of the inventions we enjoy in peaceful life first appeared, or were perfected, in wartime.

As for the field of literature, war and story-telling have undoubtedly walked hand-in-hand for millennia. It may be argued that, except for the theme of love, no other aspect of human experience has been more influential or more recurrent in literature than armed conflicts. From Greek epic to medieval sagas, from Roman epic to plays, from lyric poetry to postmodern novels, countless authors seem to agree with Ernest Hemingway when he claims that war is "the writer's best subject…since it groups the maximum of material and speeds up the action and brings out all sorts of stuff that normally you have to wait a lifetime to get".[2]

The 13 essays herein featured, by internationally recognized specialists of eight countries and different areas of study, bear witness to the urgency, fascination, and difficulty of definition of war representation. Selected with a view to providing a broad canvas of current scholarship in the field, the texts contemplate a wide array of literary genres and of modes of representation: the novel, the film, the memoir, the epic, the journalistic account, the poem, the autobiographical novel, the historiographic narrative are all treated. It concerns a subjective, but almost representative selection of articles on representation of bellicose acts in modern times.

The wide range of wars treated in these essays starts with the Canudos Civil War in the Brazilian state of Bahia in 1896-97, including new perceptions and interpretations of World War I, the Spanish Civil War of 1936-39, the Holocaust, World War II, the Korean War, the wars in the former Portuguese colonies of Africa and the Balkan Wars of the last decade of the 20th century and closes with the current war in Afghanistan, which began in 2001. The wars treated, although having different origins, like national pride, territorial expansion, fanatic religiousness, ethnic and racial conflicts, great social differences, the process of decolonization and terrorism, have one thing in common, which is their significant and constant repercussion in the print and broadcast media over a long period of time. Therefore, these modern wars have frequently been the object of new readings and reinterpretations until our days. The history of these wars could not have been written without the development of journalism, mass media and new technologies of war reportages in the 20th century.

However, this book provides neither a chronological sequence nor a thematic arrangement, and it is not concerned with each conflict's supposed historical relevance either, since it has been devised as an outlook on the variety of the research now underway in different countries, on different topics. Hence, a paper on Second World War novel may be followed by one about Korean War Poetry; a comparison between types of combat follows an analysis of literary representations of colonial wars in Africa, and so on. As professor Kate McLoughlin states in her introduction to *The Cambridge Companion to War Writing*, "it is vital that techniques and tools are found to represent war accurately: such representations might not stop future wars, but it can at least keep the record straight".[3] Such has been our goal with this publication: look for the tools and techniques, help represent war accurately, keep the record straight, for if we may lack the power of preventing war, we must at least respect its countless victims.

Finally, we would like to thank all the people who contributed to the success of this volume; our special thanks will be to Arthur Guerra, Sue Bähring, Sylvia Henkel for formatting and revising the essays, and last not least to Valerie Lange from Ibidem Verlag for the great support.

The Editors

[1] O'Connell, Robert.. *Ride of the second horseman – the birth and death of war.* (New York: Oxford UP, 1995), 5.
[2] Hemingway, Ernest. *Ernest Hemingway Selected Letters 1917-1961.* Carlos Baker (ed.). (London: Granada, 1981), 176.
[3] McLoughlin, Kate. *The Cambridge Companion to War Writing.* (New York: Cambridge UP, 2009), I.

The American Narrative of the Second World War

Thomas LaBorie Burns

I. Which Great War?

If the shattered, pitted, barbed-wire landscape of No-Man's Land is the most familiar image of the First World War, the "preeminent symbols of the Second World War are the concentration camp and the mushroom cloud".[1] In contrast to the Great War's relatively static positions of front lines and rear areas, the Second World War, as illustrated by the real and symbolic names of Auschwitz and Hiroshima, carried death and destruction to cities and civilian populations. This new spatial dimension, perhaps the war's most distinctive feature, had wide-ranging implications. For example, the apparently natural division of war into "a spatialization of clear gender territories" distinctive of the Great War – men at the front, women behind the lines – is disrupted in the later conflict. Along with the detritus and deprivations attendant on the bombing of civilian populations came refugees and displaced persons.[2]

Other boundaries were broken down by the Second World War. While the Great War was waged chiefly in Western Europe, the concentration camps were installed in Central and Eastern Europe and the atom bomb was dropped in Asia. This geographical extension attests to how far the mechanized violence of the Great War was amplified technologically as well as socially. And there was not only a larger theater and more adversary nations, but all branches of modern armed forces were fully engaged, most notably air corps. This war was a triumph of modern scientific management and technology, including newer, more lethal weapons, a quantitative leap in the destructive role of air-power, and the importance for both Allies and Axis states of bureaucratic organization and the techniques of mass production. If the Great War reversed the nineteenth century sense of human progress, it is a tragic irony that the Second World War reaffirmed the scientific progress of the twentieth.

For most people alive today, the Second World War is in fact the "great war", even if that title was once co-opted by the prior conflict, since, for most countries involved, it was a struggle for survival, while the price of defeat, as shown by occupied areas of Europe and the fate of the European Jews, was nothing less than "enslavement and death".[3] Even for Americans, for whom the stakes were not so high, this war also became the great war, the touchstone for the two other major wars – in Korea and

Vietnam – that have engaged American troops as sequels. As a character from one of Joseph Heller's novels says: "When people our age speak of the war it is not of Vietnam but of the one that broke out more than a half a century ago and swept in almost all the world".[4]

If the First World War solved very little, the Second presented solutions, or at least temporary ones: the economic catastrophe of the Great Depression disappeared and the west entered into a period of seemingly endless material prosperity; political democracy and Communism emerged as competing powers and ideologies organized around the US and the USSR, respectively; the old colonial empires disappeared or were weakened; and, unlike the world after 1919, with the reintegration of the former enemy states – Germany and Japan – into the economy, and what turned out to be, despite fears of nuclear holocaust, the peaceful co-existence of the two superpowers, "even the international scene was stabilized".[5]

Not only had its supreme importance in the history of the world but the sheer size and length of the war ensured that the most varied literary works about it would be written. As James Meek has commented: "The war is big, in time, in space, in cast. There's space for any genre".[6] For narrative fiction, in particular, more than half a century later, the war is still the source of an annual outpouring of both serious and popular novels. One reason is surely the ready availability of a perennial villain, the Nazi. Meek has suggested another: references to the war are familiar to readers, which means that narratives require less explanation, for "explanations are fatal to narrative".[7] To risk circularity, however, it may well be that the greater public familiarity with these references itself owes much to literary, and especially film, production. Unlike World War I, Vietnam or Korea, readers and movie-goers are familiar with the major names like Churchill, Hitler, and Stalin, and places such as Stalingrad, Dunkirk, Pearl Harbor, and Hiroshima have much stronger emotional connotations than the Somme, Verdun, Inchon, or Dien-Bien Phu...Such names have an almost legendary ring to them, evoking images, memories, notions, and concepts beyond their historical context.

As Dana Polan has argued, for example, the very expression "Pearl Harbor" evokes meanings far beyond the attack on the naval installation in Hawaii on that fateful Sunday morning in 1941. It signifies to Americans, among other things, the forcible entrance of their nation into the war after two years of hesitation, the treachery of the Japanese, and the inadequacy of American military intelligence, but also, in a more positive vein, the determination of Americans to fight back once they were attacked. It even suggests a "mediating unity" of the civilian population in response to the question "Where were you on December 7, 1941"?[8] Whatever answer you give offers a promise of national unity amongst an endless diversity of places and possible responses.

As this example shows, even the important dates were evocative after the fact. August 6, 1945, begins a new era, the Atomic Age. When June 6, 1944 (the Allied landings in Normandy) celebrated its fiftieth anniversary, it was still able to provoke strong emotions when the Germans were not invited to the ceremony, and again at the sixtieth anniversary, when they were. While Bernard Dick reminds us that a date "bears only a synechdocal relationship to an event, but in no way is it the event", he also observes that such dates are transmitted from generation to generation "as part of an accepted chronology" and so have their pedagogical uses even while they tend to reduce events to a mnemonic. Such dates and their related place names are evocative: "they jog the memory of those who were present and the imagination of those who were not".[9]

II. American Responses

Like those of their British counterparts, American attitudes toward the war were "more pragmatic and provided much less ground for the disillusionment of great romantic expectations; war was seen as an unpleasant obligation rather than an opportunity for individual heroism or male initiation rituals".[10] In fact, in the 1930s, the United States was in no mood to get into a war either. Isolationism was the prevailing public mood, partly as a result of the Great Depression, as all countries scrambled to save themselves at any perceived expense of the others. A number of "revisionist" historians in the Thirties held responsible government propaganda, bankers, war-profiteering businessmen, arms manufacturers, and the faulty guidance of world leaders. In a series of sensationalist investigations, in 1934 a congressional committee led by Gerald P. Nye of North Dakota called to account the "Merchants of Death" for the American intervention in a European war. Both the American and foreign literature of the war (the exception seems to be that which came out of Germany, which hardly contested it),[11] had also come to conclude that the intervention had been misguided. Such works as Henri Barbusse's *Under Fire* (1915), John Dos Passos' *Three Soldiers* (1921) and *USA* (1937), Ernest Hemingway's *A Farewell to Arms* (1929), and Erich Maria Remarque's *All Quiet on the Western Front* (1929) – to which might be added the non-fictional work by Walter Millius' *The Road to War* (1935) – all represented the Great War as a terrible mistake.

The official attitude of nonintervention can be seen in the US's refusal to intervene when Japan invaded Manchuria (1931), Italy invaded Ethiopia (1935), and Franco initiated the civil war in Spain (1936). As the Manchurian incident showed, however, non-intervention may have been read as a signal to aggressors that they would not be opposed by American forces, in which case neutrality may have been more damaging to the cause of peace than selective intervention, and, as the example of the war in Spain shows, it was now the Left that supported military intervention. But as events in Europe and the Far East became increasingly ominous, and the Fascist powers made bolder attacks on political and military stability, public opinion in the US began to polarize between the old isolationism and a new interventionism – two irreconcilable positions.

The isolationists were politically an extremely diverse group, made up of anti-Semites like the radio priest, Father Coughlin, pro-Axis sympathizers like Charles Lindbergh, anti-new Dealers like Herbert Hoover, Irish-Americans and other Anglophobes, but also pacifists and Midwestern Progressives like Robert LaFollette. The opposing interventionist camp contained more politically unified elements: Democrats, Jews, and anti-Fascists of varied type and origin, President Roosevelt and his close aide Harry Hopkins, Secretary of the Interior Harold C. Ickes, but also General Pershing, who commanded the AEF in the First World War. In 1940, organizations representing both of these coalitions were founded: the interventionist Committee to Defend America by Aiding the Allies, and the isolationist Committee to Defend America First ("America Firsters"), whose membership included Joseph Kennedy and John Foster Dulles. Reflecting the division in the nation, the bill in the House that extended military service by one year for draftees to expand the armed forces won by a single vote, 203 to 202.

Hampered by the strong opposition from initiating more direct interventionist policies, Roosevelt found various "arrangements" to aid the Allies, the most important of which was Lend-Lease: the provision of machines, food, and services, that eventually came to a total of 50 billion dollars, most of which was never paid back. When Lend-Lease became law in 1941, it seemed that the interventionists had the upper hand, but in the two years up to the bombing of Pearl Harbor, a fierce debate raged between intellectuals as well as other citizens. The interventionists saw the American participation in the European war as necessary to preserving the values of civilization against the barbarism represented by Nazism – in similar terms, in other words, to those that fueled the debate during the long waiting period before American intervention in the First World War.

Among Roosevelt's supporters of intervention were the Protestant thinker and social critic Reinhold Niebuhr, and the historian and cultural critic Lewis Mumford, two of the most important public intellectuals of the mid-twentieth century. Niebuhr had also strongly advocated intervention in the First World War, in the belief that Wilsonian democracy was a universal ideal. In the years preceding the Second World War, he was a major voice in persuading Christians to join the war against fascism by emphasizing the importance of justice in addition to traditional doctrines of Christian love. Mumford began his support for intervention in the late Thirties, joining Niebuhr in "realist critiques of liberal 'innocence'", and in taunting liberals for their "moral shallowness" in refusing to see the cult of power behind Fascism.[12] Mumford later changed his position after the atomic bomb was dropped on Japan, concluding that even despite the defeat of Germany, the war against Nazism "had made the democratic nations totalitarian".[13]

Despite initial opposition by the isolationists, no other major war involving American forces would inspire equally popular support. The First World War had provoked, and the Vietnam War would later provoke, vociferous opposition within American society. The attack on Pearl Harbor effectively put an end to isolationism and popular resistance. Once the US was in the war, the personal involvement of people who had relatives and loved ones serving in the Armed Forces blended nicely with the patriotic sentiment stirred by government propaganda, which aimed at the sale of war bonds and other appeals to raise money. As Paul Fussell comments: "In the absence of a credible positive ideology, motivation was always a problem and morale itself developed into one of the unique obsessions of the Allies in the Second World War".[14]

As can be seen in the examples of Niebuhr and Mumford, however, intellectuals had an ideology, or at least an anti-ideology and generally supported the national war effort, some of them directly by joining the armed forces. Novelists who served include Saul Bellow, Dashiell Hammett, James Jones, and Norman Mailer (the latter two could write important war novels), joined by major critics like Irving Howe, Clement Greenberg, and Irving Kristol. Other important figures from the world of the arts worked in government propaganda or intelligence agencies: poet Archibald

Macleish was for a time the director of the Office of Facts and Figures, which would become the Office of War Information. Playwright Robert Sherwood, novelist John P. Marquand, and filmmakers Frank Capra, John Ford, and John Huston worked for propaganda or intelligence agencies. These filmmakers were joined by the European intellectuals and entrepreneurs who had fled Nazism and would help to define the Hollywood pro-war film. Émigré and American scientists worked together in government laboratories to produce technical tools like radar for the war.[15] Fearing that German scientists would come up with a super-weapon, a large group of American and European physicists and engineers cooperated in the Manhattan Project, under the direction of the distinguished physicist J. Robert Oppenheimer, to develop the first atomic bomb, which would effectively put an end to the war.

The positive image of the Second World War as the "good" or just war, however, was challenged in revisionist historical works from the 1970s and 1980s, such as John Morton Blum's *V Was for Victory* (1976), which argued that the nation that had fought a war against racism and in the name of freedom had not segregated the Armed Forces (ended only by President Truman's order of July 26, 1943), interned Japanese-Americans, and severely restricted freedoms at home, as well as awarding defense contracts to large corporations, thus contributing to the postwar process of economic monopolization. The position of women during the war proved similarly ambiguous. With so many men in the armed forces, women in both Great Britain and the US benefited by the availability of work outside the home: "From a feminist point of view, in sociological terms, the wars provide the most obvious contradictions of certain assumptions about women's innate capacities".[16] Yet, in both cases, women were subjected to propaganda urging them to return to the home after the war was over to make room for the men in the workplace.

It has also been claimed that, among the American armed forces, most men, with the exception of some Jews, did not fight for ideological reasons, regarding participation in the war like their British counterparts, as a job to be done, without much discussion of what the fighting was for.[17] Blum argues that Americans had no clear idea of why they were fighting but had gone to war after the attack on Pearl Harbor. What enthusiasm there was can be attributed more to an ideology of myth than historical circumstances: soldiers fought for "the folk culture of the national past, ebullient still in their own day". Unlike the imagery of the Civil War and the Great War, in which freeing the oppressed and making the world safe for democracy were, respectively, the inspirational themes, the men of World War II "fought for blueberry pie and blond sweethearts, for the family farm and for Main Street, for perseverance and decency – for Americanism as a people's way of being".[18]

Although this statement neatly sums up many Hollywood war movies, which were themselves important sources of inspiration and propaganda, there is still a powerful collective memory of the Second World War as one that was fundamentally different from earlier and later wars. This view has been recorded in many of the testimonies collected in Studs Terkel's *The 'Good War': An Oral History of World War II* (1984): "The dedication and patriotism of the American people that was evident in World War Two just wasn't there in the others", according to a former general, and his sentiment is echoed by a number of other people, men and women, combatants and non-combatants. The attitude of the Italian-American Anthony Scarioni, who fought for the OSS with the partisans in Italy, was not uncommon: "We weren't very political, but we'd sit around the fire in our villa and argue about the war. Would it mean a better America? Would it mean an end to injustice? We were just learning about the Holocaust. We really believed in this war".[19] In the end, Fascism was defeated, the Depression ended, and the United States emerged, in contrast to an exhausted Europe, as a nation rich, powerful and unharmed. The American people felt united for perhaps the last time, and in recent years an American myth of the "great generation", the generation that fought the war, has arisen in the US, perhaps also as a result of the debacle of Vietnam.

Nevertheless, Paul Fussell has also challenged the image of the war as the Good or Just War, arguing that patriotic motives have been exaggerated: "For the past fifty years the Allied war has been sanitized and romanticized almost beyond recognition by the sentimental, the loony patriotic, the ignorant and the bloodthirsty".[20] The war claimed more civilians than soldiers and "was indescribably cruel and insane":

> It was not until the Second World War had enacted all its madness that one could realize how near Victorian social and ethical norms the First World War really was. Unthinkable then would have been the Second War's unsurrendering Japanese, its suicides and *kamikazes*, its public hanging of innocent hostages, its calm, efficient gassing of Jews and Slavs and homosexuals, its unbelievable conclusion in atomic radiation.[21]

III. The War Narratives

Nevertheless, the notion of the "Good War" is what tends to be reflected in the American literature and films of the war. Stephen Spielberg's movie, *Saving Private Ryan*, for example, begins with horrific images of Omaha Beach on the morning of

June 6, 1944, but its sad conclusion glorifies the sacrifice of the American soldiers who died in the grand effort to take back the European continent from Nazi Germany. Movies about the First World War focus, as novels and films on war always do, on the small infantry unit, but there is no grand narrative behind the ordeal, as there is in the movies about the Second World War.

It may even be said that the major difference in American narratives – whether novels or films – of the two wars is that those about the Second World War are *pro-war*. Joseph Waldheim points out, however, that this outlook began as early as the later fiction of the Great War, that which was published in the 1930s. Novels Like John Dos Passos's *1919* (1932), Humphrey Cobb's *Paths of Glory* (1935), and Dalton Trumbo's *Johnny Got His Gun* (1939) are as bitter about the Great War as the novels of the Twenties, but they reject an attitude of cynicism to register social protest. In this way, Waldheim argues, they may be seen as intermediary to the socially conscious novels of the Second World War.

> ...the 1920's anti-World War I writers stand in a cause to effect relationship to the belligerent World War II novelists. The second war was fought to protect the gains which had been won as a result of the social struggles of the 1930's – struggles which had been motivated largely by the bitter iconoclasm of the 1920's.[22]

The fiction of the war in fact accommodates contradictory attitudes, as well as a variety of subject matter. According to Eric Homberger, the American war novel is notable for its diversity: all theaters of the war, all military arms and units, both combat and non-combat are represented.[23] Historically, the important American novels of the Second World War were postwar productions. It is the historical context within which these novels were published that has affected their ideological preoccupations. For example, according to Homberger, an unexpected result of the important works of war fiction appearing in the late Forties and Fifties was "to diminish the presence of the specific causes of war, and to see it as phenomenon which was caused by man's evil nature", an ahistorical emphasis abetted by the influence of versions of Freudianism during that period. Even the "dichotomization" typical of the American war novel – in which there is a conflict between a repressive, "fascistic" character (a hostile NCO or superior officer), and a humane, individual one is related as much to postwar politics – the "opposed categories" of western democracy and eastern dictatorship – as to the character of military institutions.[24]

American writers produced a number of fine combat novels, such as Harry Brown's *A Walk in the Sun* (1946) and James Jones' *The The Thin Red Line* (1962). Four of the most important American war novels were published in the same year: 1948: Norman Mailer´s *The Naked and the Dead*, Stefan Heym´s *The Crusaders*, John Gould Cozzens´ *Guard of Honor*, and Irwin Shaw´s *The Young Lions*. Mailer´s and Shaw´s works may be considered combat novels, at the same time that both examine larger questions. Mailer is concerned with fascist tendencies in American politics, represented by General Cummings, who thinks Americans are fighting on the wrong side, at the division level, and Sergeant Croft, sadistic and lethally efficient at the platoon level. Shaw focuses on an unholy trinity of two Jews from divergent class and cultural backgrounds, and an opportunistic Nazi, but his work is less successful in its ideological discussions than Mailer's (who wanted to avoid such problems by concentrating on the Pacific War). Cozzens' novel has no combat: its action takes place at a military base in Florida, and the novel deals largely with questions of bureaucracy, for which it is a supreme fictional example, and racism in the military, which betrays the author's arrogant bias. Heym's novel (written by a European émigré) is the most ideologically sophisticated of the four. It follows an army propaganda unit across Europe into Germany after the Normandy invasion and deals with the moral compromises of the Allies in their defeat of Fascism, which may be one reason why it has received the most critical neglect. Within the historical context of the Cold War, these very different war novels share an interest in the contemporary postwar world and its conflicting ideologies. From different political viewpoints, they all tend to view the liberal humanism of the American intellectual in the postwar period as inadequate to the realities that emerged from the war.

Novelists who had done important work on the earlier war – Ernest Hemingway and John Dos Passos – and during the 1930s – John Steinbeck – did not produce distinguished examples of war novels for World War II. One measure of the slippage may be seen in Hemingway's *Across the River and into the Trees* (1950). The protagonist, Colonel Cathcart, had fought (like Lieutenant Henry of *A Farewell to Arms*) in the Italian army against the Austrians, and now returns to Venice and the countryside he knows intimately, having been badly wounded there. He was once a general but lost a regiment, although it will be made clear that his demotion was a question of incompetence at higher echelons, the old theme of real vs. false fighting-men, the latter contemptuously called "pistol-slappers".

Cathcart is fifty years old and has a heart condition that will eventually kill him but maintains himself for the task by taking drugs. Despite this apparent aging, the colonel still does Hemingwayesque things: he goes duck-hunting, points out the sights of Italy to his young driver, makes love to an eighteen year old girl in a gondola, enjoys good food and wine. He is much concerned with honor (he beats up a couple of enlisted men who fool with his young girlfriend) and is proud of his memories: in fact, he spends most of his time telling the young woman war stories. He thinks about the past battle in which he lost his regiment. The images are dutifully grim (a dead GI flattened by a vehicle, a German roasted by white phosphorus being devoured by a dog), but the old, sentimental warrior reminisces with the waiter and old fellow soldiers: "He only loved people, he thought, who had fought or been mutilated".[25]

In short, the impulse for Hemingway's writing engaging war fiction is no longer there, and critics have generally excused this novel as a work of self-parody, for which there is ample evidence in the text. When the young woman tells the colonel that he ought to write about the war, since he can talk so well about it, he disagrees: "I have not the talent for it and I know too much. Almost any liar writes more convincingly than a man who was there",[26] a statement that may be a confession of authorial failure in this particular case but that also suggests the intriguing question of whether war fiction can be written effectively by men or women who have never experienced combat, an issue Hemingway himself may have already answered in his admiration of Stephen Crane.

If the older novelists failed to adequately represent the war, younger ones would continue in the early 1960s to mine the war for metaphors adequate to postwar realities. In *Mother Night* (1961), Kurt Vonnegut Jr. takes on a central historical problem of the twentieth century – Hitler and the Holocaust – risky material to approach in Vonnegut's characteristically flip, breezy way, and does not get away with it, vulgarizing his material technically, philosophically, and ideologically.[27] The main character, Howard Campbell is in Israel in prison awaiting trial for having made broadcasts for the Nazi propaganda minister Joseph Goebbels. But Campbell is really an American counter-agent who used the broadcasts to get information out of Germany by code. Unfortunately, only the president and one or two other people know this, and so both the Israelis and the Russians want him as a war-criminal. The politics are trivialized, not by the humor, which has a critical function, but by a historical confusion in which black nationalism, European Fascism, Father

Coughlin's anti-Semitism, the right-wing John Birch Society are all conflated, although they arose in different historical periods and responded to different perceived political needs.

In *Slaughterhouse-Five* (1969), Vonnegut draws on his personal experience as a Prisoner of War in the city of Dresden and a witness to the horrific Allied firebombing of that city, February 13-14, 1945, in which 135,000 people, as he tells us, were killed. The prisoners were kept in the underground slaughterhouse of the title, which ironically saved them from being killed by the bombs of their own airplanes. The author's relationship to both the Germans and the events in the novel is problematized: he is of German stock and he appears as narrator under his own name (he mentions one of his guards in the novel as being a "distant cousin").

In perhaps the two most important novels to be published after the 1950s, Joseph Heller's now classic *Catch-22* (1961) and Thomas Pynchon's monumental *Gravity's Rainbow* (1973), the war and the postwar period are conflated, as if the war had actually never ended. Heller has described his novel as "more anti-traditional establishment than anti-war...I used the military organization as a construct, as a metaphor for business relationships and institutional structures".[28] Critics have generally responded positively to the novel's critical power, even characterizing it as "savagely radical", aiming "to expose the entire power system of the post-war world",[29] with the attack focusing on the "power elite": America's unholy alliance of the military, politics, organized religion, and big business, including multinational corporations, which proliferated after the war, gaining trading advantages by developing products at home and manufacturing them abroad. Pynchon also sees corporations as the essential components of the war machine, in this case the rocket industry of Nazi Germany but with implications for the United States.

Leaving fiction aside, far less grand but still compelling war stories can be found in the so-called factual acccunts. A varied sample of the huge body of work produced by American war journalists and correspondents can be found in the Library of America's two volume selection, *Reporting World War II* (1995), culled by the editors from articles originally published in newspapers and magazines, and including transcripts of radio broadcasts and excerpts from the diaries or memoirs of journalists that were later published as books.[30] The selections accompany the historical chronology of the war, beginning, in the first volume, with William L. Shirer on the Munich Conference that turned over Sudentenland to Hitler, in 1938, and ending, in the second volume, with John Hersey's novella-like work on the bombing of

Hiroshima, in 1945. In between are the older, established novelists who worked as war correspondents (Hemingway, Steinbeck, Marquand), along with a number of young professional journalists, some of whom, like John Hersey and Irwin Shaw, would also publish war novels, while others – Edward R. Murrow, Eric Severeid, William Shirer, I.F. Stone – would go on to distinguished careers in the news media.

A sample summary of subjects taken from the first volume alone may give an idea of the variety of writers and subject matter: Vincent Sheean, whose car breaks down in a German city before the war, reports on the petty measures of anti-Semitism he observes there; Virginia Cowles, moving out of Paris by car with thousands of Parisians, records the despair of people when their vehicles run out of gas; John Fischer reports traveling with the victorious, vainglorious Germans before the Americans are in the war as the Germans complete the destruction of Dunkirk; Edward R. Murrow registers the toughness of Londoners who can "take it" under the Blitz, while Howard K. Smithy notes that the Berliners, by contrast, can *not* take it; photographer Margeret Bourke-White tells of being behind the Russian front with partisans who attack the Germans with primitive weapons; Larry Lesueur records the ruins of the German advance to Moscow; Melville Jacoby sees an unprepared Manila undergo the first Japanese attacks; Walter Bernstein observes off-duty GIs in a dreary Alabama sin-city; Foster Hailey watches the battle of Midway from aboard one of the ships; Jack Belden retreats with General Stillwell through Burma; Mary Veaton Vorse details the daily lives of women in a Maryland munitions plant; William L. Shirer writes on the American traitors who made radio broadcasts for Fascism; Robert Sherrod, on a walk over Tarawa, details the grisly aftermath of the Marines' victory; Ernie Pyle, ever sympathetic to the plight of the common soldier, talks to the men in Tunisia and in Sicily; Martha Gellhorn writes of the fortitude of the victims and quiet competence of the staff in a Royal Air Force burn center.

Many of these journalistic pieces retain their emotional impact when read in retrospect, and yet the articles and radio talks often go beyond a mere recording of a journalist's observations and experiences: in one of the finest pieces, A.J. Liebling traces the life and exploits of a legendary soldier known as Molotov, or just "Mollie", in Tunisia; in what is perhaps the least illuminating, Robert Sherrod dogmatically informs his readers of the smallness and obsessiveness of "the Japanese mind". Writing and broadcasting from war zones and foreign cities, these non-combatant observers had a perspective on the war that neither soldier nor ordinary civilian shared. For one thing, because of the mobility they enjoyed within a given area or theater of war and the possibility of visiting other areas or theaters, they had a broader knowledge of the war that the men who actually fought it. Ernie Pyle, for example, who commented on this advantage, accompanied troops to England, Algeria, Tunisia, Sicily, Italy, France, and in the last year of the war, the Pacific islands.

On the other hand, the unarmed correspondents could not fight, and they often had to endure being targets, sometimes with alarming consequences: Margaret Bourke-White had her ship torpedoed out from under her; Richard Tregaskis was wounded by shrapnel; Richard C. Hottelet had to parachute from his burning plane. Pyle himself was nearly killed twice, first by a German bomb at Anzio and then by an accidental bombing by US aircraft at Normandy; he was eventually killed by a Japanese sniper on an island near Okinawa. Yet, as he once noted in rueful appreciation typical of the man, at least it was not necessary for the correspondent, as it was for the infantryman, to harden himself to killing.

While these journalistic pieces tend to seek a stylistic unobtrusiveness, some of them are indistinguishable from what is regarded as "literary" prose fiction. Thus, Gertrude Stein, in her impersonal, run-on prose telling how she and other people cope in a town in occupied France easily blends with her literary *oeuvre*; Hemingway's "How We Came to Paris" is a wartime version of later autobiographical fictions like *A Moveable Feast*; and Marquand's article, written aboard a battleship bombarding Iwo Jima, could stand in its own right as a short story. Even Pyle's description of Normandy after the invasion, in its lists and rhythms, sounds uncannily like a poem by Walt Whitman:

> You can sense it from the little things even more than the big things –
>
> From the scattered green leaves and the fresh branches of trees lying in the middle of the road.
>
> From the wisps and coils of telephone wire, hanging brokenly from high poles, their edges not yet smoothed by the pounding of military traffic.
>
> From the little pools of blood on the roadside, blood that has only begun to congeal and turn black, and the punctured steel helmets lying nearby.
>
> From the square blocks of building stone still scattered in the village streets, and from the sharp-edged rocks in the roads, still uncrushed by traffic.

It has been observed that the role of war journalism is not to tell the truth about war, but to humanize a dehumanizing experience. When the war correspondents cite the names and hometowns of the soldiers they talk to or share experiences with, they employ a simple way of putting a "face" on the masses of fighting men they have encountered. Another, less obvious strategy is the narrative stance adopted by many of the journalists, who take on the *persona* of a friendly but rather frightened layperson, curious and alert but carefully unobtrusive.

As for "telling the truth" about the war, the journalism in the Library of America collection seems more concerned with conveying some idea to civilians of the war's sheer horror and the human and material waste involved in waging it. In this respect, the purpose, if not the perspective, is similar to that of writers of war fiction. But engaging the larger political issues or furnishing a more historical overview is missing in the journalism, even deliberately so. What is adopted is rather a here-and-now perspective, close to the troops and near the battlefield but not – except by mishap – within it. These accounts show great sympathy for the fighting men and the support troops necessary for the waging of the war, but the war itself is taken for granted as a just and even noble enterprise, again, the familiar perception of the war as the "good war". The fictional representations, in this aspect, attempt at a greater depth of psychological truth, even when they do not question the overall enterprise as the best of them do.

One reason for this perception was the American public's ignorance of the true nature of war. For example, it eventually became clear to the military, although it could never be admitted by the political machine that sought to guarantee public ignorance and optimism, the unpalatable truth that, as Paul Fussell remarks, "men will inevitably go mad in battle and that no appeal to patriotism, manliness, or loyalty to the group will ultimately matter".[31] Another was censorship by military and political authorities and the false representation by even accredited journalists, which worked to keep the more manifest unpleasantness of daily life as experienced by the actual combatants – degrading and debilitating diseases such as dysentery and malaria, disillusionment and terror often leading to madness, and the horrific nature of war wounds and deaths such as disembowelment, dismemberment, and decapitation – from the American public: "in unbombed America especially, the meaning of the war seemed inaccessible".[32] The soldiers knew, Fussell claims, that optimistic publicity and euphemism had rendered their experience so falsely that it would never be readily communicable. They knew that in its representation to the laity what was happening to them was systematically sanitized, and Norman Rockwellized, not mention Disneyfied. They knew that despite the advertising and publicity, where it counted their arms and equipment were worse than the Germans'.[33]

In this sense, war journalism and the Hollywood war film work along similar lines. Both try to install a positive attitude toward the war in their respective audience. As in the fiction, in order to humanize the fighting-men, the emphasis is on individuals as opposed to the collective action of units and armies. The viewpoint is that "GIs were ordinary Americans with values recognizably emerging from American culture".[34] Ernie Pyle, always gives the name and hometown of the GIs he cites. Revisionist historians make an essentially similar assessment. "Whether consciously or inadvertently, the reporters tended to find in the young men they described the traits that Americans generally esteemed", as Blum puts it, who also argues that these traits were the dominant values of the culture of a people who had recently emerged from the Great Depression. Thus, in the reporters' portraits and in the movies, the myths of sports heroes and rural origins were constantly emphasized and the "cult of the underdog" from the Depression era underscored the common theme of the American fighting valiantly against greater odds.[35]

---

[1] Westbrook, Robert B. "World War II". In: Fox, Richard Wightman and Kloppenberg, James T. (Eds.). A Companion to American Thought (Oxford: Blackwell, 1995), 751.

[2] Norris, Margaret. Introductory essay to "Modernism and Modern Wars", Modern Fiction Studies special issue, 44-3 (Fall 1998), 507.

[3] Hobsbawm, Eric. The Age of Extremes: A History of the World, 1914-1991 (New York: Vintage, 1996), 43.

[4] Heller, Joseph. Closing Time (New York: Scribner's, 1994), 11.

[5] Hobsbawm. The Age of Extremes, 53.

[6] Meek, James. "Nuremberg Rally, Invasion of Poland, Dunkirk. ." In: London Review of Books (6 Sept. 2001), 28.

[7] Meek, "Nuremberg Rally, Invasion of Poland, Dunkirk…", 28-29.

[8] Polan, Dana. Power & Paranoia: History, Narrative, and the American Cinema, 1940-1950 (New York: Columbia University Press, 1986), 58-59.

[9] Dick, Bernard F. The Star-Spangled Screen: The American World War II Film (Lexington: The University Press of Kentucky, 1985), 7.

[10] Hobling, Walter. "The Second World War: American writing". In: McLoughlin, Kate (ed.d), The Cambridge Companion of War Writing(Cambridege: Cambridge University Press, 2009), pp. 212-213.

[11] This is the argument of Wolfgang Natter's Literature at War, 1914-1940 (New Haven: Yale University Press 1999), passim.

[12] Blake, Casey. "Lewis Mumford". In: McLoughlin, Companion to American Thought, p. 475.
[13] Blake, "Lewis Mumford", 475.
[14] Fussell, Paul. Wartime. Understanding and Behavior in the Second World War (Oxford: University Press, 1989), 143.
[15] Westbrook, "World War II", 751.
[16] Cadogan, Mary and Craig, Patricia. Women and Children First: The Fiction of Two World Wars (London: Victor Gollancz, 1978), 292.
[17] Erenberg, Lewis and Hirsch, Susan E. (Eds.). The War in American Culture: Society and Consciousness During World War II (Chicago: University of Chicago Press, 1996), 3-4.
[18] Blum, John Morton. V Was for Victory: Politics and American Culture During World War II. (New York: Harcourt, Brace, Jovanovich, 1976), 70.
[19] Terkel, Studs. The Good War: An Oral History of World War II (New York: Ballantine Books, 1984), 491.
[20] Fussell, Wartime, ix.
[21] Fussell, Wartime, 132.
[22] Waldmeir, Joseph J. American Novels of the Second World War (The Hague: Mouton, 1971), 43. The works of the "Twenties" that he cites reflect the attitudes of that decade even if their publication dates of two of them belong to the early Thirties: Frederick March's Company K (1933), Hemingway's A Farewell to Arms (1929) and Dos Passos's earlier work, Three Soldiers (1932).
[23] Homberger, Eric. "United States". In: Klein, Holgar. (Ed.). The Second World War in Fiction, (London: MacMillan, 1984), 173.
[24] Homberger, "United States", 174.
[25] Hemingway, Ernest. Across the River and into the Trees, 62.
[26] Hemingway, Across the River and into the Trees, 116.
[27] Karl, Frederick R. American Fictions 1940-1980: A Comprehensive History and Evaluation (New York: Harper & Row, 1983), p. 344.
[28] Meredith, James H., Understanding the Literature of World War II: A Student Casebook to Issues, Sources, and Historical Documents (Westport, Conn.: The Greenwood Press, n.d.), p. 57.
[29] Edwards, pp. 10-11.
[30] Reporting World War II, Part One: American Journalism 1938-1944; Part Two: American Journalism 1944-1946 (Library of America, 1996).
[31] Fussell, Wartime, 282. Fussell notes on the preceding page that "there is no such thing as getting used to combat", and that psychiatrists define a period of between 200 and 240 days under fire for any man to break down, depending on the exposure and intensity of his experience.
[32] Fussell, Wartime, 268.
[33] Fussell, Wartime, 268.
[34] Homberger, "United States", 199
[35] Blum, V Was for Victory, 55-60.

Tom Burns is Professor of Literature in English and Literary Studies at the Federal University of Minas Gerais (UFMG). A native of California, he served in the 82nd Airborne Division of the US Army (1961-63) and graduated in Classics from the University of California, Berkeley (1966). He spent the decade of the 1970s in Brazil, working as a dancer, model, English instructor, and translator before joining the faculty of the UFMG in Belo Horizonte. He received a doctorate from the Federal University of Santa Catarina (UFSC), in Florianopolis (1996), and has published literary criticism on a wide variety of subjects, as well as poetry and translations in Brazil and the United States. During the last ten years, he has been studying, teaching, and writing about the literature of the two world wars, and is co-editor, with Elcio Cornelsen, of the collection *Literatura e Guerra* [Literature and War](2010) from the university press. In 2005, he was a visiting scholar at Colorado State University, where he studied the literature of the Vietnam War under the noted author and scholar of that war, John Pratt. He is a co-founder of the research group NEGUE: *Núcleo de Estudos de Guerra e Literatura*.

Dead on a High Hill:
Poetry from the Korean War

W.D. Ehrhart

Every war leaves in its wake, along with destruction and misery and sorrow and death, a body of literature. From Homer's *The Iliad* to Virgil's *Aeneid*, from Philip Freneau's "The American Soldier" to Walt Whitman's "The Wound-Dresser", from Mark Twain's "The War Prayer" to James Jones's *From Here to Eternity*, war and literature are each a subset of the other. Moreover, no longer does war have to wait for a Homer or a Tennyson or a Kipling to be translated into literature. As soldiers increasingly have become more literate, there has been a marked increase, beginning in the early 20th century, in the body of literature written by the soldiers and veterans themselves.

Consider, for instance, the British poets of the Great War: Charles Hamilton Sorley, Wilfred Owen, Siegfried Sassoon, Edmund Blunden, Isaac Rosenberg. Among Americans, e. e. cummings, Alan Seeger, John Peale Bishop, and Malcolm Cowley all wrote important poems about the Great War.[1] American veterans of World War II produced such classic novels as Norman Mailer's *The Naked and the Dead* and Joseph Heller's *Catch 22*, along with poems like Randall Jarrell's "The Death of the Ball Turret Gunner", Howard Nemerov's "Redeployment", John Ciardi's "A Box Comes Home", and Richard Eberhart's "The Fury of Aerial Bombardment".[2]

The Vietnam War has produced a huge body of literature written by those who fought in it, including such canonical works as Philip Caputo's *A Rumor of War*, Ron Kovic's *Born on the 4th of July* and Tim O'Brien's *The Things They Carried*, the plays of David Rabe, and powerful poems by an assortment of poets from John Balaban, Bruce Weigl, and Walter McDonald to Yusef Komunyakaa, David V. Connolly, and Dale Ritterbusch.[3]

Even our Iraq and Afghanistan Wars are beginning to produce literature, as evidenced by Brain Turner's 2005 poetry collection *Here, Bullet* and Clint Van Winkle's 2009 memoir *Soft Spots*.[4]

Then there's the Korean War. It lasted three long years, cost 37,000 American lives (more than the Revolutionary War, the War of 1812, the Mexican War, the

Spanish American War, and the Filipino-American War combined), and has never officially ended.[5] A major American war by any definition of "major". But ask yourself to name three writers from the Korean War. Two? How about one? There is more than one reason why the Korean War is called the Forgotten War, and this is one of them.

Because if the body of literature from the Korean War is much smaller than that of the American wars that straddle it, which it is, it is far from inconsequential. It includes novels such as Pat Frank's *Hold Back the Night*, William Styron's *The Long March*, and Richard Kim's *The Martyred*, memoirs like James Brady's *The Coldest War* and Martin Russ's *The Last Parallel*, Rod Serling's play *The Rack*, and short stories such as Donald Depew's "Indigenous Girls" and John Deck's "Sailors at Their Mourning: A Memory", along with an assortment of poets whose work I will shortly discuss. Yet for much of the last fifty years, continuing to this day, this literature has been all but ignored.[6]

It is not my purpose here to explore in depth the differences between Korean War literature and the literatures of the two American wars on either side of it, the Second World War and the Vietnam War. But without going into great detail, a few observations are appropriate. The Second World War was the kind of experience that literally transformed an entire generation of Americans. One need only read Studs Terkel's *The Good War* or Tom Brokaw's *The Greatest Generation* to get a sense of that. And in its own way, though for very different reasons, the Vietnam War did that to another generation, as is readily apparent in Gloria Emerson's *Winners and Losers: Battles, Retreats, Gains, Loses, and Ruins from the Vietnam War* or Myra MacPherson's *Long Time Passing*.

The Korean War simply did not have that kind of impact. It was not the central event of the 50's, and most Americans remained untouched by it from start to finish. "People had other things to do and unless your son was there, nobody seemed to care much about Korea", writes Korean War veteran Charles F. Cole in *Korea Remembered*, and when it ended, he adds, "the Korean War vanished from view like a lost football game".[7]

The reasons are multiple and complex, but like the war itself, I would suggest that the literature of the Korean War has never been recognized or widely read precisely because that experience was not the kind of transformative experience that the other two wars were. Put briefly, as Phil Jason and I write in *Retrieving Bones*, "The Korean War did not capture the American popular imagination".[8]

But why? The soldier-poets themselves offer some possible answers. "Korea was a 'non-war,'" says William Childress, "being alternately a 'police action' and 'Harry Ass Truman's war.' Korea was no war to inspire poetry or fiction. It lacked all nobility and didn't settle a damn thing".[9] Keith Wilson calls the war "a very dirty and murderous joke".[10] Reg Saner's answers take the form of questions: "Is it because Korea wasn't officially a war, just bloody murder on both sides, while being officially termed 'a police action'? Is it because for a long time people referred to it as 'the Phoney War'? . . . Or, finally, and perhaps most likely, had World War II made us small potatoes by inevitable coparison—among even ourselves?" In spite of "all the ink spilt about poor public support for Vietnam veterans", Saner believes that "we Korean veterans got neither respect nor disrespect. Except amid our immediate families, there was no reaction".[11]

Beyond the level of popular culture, however, even within the highly specialized world of those who actually study war and the literature of war, Korean War writing, and especially the poetry, remained invisible for nearly fifty years. Paul Fussell's *Norton Book of Modern War*, for instance, includes no poetry from the Korean War, nor does Jon Stallworthy's *Oxford Book of War Poetry*, though both books include poems dealing with the Second World War and the Vietnam War. Carolyn Forche's *Against Forgetting* misidentifies Etheridge Knight as a Korean War veteran while including no one who actually is a Korean War veteran.[12] Not until after the 1999 publication of *Retrieving Bones: Stories and Poems of the Korean War* has a major American war poetry anthology included work from the Korean War.[13]

Ignored and unrecognized even by these specialists on war literature are magnificent poems by Thomas McGrath and Hayden Carruth, two of the most important American poets of the 20th century, along with the work of half a dozen veterans who fought in Korea and later went on to become prolific and serious poets. Both Carruth and McGrath are, coincidentally, World War Two veterans, not Korean War veterans. Carruth has been called "one of the lasting literary signatures of our time" by *Library Journal* and "a national treasure" by *The Nation*,[14] while the *New Republic* considers McGrath to be "one of the best American poets extant", and *Poetry East* says, "McGrath is, quite simply, one of the very best American poets".[15]

Though Carruth's "On a Certain Engagement South of Seoul" did not appear in book form until 1959,[16] the poem was probably written in 1950 and first published in *The Nation*.[17] Consisting of sixteen stanzas of loose iambic pentameter, the poem is written in *terza rima*, and begins: "A long time, many years, we've had these wars".

Carruth then goes back to his high school days "when Italy broke her peace", a reference to the 1936 Italian invasion of Ethiopia, before describing how, when he was nineteen (which would have been 1940), he "saw/A soldier in a newsreel clutch his ears/To hold his face together". Such images, "so raw and unbelievable, were "enough to numb us".

But that was before Carruth had experienced for himself the "bark and whine" of battle. Ten years later,

> . . . the news of this slight encounter somewhere below
>
> Seoul stirs my remembrance: we were a few,
>
> Sprawled on the stiff grass of a small plateau,
>
>
> Afraid.

Carruth makes that fear vivid, elucidating how war – combat – transforms literally everything, altering perceptions of self and others, warping emotions, leaving men isolated from themselves and each other:

> My clothing was outlandish; earth and sky
>
> Were metallic and horrible. We were unreal,
>
> Strange bodies and alien minds; we could not cry
>
> * * *
>
> Nor could we look at one another, for each . . .
>
> * * *
>
> . . . sat alone, all of us, trying to wake
>
> Some memory of the selves beyond our reach.

There is a weariness to the poem, a sense of sad inevitability. It is evident in the opening line, and recurs throughout the poem in lines such as "the nations undertake/*Another* campaign now . . . and we forsake//The miseries there that we can't understand/*Just as we always have*" (italics added). But this is not entirely true because Carruth, at least, does understand the miseries of those soldiers caught in that "slight encounter somewhere below/Seoul", just as he is aware of the toll combat takes on those who survive it, and even this brief glimpse

> Of a scene on the distant field can make my hand
>
> Tremble again. How quiet we are. One limps.
> One cannot walk at all. Or one is all right.
> But one owns this experience that crimps
>
> Forgetfulness, especially at night.

This is what war does to body and mind. This is the curse of memory. And for what? One war merely gives way to the next in an endless succession. And Carruth can find no saving grace, no redeeming qualities in his own experiences or the misery of others, but only a loss of certitude. Unlike many veterans, who insist on a sense of comradeship and brotherhood forged under arms, however terrible the circumstances, Carruth asks:

> Is this a bond? Does this make us brothers?
> Or does it bring our hatred back? I might
>
> Have known, but now I do not know. Others
> May know. I know when I walk out-of-doors
> I have a sorrow not wholly mine, but another's.

And here the poem ends, the questions unanswered, the sorrow unmitigated. Carruth is doubly cursed, once for the burden of his own sorrow, and again for "a sorrow not wholly mine, but another's".

McGrath's 'Ode to the American Dead in Korea", first published in 1955,[18] but almost certainly written while the war was still going on, consists of three stanzas of 14, 15, and 14 lines respectively, and is an unusual combination of rhymed and blank verse. In the first stanza, 8 of 14 lines rhyme, or four pairs of lines; in the second, 8 of 15, or four pairs; and in the third, 10 of 14, or five pairs. Five of the rhyming pairs are couplets, one couplet each in the first two stanzas and three in the last; at other times, rhymes are separated by one or two other lines. The stanzas are numbered.

How does one even begin to take apart a poem so dense, so intricate, so perfectly balanced as this one is? McGrath manages to weave into his poem the loneliness of war ("God love you now, if no one else will ever"), the bleakness of death in Korea ("Corpse in the paddy, or dead on a high hill"), the naiveté of ordinary citizens ("All your false flags were/Of bravery and ignorance"), the venality of those who take advantage of that naiveté ("the safe commanders"), the common humanity of soldiers ("ready to kill . . . your brother"), and the insignificance and anonymity of the dead ("tumbled to a tomb of footnotes") to those who send them to die ("distinguished masters whom you never knew").

And this is only in the first stanza. In the second and third stanzas, he likens those ordinary Americans who answer the call of duty to bees and moles ("happy creatures") running on "blind instinct", neatly condemns church and state ("the state to mold you, church to bless") and school, too ("No scholar put your thinking cap on"), offers perhaps the bleakest and most succinct explanation of evolution ever put forth:

> . . . in dead seas fishes died in schools
>
> Before inventing legs to walk on land[,]

dismisses the Christian belief in a benevolent and caring God ("whose sparrows fall aslant his gaze/Like grace or confetti"), implicates Big Business ("the stock exchange /Flowers"), and disparages politicians ("the politic tear/Is cast in the Forum").

Conversely, McGrath's poem pays loving tribute to the American dead in Korea "who did not know the rules". It is a lament for those who die for the interests of those who risk nothing, certainly not their own lives. Above a bleak dawn landscape, "the lone crow skirls his draggled passage home" while God blinks "and you are gone" as quickly as that. Back home, "your scarecrow valor grows/And rusts like early lilac while the rose/Blooms in Dakota". But McGrath vows that after "the public mourners" have done with their empty rituals, "we will mourn you, . . : brave: ignorant: amazed:/Dead in the rice paddies, dead on the nameless hills".

Among those who actually fought in the Korean War and later came to write about it in verse are Childress, Saner, Wilson, Rolando Hinojosa, and James Magner, Jr.[19] Magner and Saner, with eighteen books between them, have also between them no more than a dozen poems that deal with the Korean War, though some of those, such as Magner's "Zero Minus One Minute" and "To a Chinaman, in a Hole, Long Ago", and Saner's "Re-Runs", "They Said", and "Flag Memoir", are stunning. Hinojosa, primarily a novelist, is the author of *Korean Love Songs*, a 38-poem sequence that is essentially a novel-in-verse.[20] The experiences of these men in Korea, and the writing that came out of those experiences, deserve far more attention than they've ever gotten. Childress and Wilson in particular have produced work that warrants close examination.

William Childress grew up in a family of sharecroppers and migrant cotton-pickers. He joined the army in 1951 at age 18 and was sent to Korea the following year, where he served as a demolitions expert and secret courier. He subsequently earned Bachelor of Arts and Master of Fine Arts degrees, and has worked a variety of jobs from college teacher and juvenile counselor to newspaper columnist and freelance writer.

Childress's two books of poetry appeared within a year of each other—*Burning the Years* (The Smith, 1971) and *Lobo* (Barlenmir House, 1972)—and his most active years as a poet came between 1960 and 1970. A 1986 reprint combining both books, *Burning the Years and Lobo: Poems 1962-1975* (Essai Seay), includes few poems not in either of the earlier two.

Childress takes his subject matter from a wide variety of sources: the natural world and its inhabitants, the agricultural west and southwest of his childhood, the unnatural world of urban poverty and button-down America, and the whimsy of his own imagination. But war occupies a significant percentage of the total body of his published work, and his Korean War poems are wedged in between World War Two (in the form of his eight-part poem "Hiroshima") and the Vietnam War (in poems such as "The War Lesson" and "Washington Peace March, 1969").

Indeed, while those who fought the Korean War were closer in age and temperament to the veterans of World War Two, the Vietnam War seems to have been a catalyst for both Childress and Wilson, releasing pent-up feelings that had perhaps been held in check by the personal and cultural stoicism bequeathed to them by their generational older brothers and by the stultifying atmosphere of the Fifties created by Senator Joseph McCarthy and the House Un-American Activities Committee.

While Childress, for example, did write several of his best Korean War poems prior to the vast American air and ground commitment in Vietnam ("The Soldiers" in

1961 and "Shellshock" in 1962), his poems become more pointed, more cynical, and more bitter as the Sixties—and the Vietnam War—advance. And while Childress can say, with what sounds very much like pride, resentment, and envy all at once, "Korean veterans did not come home and start throwing tantrums like many Viet vets did. We simply faded back into civilian life—no monuments, and not even a doughnut wagon to meet the [troop ship] I came home on",[21] his poems suggest that the price of simply fading back into civilian life was very dear indeed.

In one of his finest poems, "Korea Bound, 1952", Childress emphasizes the unwillingness of those who are being sent to fight. The soldiers on the troop ship are "braced" against the railing as they listen to the "shrill complaining of the waves". Ostensibly free men in a democracy, they are likened to Pharaoh's slaves, and the ship itself to Pharaoh's burial tomb. And in the poem's final irony, they sail past Alcatraz Island, then a federal prison, where the prisoners' "lack of freedom guarantees their lives".

As often as not, Childress uses both rhyme and meter, sometimes altering the pattern of the rhyme scheme within a given poem, or rhyming in some places but not in others, an admixture of free verse and fixed form that is oddly pleasing and reminds me of Gwendolyn Brooks. Occasionally he gets into trouble or forces a rhyme, but for the most part he handles form skillfully.

"Letter Home", however, is free verse, and in it he assumes the persona of a young American soldier, newly arrived and still able to see beyond himself and his own misery to the misery of "children with bellies swollen,/and O, the flowers/of their faces, petals all torn". Such empathy will not survive what is to come. In "The Soldiers", Childress reminds us that "lives narrow/around living's uncertain center" and "soldiers can't be soldiers and be/human". A well constructed poem of six rhymed sestets, each line with nine syllables, it offers a cold, hard world where only the dead are resolute.

In "Shellshock", Childress moves from generic soldiers to a soldier with a name: MacFatridge. A poem about the cost of war on those who survive, it immediately suggests those men in John Huston's 1946 documentary *Let There Be Light*, which was filmed in the psychiatric ward of a military hospital—though that film was withheld from public release by the U.S. government until 1979, seventeen years after Childress's poem first appeared in *Poetry*.

Childress's empathy for his fellow soldiers is matched and more than matched by his contempt for the generals who commanded them. Both "Combat Iambic" and

"Death of a General" are scathingly unrelenting, reminiscent of Siegfried Sassoon at his angry best. And in "The Long March", a soldier pulls from a puddle

> the arm of someone's child.
>
> Not far away, the General
>
> camps with the press corps.
>
> Any victory will be his.
>
> For us there is only
>
> the long march to Viet Nam.

Here, suddenly, in the last line of a poem that begins "North from Pusan", Childress makes explicit what must have been a steadily rising horror among many Korean War veterans as the Fifties became the Sixties and the Sixties became the Vietnam War. The "we" in the third line of the poem, and the "us" above, are not just the soldiers themselves, but the American people "dumbly follow[ing]/leaders whose careers/[hang] on victory".

"For My First Son", a bitter poem over which hangs an air of resigned helplessness, appears in several variants. I prefer the version in his 1971 collection in which, after enumerating the "future of steel" toward which his son's "tiny fingers grope" – a flamethrower's blast, trenchfoot, worms, gangrene, shrapnel, empty eyes – Childress concludes:

> ... these are
>
> the gifts of male birthdays,
>
> the power and glory, and
>
> the lies of leaders send them.

"Trying to Remember People I Never Really Knew" also deals with the wreckage of war and the future that awaits male children, but this time, after detailing the fates of three men he had once known, he refuses to say if they have left sons behind or not. It is as if, if he does not acknowledge that they had sons, he might somehow protect their sons from those who would train them "as hunters of men" and the "dark forests/where lead rains fall". It is only a gesture, his trying to shield the sons from the fate of their fathers, and Childress leaves little doubt that it is a useless gesture, that those who would train them will find them in any case, but in its uselessness it is also powerfully loving and affirming of life. For whatever he might have thought when he was "still a boy [with] fists full of detonators and TNT" smiling "murderously/for the folks back home", as he writes in "Burning the Years", war and the years have taught him that "duty changes with each job,/and honor turns ashes soon enough".

"I was a regular Navy officer", writes U.S. Naval Academy graduate Keith Wilson. "I came from warrior stock, right out of the Highlands of Scotland, and the Welsh Marches".[22] He went to Korea the first time as a 22-year-old ensign in 1950, and returned from his third tour in Korean waters in 1953. "I expected nothing from war. I was a professional. I didn't, however, expect to be lied to and betrayed. I was very proud of the UN flag at our mast head when we went in to launch attacks. I thought, and still do think, that the only way I can see for the planet to survive is to have an effective world-wide government. When I found out that Korea was all a very dirty and murderous joke, Iwas silenced for many years".

Wilson got out of the navy and returned to his native New Mexico, earning a Masters degree before commencing careers in both academia and as a prolific poet and writer. Working entirely in free verse, much of his work is rooted in the American Southwest, and he has a particular affinity for Native American and Spanish-American cultures. But Wilson's experiences in the Korean War provide the foundation for perhaps his most important book: *Graves Registry*. "I started writing *Graves Registry* in the winter of 1966 in anger that our government was again fighting an undeclared war in a situation that I, from my experiences in Korea, knew we could never win", he says. "I was one of the first combat veteran officers to protest Vietnam because I knew it to be unlawful, and could only lead to another disgraceful stalemate, . . . [but] I had no poems about war at all—I had buried it inside. . . . It took the pressure of rage and fear for the young men [of the Vietnam Generation] that made me write it and itpoured out, page after page".

First published by Grove Press in 1969 as *Graves Registry & Other Poems*, it contained the Korean War poems along with poems about the Southwest. In 1992, Clark City Press published an updated edition called simply *Graves Registry* and containing the original Korean War poems, additional poems from his 1972 *Midwatch* (Sumac Press), and some fifty newer poems. Taken altogether, they weave the literary and the political into a single tableau that moves across time and geography, but my attention here must necessarily be limited to the poems dealing with Korea, which are grouped together at the beginning of the book.

The sequence begins with a love poem to his wife, "Echoes, Seafalls for Heloise", followed by three poems dealing more with the remnants and reminders of World War Two than with the Korean War. The first Korean War poem is "The Captain", in which Wilson encounters a U.S. Army officer with "the kind eyes/of somebody's uncle". But as the captain describes the raids he and his Korean Commando team conduct, Wilson records "what happened to his eyes":

> the changes when he spoke of their raids
>
> of villages flaming, women & children
>
> machinegunned as they ran
>
> screaming from their huts.

It isn't all blood and guts. One of the virtues of Wilson's poems is the way they traverse a wide range of experiences, all of them belonging to war. In ". . .*ganz in Waffen*",[23] a deck officer, firmly but without humiliating, bolsters the courage of a young sailor on the verge of breaking as their ship comes under fire from enemy shore batteries. "The Singer" recounts an incidence of accidental gunshot (in any war, though for obvious reasons it is seldom given much attention, large numbers of soldiers are killed not by the enemy but by their own and their comrades' mistakes). "Waterfront Bars" in Japan offer temporary relief to sailors between 90-day battle cruises "north of the bombline". And in "Combat Mission", three officers "in a ruined house" ten miles behind the lines drink Scotch while squatting around an oilcan stove, lifting "their cups against/the darkness, the rumbles rolling forward".

But if it isn't all blood and guts, there is plenty and more than enough of both. In "Guerilla Camp", Wilson is confronted first by the dead and wounded "from the/raid the night before", then by "a retired fighter" no older than himself whose hand has been ruined by a bullet and who demands to know 'how a man/could farm/with a hand like that". In "The Circle", Wilson's ship steams for hours through hundreds of Korean bodies floating "in faded blue lifejackets", victims of a sunken troop ship, no survivors: "We sailed on. I suppose that's all/there is to say". But one body in particular remains fixed in his mind:

> God knows why
>
> but his ass was up instead
>
> of his head; no pants left,
>
> his buttocks glistened
>
> greyish white in the clear sun.
>
> the only one.

Whatever illusions of service and nobility Wilson entered the war with are evaporating. By "December, 1952", once again "back in the combat zone", he recalls the heroism of great naval commanders of the past and the grand enterprise to which he had thought himself attached:

> A blue United Nations patch on the arm, a new
>
> dream. One World. One
>
> Nation.
>
> Peace.

But now he realizes that nothing has changed since the days of Nelson and Farragut, that "the old bangles" still work, allegiances are still bought, and "tracers hit a village,/the screams of women, children/men die". And while the "New York Stock Market [rises] and cash registers/click", Wilson is finally forced to confront

> the cost of lies, tricks
>
> that blind the eyes of the young. *Freedom.*
>
> Death. *A life safe for.* The Dead.

"Commentary" is equally scathing, a recitation of what has become, for Wilson, only the squandering of lives, especially Korean lives, in the name of Americans back home

> whose enemies
>
> are always faceless, numbers
>
> in a paper blowing in the
>
> Stateside wind.

How many bodies would

fill a room

living room with TV, soft

chairs & the hiss

of opened beer?

We have killed more.

The children's bodies alone

would suffice.

Wilson's poems are not about the big battalions and the pitched battles, but about coastal operations and guerilla raids, shattered villages and shattered ideals. They are peopled by Americans, yes, but also by Koreans and Japanese, refugees and cripples, and by warriors, yes, but also and more so by the defenseless and the innocent who always become the wreckage of war. They are Wilson's explanation of how he began life expecting to kill people and ended up dedicating it to teaching people instead.

So there is indeed a poetry of the Korean War, and there are at least three good reasons why it should not be ignored, dismissed, or forgotten. Firstly, it offers valuable insights into the Korean War itself and the experiences of those who fought it. As I wrote a quarter of a century ago about the poetry of the Vietnam War:

> Scholars and politicians, journalists and generals may argue, write and re-write 'the facts.' But when a poem is written, it becomes a singular entity with an inextinguishable and unalterable life of its own. It is a true reflection of the feelings and perceptions it records, and as such it is as valuable a document as any history ever written.[24]

This is no less true of the poetry of the Korean War.

Secondly, much of this poetry is first-rate writing, be it war poetry or not, as I hope I have demonstrated with the poems I have discussed here. Good writing is always worthy of attention, and the best of these poems can stand up to the best poetry written about any war in any generation.

Finally, the poetry of the Korean War helps to make sense of what otherwise appears to be a baffling and mystifying juxtaposition. The poets of World War hardly celebrate or glorify their experiences. Jarrell's ball turret gunner is "washed out of the turret with a hose". Nemerov's cat "vomits worms" in "Redeployment". Ciardi's "A Box Comes Home" with Arthur inside. Eberhart's students in "The Fury of Aerial Blombardment" are "gone to early death". Yet none of these poets suggests that the war they fought was unnecessary or unjustified, let alone that it was wrongheaded, arrogant, evil, unforgivable.[25]

But only a generation later, Vietnam War poets do exactly that. Jan Barry compares American soldiers to the Mongol hordes in "In the Footsteps of Genghis Khan". Steve Hassett compares them to Hessian mercenaries in "Christmas". In "The Hooded Legion", Gerald McCarthy wonders, "What hand did not turn us aside?" Bryan Alec Floyd's "Private Jack Smith, U.S.M.C". came to feel "that his politicians were garbage/who should have been wasted".[26]

But an examination of the poetry from the Korean War suggests that this transition from "Good War" (or at least necessary and justifiable war) to "Bad War" is not so abrupt as it seems. In "Combat Iambic", Childress writes of his commanding general, "I pray Beelzebub, Lord of the Flies,/to rear his maggot children in your eyes". In "A Matter of Supplies", Hinojosa coldly observes, "we're pieces of equipment/to be counted and signed for". Saner's American flag in "Flag Memoir" flutters over a hometown stadium, "Explaining. Trying to Explain". And Wilson, in "December, 1952", laments, "It is when the bodies are counted/man sees the cost of lies, tricks/that blind the eyes of the young".[27] If the Korean War poets are closer in age to their World War II counterparts, they respond to their experiences in the Korean War with a sense of disillusionment and betrayal that much more closely resembles the poets of the Vietnam War.

At the larger historical level, to skip from World War II directly to the Vietnam War is to fail to understand both the Vietnam War and the Cold War within which the Vietnam War unfolded, the parameters for each having been determined by the Korean War. Just so, on a literary level, there is much to be learned from the poetry of the Korean War, and much to be appreciated. Yet for most readers, students, teachers, and scholars, this literature remains, in Tom McGrath's words,

> dead on a hill,
>
> Dead in a paddy, leeched and tumbled to
>
> A tomb of footnotes.[28]

[1] For these American poets, see, respectively: "I sing of Olaf glad and big," "Rendezvous" and "On the Aisne," "In the Dordogne," and "Chateau de Soupir, 1917". See Hedin, Robert. (Ed.) *Old Glory* (New York: Persea Books, 2004). The work of the British poets can be found in multiple sources.

[2] An excellent selection of American poetry from World War II, including these poems and poets, can be found in Stokesbury, Leon. (Ed.) *Articles of War* (Fayetteville: University of Arkansas Press, 1990).

[3] Many of the Vietnam War poets are represented in Ehrhart, W.D. (Ed.) *Carrying the Darkness* (Lubbock: Texas Tech University Press, 1989). For Connolly's poems, see Connolly, David V. *Lost in America* (Woodbridge: Vietnam Generation & Burning Cities Press, 1994).

[4] Alice James Books and St. Martin's Press, respectively.

[5] A truce was signed in July 1953, but there has never been a peace treaty ending hostilities.

[6] Depew's and Deck's stories, along with other stories and a solid selection of the poetry, are included in Ehrhart, W. D. and Philip K. Jason. (Eds.) *Retrieving Bones: Stories and Poems of the Korean War* (New Brunswick: Rutgers University Press, 1999).

[7] Cole, Charles F. *Korea Remembered: Enough of a War!* (Las Cruces: Yucca Tree Press, 1995), 212 & 273.

[8] Ehrhart and Jason, *Retrieving Bones*, xix.

[9] Ehrhart, W. D. "Soldier Poets of the Korean War" In: *War, Literature and the Arts*, vol. 9, #1, Spring/Summer 1997, 33. This special edition of *WLA*, which I guest-edited, is the first substantial exploration of any kind into the poetry of the Korean War.

[10] Ehrhart, *WLA*, 9/1, 33.

[11] Ehrhart, *WLA*, 9/1, 39-41.

[12] See Ehrhart and Jason, *Retrieving Bones*, xlii, for a detailed discussion of Etheridge Knight.

[13] Both Hedin's *Old Glory* and Lorrie Goldensohn's *American War Poetry* (New York: Columbia University Press, 2006) include substantial sections on Korean War poetry, and both acknowledge in print their debt to my research on the poetry. (Phil Jason's interest was in the fiction of the Korean War, and it was his expertise in that genre that enabled us to do an anthology combining fiction and poetry.)

[14] Both quoted in Martha T. Mooney's *Book Review Digest 1992*, 322.

[15] *New Republic* quoted in *Contemporary authors New Revision Series*, v.6, 341. *Poetry East* quoted in the 1999 Copper Canyon Press Catalog (www.ccpress.org).

[16] Carruth, Hayden. *The Crow and the Heart* (New York: Macmillan, 1959).

[17] In a letter to WDE dated December 9, 1999, Carruth writes: "I can vaguely recall writing the poem you ask about, 'On a Certain Engagement South of Seoul,' and I'm quite sure it was after I read a newspaper account of a group of soldiers who got lost somewhere and were ambushed, and it made me think of feelings I had had as a GI in WWII. I think this was in about 1949 or 1950, but I can't be sure of that. [Note: It could not have been in 1949 since the Korean War did not begin until June 1950.] It might have been originally published in *The Nation*, because I was writing for that magazine then and the topic would have been congenial to the editors there, but again I can't be sure".

[18] McGrath, Thomas. *Figures from a Double World*. (Denver: Swallow Press, 1955).

[19] All of the poems by these Korean War veterans can be found in Ehrhart, *WLA*, 9/1. A smaller selection of their poems is included in Ehrhart and Jason, *Retrieving Bones*. These poets are all, of course, Americans. Though 60,000 British troops served in Korea between 1950 and 1953, I know

of no significant poetry written by British veterans of the fighting. If it exists, I would be grateful to have it brought to my attention.

[20] Hinojosa's original *Korean Love Songs* (Berkeley: Justa Publications, 1978) is long out of print, as is a 1991 German-English bilingual edition published jointly by the University of Osnabruck and VC-Verlagscooperative. The entire sequence appears in Ehrhart's *WLA, 9/1*, but that, too, is now not easy to obtain. A small selection from the sequence appears in Ehrhart/Jason's *Retrieving Bones*.

[21] Letter to Ehrhart dated June 13, 1997.

[22] This and subsequent statements by Wilson are taken from his letter to Ehrhart dated February 21, 1997.

[23] The title means "complete in armor". This and the German epigraphs that Wilson uses with a number of his poems come from Rainer Maria Rilke's *The Lay of the Love & Death of Coronet Christopher Rilke*.

[24] Ehrhart, W. D. *Carrying the Darkness:* The Poetry of the Vietnam War. (Lubbock: Texas Tech University Press, 1985), p. xxvi.

[25] See Stokesbury, *Articles of War*.

[26] See Ehrhart, *Carrying the Darkness*.

[27] See Ehrhart and Jason, *Retrieving Bones*.

[28] Ehrhart and Jason, *Retrieving Bones*, vii.

W. D. Ehrhart is editor of Carrying the Darkness: The Poetry of the Vietnam War and Unaccustomed Mercy: Soldier-Poets of the Vietnam War, guest-editor of I Remember: Soldier-Poets of the Korean War, and co-editor of Retrieving Bones: Stories and Poems of the Korean War. A former Marine Corps sergeant, veteran of the Vietnam War, and author or editor of nineteen books of prose and poetry, he holds a Ph.D. from the University of Wales at Swansea, and teaches English and history at the Haverford School in suburban Philadelphia, PA.

The dark song of the night of war
António Lobo Antunes' *Os Cus de Judas*[1]

Olinda Kleiman

A significant example, for its very uniqueness, of the Portuguese literary production about the colonial war in Africa, in the years following the end of the conflict, *Os Cus de Judas* offers through the particularities of its writing an interesting insight on the research carried out during the latest decades to develop analytical principles on how the experience of fighting is narrated. Interested myself in those issues, I follow the lead of the work of Jean Kæmpfer, whose results have been presented in his *Poétique du récit de guerre*.[2] Kæmpfer proposes a distinction between two types of narrative: one, "classical", characterized by its "imperial" writing, is subordinate to a total devotion to lofty heroes; the other, "modern", or "idiotic", unfolds around an insignificant character, who is directly involved in the fighting.[3] Kæmpfer is interested in the latter, and so shall I.[4]

One of the remarkable aspects highlighted by the critic is the curious paradox that permeates a set of works: even though each one claims "an irredentist singularity", they all abide by the law of a genre that evades the application of models. In his attempt to unveil this "law of the law of the genre" (Derrida), Kæmpfer identifies three features, of a narratological, thematic, and dialogic nature, that make up the modern war narrative. Narratologically, the texts adopt "a strict restriction of point of view"[5]; resorting to the approach inaugurated by *The Charterhouse of Parma*, "they deliberately stick to the perspective of a character overtaken by the events" and rest on this prior realization: "in short, war was everything one did not understand" (Céline). Thematically, they develop the plot around a "hero" who moves inside the chaos; the verbalization takes on the mode of a "personal point of view" in order to convey an experience of "radical depersonalization".[6] Recalling the paradox previously mentioned, I would add that the microcosm where this character with a limited view evolves constitutes the location, also limited, of an individual experience whose meaning is only found in the collective nature it is capable of taking on. Finally, in dialogic terms, these works stand out because of a strong controversial component: establishing an intertextuality with the "classical" narratives, they vilify their glorifying discourse, by contrasting them with a fully horrific truthfulness of facts, lived and visible. They thus attempt to redress the excessive bias of their own narrative, which must be credible if it is to convey war "as it really is", "as close as possible to an experience which acute subjectivity renders questionable, even irrelevant in face of History".[7]

Kæmpfer is notably not alone in having shown that though the extreme experience of war is indescribable, the indescribable nevertheless possesses– another paradox – "its tropes, its topics, even its commonplaces".[8] He takes an important step towards a systematization and, granted that the representation of war follows certain general principles, according to modes and codes widely shared, the typical traits he points out are pertinent. I propose to test these concepts by analyzing *Os Cus de Judas*, viewed as an example of the "modern" war narrative.

The test of experience

As with many other works that aim at fictionalizing the experience of war, *Os Cus de Judas* presents itself as a memory novel. Since its publication in 1979, no one has questioned whether this is a book about the colonial war that is not talked about – and therein precisely lies the problem. The author himself has provided some remarks in this direction.[9] The African war is surely the central issue and the inconceivable experience the driving force of the story – an experience which, at the particular time in his life when the man aspires to become a writer, shapes the novel, according to a rule that seems well established. It is the same with most war narratives, produced by authors who have known the battlefield. To verbalize a limit situation, facing death in its own realm, risking one's life, and having the duty, or the power, to kill, seems to be an inescapable need for those who have lived this "terebrant experience".[10] Everything unfolds as if the awareness of the unimaginable – to hold the power over life or death – and the encounter with death, always on the lookout, had prompted the novelist to search in creative invention an awakening of the vital forces, as if committing his experience through words were indispensable for life *afterwards*. Lobo Antunes clearly says so in an interview with Thierry Guichard:

> I came back from the war in 1973. There were three things I had to talk about in order to feel relieved: guilt (towards my daughters), war and psychoanalysis. Hence the trilogy.[11]

In addition to the cause-effect link between war and writing, this statement makes two other connections: between work and biography, and between writing and psychoanalysis. Lobo Antunes has always been open about this: the novel is strongly based on the experience he lived, where war takes on the most extreme shape, thereby exemplary in its literary form. He insists on that in more recent interviews,[12] when he evokes a sort of persistent pain, imposed by the writing, at the same time a therapy, a search for the self and an ordeal. How not to link the pain that feeds itself on being told and the pain of war, recalled day after day by a character-narrator who nurtures his torment, narrative after narrative, retold by the writer, a kind of endless repetition one seems not to be able to evade? *Os Cus de Judas* bears witness to this repetition, common in war narratives, as a torment-therapy, also as a testimony to these "stubborn facts" that overload private memory and are denied by public memory, which so refuses to give sense to the trial and the existence of the victims. It is in this "divorce between public and private word",[13] with the excess of the former compared to the emptiness of the latter, that the pangs of anguish set in the foreground of the work are condemned to maintain themselves.

As it displays a "remembering conscience", the novel rebuilds in the present of the verbalization, contaminated by the "current conscience",[14] a past whose edge is located in the rupture brought about by experience:

> At this point in my narrative I am invariably disturbed, whatever, it was six years ago and I am still disturbed: [...] I ve begun this painful learning of anguish.[15]

This narrative of "learning the anguish", which is its substance and makes it a novel of initiation, speaks of this crucial moment in an existence "between the rupture by time and the writing of the story",[16] which is but the reconfiguration of the ordeal lived by the author. The author does not identify himself with the narrator. He creates the conditions for such an identification: similarities in private life[17] – profession, date of marriage, name of the wife, divorce...; itinerary of the narrator's mobilization grounded on Lobo Antunes'; wartime images re-enacted in fiction according to the words of the writer; coincidence between the time of the narrative – the narrator's time – and the time of the writing, or of publication – the author's time. "I is [may be] another", but the bias of an aesthetics of confusion is a deliberate choice. This narrative strategy has two intentions: to "de-particularize" a too particular ordeal in order to speak of being in its universality; to instill the strength of authenticity, verifiable in the actual life – Lobo Antunes' publicly known life – into the story of a human experience that is unbelievable because it is humanly impossible. By placing itself in the fusion-confusion between reality and fiction, the novel can make its ethical choices, its threefold approach: reflexive, as exploration of the depths of the soul and reflexion about being in the world, social, as testimonial solidarity, political, as a scream of protest, asserting the authenticity of the facts, placing the official discourse against its indignant arrogance:

> The napalm bombs were covered by oil and the government solemnly stated In no case would we resort to such a cruel method of extermination, I saw the bombs being covered in Gago Coutinho.[18]

This book, the second in a rich work whose beginning puts the theme of war at the center of the stage, only appeared six years after Lobo Antunes' return, the very date at which the narrator is supposed to tell his story. Neither this narrative, nor the novel itself may be taken as the verbal explosion at the exit of "hell". Showing the war at close range requires looking at it from afar. Turning it into fiction calls for a distance, without which, so the writer says, it cannot be written with a lived reality:

> It takes distance to put things into writing, one cannot write in the heat of the moment, one risks being a pamphleteer.[19]

Imaginative recreation by anamnesis, the novel, reflexive and not polemical, benefits from a global approach to time and to the facts through which it thinks about the war. Author and narrator have this distance of years that affords them the possibility of thinking of a before, a during and an after the war, in order to build the narrative. The story then assumes its real meaning in the field of ruins on which it is built: the "ruins of the empire"[20], the ruins of an existence undermined by the war and an impossible return in which the fate of a generation is mirrored, the ruins of a revolution, long awaited and aborted, that paved the way for the collective amnesia and threw an abject nation into apathy – oblivious of its dead and unable to look at the face of its victims and to dress its wounds. It is within this context of post-colonial dysphoria that the reconstruction of the broken being takes place, in the vain attempt to understand and communicate, which is also the vain attempt to reinstate and reopen from the past an inaccessible or blocked present and a denied future, and heal the tumours of this present infected by the past.

War and its representation: the "idiotic" discourse

> *It is a tale told by an idiot, full* of sound and fury, signifying nothing
> William Shakespeare, *Macbeth*, V, 5.

A war narrative, *Os Cus de Judas* is also a discourse about war. Conceived in opposition to "imperial" writing, it stigmatizes the authoritarian voice to which it refers. It takes the posture of the "idiotic" discourse and the narrator incidentally calls attention to it – "I don't know if what I am going to say sounds idiotic"[21] – as it also sides with the ideological stand associated with it. It does not tell the war in its glorious majesty but rather in its huge senselessness. It is carried by a single voice and enunciated in a single mode: a first-person narrative making the choice of singularity. The novel constructs itself within a nondescript character, who is neither hero nor ordinary man – war denies him to be either of them. The subject is both agent and object of the narrative; he sometimes places himself at the center of the narrative and at the center of the war he has made, and this experience creates the subject-matter for a one-way dialogue with a woman, met for one night only in a bar. The narrative, interspersed by "coitus as sad as the Lisbon nights",[22] lasts for this single night, between their meeting and their separation at dawn. However, what is announced as a deliverance through the word takes on the shape of a nightmare haunting a spirit troubled by the commotion of war. It is the narrative, reiterated night after night, of an anguish that can never be fully told and can never end, the "passion" (Kæmpfer) of a man condemned to an obsessive confinement, locked up in his obsessions.

This discourse, which could be placed in the category of the "autistic" narratives,[23] were it not for its volubility induced by alcohol, displays the mark of degradation in its nature as well as in the conditions of its enunciation. It brings together two outcasts, two barflies, in a place symbolic of a moral decline, where the "lost souls", the wrecks of life are to be found. It is said in the night, thus showing how it belongs to the zones of shadow and terror of the individual, to the realm of the nightmarish and unreal: "I start to think that [...] I am telling you [...] a made-up story".[24] A depressive monologue, it clings to the speaker's depression, to a confinement to which it contributes. It does not tell of its effects on the silent interlocutor. One is led to believe there none, and this is the problem. The silence of the woman makes sense. It articulates the narrative in the gap between the "sound and the fury" of the "idiot" and the silence opposed to him. It is in the symbolic value which both may take, at the same time, within the system of representation of war, that the passive presence of the woman, and the wall of silence into which the narrator bumps find their deep meaning. The narrative, which is indubitably concerned with war and its human disasters, is actually addressed to somebody, and this constitutes the movement toward life of a war survivor who has broken up with society. It is the gesture as well, the word through which the war, which lacks the words to tell itself, will find the voice to tell itself, but not to be understood since it is beyond understanding. This is the first deep resonance of the silence, which will never be broken. The presence of the woman, as a woman and in the sexual role assigned to her, sets the other axis of rupture that interests both the author and his narrator: the relation of love, precluded in the very idea of its possibility. Without it, the sexual relation will hardly taste better than "coitus as sad as the Lisbon nights", even supposing that it does not turn itself into a degrading continuation of warlike habits.

Besides the clear symbolism of a family future mortgaged by experience, which has once again brought into touch two beings now strangers, the incomprehension between the night woman, a substitute for a the wife, and the narrator affects society as a whole. Metonymically, this woman stands for the Other who has not fought in the war and who is not only different but actually indifferent: "Why the f... is this not talked about"?[25] This difference-indifference justifies the narrator's discourse, as a word incessantly renewed in its principle, if not in its terms, never being echoed. The trauma of war places its victims before a double aporia determined by the initial realization: "War, in short, was everything one did not understand". It demands to be understood, even if it is not understandable because it has no sense; it must be conveyed, even if it is unspeakable and incomprehensible. Silence and narrative jointly make up the answer, a non-answer, to these aporias, the mark of a fracture that affected an existence, a couple, a nation. Hence this endless flow of words, induced by the void, which persists in its efforts to make understood what it itself does not understand, endlessly throwing in "do you see?" to an interlocutor summoned to understand, and exhausting itself in repeating in the empty space a meaningless "strange story".[26]

"To write a novel is to build up a delirium", the novelist explains.[27] By putting this aesthetically operating paradox into practice, *Os Cus de Judas* builds up its narrative into the "discourse of the grandiose solitude of a drunkard".[28] The words are those of an inebriated narrator, who looses himself in ethylic ramblings but also displays his lucidity and his skills to adjust the effects of alcohol to the needs of his rhetoric. As his eloquence grows in parallel with his level of alcohol, he puts into words and shapes the full load of his memories, brought back to his mind from the time of war, eight years before. His narrative displays a studied architecture: divided into twenty-three chapters corresponding to the twenty-three letters of the Portuguese alphabet, as if to tell the war from A to Z. The novel does not open with images of war. One has to wait for the very last words of the chapter for them to break out, allusively by means of the strong image of a farewell at the docks. Meanwhile, the narrator will have set in motion a whole process of relation to the past, based on his childhood – the zoo across the street from his parents' house, the family environment and its frame of mind – but also addressing the present and the fear of the future, intertwining time and subjects, all adorned with the most absurd meditations on being in the world.

The link with the war is not directly made. But it is there, in this verbal hallucination. The narrative modes determined in this opening chapter will be present throughout the work. The muddle of all levels will intensify, so much so that it will include the spatial dimension, creating a semantic maze representative of the war's absurdity and the mental confusion it brings about. The presence of the war, *in absentia* or almost, is stated at every turn, meaning that it is not taking place in Africa only. It wormed its way everywhere. It is in the present time, a bloated present, which includes the future of a whole generation. The narrator does not refrain from telling this to his interlocutor, whom he includes in the category of the "war casualties". But above all – and this is probably the meaning that this chapter introduces in order to make it one of the nodal aspects of the novel –, it was already inscribed in the past of a colonial Lisbon, symbolically represented by the house of the narrator's sinister family. Trapped between an undertaker's shop – a gruesome omen of the coffins to come – and the zoo where wild animals, though domesticated, are crammed behind bars, foreshadowing animalized soldiers, imprisoned by barbed wire, the house is the fitting setting for a family in need of war and heroes, like the family of the narrator who is thrown into war for the sake of clerical and patriotic ideals, fiercely upheld by a posse of old and formidable aunts.

The portrait, extended to the nation, is vitriolic. The words and the images encompass everything and everybody in the same realm of darkness taken in by the angry and desperate look of a man more dead than alive, in search of a unity that has been taken away from him, and instead condemned to relive an unbearable past. This narrative of past memories is carried out by a nameless character. One is tempted to conceive this anonymous voice as the rebellious voice of all soldiers. It is and it is not. During a war, each person lives his own experience, like the others, at the same time as the others, but in loneliness and abandonment. Therefore this man is primarily himself, merging into the image of the other. This is also the reason why *Os Cus de Judas* does not have a plot. If the writer is to be believed, a novel does not tell a story; it explores human nature, to the depths of the mystery of the unconscious.[29] In this sense, *Os Cus de Judas* does not tell a war story but opens up to "the knowledge of hell" putting into words an extreme situation so absurd that it cannot be explained:

> [...] who can decipher this absurdity [...] a dark month-long tunnel, where I fall mooing, a wounded ox that does not understand, that does not understand, that does not manage to understand.[30]

The narrator faces a real challenge, to be analyzed in chapter S. It stems from the need to speak, since "one cannot understand what is not spoken",[31] but this need comes up against an impossible translation into words:

> The urge to write and the torturing panic of not being able, of not being able to translate into words what I wish I could scream into everyone else's ears.[32]

Putting war into words

War is the unspeakable that must be spoken: putting war into words is a paradoxical act, besides an act of violence that one does to oneself. Words must translate a "hallucinating"[33] reality: the narrative must bear the imprint of the hallucination. War is murdering noise and fury: the verb can only be noisy and murderous. War is unnameable mud and abjection: the only possible answer is obscenity. Paradoxically, then, words strive to narrate the unnarratable, in a raging discourse. The reader dives into it and does not come out. This hallucinated word, expression of a "furious" rebellion, that melts everything into "its huge stupor of gunpowder", answers the need to say everything, the war's raw reality, its absurdity, the responsibility of those who decree it, the pain of those who make it and lend themselves to be moulded to it; it becomes outrageously obscene in order to yell how scandalous it is. Apparently stunned, but in fact the product of an elaborate ordering, the narrative it conveys resorts to complex, at times contradictory processes. It generally follows a chronological order, tracing the verifiable stages of a path of initiation that works like a descent into Hell, towards the "cus de Judas". However, dependent on the fantasies of memory and of a subjective perception pushed to its paroxysm, it mixes the factual and the gloss in its dread of taking a stand and commenting on the uncommentable, brings in distortion, moves on through bewildering analogies, building up a whole reminiscent of the stream of consciousness and the Faulknerian way of probing into the mysteries of human nature and its fierce inhumanity. Everything is subjected to the merciless gaze of a "ghost" back from the war who has learned about the world through his contact with horror and who smoothes everything towards the abject in a cynical answer to the family's "vigorous prophecy": "fortunately the troops will turn him into a man".[34]

Obscenity is one of the striking features of this male voice. It is a commonplace of the narrative as it seemingly imposes/ in which it seems to impose itself by the force of its effects. Its manifestations, lexically speaking, are both numerous and manifold: they deal with scatology – turd, shitting, feces, shit, defecation, bog, intestine, bowel; the anal – asshole, arsehole, bum, anus, anal, arse, haemorrhoids; sex and sexuality – pubis, vagina, penis, testicles, balls, dick, to fornicate, to fuck, to fuck someone's brains out, to bugger; insults – goddamn mother fucker, cocksucker, son of bitch, bastards, pricks. Lobo Antunes explores the artistic, ideological, and semantic potentialities of this field. The choice for an aesthetics of the obscene, which blends with that of the incongruous, is a discursive strategy adapted to the "idiotic" narrative, for it belongs in the displaced discourse as one of its major resources. It can be found at the core of uncommon images, seldom gratuitous. I shall mention one, which does not come casually from the creative imagination of a psychiatrist, a keen observer:

> We would ophthalmologically observe the anal conjunctivitis of mandrills whose eyelids swell because of inflammable haemorrhoids.[35]

The hypothesis herein advanced, as an unreal invitation, to a liaison itself unreal, for it is subjected to an unachievable condition, is not unsavoury indeed. It is not meaningless either. Herein we find expressed, through the grotesque, the awareness of how impossible it is to have a sexual intercourse if not an animal one:

> Who knows if we will end up making love, frenzied like two rhinos with toothache.[36]

At war, sexuality is but one of the manifestations of barbarism; but it stands so much for the savagery of men that in the narrative it functions as a metaphor of war and of the relationships with the other. War and sex go together, hence this narrative that joins war and love, hence also the role of the woman, standing for the couple's inescapable rupture.

A world of men without women, war is a world castrated and of castration, like those who "invent" it, Salazar, the "castrated man",[37] and his "eunuch ministers",[38] producing degenerates of despicable practices. Onanism, the "alphabetization" method of the idle soldiers is "the daily exercise", one of the few *savoir-faire* that the army instills in the "barracks rut".[39] The other is killing, both forming an unswerving duo: "we masturbated and we shot".[40] There are plenty of references to masturbation as an endless occupation. They tell of the war's imbecile sterility. They also illustrate the idea of frustrated sexuality that is perverted into generalized depravity, natural to a "perfect Portuguese" who "boasted about fornicating".[41] Virile manifestations take on varied shapes, in consonance with bellicose behavior. It ranges from sordid promiscuity to the rampages of sadistic violence. The collective rape of Sofia is the most despicable example, associating verb and act, both PIDE-like and unbearable:

> We worked on her for the guys to change the oil, and next, we gave her the ticket to Luanda.[42]

The theme of sexuality and its metaphorical approach fit the issues of war, in the representation of this male world's turpitude and perversion, as opposed to the family vow. But that is not all. Having become this dreamed-of man, after this leap "from solemn communion to war",[43] the narrator can bring things back into place with the 'Portugal' family, incarnated by the family microcosm. He carries this out in a cynical fashion by applying the lessons of the army: the low language of the barracks, the fitting institution for the education of the children from good families. It is in the sexual metaphor, extended into the field of scatology, that he finds the semantics of violence for a powerful development, whose main display of aggressiveness lies precisely therein, in the use of obscenity, transgressive and taken as such in the very circle he belongs to. This outburst of violence, the product of a long built up resentment, spills over everything, providing an ignominious view of the "world-the-Portuguese-has-created".[44] Mete Lenha's café[45] – a paradigmatic representation of this world – is the mirror in which all "sons of bitch",[46] "cocksuckers",[47] "pricks"[48] can see themselves: the politicians who pull the strings from the *salons* of Lisbon or the staff officers concealed in the air-conditioned offices of Luanda, the narrator's family, ready to sacrifice their own for "their Christofle silverware", the smart idlers of the Movimento Nacional Feminino, in cahoots with the Church and the dictatorship:

> The ladies of the Movimento Nacional Feminino sometimes came to entertain the menopause mink coats, by handing out medals of Our Lady of Fátima and keychains with Salazar's effigy, accompanied by nationalistic Our Father and threats of the biblical hell of Peniche, where the PIDE agents were more efficient than the poor devils holding forks in catechism. I always thought that their pubic hair was made of fox fur and that, when they got excited, drops of Ma griffe flew from their vaginas.[49]

The narrator finds a "shitty country", when he comes back on leave – "a shit and shitty country".[50] Shit overflows. It has entered the inside of the soldiers. The narrator repeats *ad nauseam*, in a cry of paroxysmal revolt:

> We carried twenty-five months of war in the guts, twenty-five months eating shit and drinking shit, and fighting for shit, and falling sick for shit, and falling down for shit, over the guts.[51]

which has its counterpart in the "dumbfounded"[52] reiteration before the first corpse, the one that lends face, name and reality to death:

> The nurse who helped me kept saying fuck fuck fuck [...], Fuck fuck fuck I replied to the nurse [...] we all said fuck with the mouth shut.[53]

Since words are powerless, obscenity is the possible response; through its meaningful force, it expresses all aspects of war with the required brutality. The choice of a text overflowing with the need to say everything about a war whose ineffability it feels incessantly, and wishing to shock through scandal, appears already in the title, quite puzzling in fact. "Cu de Judas", – literally "the asshole of Judas" – is a set phrase meaning "in the middle of nowhere". Lobo Antunes uses it in a letter to his wife in order to name the "land at the end of the world"[54], a geographical location, on the border of Eastern Angola. For the author, it includes the sense of treason, conveyed by the name "Judas".[55] Thus, beyond its usual meaning, the phrase becomes significant in the characterization of the soldiers, at once traitors for their compliance, and betrayed, sent to their death by the warlords and by their fellow countrymen who close their eyes. At no time does the text employ it in a sense other than topographical. If it affects the soldiers, it can be only through semantic contamination. But it is quite conceivable that the author, haunted by the search for the "bomb, for the festival of words", for the "fucking sentence" and its effects, may have been seduced by a set phrase with a definite meaning, which can however take on another one in the poetics of the text, by analyzing the terms that form it. Something which the author does not fail to do as is shown by the passage: "Who has stuck me, with no warning, in this cu de Judas?",[56] where the verb "stick" is not meaningless.

According to Luís Madureira, the title conveys the idea of sodomy, a vector for a representation of Portuguese colonialism, sterile, reversing the notion of empire as "productive penetration", in the spirit of Gilberto Freyre's Lusotropicalism.[57] However, no such semantic network is identifiable in this sense and it is surprising that a text that does not shy away from violence and subversion, and possesses is own key as Lobo Antunes claims,[58] is so discreet about possible sodomistic, and especially homosexual, practices. It is not inconceivable that sodomy may have compensated for the masturbative loneliness and sodomization may have been a means of oppressing the most fragile soldiers, an aspect of the violence of the barracks found in *Fado Alexandrino*. Nothing of the sort here. The semantic network is built around obscenity, which is operating in itself. "Cu de Judas" speaks of the asshole, undeniably. If it says anything else, through poetic resemanticization, this cannot be anything but a symbolic sodomization of the poor devils, the victims of all possible betrayals, the "buggers" of the war.[59] Must it be therefore necessarily interpreted in terms of sodomy? Can it not be kept at a metaphorical level? The same signified is expressed through other signifiers: "Who fucked us?", for instance.[60] The word need not be translated into actions. Obscenity, the violent instrument of a violent rebellion, must be taken at face value. Sexual, anal, scatological metaphors are never entirely unrelated and they operate collectively to express "this shit of a war", its dehumanized world.

Images of chaos

The strategies to depict war are placed under two registers: one, abstract, produces depersonalized images, leaning towards universalization in a reflexive design; the other, concrete, carried by the physician's experience and extremely personalized, leans towards a realistic representation, through allegedly truthful images, so as to bear witness and express condemnation. Modelled on the "idiotic" discourse, they reverse the paradigm of the heroic narrative. In the first case, the images, linked to the natural environment, oscillate between a hostile setting and tortured landscapes, *silva horrida* and a fascinating nature. They are organized around a threefold dialectical relation between war and landscape, the authenticity of Africa versus "world-the-Portuguese-has-created", an interior landscape and a physical landscape.

Many of them are commonplace and establish an aggressive setting, built on a limited number of schemes: an immersion into a strange world, with its aggressive difference, especially climatewise; a world evoking the concentration camps – barbed wire, promiscuity, fields of ruins; a hostile environment, swept by rain and wind, menaced by violent storms, "swarming with insects",[61] annoying flies,[62] bloodthirsty mosquitoes;[63] a repugnant place – overbrimming with filth, bloodthirsty dogs, vermin, worms, fat rats.[64] This setting, with its realistic traits, is to be interpreted as a metaphor of the aggression of war, death and its accompanying decay: the stench of death-manure, rot, mud reminiscent of the "historic mud of Verdun",[65] scavengers, crocodiles, and other hyenas.[66] Other images, some original, others topical, complete them, in a game of opposition, mirroring the narrator's ambiguous relation to space, between rejection and bewilderment. The African space – the location for a forced exile and a war site – provokes disgust. It is marked by the stamp of rudeness and of grotesque: such is the case of the Mete Lenha's café, of the "cus de Judas", but of Luanda as well, a caricatural icon of the "world-the-Portuguese-has-created".

Conversely, there is authentic Africa with its vast spaces,[67] its starry nights,[68] its majestic dignity.[69] The contrast assumes a symbolical value in a passage which exhibits both the depravity of a Portuguese "junior officer" who rapes an African woman and the majesty of the plain where the rape is set.[70] Like the men, the land also watches helplessly the outrages inflicted on its own people, bears the cruel marks of war; like the men, it holds the unleashed brutality, the powerful madness of the general destruction. Like the men, it is both the victim and the executioner. Because of its cataclysmic savagery, joining water and fire in one Apocalyptic vision, the Cambo illustrates this double nature, and the dichotomy, translating the co-existence of the beautiful and the frightening, appears with its evident ontological projection in the distribution between trees and animals, the former as symbols of human suffering, the latter of human ferocity.[71]

Metonymical representations of the site of the war, of the ruined landscapes which, according to hermeneuticians, constitute the main characteristic of the new poetics of war narrative,[72] the trees, present throughout the novel acquire a steady importance towards the end. Two types of trees gain a strong metaphorical value: the eucalyptus and the mango trees. The former mostly refer to the stay in the east; the latter are restricted to the north. Maybe one can see there a link with the real world, but one cannot rule out that each of them takes a different meaning. Both bear witness to a suffering nature, but whereas the mango trees belong to the African world and keep watch, sentinel-like, at the door of *tia* Teresa's house, the role of the eucalyptus is less clear. Do they stand for the "world-the-Portuguese-has-created", as they guard the brothels of Malanje?[73] Do they belong to the world of the war, standing for both Africa and the Portuguese barracks, the "dismal witnesses of a duel" that overwhelms them, a representation of the soldiers from both sides?[74] Are they the signs of a growing common resistance biding its time, as the wrathful tension that elongates their silhouettes indicates, when the first death among the Portuguese takes place?[75] Their symbolism links them with the night of the war, simultaneously inscribing them in the majestic beauty of a legitimate and dignified resistance, on the African side,[76] and of a communion with the Portuguese soldiers as they nervously wait for battle.[77]

Together with "the huge wall of the mango trees of Marimba",[78] whose "tragic branches"[79] share the fate of other trees, violently "uprooted from obscurity" by the lights of a foreign civilization,[80] the eucalyptus of Ninda are poetic images of the war, representative of "the murderous violence on the pregnant land of Africa".[81] These images take part in the conventional seme of the tortured earth, which they enrich particularly by the implementation of this process of inversion, one of whose manifestations is the reification of men, the humanization of things.

The mango trees of Marimba are perhaps the most elaborate expression of this process. But the full significance of the latter cannot be accessed by only reading *Os Cus de Judas*. Three layers of meaning are formed. The first one, linked with the idea of "tragic branches", carries the suffering of the landscapes and, by analogy, of men; the second, backed by the term "rumor",[82] juxtaposes the cry of pain and the deafening noise of the war, but stretches it beyond the time of war, in an ongoing noise that maintains the trauma; the third, arising from the narrator's analysis, assigns to the mango trees the role of a shield against war and its casualties, at the doorsteps of *tia* Teresa's hut:

> At aunt Teresa's hut, when the door was locked and the shutters closed for a tabernacle intimacy, the war moved amidst the mango trees, escorting its dead heroes and its fake patriotism made of stucco and plaster, not daring to walk in.[83]

These senses interfere and build up a powerful meaning reinforced by a system of echoes in the subsequent writings. A sentence, from a recent work – "I forbid to have X-rays taken, to prevent the trees of Africa from trembling in the film"[84] –, specifies the deep implications of a metaphor whose aim is not only to represent the din of the war during the war but the whole of the war, taking hold of the individual, forcing upon him the memory of the memory of pain and preventing him from forgetting.

I shall not dwell upon the process of animalizing the human, whose models are common in war narratives since early Greek epic. One singular metaphor, of specific relevance, shall suffice. From the traditional man-animal association, operating throughout the narrative, one metamorphosis takes place, brought about by the man-fish representation:

> We were fish, you know, mute fish in cloth and metal aquariums, both fierce and tame, trained to die without protest, to lie quietly in the troop coffins, to be welded inside, to be covered by the National Flag and sent back to Europe in the ships' hold, dog tag in the mouth to prevent the cry of rebellion.[85]

This image is to be related to that of the lost fishlike gaze of the silent woman. What is involved, as we have seen, is precisely this silence, and everything it implies: the indifference, the obedience, and the cowardice that made possible such "ferocity" against the other, the "submissiveness" to the true enemy, the making of one's own coffin. The metaphor, simple in itself, unfolds into a complex reasoning about the behavior of the military and the politicians, the civil "worms", the women and men who have remained and who have all played their part in the national cowardice. If the war happened, the responsibility must be found in everybody's complicity.

These metaphors belong less to the narrative than to the comments that accompany it. They are thoughts about the war. Others take over from them and speak of the war in its cruel reality. They wish to be strikingly true to life. Plucked from life, they say that "everything is real, even the throes of death". There are no descriptions of battle scenes, no heroic actions or figures, only violence in all its forms, beheld, performed, endured, self-imposed: the sadism on the part of the PIDE and the Blacks employed/enrolled? by the colonialists, engaged in collecting ears or sticking ice cubes into the rectum of the enemy; the sadism of the narrator, who shapes his behavior according to those he condemns: "fourteen stitches in the agent's asshole, taking my time, sticking with relish the needles into the flesh"[86]; perverse sexuality, noted in calendars but also practised on women; mauled bodies: the amputation of the MPLA soldier's leg and the ensuing photographic session, blood, paradoxically always missing and always excessive; omnipresent death:

> Pereira's coffin, Carpinteiro's coffin, Macaco's coffin, murdered by a mine fifty meters away from me.[87]

Lobo Antunes does not dwell on descriptions. When they are found, they are striking, as shown by the accident to the medical sergeant "sitting on the track staring speechless at his own intestine he was holding in his hands, something yellow and big and disgustingly hot between his hands"[88] and the suicide of the soldier of Mangando.[89] The author is more concerned with the reactions that the extreme violence of watching murder and death or killing produces on the soldiers who behold their own death in the death of the other: "After all, is this the aspect of our death?".[90] Familiarity with death, not with the idea of death but with its actualization, makes the experience all the more terebrating as it is accompanied by the humiliation of discovering oneself: the frailty of the body, tangible in the corpses around, the powerlessness to fix the unfixable, death drives leading to the most despicable acts, the insurmountable fear of being afraid, the abjection of one's own cowardice.

When it is over, the experience lived as an unprecedented experience creates the narrative, a paranoid recollection of an impossible, although extremely real past, branded with the stamp of its uniqueness, and thus both incomprehensible and unspeakable. The hallucinated speech moulds itself on the madness of the war, in order to think it through, by means of a deceptive trick. The discourse, based on a kind of abandonment and wearing the mask of alcoholic rambling, is in fact the elaborate discourse of a physician, in charge of bodies and souls alike. It is enunciated by an *I* who never names himself, but, nonetheless, insistently and precisely asserts his situation. The void opened by anonymity swallows up the author's name, written on the cover, and refers back to the person of Lobo Antunes. The overcrowded memory of the alienated narrator-physician, in search of these primordial space and time, is also the memory of Lobo Antunes, the empirical individual who lived through the twofold ordeal of war and of a difficult readaptation; the same overflowing memory is also the memory of the author, a psychiatrist, aware of the traces that an extreme experience imprints on the body, as shown by the trees of Africa, almost thirty years after the return from the war. The clinical image is fortunate for its aesthetic and semantic power. It suggests the link with the war, with time and space, the time and space of the war and the past, but those of the present as well, the *hic et nunc* of a daily life that must be lived despite everything, the link, in the past but above all in the present, with the other and with one's own otherness. "Who came here cannot return the same"[91], says the narrator.[92] It is also what Lobo Antunes writes to his wife:

> I look at myself in the mirror and see a stranger. But on the outside I am the same, I guess. It is in the inside that I have changed.[93]

Both speak the same language. Others recognize themselves in it, as testified by the immediate success of the book. The private word has entered the public realm, denouncing, with the scandal of the war, the scandal of the general, moral, intellectual, political cowardice and promoting memory against oblivion, for "battles only exist through the people who fight them, and have no other location but the stories that tell them".[94]

---

[1] The novel has been published in English as *The Land at the End of the World* (W. W. Norton & Company, 2011)

[2] Kæmpfer, Jean. *Poétique du récit de guerre* (Paris: José Corti, 1998).

[3] Antunes, António Lobo. *Os Cus de Judas* (Lisboa: Editorial Vega, 1979), 13.

[4] This text offers a condensed and altered version of a study published in 2010. "La rumeur des manguiers de Marimba. Poétique de la guerre: *Le Cul de Judas* d'António Lobo Antunes". In Kleiman, Olinda, Pascal, Anne-Marie, Rousseau, Philippe (ed.). *Poétique de l'écriture d'une expérience de guerre – la littérature postcoloniale en langue portugaise*. (Saint-Étienne: Publications de l'Université de Saint-Étienne, 2010), 91-119.

[5] Antunes. *Os Cus de Judas*, 9.

[6] Antunes. *Os Cus de Judas*, 10.

[7] Antunes. *Os Cus de Judas*, 10.

[8] Antunes. *Os Cus de Judas*, 8.

[9] Cf *Diário popular*, October 18, 1979; Guichard, Thierry. *Le Matricule des anges* (Montpellier: n°23, juin-juillet, 1998), 9. Later, Lobo Antunes will repeatedly say that war is not the subject matter of the book. Cf Blanco, María Luísa. *Conversations avec António Lobo Antunes* (translated by Michelle Giucicelli, Paris: Christian Bourgois, 2001/2004), 133, 166.

[10] Riegel, Léon. *Guerre et littérature* (Paris: Klincksieck, 1978), 172.

[11] Guichard, Thierry. *Le Matricule des anges*, 8-9.

[12] Blanco, *Conversations avec António Lobo Antunes*, 98.

[13] Kæmpfer, *Poétique du récit de guerre*, 33.

[14] "Au lieu de parler du passé le plus lointain, détaché de la conscience remémorante, on laisse cet autrefois se dire à travers une conscience actuelle; le passé est revécu dans le présent". Rousset, Jean. *Narcisse romancier* (Arud Santos, João Camilo dos. "Alguns aspectos da técnica narrativa em *Os Cus de Judas* de António Lobo Antunes", *Cahiers d'Études Romanes*, 10, 1985), 247, note 13.

[15] Antunes, *Os Cus de Judas*, 58.

[16] Ricœur, Paul. *La Mémoire, l'histoire, l'oubli* (Paris: Seuil, 2000). "Entre la déchirure par le temps ailé et l'écriture de l'histoire et son stylet". Handwritten note on the photo of a sculpture group representing Chronus and History.

[17] The publication, authorized by his daughters, of the war letters Lobo Antunes wrote almost every day to his wife, during his mobilization in Angola, makes an interesting document that allows to observe to what extent fiction owes to biography in this particular case. Antunes, António Lobo. *D'este viver aqui neste papel descripto* (Lisboa: D. Quixote 2005).

[18] Antunes, *Os Cus de Judas*, 106.

[19] Blanco, *Conversations avec António Lobo Antunes*, 125.

[20] Ribeiro, Margarida Calafate. *Uma história de regressos. Império, Guerra Colonial e Pós-colonialismo* (Porto: Afrontamento, 2004).

[21] Antunes, *Os Cus de Judas*, 9.
[22] Antunes, *Os Cus de Judas*, 11.
[23] Kæmpfer, *Poétique du récit de guerre*, 11.
[24] Antunes, *Os Cus de Judas*, 67.
[25] Antunes, *Os Cus de Judas*, 67.
[26] Antunes, *Os Cus de Judas*, 35.
[27] *Le Monde*, november 1998.
[28] Antunes, *Os Cus de Judas*, 187.
[29] Antunes, António Lobo. "Ao negrume do inconsciente, à raiz da natureza humana". In: Antunes, António Lobo. *Segundo Livro de Crónicas* (Lisboa: D. Quixote, 2002), 109.

[30] Antunes, *Os Cus de Judas*, 42.
[31] Antunes, *Os Cus de Judas*, 155.
[32] Antunes, *Os Cus de Judas*, 155.
[33] Antunes, *Os Cus de Judas*, 41.
[34] Antunes, *Os Cus de Judas*, 15.
[35] Antunes, *Os Cus de Judas*, 11.
[36] Antunes, *Os Cus de Judas*, 27.
[37] Antunes, *Os Cus de Judas*, 63.
[38] Antunes, *Os Cus de Judas*, 105.
[39] Antunes, *Os Cus de Judas*, 17.
[40] Antunes, *Os Cus de Judas*, 125.
[41] Antunes, *Os Cus de Judas*, 18.
[42] Antunes, *Os Cus de Judas*, 157.
[43] Antunes, *Os Cus de Judas*, 116.
[44] Antunes, *Os Cus de Judas*, 125.
[45] Antunes, *Os Cus de Judas*, 40.
[46] Antunes, *Os Cus de Judas*, 106.
[47] Antunes, *Os Cus de Judas*, 110.
[48] Antunes, *Os Cus de Judas*, 67.
[49] Antunes, *Os Cus de Judas*, 19.
[50] Antunes, *Os Cus de Judas*, 89.
[51] Antunes, *Os Cus de Judas*, 172.
[52] Antunes, *Os Cus de Judas*, 44.
[53] Antunes, *Os Cus de Judas*, 59-61.
[54] "Estou mesmo a ver que vou chupar 8 dias sem correio, e sem poder escrever, no cu de Judas". Antunes, *D'este viver aqui neste papel descripto*, 270.
[55] Uteza, Francis. "Lobo Antunes: le point de vue de l'écrivain". In: *Quadrant*. (Montpellier: Université Paul Valéry, Centre de Recherche en littérature de langue portugaise, 1984), 154.

[56] Antunes, *Os Cus de Judas*, 42.
[57] Madureira, Luís. "The discreet seductiveness of Crumbling Empire – Sex, violence and colonialism in the fiction of António Lobo Antunes", *Luso-Brazilian Review*, XXXII. (University of Wisconsin, 1995), 25.
[58] Antunes, *Segundo Livro de Crónicas*, 109.
[59] I subscribe to M. C. Ribeiro's analysis, *Uma história de regressos. Império, Guerra Colonial e Pós-colonialismo*, 278 sq.
[60] Cf also "Dava o cu para estar longe dali" Antunes, *Os Cus de Judas*, 165; "'Estamos tramados' e 'estamos lixados' é a frase corrente". *D'este viver aqui neste papel descripto*, 291.
[61] Antunes, *Os Cus de Judas*, 51.
[62] Antunes, *Os Cus de Judas*, 39.
[63] Antunes, *Os Cus de Judas*, 28.
[64] Antunes, *Os Cus de Judas*, 40.
[65] Antunes, *Os Cus de Judas*, 18.
[66] Antunes, *Os Cus de Judas*, 40.
[67] Antunes, *Os Cus de Judas*, 33.
[68] Antunes, *Os Cus de Judas*, 152.
[69] Antunes, *Os Cus de Judas*, 156.
[70] Antunes, *Os Cus de Judas*, 179.
[71] Antunes, *Os Cus de Judas*, 171.
[72] Kæmpfer, *Poétique du récit de guerre*, 210.
[73] Antunes, *Os Cus de Judas*, 180.
[74] " […] allongé dans un trou à attendre la fin de l'attaque, regardant les silhouettes figées des eucalytus coiffés de leur haut-de-forme, identiques à de funèbres témoins de duel" (52).
[75] "Nunca os eucaliptos de Ninda se me afiguraram tão grandes como nessa tarde, grandes, negros, altos, verticais, assustadores" Antunes, *Os Cus de Judas*, 59. "Os eucaliptos de Ninda não cessavam de aumentar" Antunes, *Os Cus de Judas*, 60.
[76] Antunes, *Os Cus de Judas* 122.
[77] Antunes, *Os Cus de Judas* 51.
[78] Antunes, *Os Cus de Judas*. 160.
[79] Antunes, *Os Cus de Judas*. 132.
[80] One may compare: "Candeeiros gagos […] aclaravam de viés o renque das mangueiras, arrancando ramos trágicos do escuro" Antunes, *Os Cus de Judas*, 132 and "Os faróis do carro arrancavam as árvores do escuro puxando-as violentamente para si" Antunes, *Os Cus de Judas*, 161.
[81] Antunes, *Os Cus de Judas*, 167.
[82] "Um grande rumor de trópicos ensanguentados cresce-me das vísceras que protestam" Antunes, *Os Cus de Judas*, 175; "Parece-me ouvir o rumor das folhas das mangueiras de Marimba e o seu imenso perfil contra o céu enevoado do cacimbo" Antunes, *Os Cus de Judas*, 188.
[83] Antunes, *Os Cus de Judas*, 176.
[84] Antunes, *Segundo Livro de Crónicas*, 217.
[85] Antunes, *Os Cus de Judas*, 101.
[86] Antunes, *Os Cus de Judas*, 135.
[87] Antunes, *Os Cus de Judas*, 61.
[88] Antunes, *Os Cus de Judas*, 102.
[89] Antunes, *Os Cus de Judas*, 160.
[90] Antunes, *Os Cus de Judas*, 105.

[91] Cf. "Celui qui a été ne peut plus désormais ne pas avoir été: désormais ce fait mystérieux et profondément obscur d'avoir été est son viatique pour l'éternité". Vladimir Jankélévitch, cited by Ricœur, La Mémoire, l'histoire, l'oubli, epigraph.

[92] Antunes, *Os Cus de Judas*, 125.

[93] Antunes, *D'este viver aqui neste papel descripto*, 221.

[94] Kæmpfer, Poétique du récit de guerre, 32.

(Translated from french to english by Luis Gustavo Leitão Vieira)

Olinda Kleiman is professor of Portuguese language and literature at the Université de Lille 3, France. Head of the Portuguese studies department in this university and co-editor of the publication Poétique de l'écriture d'une experience de guerre – La littérature postcoloniale en langue portugaise (Saint-Étienne: Université de Saint-Étienne, 2010). Kleiman, in addition to being a renowned scholar specializing in Gil Vicente's theater, has several relevant publications in the field of war literature, such as "La guerre coloniale dans la poésie de Manuel Alegre : entre exorcisme et idéologie" ; "Dé-chanter la guerre: aspects de la poétique de l'écriture de la guerre", with Philippe Rousseau ; and "La rumeur des manguiers de Marimba. Poétique de la guerre : Le Cul de Judas, d'António Lobo Antunes", to name a few.

War Imagery.
On the First Edition of Ernst Jünger's *Storm of Steel*[1]

Oliver Lubrich

Ernst Jünger's *Storm of Steel* (1920)[2] contains remarkably few explicit reflections on World War I. A mere two dozen direct statements appear amid a hundred intertextual references and many hundreds of verbal images, which generate a multitude of meanings. This essay will analyse Jünger's language of imagery and decode its implied semantics. How does Jünger metaphorically stage the war? And what messages does he convey through his images?

1. The Use of Metaphors

In the first pages Jünger lays down tracks for his readers to follow throughout the rest of his book.[3] Through a metaphorical vocabulary of description, the text takes on additional levels on which the subject matter is represented figuratively. Metaphorical imagery renders the incomprehensible coherent.[4] Jünger translates his war-time experience into an elaborate language of metaphors, which correspond to semantic codes that allow for alternative interpretations.[5] He performs his theme, as it were, in a variety of keys.

Each word, according to Nietzsche or de Man, offers manifold readings as we need to distinguish between its 'literal' and 'rhetorical' meanings.[6] As soon as certain figures proliferate, they enter into a relationship of reciprocal corroboration and clarification. Tropes interact. Single metaphors (in the extended, Aristotelian sense)[7] link themselves to chains of meaning. When these individual threads merge into cross-referential networks, they constitute significant subtexts. Out of individual, scattered elements emerge sequences and structures. These are not strictly separated but rather meet and overlap. Various subtexts complement each other to generate comprehensive systems of signification.

In *Storm of Steel*, we can distinguish four such semantic fields: Jünger codifies the war as an event of *nature*, as economic *practice*, as a phenomenon of *culture*, and, by means of anthropomorphism, as a *person*.[8]

The First Field: Nature

War is configured as a natural event:

(1) Cosmos. On the highest level war is astronomical: a large missile appears as the *sun*, explosions as *planets*, and a fighting position has the shape of the *moon*.

(2) Weather. The title itself, *Storm of Steel*, transforms the war into a meteorological incident. And this motif runs from beginning to end: a bombardment or offensive are described as *storm, tempest, hurricane* with *thunder, lightning, clouds*, as *wind, hail* and *rain*, heavy *patter*, light *shower*, and even *snow*. They are prefigured by the suggestion that "something is hanging in the air" (35, 45). They erupt and then slacken. A kind of dew remains, representing human blood. The solitary man sees himself "face to face with an outburst of the elements" (51-52). As an artificial event, war crowds actual nature from the foreground: "It appears", Jünger writes about an attack in the spring, "that even the laws of nature are no longer valid; the air glimmers as on a hot summer day" (144).

(3) Water. Soldiers felt in their trenches as if they had been hurled by a typhoon onto an *island* or threatened on a *ship* in distress. The battlefield is then the *sea*, the unevenness of the terrain evokes *waves*. As an officer, Jünger was the "Captain" (163). The movements of his assault troops through the fog of the no man's land become "odysseys" (119). In extension of this imagery, he turns fortifications into *coastlines* and walls of defense into *dykes*, against which wash up the sea of enemy fire and surge of attacks like breaking waves, approaching and receding again with the regularity of the *tide*. Troup movements he visualizes as *rivers* that flow from the hinterland towards the front, where they are dammed up, before gushing into the death zone and rolling up over enemy lines. Soldiers are carried away as if by a *current* or *maelstrom*. And even suffering is captured by the same imagery: blood seems to flow like water.

(4) Land. Alternatively to the depictions of water and the sea, the battle zone morphs into various landscapes: *deserts, fields, forests, hillocks, geysers*, and *volcanoes*. While real "farmland transforms into desert" (60), inversely, the battle zone becomes a "field". Detonations turn into a "forest of impacts" (94). Shells that land on soaked earth yield "high-spouting mud geysers" (98). The ruins of villages become "massive hills" (50). Cannonades make "the earth tremble" (143) like an earthquake – or like "volcanic explosions" (144). At the end, artillery has created a new form of landscape: the "sinkhole landscape" (121). The soldiers adjust themselves to this metaphorical representation: like *plants* they "graft together" in the trenches (25), being "a thorn in the enemy's eye" (80).

(5) **Animals**. War resembles a wilderness of fauna. Jünger reimagines soldiers, tanks, airplanes, guns, and shells as animals. Men become *tigers*. They fight delirious, like "werewolves that rush howling through the night" (146). Those who rob the fallen behave like "hyenas" (142). The shock troop commander hides in a "foxhole" (53) A dying man "stretches almost cozily like a cat" (158). With varying connotations, Jünger describes soldiers as *dogs, pigs, moles, hedgehogs, chickens, seals, amphibians, lizards, snakes,* and *ants*. He occasionally even notes which animal traits are missing: "I'm no owl that can find my way in the dark!" (114) Man is transformed into an animal, hands become *claws*. Human beings activate their "baser instincts" (71). Sometimes they must be "reined in" (174) like *horses*. On entering a battle fighters feel like "wild animals torn out of their dens" (143). As if *insects*, they move in swarms. As if *birds*, they flit apart or settle into their nests. They struggle until they "collapse like an exhausted animal" (102). The wounded emit a "howl" (15) "as if they were skewered on a spit" (86). The decomposing dead are transfigured into *fish*. And even war itself is an animal, showing its "talons" (2). Cannons are like *wolves*: they *howl, spit, bay, roar,* and *devour*. One perceives their bird-like fluttering or their mole-like grubbing in the earth. Gunfire generates the impression of a swarm of *bees*. Hand grenades look like *eggs*. Trenches and paths take on the shape of *snakes*. Tanks move like "great awkward beetles" (165). The infantryman experiences airplanes ominously circling overhead as *vultures*, while he conceives of his own side's machines as *flamingos* and the humming of motors reminds him of *mosquitos*.

The Second Field: Practice

Planets, weather, water, landscape, and the animal world all lie outside of human affairs. A second order of images brings just this, various forms of human experience, to the fore.

(6) **Hunting**. One of the earliest forms of organized activity is the hunt. Jünger sees the conflict as a hounding or driving hunt, in which the roles of hunter and prey are continually interchanging. He stages various scenes accordingly: *lying in wait, stalking,* or *entrapment*. Men "leapt here and there like hares" (100); when they had been hit, they "did cartwheels like a shot rabbit" (179). "With the swelling joy of a

huntsman, I saw that we had made a tremendous catch" (129). Again and again he uses *jagen* as a control word, with regard to guns and bullets as well: a mounted battery "charged ahead" (*vorjagten*) (126), "one explosion chased after another" (*jagte*) (97).

(7) Animal husbandry. Three images are derived from the realm of livestock breeding: the courageous individual who rises up out of the spineless *herd*; the enemy fire that repulses troops like *cattle*; and soldiers being *slaughtered* like animals.

(8) Agriculture. Various images turn the war into agriculture. First, the combat area goes from being a natural landscape, as we have seen, to being a plowed *field*. The armies till the soil; by levelling the ground with their shells they plow and furrow, churn up and circulate the earth, as if working it with hoes. Then they plant and sow. Soldiers are imagined as objects of this farming process: as soon as they rise in bloom, they are *harvested*, mowed down. Their bodies die and enter into the natural cycle of the material world as *fertilizer*. Early on, one encounters bullets as "seeds of lead" (85); later, hand grenades appear "lemon-shaped" (110). At the end, despite defeat, Jünger is able to reap his individual "fruits of victory" (153), when he is served "lemonade" (181) in the hospital – and awarded the medal "Pour le Mérite" (181).

(9) The trades. "War is the hardest trade of them all", soldiers are "its masters" (71). They work on one another with hammers and anvils, with pliars and screws; they emboss, they plane, they drill. The military doctors "exercised their bloody handiwork" (64). Beside *locksmith* and *carpenter*, two other industries are named: the *miller* and the *watchmaker*. The war itself becomes a mill in which men and things are pulverized. In their shelters, soldiers suffer under the "clockwork" of falling drops (VI). On the battlefields, gradually they become blunt like worn out tools.

(10) Mining. Static warfare is comparable to mining to the extent that trenches and bunkers appear to be *tunnels* that the soldiers dig as if they are *miners*. They spend their lives "miserably underground" (V), inside the holes they have dug deep into the earth.

(11) Industry. By mechanizing and modernizing his images of economic activity, Jünger frames the war as industrial production. This representation functions on two levels: seen at large, the battlefield is a *factory*, in which innumerable levers (and gears) become active and one little wheel locks into another. Within this factory one finds various instruments, mechanisms, and processes at work: machines, devices, technology, matter, and energy. But what kind of factory is it? What does it produce?

The only concrete motif that Jünger develops is that of an *ironworks* which manufactures plates. This metaphor takes on many contours as he applies it to different aspects of the war: to tanks, bullets, gas – and troops. The soldiers are treated here not only as factory *workers*, but also as *raw material* that, once melted, is turned into steel and subsequently into a product. (They are continually being "hauled" somewhere, "loaded" and "unloaded".)

(12) **Labor**. Within the term "labor" Jünger labels the jobs in the trenches and behind the front lines, specifically, digging out fortifications, advancing towards enemy lines, shooting and killing – as well as retrieving corpses from the debris and mud. The motif is not limited, however, to manual labor or industrial jobs, but rather extended to administrative and freelance work. The war becomes a professional activity where civil servants and private sector employees have their areas of specialty and enjoy their evenings off after long "hours at the office".

(13) **Economy**. One can also understand the war, more abstractly, in the context of trade and finance – as a phenomenon of capitalism. Jünger uses a broad palette of economic terms to illustrate individual aspects: *business*, *money*, *cost*, *price*, *savings*, *budget*, *tax*, *customs*, *export*, *barter*, *contract*, *sale*, and *receipt*.

The Third Field: Culture

The war is integrated into collective worldviews and staged according to respective cultural practices.

(14) **Religion**. Jünger places events in supernatural metaphysical contexts. War is holy. The experience of it corresponds to a religious ordeal, its progression to a sacred ceremony. The battlefield becomes a destination of pilgrimage to which one journeys in order, full of "awe" (1), to receive a "blessing" (156), to accept a "prophecy" (163), to participate in a religious service, or to lead a hermetic existence. The (Christian) theological categories that Jünger introduces are *hell* and the *devil*, miracles, angels, and the "hereafter". With no earnest references to a 'God' that go beyond the level of idiomatic figures of speech, that concept remains metaphorical.

(15) **Ritual**. The activity that conforms to a religious worldview is that of ritual. War becomes a cult. If it is a *sacrificial* rite, then the soldiers are those to be sacrificed and the officers function as presiding priests.

(16) **Festival**. A form of celebration divorced from religious cult is the festival: as a "bloody festival" (173), it preserves the deadly aspect of the rite, as a "Shrove

Tuesday from hell" (52), it retains a Christian dimension. As an orgy, it keeps its ancient, carnal and sexual connotations.

(17) Theater. Jünger conceives of the war as a "play" or "spectacle". In generic terms, he defines this more exactly as a "drama" (25), as a *tragedy* with acts, scenes, interludes, stage design, and a curtain. *Masks* play a particular role: as mask-like faces, death masks – and even gas masks. In a self-referential passage, Jünger even questions his own effort at theatricalization: "today it smacks somewhat of theater" (101).

(18) Music. Jünger describes the noise of battle as a kind of music that one hears in different keys, pitches, tonalities, and songs, with melody, beat, refrain, and overture, and conducted by the commanders of the artillery. He singles out four instruments: whistles, drums, bells – and a lyre.

(19) Dance. While armies provide the music, the battlefield offers the space for a "dance floor of death" (166). As the bombardment started, writes Jünger, "the dance [...] began" (39). Everything seems to dance: strafing, fire, remnants and smithereens, earth, panicked people, the dead, compass needles, and objects in the sweltering air.

(20) Literature. In addition to the dramatic, Jünger highlights the prosaic aspects of war. Individual types of prose that retain a particular function are the fable, the fairy tale, the adventure story, and the frontier novel. The action tends towards the magical or fabulous. The author especially develops the aesthetics of gothic horror: events are spectral, mysterious, fantastical – a phantom, an apparition full of "shadowy figures". The motif of the treasure hunt comes up again and again. The American frontier, called up by mention of the popular writer Karl May (36), a "bivouak" (57) and a "stake" (143), also qualifies as an interpretive model: the "wild west" (25) is a space, in which strength determines right, where friend and foe encounter one another in proverbial enmity as "cowboys" (162) and "Indians" (6).

(21) Visual arts. Jünger uses aesthetic categories to evoke the "artist's gaze" (169) of a soldier in the trenches surveying the enemy's position, the "ingenious" (69) talent for destruction, the "brilliantly constructed hell-machines" (72) – and even the "grotesque" (135) view of the devastation. As with the other arts (theater, music, dance, literature), the visual arts (such as sculpture or the art of the goldsmith) take shape metaphorically. The motif of *sculpture* refers to the way that soldiers were "molded" (8). A person can only become truly statuesque, however, when he has been "petrified" (124) by the sight of horror, as if by the glance of the Gorgon.

Ammunition, in turn, takes on the morbid character of ancient pieces of art: "The shells and splinters of grenades that lay strewn all about were covered with a beautiful green patina" (43).

(22) Painting. War is presented as the object of an aesthetic experience. It can be beheld as a painting. "The landscape was picturesquely adorned by the many participants of the war" (9). Again and again Jünger describes events as an "image" or "picture" whose details are contained as if within a frame.

(23) Architecture. Architectural elements appear throughout: the effects of bullets evoke *towers, columns, locking, bolts, chains, walls, vaulting, arcs,* and *fountains*. The bearing of soldiers (as pillars, bars, or chains), the appearance of fortifications (as a terrace or cabin), the nature of the battlefield (as carpet) are depicted with the same imagery.

(24) Sport. The author calls upon two areas of athletic competition in developing his metaphorical language: sports involving a *ball*, in which hand grenades take on a central role, and sports of *combat* such as wrestling, boxing, and fencing.

(25) Games. Various sorts of games serve as models for understanding: *strategic games* such as chess, *games of chance* like cards, dice, or lottery, *shooting games* involving target shooting and the shooting gallery at a fairground. Another group are *children's games* such as throwing snowballs, bowling, rattles, and other toys. In view of a massive offensive, Jünger writes that even "the greatest of the battles" that he faced seemed in retrospect "more like childsplay" (143). And occasionally soldiers would experience themselves along those lines: during the battle they feel lost like children; in mourning for their killed comrades they weep like children; and in death they take on the appearance of children.

(26) School. The idea of school pervades the text as a leitmotif: the first month was "a good school" (7). The street of a locality where officers are housed "took on the appearances of a students' stomping ground" (91). Eagerness for battle comes across as the "rowdiness" (131) of students. "The school of war is thorough, but its fees are high" (142).

(27) Civilian life. Elements of bourgeois, everyday life are scattered throughout: the territory covered by war is a *fairground*, stormed dugouts are *junkyards*, and occupied villages *lunatic asylums*. The war has "imprinted" the terrain with its "stamp" (28). A dugout "leaked" "like a watering can" (28) – or got "crushed like a matchbox" (69). Military operations recall sweeping and mopping, combing and shaving, visiting and receiving guests. Jünger portrays one officer as an "awkward neighbor" (30). Splinters take on the shape of needles. A charred uniform looks like tails. The bodies of the wounded and dead Jünger describes as *household tools*: "The head had been knocked clean off of one man and the trunk of his neck looked like a great bloody sponge" (76). "Another, with a triangular rag hanging from the back of his skull, emitted constant, harrowing cries" (15).

FOURTH FIELD: Person

Through anthropomorphisms, the war is personified.

(28) Subject. War and death appear as allegories: as a sinister being, a demon that stands expectant between the two armies, waiting for people to run into its arms; that utters warning cries or mutters gloomily; that grimaces, casts a shadow, and takes pleasure in death. They also appear in the guise of a knight, hunter, or blackguard (with a cudgel). This *monster* is not only abstractly allegorised, but also concretely imagined: as a taloned, fire-breathing *dragon*, on the look-out for his next victims that he will catch and devour. As soon as a mythical *demon* is introduced, the effects of battle can be rendered as hits, strokes, clashing, stamping, tramping, hacking, or blowing. We apprehend the war as a struggle between two people, each embodying an entire army. The opposite side is conceived of in the singular form, as *the* enemy. And likewise, the German army takes on the shape of a single person that uses its *hand* or *fist*. Platoons are reimagined as a collective bodies. Other details convey more personifications: tanks appear as "giants" (165); grenades blink and gurgle, spit, run riot, throw, grab, bite, slay. And even the terrain is described in anthropomorphic terms. Gravel pits yawn. "They spent their days in the bowels of the earth" (VI). Everything takes on a monstrous character.

(29) Eating. The war is the scene of a meal, the process of feeding: eat and be eaten. The soldiers are "bloodthirsty". They guzzle away, tasting the horror. At the same time they become a form of nourishment: they lie on a plate (even the enemies' steel helmets remind one of plates) and get devoured. Disaster is brewing in an oven or a pot bubbling on the stovetop.

(30) Sex. Jünger's experience of war has a sexual structure. In the course of mobilization and the first encounters with battle, he loses his innocence. An assault unit's operation takes on the dramaturgy of copulation: from passionate *anticipation* to *foreplay*, *thrusting*, and *penetrating* enemy positions, and finally the *subsiding* of arousal once the action has ended. Jünger repeatedly describes the sequence of battle with the terms of a sex act: lust, desire, position, climax, and gratification. A 19-year-old's "first time" has special meaning. After a day of rest he feels "as if" he is "new born" (17). The war becomes an erotic experience, the battlefield the location of a "rendezvous of combat troops" (73). We are to read injuries (as in a kitschy fantasy) as the darts of love – or as brutal penetration. "Tearing off my shirt, I saw that I had taken a shot diagonally across my heart" (159). Jünger is saved by a *Gefreiter* [sic!] (i.e. a private – with overtones, via alternate meanings of the verb *freien*, to court) called *Hengstmann* [sic!] (i.e. Studman), who takes him in his arms and, like a knight with his damsel in distress, carries him to his own ranks, whereupon the saviour himself is shot: "Hengstmann sank down gently under me" (180). A homoerotic interpretation is not far-fetched: interaction between comrades can be read as "our intercourse" (8) or as a cohabitation of partners: "we shared our household" (8). There are intimate chance encounters: "I nestled involuntarily against a man who lay next to me on the pallet" (93). When they intrude on another unit in their quarters, those men "come running in their negligees" (79). Explicit sexuality does not occur, however. "There was no place for the erotic" (18). But speech substituted for reality in the soldiers' conversations all the more: "the erotic played a central role" (136). Actual women are almost entirely absent. At the most they appear as nurses; and here they elicit a strange agitation in the inexperienced soldiers: "the female being confused me in those days, when the fate of a battle had thrown me into a bed at the hospital. From the masculine, purposeful, practical business of war one emerged into an atmosphere of undefinable radiance". (181)

(31) Conversation. The war appears to follow the rules of conversational communication: cannons talk, entering a dialogue whose course is defined by statements offered and answers made in reply. A bombardment is to be understood as a *greeting*. "Sometimes the artillery fire stopped speaking" (167).

(32) Cyborgs. *Storm of Steel* charts a military anthropology. War defines "human nature" (103). The author imagines the individual soldier as well as whole units as technoid organisms, as cyborgs. The spine, bones, and fists are made of iron rather than flesh. People function as automatons, man-machines. The battle takes place between partly organic, partly technological figures, "between two brazen powers" (167).

On the whole, the following structure of metaphorical fields and codes emerges:

NATURE	PRACTICE	CULTURE	PERSON
(1) Cosmos	(6) Hunting	(14) Religion	(28) Subject
(2) Weather	(7) Animal husbandry	(15) Ritual	(29) Eating
(3) Water	(8) Agriculture	(16) Festival	(30) Sex
(4) Land	(9) The trades	(17) Theater	(31) Conversation
(5) Animals	(10) Mining	(18) Music	(32) Cyborg
	(11) Industry	(19) Dance	
	(12) Labor	(20) Literature	
	(13) Economy	(21) Visual arts	
		(22) Painting	
		(23) Architecture	
		(24) Sport	
		(25) Games	
		(26) School	
		(27) Civilian life	

2. Semantics

Storm of Steel can be broken down into 32 metaphorical codes. The images generated by this language provide a gloss of mutually complementing, supplanting, and varying meanings. What does each of these signify on its own?

As an astronomical, meteorological, nautical, or geological phenomenon, the war seems to follow the laws of nature, removed from human influence and responsibility. But is war natural?[9] Should we critique this naturalization as an ideological treatment?[10] Does a reactionary fear of the disintegration of hierarchical order find expression in the metaphor of the flood, for example?[11] Or should the naturalization "not be prematurely dismissed", since, at least, it establishes a cognitive paradigm, creates distance, and positions the subject against the war as an object of reflection?[12]

In the animal world, war remains in territory that we cannot morally sanction. It is at least personalized, however, through animal protagonists whose behaviour is, to some extent, symbolically analogous to human conduct that we can interpret and judge. Yet the interpretation of this analogy is ambiguous: although Jünger himself uses the term 'fable,' his text does not offer a *fabula docet*. On the one hand, conflict in the animal kingdom is associated with Darwinian principles of the 'struggle for life' and 'survival of the fittest.' On the other hand, Jünger's animal images are not coded with racist overtones, such that noble beasts fight against those of a lower order, or even coded with aristocratic values, since assault troops appear as "tigers" but are nonetheless described in the next moment as "ants" fleeing from a grenade or as "moles" burrowing in the earth. When war draws out man's bestial qualities, we are encouraged to read this critically: as *anti*-war imagery.

War is integrated into the sphere of human activity as a hunt, as animal husbandry, and as agriculture. Hunting and livestock breeding are located between the zoological-natural and the human-technical worlds. Both imply violence: man kills animals during the hunt or at the slaughterhouse. Insofar as people assume the role of animals, as hunted, or as raised and slaughtered livestock, Jünger's images from the animal world are extended here.[13] As a process of agriculture, by contrast, the war becomes a peaceful affair. It is both organized and productive and has therefore positive connotations. And yet, all three areas – hunting, raising livestock, and cultivating the land – seen from an anthropological perspective, imply the management of aggression and violence: the potential for aggression which a hunting party steers towards the animal, a breeder can channel onto the victim during ritual slaughter.[14] An agricultural society relies on the development of substitute activites such as symbolic rites that facilitate an equivalent release without bloodletting and that correspondingly strengthen social cohesion. When unsuccessful, such a society runs the risk of an outbreak of uncontrolled violence: a war.[15]

Both the soldier as technician[16] and the war as labor[17] are manifestations of modernity. Jünger's modernity is destructive, in that it annihilates what has been; yet it also creates something new. From a cynical perspective, death and suffering appear to be the sacrifice necessary for progress to occur. In *Der Arbeiter* (1932)[18] Jünger pursued this imagery further by rendering the Worker a social-utopian figure. The labor motif became totalitarian, whereas Jünger's earlier concept of military professionalization as a *job*, in contrast to a patriotic 'People's Army', had still mitigated totalitarian nationalism.

Jünger does not invest different forms of economic activity with moral distinctions, such as making agriculture, mining, and industry positive (productive), while devaluing trade and, above all, finance as negative (not productive) – as was the case in anti-semitic discourse.[19] The war, of course, took place in the context of the warring countries' real economies. Through his imagery Jünger points to an actual relationship. Later, in his concept of "Total Mobilization", he will turn the war into a paradigm for a totalitarian society.[20] On the other hand he makes its economic aspects visible: capitalism appears as a war-like business; war as a continuation of economic activity by other means. In this sense, Jünger's interpretation is in accord with the imperialism and war theory of Marx and Engels, not to mention Lenin.

By asserting its metaphysical character, war is once again withdrawn from the realm of human responsibility. The possibility of interpreting it rationally is called into question. If it is part of a divine plan, it seems just as inevitable as if it is an act of nature. It possesses a deeper meaning. One could certainly also perceive this posture as the understandable reaction of a soldier on the front: Hermann Knebel sees the "connotative connection with metaphysical concepts" as an attempt to offset the "minimization of the subject through the maximization of the technological impact of war".[21]

Ritual sacrifice is collective violence. As opposed to murder, pogrom, or assault, this is religiously legitimate, channeled violence in the service of a community, violence that can be understood as a source of cultural development.[22] By using the sacrifice metaphor Jünger implies a complex meaningfulness, a psychic, social, and civilizational expedience that hardly approaches the reality of war. But he nonetheless positions war within certain conventions. A sacrifice is no ordinary murder.

As a celebration, war becomes something enjoyable, in contrast to ritual killing. Like a sacrifice, it occurs outside of everyday life in a symbolically demarcated time and space. As an artistic performance, it becomes unreal– even while theater at its origins preserved the memory of the sacrificial rite. The performance gives the viewer the chance to position himself not on the stage but outside of the story, in the "foyer of death".[23] The motif of the world-as-theater as it appears in medieval mystery plays, in Shakespeare ("all the world's a stage…"), or in Calderón's *El gran teatro del mundo*, yields a complex allegory: if the world is a stage and life is a play, then 'God' takes on the functions of the author, director, and critic, who judges, after death when the curtain has fallen, how well people have played their roles, how closely their behavior has conformed to religious source texts, and who assigns them their new places outside of the theater, in real, eternal life. Jünger, by contrast, offers us no comparable narrative.

Musicality suggests harmlessness as well as perfect predictability. Harro Segeberg read Jünger's dance metaphor – in line with Kleist's essay *On Puppet Theater* – as the perfection of mechanized man.[24]

The image of the soldier as a sculpture anticipates the monumental commemoration of heroes and, by describing the depicted object as gruesome, the establishment of anti-war memorials: both Arno Breker and Käthe Kollwitz at once. What is provocative about Jünger's painting motifs is that he reclaims the indifference of the distanced observer whose lack of involvement seems to scoff at the horror of collective violence. In modern literature, however, catastrophic war images are often represented ecphrastically, in the form of paintings depicting violence, as apocalyptic visions.[25] It is precisely the *evidentia* of the picture that permits an author to communicate horror effectively. Jünger's images remain, despite all the aestheticizing, images of atrocity.

Architecture is *the* constructive profession *par excellence*. War is *the* archetypal destructive event. The inadequacy of this figurative language is apparent. It does have a discursive index though: Christoph Asendorf situates the visualization of trajectories in the context of avant-garde ideas from architecture, design, urban studies, anthropology, and technology, that coincide with the military motif of the flow line, parabola, or flight path.[26]

As a theatrical, musical, dance, pictorial, literary, or architectural phenomenon, war possesses an aesthetic value.[27] Critics have long considered Jünger in relation to aestheticism, in particular to Nietzsche.[28] Walter Benjamin advanced two general theses: that fascism "boils down to an aestheticization of political life;" and that "all efforts to aestheticize politics culminate at one point. This one point is war".[29] In a review, he spoke directly about Jünger, suggesting of him exactly this: "a wanton transfer of the thesis 'art for art's sake' onto war".[30] On the other hand, as Karl Heinz Bohrer has shown, Jünger's "aesthetics of horror", in which the moment of sharper awareness takes on a particular meaning, can be understood as modernistic and diagnostic.[31]

The motif of athletic competition implies that war is harmless, but also that it is executed according to the idea of fairness. If war is a sport and the soldiers are athletes, then there must be a system of rules: international law. Jünger thus counteracts the nationalistic doctrine of hate and objects to fighting the "total" war of Ludendorff's theory.

Thought of as a game, war would also be harmless, even pleasurable. Ulrich Prill sees a general "ludic attitude"[32] in Jünger's works. By connecting the motif of the game with that of childhood, however, Jünger ventures a serious critique: war is like the action of children – pre-rational, egotistical, cruel. To designate it as a sort of school seems at first trivializing. But then Jünger does not specify what the soldier might actually be learning. He learns just this perhaps: that war is horrible and criminal.

The remaining metaphors from civilian life are not invested with such ambivalence. Josef Peter Stern criticized the savageness of Jünger's "Embattled Style" as a mannerism and lamented the reverse invasion of military imagery into civilian territory in *The Worker*: "a piece of prose is not a 'military exercise,' nor do 'guns speak,' except by way of worn-out metaphor".[33]

As a person, war becomes a subject – and as such we can judge it. When Jünger portrays it as monstrous, this can hardly be read as a positive appraisal. Soldiers must adopt an attitude in the face of it: fear, disgust, rejection. Understood as the process of food intake, war would be necessary in ambiguous ways: soldiers are part of the food chain, of the circulation of matter. This may be a vulgar sort of Darwinism – but also cynicism.

When the battle takes on sexual overtones, it is libidinous, lustful, and once again, necessary. Played out between men, this sexuality is homoerotic. It can be seen as an overcoming of differences.[34] The erotic relationship to the enemy amounts to a sado-masochistic perversion, and yet also to a certain connection and equality.

War staged as a discussion, as a civilized form of interaction, is indeed so hair-raising that one must ask the question again: is this intended to be provocatively naïve, trivializing, and ideological, or ironic and subversive? Is the representation of war through metaphors of communication a way of disavowing the one or the other?

The cyborg motif is not *per se* reactionary. Matthew Biro distinguishes progressive and regressive variants from the Weimar period.[35] Jünger stands for the endorsement of a technology that transforms mankind imperiously, in contrast to the critical representation Raoul Hausmann produced or to the ambivalent and self-reflexive work of Fritz Lang. *Storm of Steel* connects the motif with a sharpening of the senses, the *Total Mobilization* with the technological transformation of the world, and the *Worker* with the epiphany of a new man under a cybernetic state.[36]

By imparting additional levels to his text through numerous images and references, Jünger distinguishes his work as *modern* literature, characterized by increased self-referentiality and self-reflection. By exposing the artistic character of his writing, he counteracts both an aesthetic and a political ideology that he appears in other respects to be advancing. Self-referentiality and manifest artificiality tend to be anti-authoritarian.

By naturalizing, pragmatizing, culturalizing, and personifying the war, Jünger makes it interpretable. Each metaphor possesses a common denominator with its object that facilitates the transfer. It generates problematic significance, however, when it produces excesses of meanings. The ideological dimension of metaphorical interpretations requires scrutiny. For their implications are various: trivialization and distortion, fatalism and responsibility, glorification and subversion. Jünger's metaphors contain ambivalence, a cynical, ironic, or critical potential.[37] His methods are anything but straightforward.[38]

The temptation arises to read the later Ernst Jünger into this very first text and to see the first edition of *Storm of Steel* before a background of subsequent editions.[39] The controversy around the author threatens to overshadow the reading of the work.[40] The myth of his person has impeded an impartial reception. In fact, however, the 1920 text offers the possibility not to rediscover the fully-developed war-glorifier and proto-fascist,[41] but rather to observe his genesis. The nationalistic and totalitarian leanings are only nascent here. We can recognize the first signs of ideas that will evolve into full-fledged positions later. But alternative potentialities emerge that are either simply abandoned or that the author suppresses and then to some extent later tried to revive.

3. Functions

Linked to the problem of how to interpret Jünger's imagery are further questions: 1. Can we distinguish types of metaphors? 2. What overall impression do these verbal images generate? 3. What relationship do they have to one another? Is there an overarching system? Do the tropes contain a collective interpretation of the events of the war? 4. Are they interconnected? Do they overlap? 5. Can we observe development? 6. Are they allocated to the warring parties in specific ways? 7. How do the metaphors relate to non-metaphorical uses of the same words? 8. Is the verbal imagery reflected on a meta-level? 9. Which metaphors appear in the text that are not further developed? And are there metaphors that Jünger significantly avoids? 10.

How appropriate are the author's chosen images? 11. What insights do they convey? 12. And does Jünger make use of a (proto-) fascist or national-socialist language?

(1) Types. Considered formally, Jünger's images are of various kinds; according to their degree of obviousness, different types can be distinguished: reflected images (comparisons, framed by corresponding formulations); explicit metaphors (recognizable as such, the figurative dimension not being absorbed by pragmatic meanings); and implicit metaphors (whose literal meaning obscures the metaphorical, which is accessible only upon attentive examination and in the context of similar images).

(2) Frequency. All three types seem to appear in Jünger's text with much greater frequency than is, on average, the case in literary texts. The overall impression is, to begin with, a purely quantitative one of prodigious density, metaphoric sprawl. We can understand this as a symptom: the extraordinary discordance of his war experience leads to a variation of interpretive attempts that express themselves implicitly – and possibly in part unconsciously – with a proliferation of verbal images. This very plurality is evidence of the impossibility of coming to terms with the subject and depicting it in language.[42]

(3) Relationships. How do the areas in which the metaphors move about relate to one another? They complement each other synchronously, as levels of sublimation: from the simple (weather, agriculture, ritual, eating) to the complex (animals, economy, literature, dialogue). Furthermore, diachronic links and continuities ensue, whose logic seems to be one of implicit social, economic, and cultural history: in social and economic terms, Jünger understood the war as a hunt, as animal husbandry, agriculture, skilled manual labor, mining, industry, finance and trade; culturally, he interpreted the war in different evolutionary stages as ritual, celebration, sports, theater, music, dance, sculpture, painting, architecture, and literature.

(4) Interference. How do the images and meanings interact with one another? They yield more or less complicated combinations, whose elements are often incompatible – for example the motifs of bodies of water and of dance ("the waves of the storm danced like a line of ghosts through white, undulating vapors". [146]), landscape and architecture ("through a forest of artillery fountains as high as church towers" [97]), the animal world and landscape design ("soil sprang up in spitting fountains" [105]). In a single word like *Garbe*, Jünger superimposes multi-layered meanings: the image from agriculture of a bundle of grain overlaying the idea of the flames of fireworks (*Garbe*, i.e. "sheaf"); the aesthetic concept of deportment, of jewelry and of garments (*Garbe*, i.e. "garb"); and the depiction of pieces of meat from the butcher (*Garbe*, i.e. "truss").[43] The war is thus freighted with meanings that intersect and come into conflict with one another. Jünger drives his metaphors to the outer bounds of their functional capacity.

(5) **Variation**. How are metaphors allocated throughout the text? A quantitative analysis would show where the emphases lie, by examining the statistical frequency and distribution of individual images. More important, however, is the qualitative question: what subjects does Jünger treat metaphorically, when and where? Clusters of metaphors appear on the first two pages of the foreword as well as the first page of the main text, where the motifs are introduced. An abatement that we might expect, due to the writer's increasing familiarity with the experience that he recalls, does not occur. But the frequency varies: first it grows denser as the subject turns to combat operations, and subsequently decreases when the author begins describing sojourns far from the front. The intensity of the figurative language indexes the intensity of horror. There is, however, one remarkable moment in which the imagery is temporarily broken off: at the beginning of the chapter "The Great Battle", a climax of the text, Jünger describes how his company is hit by artillery shelling while gathered in a pit in anticipation of an attack (140-141). The effect of the shells is devastating: of more than 150 men, only 63 escape death or grave wounds. Lieutenant Jürger reacts by "leaping up and running aimlessly into the night" (141). He then suffers a nervous breakdown: "I threw myself to the ground and broke into spasmodic sobs as people stood somberly around me" (141). He suggests that this experience would become traumatic for him: "one never forgets such moments" (141). This is a scenario of shell-shock. Significantly, none of the usual figurative language plays a role here. The chains of tropes are interrupted. In the panic it is no longer possible to form metaphors.

(6) **Deconstruction**. Every war is based on a friend-foe distinction. On the one hand, Jünger seems regularly to reserve metaphors of a pejorative nature for the enemy. Thus the English appear as "pigs" (22, 159). On the other hand though, he employs a stereotypical animal metaphor to describe himself and his comrades: the "front-swine" (28, 93). He expressly uses the "scoundrel" meaning of the word "pig" (*Schwein*) for both sides: "'il y a des cochons aussi chez vous!'" (28) (i.e. "there are pigs on your side too!"), an English officer calls out to him as they converse across the no man's land after a German soldier broke a cease-fire. Jünger later makes this

sentence his own: "there are pigs everywhere" (62). Conversely he turns the English insult, "the Huns" (153), back onto the enemy, with a denigrating meaning, calling them the "Hun-mongous English" (*hünenhafte Engländer*) (179).[44] By using the same images for both sides, he overrules the opposition this imagery appeared to confirm. The antagonism that motivates the war dissolves.

(7) Referentiality. The author presses this metaphor further by describing not only how these "pigs", the German soldiers, engage with other pigs, the English, but also with the real swine that nourish them: they eat "pork meat" (93). Metaphors collide with their real counterparts. The effect is a confusion of literary tropes and extra-literary reality.

Jünger appears to have sought just this result. He offers up corresponding real-life equivalents for nearly all the areas that inspire his figurative language. So, for example, a "mill" (45), a "mine" (19, 43), a lime works (called "Chez-bontemps", 78), a phonograph (154), "the iron scaffolding of a destroyed sugar factory" (135), a "chapel" (165), a photographic "image" (147), an actual conversation with the enemy (131), and an extremely realistic "giant figure [...], swinging a white cudgel" (85). The boundaries become blurred between an allegory of the war and images transmitted from the war into reality. The soldiers celebrate a "libation" (79) when they get drunk. They do not just make metaphorical but also real music. Jünger himself "drummed with his feet to warm them against the tunnel's edge" (135). "Christmas songs" are "drowned out by MGs" (29). Sleeping soldiers are likewise "disturbed by [...] swarms of mosquitoes and shelling" (97). Jünger does not just describe himself as, but he also pretends to be, an animal – when in danger, in the dark: "I [...] emitted a sequence of nature sounds" (38). After "lemon-shaped hand grenades" (110) threatened his life, the wounded receives "lemonade" (181).

The idea of school pervades the text in manifold ways, figurative and literal: schools in the war zone, training for soldiers, schoolchildren and teachers, as well as memories of school. Games make their way into the text when in fact soldiers play them, for example card games; but also when, for instance, "in horrific contrast" they spot "a child's toy" (19) between army positions. Jünger's shock troops use baby carriages that had been left behind as a means of transport (73). And finally, there were children living in the combat zone: "unsuspecting children played" (18). Aesthetic images confront woeful reality.

The multiple meanings of the mask are particularly strange. When mention is made of a mask, the reader must deduce meaning from the context: Is it a gas mask, a mask of war, a mask-like face, a death mask, or an actors' mask? At the same time, the motif is self-reflective: it points to Jünger's own process of *masking* reality – with images. "I put the mask on" (42).

In the area of nature, it becomes clear to what extent metaphorical and literal meanings overlap – and how both come into conflict with alternate meanings of the same words. The weather provides obvious examples of phenomena that correspond to images Jünger uses to stage the war: rain, snow, storm, and sunshine. Occasionally their real and metaphorical dimensions come into contact with one another: "a storm mounted, its claps of thunder drowned out by the emerging noise of a new barrage of enemy fire" (107). It is far from clear which meaning we should read as primary in the case of these ambiguous words; whether, for instance, when he writes about a "spring awakening" (137), Jünger refers to the spring season that is in fact beginning or to the major German offensive that is just taking off. Alternative usages of the same vocabulary operate on another level. For example the word 'rain' is used in the phrase "rain of flowers" (1), 'hail' in "a hail of insults" (163), 'shower' in "shower of death" (52), 'thunder' in the exclamatory cry "*Donnerwetter!*" (40), and lightning in "lightning-quick, logical astuteness" (36).

Jünger's nautical imagery gains surreal authenticity when "naval cannons" (45) actually come into operation; when soldiers nearly "drown […] in mud" (121) on rain-drenched terrain; when "a dirty stream filled up my hollowed-out seat, gurgling right up to the top" (103); and when the author finds fossilized "mussels, starfish" (108) in a trench.

Hunting is reflected on different levels. A command to "preserve the French hunt" (125) is literal. The regimental reserve is put up in a forester's lodge that gets christened the "'Pheasant House'" (3). More burlesque variations on the hunting theme appear, such as the "lice hunt" (9) and the "rat hunt" (38). Single stage-props establish the link between real and metaphorical dimensions: "a long, green hunting whistle in his mouth, dangling a musket", a soldier paces "through the machine-gun fire as if he were going on a hare-hunt" (152). In military jargon, one branch of the service is called the "hunters" (151, 152).

Actual animals also make appearances: a mole, rats and mice, flies, lice, earthworms, ducks and coots, fish, a pike, a sheepdog, a terrier, hares and partridges. There are eggs and a goat pen. "Snails and moles lay about", dead, after a gas attack (43). Jünger depicts himself as a researcher of beetles, an "entomologist" (108). He seems to perceive certain animals – like the gunfire that they represent – as irksome:

"a lark soared over us and annoyed us with its warbling" (86). What confuses him appears to be the contradiction between these real phenomena and the military meaning assigned to them: "a lark soared; I found its warbling an intrusive contrast, it unsettled me" (22).

Figurative language dissolves into actual reality: real schools, games, and toys; mills, mines, and factories; masks and songs; natural phenomena; hunts and animals; all corrode Jünger's metaphors from the margins, calling their figurality into question. And they interfere with the metaphors' function by exposing their inappropriateness.

(8) In/appropriateness. How appropriate are Jünger's images to their referents? Clearly war is neither a concert nor a building and certainly not a conversation. The contrast is shocking. It shows us the incomprehensibility of war and the impotence of language to describe it. *Storm of Steel* is the most laborious effort to extract meaning from violence through imagery; and at the same time, by making the intricacy of this attempt discernible, Jünger concedes its failure. Gert Mattenklott spoke of Jünger's *Workers* as a "tragic type, dependent on fictions to be able to endure life".[45] This sentence could be modified to apply to Jünger's first book: Ernst Jünger is dependent on metaphors that help him endure the horrors of war. His metaphors have a protective function. The more intense the terror, the greater the frequency of images.

(9) Approximations and alternatives. Aside from the chains of motifs and fields of images, single metaphors appear, which are not incorporated into a network structure. Some possible areas of meaning are left unexploited, some imaginable interpretations remain in the background. There is, for instance, the motif of execution ("last meal before being hanged" [110]), whereby the war could have been understood as a mass killing by a tyrannical authority; or that of murder ("the murder weapon" [131], "the instrument of murder" [164]), in which we could see the war as a crime; or further, that of illness and medicine ("plague" [VI], "bullet-injection" [158]) that permit us to conceive of the war as an epidemic crisis of reason; or that of whips and shackles ("whipped up" [157], "shackled" [178]) that might depict it as an act of sadomasochism. Beyond these, there are isolated, sterile metaphors – images that are sometimes explored in other places: for example "radiation" is elaborated in later texts,[46] electricity ("opposite poles" [167]),[47] archaeology, and the nightmare. There are, additionally, significant images that do not appear at all, although they would be easily integrated into existing fields: for instance, that of the flood, which would have amounted to an apocalyptic vision;[48] or the marionette (that gets developed in Jünger's *The Battle as Internal Experience*), which could symbolize the imbecilic quality of military obedience.

(10) Self-reference. Not only does Jünger generate military metaphors, he also thematizes this act of creation as a linguistic practice. He draws our attention to the proliferation of tropes by putting them in quotation marks, marking them as "socalled" or explaining their origins: dugouts he calls "'dripstone caves'" (5), "'to the men's room'" (5), or "'Columbus's egg'" (96), the field kitchen's vegetables are "'barbed wire'" (5) or "'crop damage'" (5), a ruin with a view of the front he calls "'Bellevue'" (19), and the commander's residence, "having been shelled to pieces, [...] had probably earned its name, 'Rat Castle'" (97). The soldiers termed war gas "'attack perfume'" (162), antitank barriers "Spanish cavaliers" (111), certain hand grenades "egg grenades'" (111) or "bottle mines" (171). Bullet shields are "so-called Siegfried plates" (163). An improvised table becomes a "so-called table" (163). "Tanks [...] bore largely facetious, threatening, or lucky names and war paint" (165). "To describe the seething of distant artillery thunder we'd minted the phrase, 'it's humming'" (174). Soldiers brought "a signboard" to one trench "with a half-obliterated inscription, 'Keep away, dragons'" (127). Individual passages about the front contain names rife with connotations, for example "the desolate area that we had christened 'Wallachia'" (162). A 'colleague' "named his ridiculous little dugout" after a character from a novel, "'Villa Leberecht Hühnchen'" (38). Sleeping is referred to as "'breathing startorously' as it's known in the technical lingo" (22) (while conversely, in Jünger's prose, the rattling breath of the dying man is tantamount to the snoring of a sleeping man: "his snoring death rattle" [157]). Finally, Jünger 'marks' even the rhetoric of commands and reports: "as the lovely command formula goes..." (178).

In all these places the author points to a practice which is normal in war: the formation of soldiers' jargon; but he at once distances himself from this jargon by setting it inside quotation marks, in order to replace it with his own figurative language. This distancing of the literary from the trivial imagery is what differentiates *Storm of Steel* from a conventional work of war writing of the kind that was published *en masse* in the 1920s.

As he considers the soldiers' terminology from a certain distance, Jünger implements his own metaphorical language on different levels: as images of the war (the primary metaphorical level), alternative images from the same material (the secondary level), proper names (between signs and reality), and corresponding things (depicted reality).

(11) Epistemology. *Storm of Steel* poses an epistemological question: what functions do verbal images have in appropriating reality? How does figurative language shape our perception, recognition, understanding, and thinking? To what extent is our reality constructed by tropes? What communicative function do they have? Do they have the heuristic value of a provisional modelling?[49] What existential, psychological mechanisms does the creation of metaphors follow?

(12) Fascism. Is Jünger's language, after all, fascist? Russell Berman defines *ekphrasis*, the privileging of pictorial seeing over the written word, as a strategy of fascistic representation (in Leni Riefenstahl's *Triumph of the Will* and Jünger's *Worker*). His thesis is "the descriptive rhetoric of fascist representation".[50] Is Jünger's imaging fascistic *per se*? Perhaps more fitting is a more concrete question: which of Jünger's images – or to be more exact, which of their elements and implementations – correspond to a national-socialistic vision? The image of the *tiger*, for example, appears in World War II in the appellation of a combat tank; the motif of *knighthood* in the SS's self-staging; the idea of *human sacrifice* was used in propaganda after the defeat at Stalingrad; the nihilistic *death cult* formed a central element of the era's *weltanschauung*.[51] Some images that served Jünger in his descriptions of his war had sinister afterlives.[52] They reinforced ideological concepts ('total mobilization,' 'worker,' 'inner experience'). Historically, in the attempts to cope with the First World War, we can observe the evolution of fascism as it emerges. Ernst Jünger's language is *partially* and *potentially* fascist.

The simplest method of assigning meaning to the war is explicit ideology: its justification, through a superordinate authority (a God, the Führer, the Kaiser, the people, the nation, the state, the army, a command) or an abstract principle (patriotism, freedom, faith, progress, peace). Jünger's texts are illuminating insofar as they broadly eschew those sorts of constructions. Instead, we can perceive an indirect strategy of processing the war – the radical 'other' of civilized life – by means of language: through a poetic economy of multiple figurations. The title itself betrays this technique of cumulative imaging: War = *Storm* + *Steel*. The deep confusion that the experience provokes seems to demand a mode of literary interpretation that, rather than explicit in its messages, is implicit in its design, and therefore subtler and more flexible. The generation of metaphors serves the purpose of rationalization and comprehension.

Through his excessive creation of competing metaphors, Jünger tests divergent options of understanding. On one hand, he awards the war deeper, positive significance; and on the other, he calls that very meaning into question. *Storm of Steel* is more a kaleidoscope of various efforts at interpretation than an authoritarian glorification. In sum, the text is about the incomprehensibility rather than the magnificence of war. In its contradictions, the book, as a document, can be read in two ways: one, it permits the reconstruction of a certain fascination and the observation of ideological thinking at its origins, states of mind that would later contribute to national-socialism; and two, it offers an occasion to see the horror of the war reflected in the attempts to deal with it linguistically.

In the first edition of *Storm of Steel*, Jüngerian war imagery can be analyzed in terms of codes, differentiated by types, and described according to its density. Its metaphors can be examined according to their relationship, interference, and variation. They connote different positions and get tangled up even as they overlap or conflict with each other. Together, they produce an effect that we can read as a sympton of uncertainty.

---

[1] The following essay is the revised English version of: Sprachbilder des Krieges. Zur ersten Fassung von Ernst Jüngers In Stahlgewittern. In: *Pandaemonium Germanicum* 16:2 (2010), 53–88. Translation by Maggie Bell.

[2] The publication from 1920 was the first of seven versions each of which was the result of substantial revisions by the author: Jünger, Ernst. *In Stahlgewittern*. Aus dem Tagebuch eines Stoßtruppführers (Hannover, 1920). (All citations from this edition will be indicated by a page number in parentheses. Like all quotes from other sources, they have been newly translated into English.) The subsequent six editions appeared in 1922, 1924, 1934, 1935, 1961, and 1978: *In Stahlgewittern*. Aus dem Tagebuch eines Stoßtruppführers (Berlin, 1922, 2nd edition; Berlin, 1924, 3rd edition); *In Stahlgewittern. Ein Kriegstagebuch* (Berlin, 1934, 4th edition; Berlin, 1935, 5th edition); *In Stahlgewittern*. In: *Werke*, Volume 1, 11-310 (Stuttgart, 1961, 6th edition); In: *Sämtliche Werke* 1, 9-300 (Stuttgart, 1981[27], 7th edition). – Hermann Knebel examined the modifications which were considerable both qualitatively and quantitatively. Knebel starts from the premise that Jünger developed a "generative center" (the idea of "regressive modernization" worked out by Harro Segeberg) in each case in a different way. The goal shifts from the recollection of a war veteran, to the agitation of a revolutionary nationalist, to the humanistic literature of an elite writer. Knebel, Hermann. 'Fassungen': Zu Überlieferungsgeschichte und Werkgenese von Ernst Jüngers *In Stahlgewittern*. In: Segeberg, Harro (Ed.). *Vom Wert der Arbeit. Zur literarischen Konstitution des Wertkomplexes 'Arbeit' in der deutschen Literatur (1770-1930)* (Tübingen: Niemeyer, 1991), 379-408. – See also Kunicki, Wojciech. *Projektionen des Geschichtlichen. Ernst Jüngers Arbeit an den Fassungen von "In Stahlgewittern"* (Bern: Peter Lang, 1993).

[3] The subtitle, *Aus dem Tagebuch eines Stoßtruppführers* ('from the diary of a shock troop leader'), refers to an actual journal written during the war. The original diary remained in Jünger's private

possession until his death. It appeared at last, 90 years after the first edition of the literary work it inspired, as *Kriegstagebuch 1914-1918*, published by Kiesel, Helmuth. (Stuttgart: Klett-Cotta, 2010). John King had previously compared the manuscript with the printed version: King, John. *"Wann hat dieser Scheißkrieg ein Ende?"* Writing and Rewriting the First World War (Schnellroda: Antaios, 2003).

[4] See Blumenberg, Hans. *Paradigmen zu einer Metaphorologie* (Frankfurt: Suhrkamp, 1960); Blumenberg, Hans. *Die Lesbarkeit der Welt* (Frankfurt: Suhrkamp, 1981); Lakoff, George / Johnson, Mark. *Metaphors We Live By* (Chicago: Chicago UP, 1980).

[5] Hermann Knebel alludes to Jünger's way of "embedding the events of the war in meaningful discourse", implicitly, "via representational technique" (Knebel, 'Fassungen', 391). Harro Segeberg speaks of an "intentionally composed text with suggestively arranged verbal images". Segeberg, Harro. "Regressive Modernisierung". In: Segeberg, Harro (ed.). *Vom Wert der Arbeit.* Zur literarischen Konstitution des Wertkomplexes 'Arbeit' in der deutschen Literatur (1770-1930) (Tübingen: Niemeyer, 1991), 337-378: 344-345. The most comprehesive study (of Jünger's literary works up to 1933) is: Verboven, Hans. *Die Metapher als Ideologie.* Eine kognitiv-semantische Analyse der Kriegsmetaphorik im Frühwerk Ernst Jüngers (Heidelberg: Universitätsverlag Winter, 2003), 15-27 (methodical section).

[6] Nietzsche, Friedrich. "Ueber Wahrheit und Lüge im aussermoralischen Sinne" [1873]. In: Colli, Giorgio and Montinari, Mazzino (Eds.). Nietzsche, Friedrich. *Kritische Studienausgabe.* 15 Volumes, Volume 1 (Berlin/Munich: De Gruyter/dtv, 1988), 873-890; De Man, Paul. "Rhetoric of Tropes" (Nietzsche). In: De Man, Paul. *Allegories of Reading.* Figural Language in Rousseau, Nietzsche, Rilke, and Proust (New Haven: Yale UP, 1979), 103-118.

[7] Aristotle. *Poetics*, 21-22; *Rhetoric*, III.2, 4, 10, 11.

[8] The author must forego citing individual pieces of evidence, an exhaustive survey of which underlies the following paradigmatic reconstruction. See Lubrich, Oliver. *Das Schwinden der Differenz. Postkoloniale Poetiken* [2003] (Bielefeld: Aisthesis, 2009), 148-224; see also the selections pertaining to *Storm of Steel* In: Verboven. *Die Metapher als Ideologie*, who proposes an alterative structuring: 29-35 (water), 55-61 (fire), 81-85 (music), 96-97 (theater), 110-115 (production), 148-152, 167 ff., 175 ff. (transformation), 182 ff. (hunt), 190-191 (delirium), 195 ff. (the supernatural), 203 ff. (space).

[9] Poncet, François. "La vague, Leitmotiv Jüngerien". In: Beltran-Vidal, Danièle (Ed.). *Images d'Ernst Jünger* (Bern: Peter Lang, 1996), 85-104.

[10] Kaempfer, Wolfgang. *Ernst Jünger* (Stuttgart: Metzler, 1981), 68.

[11] Theweleit, Klaus. *Männerphantasien* [1977], 2 Volumes. Volume 1: Frauen, Fluten, Körper, Geschichte. Volume 2: Männerkörper. Zur Psychoanalyse des weißen Terrors (Munich: dtv, 1995).

[12] Knebel, "Fassungen", 392.

[13] Rolf Schroers sees the motifs of hunting and trapping (as well as those of travel and the mirror) in the context of the 'stereoscopic' search for a deeper meaning behind those phenomena, as developed in later writings. Schroers, Rolf. *Der kontemplative Aktivist.* Versuch über Ernst Jünger. In: *Merkur 3* (204), 1965, 211-225: 220-224.

[14] Burkert, Walter. Homo Necans. *Interpretation altgriechischer Opferriten und Mythen* [1972] (Berlin/New York: De Gruyter, 1997), 8-96 ("Opfer, Jagd und Totenriten").

[15] Girard, René. *La violence et le sacré* (Paris: Hachette, 1972), 63-104 ("La crise sacrificielle").

[16] Regarding the typology of 'soldier,' 'worker,' 'tyrant,' 'aesthete,' and 'anarchist' in Jünger's works, see Merlio, Gilbert. "Les Figures du pouvoir chez Ernst Jünger". In: David, Claude (Ed.). *Les Songes de la raison* (Bern: Peter Lang, 1995), 418-434: especially 419ff.; and Merlio, Gilbert. "Les images du guerrier chez Ernst Jünger". In: Beltran-Vidal, Danièle (Ed.). *Images d'Ernst Jünger* (Bern: Peter Lang, 1996), 35-55.

[17] Negt, Oskar and Kluge, Alexander. *Geschichte und Eigensinn.* (Frankfurt: Suhrkamp, 1981), 797-860.

[18] Jünger, Ernst. "Der Arbeiter" [1932]. In: Jünger, Ernst. *Sämtliche Werke* 8, 9-317.

[19] Adorno, Theodor W. and Horkheimer, Max. Elemente des Antisemitismus. Grenzen der Aufklärung. In: Adorno, Theodor W. and Horkheimer, Max. *Dialektik der Aufklärung* [1944] (Frankfurt: S. Fischer, 1983), 177-217.

[20] Jünger, Ernst. Die totale Mobilmachung [1931]. In: *Sämtliche Werke* 7, 121-141.

[21] Knebel, "Fassungen", 392.

[22] Burkert, Walter. "Griechische Tragödie und Opferritual" [1966]. In: Burkert, Walter. *Wilder Ursprung. Opferritual und Mythos bei den Griechen* (Berlin: Wagenbach, 1991), 13-39; Lorenz, Konrad. Das sogenannte Böse. Zur Naturgeschichte der Aggression [1963] (München: dtv, 1983).

[23] Krull, Wilhelm. Im Foyer des Todes. Zu Ernst Jüngers In: Stahlgewittern und anderen Texten über den Ersten Weltkrieg. In: Arnold, Heinz Ludwig (ed.). Ernst Jünger (Göttingen: Text + Kritik, 1995), 27-35.

[24] Segeberg. "Regressive Modernisierung", 356-357.

[25] Buch, Robert. The Pathos of the Real. On the Aesthetics of Violence in the Twentieth Century (Baltimore: Johns Hopkins UP, 2010).

[26] Asendorf, Christoph. Totale Mobilmachung / Total Mobilisation. In: Daidalos 47, 1993: 90-95. Asendorf refers to a place in the seventh edition (166): "Our camp was now such that we sat under the firebell the way we would sit under a tightly woven basket". In addition to Ernst Jünger, Le Corbusier and Peter Behrens, among others, are the focus of this study.

[27] On the dandy motif: Jünger, Ernst., Sturm [1923]. In: Sämtliche Werke 15, 11-74; see Plard, Henri. Une œuvre retrouvée d'Ernst Jünger: Sturm (1923). In: Études Germaniques 4 (92), 1968: 600-615.

[28] See Kaempfer, Wolfgang. Das schöne Böse. Zum ästhetischen Verfahren Ernst Jüngers in den Schriften der dreißiger Jahre im Hinblick auf Nietzsche, Sade und Lautréamont. In: *Recherches Germaniques* 14, 1984: 103-117; Ohana, David. Nietzsche and Ernst Jünger: From Nihilism to Totalitarianism. In: *History of European Ideas* 11, 1989: 751-758.

[29] Benjamin, Walter. "Das Kunstwerk im Zeitalter seiner technischen Reproduzierbarkeit" (3rd Edition) [1936-1939]. In Tiedemann, Rolf / Schweppenhäuser, Hermann (eds.). *Gesammelte Schriften*. 7 volumes in a set of 14, Volume 1.2. (Frankfurt: Suhrkamp, 1977), 471-508: 506. See also Hillach, Ansgar. *The Aesthetics of Politics*: Walter Benjamin's Theories of German Fascism. In: *New German Critique* 17, 1979: 99-119.

[30] Benjamin, Walter. "Theorien des deutschen Faschismus Zu der Sammelschrift Krieg und Krieger. Herausgegeben von Ernst Jünger" [1930]. In: Tiedemann-Bartels, Hella (ed.). *Gesammelte Schriften*. Volume 3 [Kritiken und Rezensionen] (Frankfurt: Suhrkamp, 1991), 238-250: 240. Benjamin criticized the technological intensification of idealism, employing an imagery for his argument that does not occur in Jünger: "so weit man über den Grabenrand blicken konnte, war alles Umliegende zum Gelände des deutschen Idealismus selbst geworden, jeder Granattrichter ein Problem, jeder Drahtverhau eine Antinomie, jeder Stachel eine Definition, jede

Explosion eine Setzung, und der Himmel darüber bei Tag die kosmische Innenseite des Stahlhelms, bei Nacht das sittliche Gesetz über dir. Mit Feuerbändern und Laufgräben hat die Technik die heroischen Züge im Antlitz des deutschen Idealismus nachziehen wollen. Sie hat geirrt". (As far as one could see over the edge of the trench, all of the surroundings became the terrain of German idealism itself: every shell crater a problem, each stretch of barbed wire an antinomy, every spike a definition, every explosion something posited, and the sky overhead – by day, the cosmic interior of a steel helmet, by night, the moral law that reigned above you. With firing lines and communication trenches, technology wanted to trace the heroic features of German idealism's countenance. It was mistaken.) Benjamin, "Theorien des deutschen Faschismus. Zu der Sammelschrift Krieg und Krieger. Herausgegeben von Ernst Jünger", 247

[31] Bohrer, Karl Heinz. *Die Ästhetik des Schreckens* (Munich: Carl Hanser, 1978), 138-403. For a critique of Bohrer's modernistic interpretation of Jünger: Hemmerich, Gerd. Ernst Jünger: Ein moderner Autor? In: PESCHEL, Dietmar (ed.). Germanistik in Erlangen. Hundert Jahre nach der Gründung des Deutschen Seminars (Erlangen: Universitätsbund Erlangen-Nürnberg, 1983), 389-396.

[32] Prill, Ulrich. *"mir ward Alles Spiel"*. Ernst Jünger als homo ludens (Würzburg: Königshausen & Neumann, 2002), 31-48: 33.

[33] Stern, J[osef] P[eter]. The Embattled Style: Ernst Jünger, In Stahlgewittern. In: Klein, Holger (ed.). *The First World War in Fiction*. A Collection of Critical Essays (London: Macmillan, 1976), 112-125: 119, 225 (footnotes).

[34] See Segeberg, "Regressive Modernisierung", 347.

[35] Biro, Matthew. The New Man as Cyborg: Figures of Technology in Weimar Visual Culture. In: *New German Critique* 62, 1994: 71-110, especially: 97-110.

[36] See also Pekar, Thomas. "'Organische Konstruktion'. Ernst Jüngers Idee einer Symbiose von Mensch und Maschine". In: Strack, Friedrich (ed.). *Titan Technik*. Ernst und Friedrich Georg Jünger über das technische Zeitalter (Würzburg: Königshausen & Neumann, 2000), 99-117; on the technologization of nature: Mottel, Helmut. *Technische Paradiese* – Zur poetologischen Funktion der Meta-Phorisierung technischer Perfektion im Werk Ernst Jüngers. In: Strack, Friedrich (ed.). *Titan Technik*. Ernst und Friedrich Georg Jünger über das technische Zeitalter (Würzburg: Königshausen & Neumann, 2000), 225-242.

[37] By considering *metaphor as ideology* and warning of the "metaphorical dangers of language", Verboven developed the thesis that Jünger's "language and thinking" are "molded" in such a way by the "structure" of his metaphors, that they constitute, "in their entirety […], an ideology or philosophy of war simply poured into literary form, "an ideology embodied in a literary language","a legitimization of war and […], thus, a clear ethical (ideological) choice", which can be seen as internally coherent; According to Verboven, Jünger is "trapped within his metaphorical models" (Verboven, *Die Metapher als Ideologie*, 245-252). In contrast to this approach, the contradictions within Jünger's imagery should be examined.

[38] Roger Woods saw symptoms of psychic and political disturbance in the tensions between Jünger's euphoric expectation and disillusionment, the feverish search for meaning and meaninglessness, the soldierly sense of community and isolation, delirious fighting and despair at the military leadership: "One overlooked aspect of Jünger's portrayal of the First World War is the range of attitudes (often irreconcilable) which underlie his thinking". Woods, Roger. "The Conservative Revolution and the First World War: Literature as Evidence in Historical Explanation". In: *The Modern Language Review 1*, 1990: 77-91: 80.

[39] Eva Dempewolf has studied the shifts between the editions historically, in view of Jünger's biographical circumstances and political intentions, and in doing so has also observed the modifications of various species of his imagery. Dempewolf, Eva. Blut und Tinte. *Eine Interpretation der verschiedenen Fassungen von Ernst Jüngers Kriegstagebüchern vor dem politischen Hintergrund der Jahre 1920 bis 1980* (Würzburg: Königshausen & Neumann, 1992), 13, 30, 191, 194, in particular: 78-160. Hans Verboven has not only compiled a comparative study of the different editions (Verboven, *Die Metapher als Ideologie*, 253-262), but also reconstructed the development of war imagery throughout Ernst Jünger's entire early work and conceptualized it theoretically (as expansion, escalation, standstill, and regression, the metaphorization of comparisons or the extension of imagery into non-war-related areas).

[40] On the controversy surrounding Jünger: Moreno Claros, Luis Fernando. "Un centenario polémico: Ernst Jünger en Alemania". In: *Revista de Occidente* 175, 1995: 129-149. For a liberal reception: Lehner, Kurt M "Vom Stahlgewitter zum Anarchen. Ernst Jünger – ein politischer Denker?" In: *Liberal* 2, 1995: 81-87.

[41] Bernhard, Hans-Joachim. 'Die apologetische Darstellung des imperialistischen Krieges im Werk Ernst Jüngers". In: *Weimarer Beiträge* 2, 1963: 321-355.

[42] On the level of content, Hans-Harald Müller describes how Jünger's attempt to interpret his war experience individualistically and heroically comes into conflict with the necessity of describing a de-individualized event; this "led Jünger [...] right to the edge of the insight that the motifs and feelings underlying this experience are not communicable". Müller, Hans-Harald. "'Im Grunde erlebt jeder seinen eigenen Krieg.' Zur Bedeutung des Kriegserlebnisses im Frühwerk Ernst Jüngers". In: Müller, Hans-Harald und Segeberg, Harro (ed.). *Ernst Jünger im 20. Jahrhundert* (München: Wilhelm Fink, 1995), 13-37: 18-24, 23.

[43] GRIMM, Jacob and Wilhelm. *Deutsches Wörterbuch*, Leipzig: Hirzel 1878. Entry "*Garbe*".

[44] The German word "Hüne" (giant) is derived from "Hunne" (Hun, lat. *Hunnus*).

[45] Mattenklott, Gert. "Das Neue im Alten: George, Jünger, Benn". In: Der Neue Mensch. Obsessionen des 20. Jahrhunderts (Stuttgart: Cantz, 1999), 27-35: 30.

[46] See Porath, Erik. "Strahlungen Ernst Jüngers. Anmerkungen zu einem Tagebucheintrag". In: *Wirkendes Wort* 2, 1995: 241-257: 252-253; Hüppauf, Bernd. "Unzeitgemäßes über den Krieg. Ernst Jünger: Strahlungen (1938-48)". In: Wagener, Hans (ed.). *Von Böll bis Buchheim*: Deutsche Kriegsprosa nach 1945 (Amsterdam/Atlanta: Rodopi, 1997), 13-47: 22.

[47] Helmut Lethen observes how Jünger introduces a new sort of imagery in *Der Arbeiter*: "he changes the central techological metaphor. Jünger is one of the first writers to move the model of electric circuitry into the center if an analysis of society". Lethen, Helmut. Verhaltenslehren der Kälte. Lebensversuche zwischen den Kriegen (Frankfurt: Suhrkamp, 1994), 187-215 ("Jüngers Fall ins Kristall").

[48] As an apocalyptic interpretation: Gerhards, Claudia. *Apokalypse und Moderne*. Alfred Kubins "Die andere Seite" und Ernst Jüngers Frühwerk (Würzburg: Königshausen & Neumann, 1999), 74-123.

[49] Is already true for the first work, what may be said about the texts of the thirties and forties, namely, that Jünger's process corresponds to a "meditation 'wandering' through symbols and signs"? Sader, Jörg. *'Im Bauche des Leviathan'*. Tagebuch und Maskerade. Anmerkungen zu Ernst Jüngers Strahlungen (1939-1948) (Würzburg: Königshausen & Neumann, 1996), 223.

[50] Berman, Russell A. "Written Right Across Their Faces: Ernst Jünger's Fascist Modernism". In: Huyssen, Andreas / Bathrick, David (eds.). *Modernity and the Text*. Revisions of German

Modernism (New York: Columbia UP, 1989), 60-80: 64. See Rausch, Jürgen. "Ernst Jüngers Optik". In: Arbogast, Hubert (ed.). *Über Ernst Jünger* (Stuttgart: Klet-Cotta, 1995), 49-72; Boehm, Gottfried. "Fundamentale Optik". In: Figal, Günter / Schwilk, Heimo (eds.). *Magie der Heiterkeit* (Stuttgart: Klett-Cotta, 1995), 9-24.

[51] "Jünger's metaphorical archaism, the fossil-like character of his imagery, converge with the tendency that could have belonged to the basic trends of European fascism". (Kaempfer, Wolfgang. "'Der Tod ist ein Meister aus Deutschland.' Zu einem Leitmotiv im nihilistischen Schrifttum Ernst Jüngers". In: *Recherches Germaniques 6*, 1976: 136-151: 149.)

[52] Kunicki observes, for example, an "accentuation of the mercenary style" in the first and second editions and the "fading" of that style in the third and fourth (Kunicki, *Projektionen des Geschichtlichen*, 54-55, 156). Jünger's depiction of war changes considerably between the two World Wars. Ernst Keller recognized a transition from aestheticization and apology to self-reflection and critique: Keller, Ernst. "Wrestling with an Old Trauma: Ernst Jünger's Changing Perception of Destructiveness". In: *AUMLA* 81, 1994: 21-31. Jan Philipp Reemtsma analyzed Jünger's "disturbed moral state of mind", "self-loathing", und "denial mechanism", on the basis of "omissions" in the Causasus diary, as a technique of "fading": Reemtsma, Jan Philipp. "'Es schneet der Wind das Ärgste zu'. Ernst Jünger im Kaukasus". In: Reemtsma, Jan Philipp. *Mord am Strand*. Allianzen von Zivilisation und Barbarei (Hamburg. Hamburger Edition, 1998), 316-347: 320-321, 329-330. Lothar Bluhm sees Jünger's orientation towards nature (and art) as inner emigration: Bluhm, Lothar. "Natur in Ernst Jüngers Tagebüchern aus dem Zweiten Weltkrieg". In: *Wirkendes Wort 1*, 1987: 24-32; similarly: Bluhm, Lothar. "Ernst Jünger als Tagebuchautor und die 'Innere Immigration'. Gärten und Straßen (1942) and *Strahlungen* (1949)". In: Müller, Hans-Harald / Segeberg, Harro (eds.). *Ernst Jünger im 20. Jahrhundert* (München: Wilhelm Fink, 1995), 125-153; see Bullock, Marcus. "Fallen Altars Are Occupied by Demons: The Disenchantment of Ernst Jünger". In: Grimm, Reinhold / Hermand, Jost (eds.). *1914/1939*. German Reflections of the Two World Wars (Madison: Wisconsin UP, 1992), 70-90: 89.

Oliver Lubrich is Professor of German and Comparative Literature at Universität Bern in Switzerland. Previously, he was junior Professor of Rhetoric at the Peter Szondi "Institute of Comparative Literature and the Cluster of Excellence "Languages of Emotion" at Freie Universität Berlin. He has been a visiting professor at University of Chicago; California State University, Long Beach; Tecnológico de Monterrey, Mexico; and Universidade de São Paulo, Brazil. – Oliver Lubrich published books on *Shakespeare's Self-Deconstruction* (2001) and *Post-Colonial Poetics* (2004, 2009²). He edited/co-edited Alexander von Humboldt's *Central Asia* (2009), *Kosmos* (2004³) and the first German version of *Vues des Cordillères* (2004²), the Chimborazo Diary (2006²) as well as the ethnographic and political essays (2009, 2010). In his current research project he documents international testimonies from Nazi Germany: *Reisen ins Reich* (2004, 2009²); *Berichte aus der Abwurfzone* (2007). (*Travels in the Reich* was published by the University of Chicago Press in 2010.)

Through an Enemy Land:
On Space and (In)visibility in Euclides da Cunha's *Os sertões*

Javier Uriarte

There is an extended belief that the history of Brazil – unlike that of other Latin American countries – is characterized by a long peace. However, this is clearly untrue. Brazil was involved in many wars, civil or international.[1] And, as was the case of other Latin American states, in Brazil war was a crucial element of modernization. In this particular aspect Latin America did not represent an exception to Charles Tilly's classical statement that "war makes states".[2] For him, "governments stand out from other organizations by their tendency to monopolize the concentrated means of violence".[3] In the last years of the 19th century, the Brazilian state apparatus became finally consolidated. This process was marked by one of the most remembered civil conflicts in the history of the country, the Canudos War (1897).

This war was one of the most tragic events in late 19th century Latin American history. A gigantic army sent by the Brazilian government (composed of more than ten thousand soldiers), supposedly defending the newly founded Republic, reduced to ashes the city of Canudos, in the country's northeastern backlands known as the *sertão*.[4] The outcome of the war was an outright massacre: apart from the thousands who died in combat, all remaining prisoners were immediately executed once Canudos was defeated. The best known account of this war is Euclides da Cunha's *Os sertões* [*Rebellion in the Backlands*] (1902),[5] one of the most complex works of the Brazilian literary canon, and one of the first books about war published in the 20th century.[6] However, it would be highly reductive to define Euclides' work as just a book about this war. Its complexity resides in the fact that it traverses different literary genres and discursive forms; it complicates the –never crystal clear– boundaries between history, fiction, and literature; it makes use of different 19th century scientific discourses, including history, sociology, geology, and biology; it is partly a travelogue, a journalistic chronicle, a piece on military strategy, and an anthropological essay. Most importantly, it seeks to offer an interpretation of "Brazilianness": in this sense, *Os sertões* can be seen as inaugurating a genre dear to Brazilian – and Latin American – intellectuals: the essay of national interpretation.[7]

The exact population of Canudos has not been established with precision, but it seems safe to say that it was not an insignificant town.[8] Its inhabitants were *sertanejos* (that is, people from the *sertão*) who followed a *caudillo*-like religious leader known as Antônio Conselheiro, whose real name was Antônio Vicente Mendes Maciel. The *Conselheiro* (or Counsellor) – as he was popularly known – was a mystic and millenarian leader who preached against the Republican system, which he considered sinful, asking his followers not to pay taxes to the government.[9] His followers came from different northeastern regions, but had in common their poverty, marginality and hunger. For them, the new republican system did not offer anything new or good; there was no tangible difference between the imperial system and what was understood by the Brazilian elites as the finally achieved political modernity. In the beginning, the government did not take this rebellion seriously, and sent two successive expeditions which were easily defeated by the *sertanejos*. Even a third expedition, significantly bigger and under the leadership of the respected and feared general Antônio Moreira César, ended in disgrace. This explains the national dimensions that the support for the fourth expedition achieved. It also explains the hunger for death and revenge that propelled it.

Euclides da Cunha was sent to the front, as a war correspondent, by the journal *O Estado de São Paulo*, and he witnessed only the last weeks of the combat. However, his book, published five years later, is not a simple testimony or account of the war. It is the consequence of thoughtful and comprehensive readings in many different fields, and of profound reflections: the result is not a harmonious totality, but a beautifully written text almost illegible for its richness, frequent, contradictions, and tensions.

The resistant attitude maintained by the inhabitants of Canudos towards the official taxation policy represented an obstacle for the process of state modernization that was taking place in Brazil after the fall of the imperial system. One of the key operations in this consolidation of the state's bureaucratic apparatus consisted precisely in being able to transform every individual into a taxable subject. Part of extending the state's control over its subjects to the most unknown regions (unknown to the state, of course) was to incorporate all of these spaces and its inhabitants into the cadastral map it sought to draw as precisely as possible. James C. Scott insists on the fact that taxation is one of the main objectives of the state's gaze on its spaces and citizens: "[State agents'] abstractions and simplifications are disciplined by a small number of objectives, [...] the most prominent of these were typically taxation, political control, and conscription".[10] The Canudos rebellion ignored the authority of the state and rejected its logic and appropriative gaze. Thus, through the massacre perpetrated there, the state sought to re-appropriate (ie, territorialize) a space and a monologic discourse, while establishing new (and possibly immovable) symbolic and geographic boundaries for the state. The consolidation of the Brazilian – and more generally, Latin American – state apparatus in the end of the 19th century implied a strong centralization and militarization. In order to achieve this, the state had to obtain a monopolistic control over all spaces and over the displacements through them.

I propose to read *Os sertões* as a text about the relations between power, space, and movement. The text is divided into three parts: "A terra" ["The Land"], "O homem" ["The Man"], and "A Luta" ["The Fight"]. The forms that movement and spatiality adopt in each of them are multiple. Focusing on the first part of the book, "The Land", this essay will discuss the ways in which war is narrated through descriptions of space. It will examine the forms of seeing and understanding movement in these moments of conflict. I frame war as a key element in what James C. Scott calls the state's operations of legibility and simplification.[11] It implies, thus, a complete reconfiguration of spaces. This is connected to the description of the *sertão* as a desert[12] that remains foggy to the eyes of the state. This uncertain status of the backlands, as a Brazilian territory nonetheless somewhat exterior to the law of the state, is important in my analysis. War becomes the necessary instrument for the state's internalization and incorporation of these territories into the modern space of the nation. The Canudos war can thus be read as the triumph of the immobilizing and fixing logic of the modern state over the constant movement and ubiquity of the man of the *sertão*. I suggest that Deleuze and Guattari's notions of war machine and nomadology can prove productive in this reading of Euclides' major text. In the chapter "1227: Treatise of Nomadology – The War Machine" titled of *A Thousand Plateaus* (1982), Deleuze and Guattari conceive the nomad as the one who opposes, through the use of violence, the also violent imposition of the modern state. The latter seeks to suppress or control all movement, and to fix its subject's identities: "settling, sedentarizing labor power, regulating the movement of the flow of labor, assigning it channels and conduits [...] this has always been one of the principal affairs of the State".[13] To this regulating desire the nomad opposes movement, an incessant fluidity, and what Deleuze and Guattari call "heterogeneity and becoming". I am not referring, of course, to the literal meaning of nomadism, since Canudos was evidently a settlement of people in a given location. The Canudos settlement brought in fact an end to more than ten years of the Conselheiro's wanderings throughout the Brazilian northeast. What is more, the *sertanejos'* fierce resistance to the very end, their refusal to escape in order to save their lives while death became all but certain, is evidence of their strong will to hold to a place, to defend their own immobility. In my reading, nomadism is about reclaiming one's own capacity to freely occupy the space, to move (or not) through one's own space. This essay explores a certain nomad logic of relating to space, of constituting oneself into a war machine, as Deleuze and Guattari would put it. Juan Pablo Dabove has insisted on this: "[e]ven though it [Canudos] represents the end of wandering for Conselheiro's followers (and life in a city is the opposite of nomadism), at its core it conserves a nomadic imprint, an air of the warrior's headquarters".[14] If the *jagunços*, as they are dismissively called by Euclides, resist without abandoning their city, it is also true that they keep leaving it, turning the *sertão* into the real space of war. Thus, *Os sertões* represents opposing forms of conceptualizing space and of moving through it. The narration of war is inextricably linked to the forms in which movement is articulated, and space is seen, described, and conceived.

While the mobile and nomadic logic of the *sertanejos* implies a form of resistance to the state's unifying mould – which tries to codify all movement, to give it a course and a sense –, their stubborn permanence in Canudos constitutes a vindication of stasis. I propose to read this vindication as a different form of resistance, related to Mary Louise Pratt's recently developed notion of the *stayer*, which constitutes a critique of the western association between movement and liberation. Pratt suggests that stasis can be liberating. Thus, to stay could constitute a form of resistance: "I propose to examine staying as an epistemological construct, in relation to movement, as a way of disrupting the identification of mobility with freedom, and of the traveler with the knowing subject".[15] Thinking of the struggles of contemporary indigenous groups in Latin America, Pratt mentions the importance of what she considers a new human right: el *derecho de no migrar* ["the right not to migrate"].[16] The foundation of Canudos does not relate exactly to this right, but rather to the possibility of carrying out a *voluntary* migration. Levine affirms that Canudos was formed by a gigantic migration which took place within the *sertão*.[17] This massive displacement transformed the new city into an alternative to the coastal urban centres. This new direction of the migratory movement implies a detour with respect to the expected route, a change in the direction produced by the country's economic forces. The inhabitants of the *sertão* decide to march towards what – from a lettered vision – was the epitome of the anti-city, what Dabove has called "a nightmare of reason".[18] From a modern coastal perspective, the foundation of Canudos implies a "deviated" trajectory, not only in the moral and economic senses of the word, but also geographically: it represents a journey "backward". It is another form of opposing the "involuntary mobility" described by Pratt, which would characterize the social history of Brazil and of many Latin American countries for most of the 20th century. It is a subversive mobility, which resignifies the national space and the very causes and dynamics of migration.

This dialectic tension between stasis and mobility adopts different forms in the three parts of *Os sertões*. At times, the space is seen as alien, unknown, strange. As a consequence, the narration looks for ways to dominate or domesticate it. Although in this essay I concentrate in the *strategies for seeing* displayed in the first part, I would like to quickly point out the continuities of these strategies in the second and third parts. In a word, I wonder how the city and its dwellers are described, and then how movement becomes an essential part of what I like to call an *invisible war*. The larger argument I am making is that war can be read through notions of (in)visibility. Of course, the visual aspect of war is connected to knowledge and understanding: trying to *see* means, for the narrator, to struggle to make sense of war and of the Other he encounters in the *sertão*.

In the second part, "The Man", Canudos is described as aberrant. If the territory and the landscape are, as we shall see, *anti-natural,* the narrator sees Canudos also as contradictory and as the antithesis of the lettered city imagined by the intellectual elites.[19] In this city it is no longer possible to distinguish the urban space from the countryside: this opposition, which has characterized to a great extent the construction of Latin American countries until today, becomes meaningless in Canudos. It is a space of continuities, not of interruptions, obstacles, or oppositions. This is another way of understanding the relation that this nomad city establishes to the surrounding *sertão*. This is important because the urban-rural distinction is also constitutive of the modern state, whose authority emanates from an urban centre that makes use of the countryside through a relation of domination. In "The Fight", the final part, some interesting notions of spatiality appear in moments of military confrontation. For example, war is present through the *absence* of actual clashes. The Canudos warriors' strategy is to avoid the fight by provoking something akin to a guerrilla war. They make an invisible war. This form of combat is narrated in *Os sertões* through the gaze of a civilized eye that is never completely capable of *seeing*. This eye is initially out of focus, and needs time to adjust itself to the scenes it finds.[20] The space of the *sertão* hides zones of invisibility for an eye that is not prepared to understand and narrate what it witnesses. The originality of the narrator's perspective here is that he presents these deficiencies as his own; he acknowledges his own incapacity to give sense to what he witnesses. In a sense, *Os sertões* can be seen as the narration of a process by which the eye finally *sees*. This invisible quality that the spaces and its inhabitants adopt for the supposedly civilized eye is what allows Leopoldo Bernucci to compare Euclides to foreign travelers: "Adopting the role of the ethnographer and of the researcher of the land, the author's dazzled gaze makes us recall the decisive moments lived by Léry, Saint-Hilaire, Spix, Martius, and others. It is a new discovery by an audacious *traveller,* who, in the end, discovers himself".[21] The relationship between the Latin American intellectual elites and Europe, whose perverse functioning in Brazil was famously pointed out by Roberto Schwarz,[22] can be translated as a certain closeness that Latin Americans felt towards the European intellectual and social world, even if – as was the case with Euclides – the person had not actually travelled. Euclides probably felt more "at home" in Europe than in the Brazilian backlands.[23] This can explain the fact that the narrator's voice and gaze remain alien not only to the described object, but also increasingly with respect to themselves. Not only the space and its people are uncanny, but *Os sertões* is also a voyage into a self (and a nation) which becomes increasingly unrecognizable.

This article suggests that *Os sertões* can be read as the narration of a process of "visibilization". Through what I call the rhetoric of confusion, the narrator seems to acknowledge the shortcomings of his own voice. He carries out a critique of his previous perspective incorporating this opacity as a constitutive part of his writing.[24] The narrator's own incapacities constitute thus a formidable literary strategy: what he narrates is, to a large extent, his own blindness. This is a powerful way of expressing the impotence of urban knowledge to make sense of the space of war (a war which has its origins precisely in the modern city). The book ends with an illumination: what becomes visible – while remaining unexplained – for the narrator is the utter criminal character – and senselessness – of war: "The campaign in question marked a backward step, an ebb in the direction of the past. It was in the integral sense of the word a crime and, as such, to be denounced".[25] The other conclusion expressed in this quotation has to do with the relations between war and *time*: the Canudos campaign was not a way of bringing modernity to the backlands, or of incorporating them to the creed of progress and order, as the narrator believes in the beginning; on the contrary, it was just an unnecessary massacre.

Here lies the difference between the narrator and the state whose logic he reproduces in the beginning. While for the state war is the simplifying element *par excellence* because it makes the otherwise opaque *sertão* become visible, for the narrator it is a source of uncertainty and disorientation. After witnessing war, the narrator will no longer be able to identify himself with the ideology of the state.[26] If Canudos became legible for the state, this legibility constituted a form of desertification: once the massacre had taken place, the site was burned with the intention of not leaving traces of the former rebellious city. As we have seen, while the origins of the word "sertão" are connected to the desert, it was clear that Canudos was not a void before the war; the connection between the terms proves then ideological. With war, what used to *be called* a desert was *transformed* into one.[27]

In the book's first part, "A terra", the description of the backlands functions as a form of introducing the narration. The description incorporates references to books of geology, travel narratives, and maps. Here, the narrative voice tries to give an order to the space of the *sertão*; this is like drawing a map through description (several maps accompany the text). The beginning of the book is particularly impressive: the gaze penetrates into the country's northeast through what Leopoldo Bernucci has called a "telescopic gaze" ["visão telescópica"].[28] This first section incorporates also the rhetoric of travel and gives the text a particular *direction*. The discourse is constructed in a way that it gradually approaches Canudos, so that the site of the conflict becomes the ultimate destiny of the voyage. This *crescendo*, which characterizes the tone of the text, is combined with a constant use of anticipation: the conflict is already present in the initial descriptions of spaces. If for Georges Van den Abbeele, "a journey organized in terms of its destination makes of that destination the journey's conceptual point of departure, its point of orientation",[29] then the first part situates Canudos as the space from which to think and organize the na(rra)tion, and in this sense it anticipates the operation of de-centering (or re-centering) that Euclides' book seeks to perform. To think the country *from* a Canudos perspective is the intellectual task that *Os sertões* seeks to propose. This task, however, is never fulfilled and remains incomplete, beyond the work's horizon of possibility. It is in this failure, however, where its greatest merit resides. As Jens Andermann has stated, "by narrating the collapse of representation, *Os sertões* permits representation to recommence".[30] From this perspective, *Os sertões* can be read as the narration of an epistemological effort seeking to change the site from which to look at the nation.

In this section there are many allusions to the figure of the traveller, the walker or even the more telling one of the observer. All of them imply an external perspective. The narration develops as the voice penetrates into the land, and it uses such words as "to advance", "to open", "lines of penetration", "traverse", "go through".[31] There is a conquering logic in this movement forward. These first pages show us a mobile subject before a static territory. For example, in an original representation of a travel scene, the narrator incorporates his reader in the fictitious entrance: "This is the exceedingly beautiful region of the Campos Gerais, an expanse of undulating hills – an enormous stage where the rude company of vaqueiros, or cowboys, holds forth. *Let us cross this stage*".[32] Almost immediately, however, tension appears, already as an anticipation of the conflict to come: "In the vicinity of Quirinquinquá, however, the earth takes on a more varied aspect".[33] The opening and seemingly victorious impulse of domination is soon interrupted; the land becomes invisible, it *moves away*. The initial gaze that sees and dominates it all uses even the topic of the land as sea, which was frequently present in the descriptions of Latin American plains since Humboldt.[34] For Euclides, however, the sea adopts new connotations, since it constitutes the origin of the *sertão*. That is to say, the latter is not just metaphorically a sea, but it *was literally* one: "we beheld them [the backlands] emerging in their geological modern form from a vast Tertiary sea".[35] If these lands are the result of the past, they also are still a form of that past: they belong thus to a different time. The *sertão* is for Euclides the space of the origins, and the narrator will end up recognizing the true "Braziliannes" of its inhabitants.

Conceived as a desert, the *sertão* adopts the ideological connotations attributed to the idea of the "desert" through 19th century Latin America. It is the space of otherness, an absolute exteriority, without inhabitants or order. *Os sertões*, however, does not offer a coherent description of this space. Its status changes throughout the book. The first part describes a void: it constructs the space as if it were really deserted. The second part shows us an inhabited desert, in which men are not distinguished from the landscape. The third part narrates the desertification brought by war, the return of the void. However, these moments should not be read as independent, since war is present from the very beginning. The first symptom of disorder is the absence of paths: for the civilizing logic, it is important to regulate space and movement; to establish *how* one moves forward is as important as the very fact of moving. As Deleuze and Guattari have affirmed, canals and conducts are seen as a necessity for the instauration of the modern state. The most palpable way to dominate the territory is to plan routes and paths, and the railway seems to be the most appropriate way to give order to space. However, the traditional routes remain unchanged in the *sertão*. Talking about a path that is three centuries old, the narrator explains: "They did not alter it in the least, and civilization later has not changed it by laying down alongside the bandeirante's trail the track of a modern railway".[36] The presence of the railway is not able to inaugurate new routes to traverse that place, which remains alien. Its impenetrability makes it become untouched by the modernizing forces. The existing routes "would in either case invariably skirt and contrive to avoid this desolate and sinister region, thereby sparing themselves the hardship of crossing it".[37] These adjectives do not really describe the landscape but the mental state of a subject for whom this geography that resists incorporation remains "sinister", "desolated", and "torturing". The *sertão* is disorienting because there is no state there: there are nothing but obstacles which make the idea of travel impossible. The "lines of penetration" can only serve to mark "the confines of a desert".[38] The desert could be defined, thus, as that space that cannot be *travelled*. The enthusiastic rhetoric that sought to conquer and discover, that powerful gaze which in the beginning seemed to fly over the *sertão*, stops here to look from afar or from the outside. If to travel is to see, then the *untravelled* desert is that which remains invisible.

The discourse that in the beginning portrays itself as mobile seeks to immobilize. This is why it creates a monotonous and void territory: "Advancing swiftly, especially along those stretches marked by a succession of small knolls, of precisely the same form and arrangement, all of them, even the most rapid traveler has a sensation of immobility. The same uniform landscapes against the same unvarying horizon, which recedes as he advances".[39] In this antithetical construction the elements alluding to movement ("swiftly", "rapid") appear together with their opposites ("immobility", "uniform", "unvarying"), creating thus a form of tension that will characterize the text as a whole. The quote can also be read as seeking to "domesticate" the only vestige of mobility: undulation.[40] This undulating movement, which could be seen as altering an almost perfect linearity, is "small" and monotonous. This constant succession of undulations does not seem to change the idea of total uniformity: the line predominates in the end. In this quote we could also read the opposition between an active subject and a passive land. However, the latter is not really immobile, but the traveller himself. It is the land that, stubbornly unchanging, transmits its immobility to the traveller. In the end, it is the space that imposes its own rhythms to him; it domesticates and stops him. Once again, the space deactivates the strategies of domination developed in the text, and resists the attempts aimed at its transformation.

The *sertão* is the scenario of what Euclides calls "the martyrdom of earth".[41] We can see that there is a fight between the land and the climate, which punishes and tortures the former. This conflict in nature adopts different forms. At a certain point, the landscape changes and the vegetation appears monstrous: several plants called "friar's head" ["cabeça de fraile"] are described as giving "the singular impression of bloody, decapitated heads tossed here and there, without rhyme or reason, in a truly tragic disorder".[42] Again, other heads – this time human – will appear later on.[43] The conflict in nature announces the war. I am interested in this imagery as an announcement of the human conflict because it is related to a textual construction that gives one single direction to every element. War is inevitably present, even if it is narrated afterwards. War imposes thus a way of looking at space and of narrating it.

In this first part, nature is seen as aberrant, as *anti-natural*.[44] This is connected to the problematic will to extinguish the desert, to eliminate it, to make it become "normal". It seems necessary for the state to "correct" the deviations of nature in order to make it productive and to insert it again within the logic of the modern state. The "domestication" of the "wild" waters could be the best example of this logic. Water does not seem to be a solution for the many problems caused by the sun and the drought, because it sterilizes the land and makes it inapt for agriculture. The arrival of water is excessive, uncontrolled and destructive. Man should re-establish equilibrium among these extremes; he must "civilize" nature. The entire first section ends with this project:

> If certain of our valleys, intelligently selected at frequent intervals throughout the entire extent of the backlands territory, were to be walled in, three consequences would inevitably follow: (1) there would be a considerable attenuation of the drainage of the soil, with its lamentable effects; (2) fertile border regions for cultivation would be formed within the network of conduits; and (3) there would be created a state of equilibrium against the instability of the climate, for the reason that the numerous small reservoirs, uniformly distributed and providing an expanded surface for evaporation, would naturally, in the course of time, come to have the moderating influence of an inland sea[45]

The quotation is revealing. It is coherent with the military project, since both seek to extinguish the desert. This is about territorializing the space by inserting it within the logic of capitalist production. Fluidity and movement must be then organized, given a route:

> "the State needs to subordinate hydraulic force to conduits, pipes, embankments, which prevent turbulence, which constrain movement to go from one point to another, and space itself to be striated and measured, which makes the fluid depend on the solid, and flows proceed by parallel, laminar layers".[46]

Euclides' project is based on two moments: first, it is about stopping all movement, in order to direct and resignify it afterwards, making it useful and productive. Finally, stability and uniformity are achieved. When referring to the modernizing interventions of the state in space in order to simplify it and to make it legible, Scott affirms: "The organization of the natural world was no exception. Agriculture is, after all, a radical reorganization and simplification of flora to suit man's goals".[47] The importance of agriculture is thus seen in *Os sertões* in this anxiety about organizing the natural chaos and giving a new meaning to water by transforming it into a "resource": "utilitarian discourse replaces the term 'nature' with the term 'natural resources' focusing on those aspects of nature that can be appropriated for human use"[48] This project's simplification of movement reveals a subject which feels actual horror towards a fluidity felt as exterior. Continuing with the line of reasoning displayed by Deleuze and Guattari in the quote above, in order to control this fluidity the subject has to think in terms of the solid.

---

[1] One of them, the War of the Triple Alliance (1864-1870), also known as the Paraguayan War, was one of the bloodiest conflicts in the history of the continent: Paraguay lost the majority of its population in it. See Whigham, Thomas L. and Barbara Potthast. "The Paraguayan Rosetta Stone: New Insights on the Demographics of the Paraguayan War". In: *Latin American Research Review*. 34:1 (1999), 174-186. It is also important to insist on the fact that the difference between civil and international war was not always clear, especially during the 19th century.

[2] Tilly, Charles. "War Making and State Making as Organized Crime". In: Besteman, Catherine. (Ed.). *Violence: a Reader*. (New York: New York University Press, 2002), 36.

[3] Tilly, "War Making and State Making as Organized Crime", 38. This is not far from Max Weber's classical conceptualization of the state as system of domination: "a relation of men dominating men, a relation supported by means of legitimate (i.e., considered to be legitimate) violence". Weber, Max. "Politics as a Vocation". In: Besteman, *Violence*, 14. In order to make this domination possible, the state needs to have the monopoly of that legitimate violence: "a state is a human community that (successfully) claims the *monopoly of the legitimate use of physical force* within a given territory". Weber, "Politics as a Vocation", 13 (emphasis en original). This article

explores the moment in which – through war – the Brazilian state successfully achieved this monopoly of violence.

[4] The proclamation of the Republic in 1889 constitutes, together with the 1922 declaration of Independence, the key political event in 19th century Brazilian history. This moment coincides also with the final and successful push for modernization of the state apparatus.

[5] I am giving the title of Samuel Putnam's 1944 translation of the book, which is the first and most cited one (Chicago: University of Chicago Press, 1964). *Os sertões* was recently republished in English as *Backlands: The Canudos Campaign* (New York: Penguin Books, 2010), with a new translation by Elizabeth Lowe. I will be using Putnam's translation throughout this essay.

[6] *Os sertões* is not the *only* narration of this war, however. Many other books relating the war from different perspectives were published before it. Some examples are *Os jagunços* (1898), by Alfonso Arinos, *Última expedição a Canudos* (1898), by Emídio Dantas Barreto, and *O rei dos jagunços* (1899), by Manoel Benício. On the relations between Arinos' book and *Os sertões*, see Walnice Nogueira Galvão's "De sertões e jagunços" (In: Galvão, Walnice Nogueira. *Saco de gatos*. Ensaios críticos. São Paulo: Duas Cidades, 1976, 65-85), and Leopoldo M. Bernucci's "Os palimpsestos da história" (In: Bernucci, Leopoldo M. *A imitação dos sentidos*. Prógonos, contemporâneos e epígonos de Euclides da Cunha. São Paulo: Edusp, 1995, 65-84). Adriana Michéle Campos Johnson sees the accounts by Arinos and Benício as alternative visions of the war. See "Another Canudos", the fifth chapter of her *Sentencing Canudos. Subalternity in the Backlands of Brazil* (Pittsburgh: University of Pittsburgh Press, 2010).

[7] These texts try to find a specificity for national culture; thus, they discuss the origins of a given country's people, pointing out their most salient features, trying thus to find a consistent explanation for their behavior, political decisions, or historical changes; many times, this explanation is sought in the country's cultural production (for example, its music or literature). In this line we could cite – just in Brazil – Gilberto Freyre's *Casa grande e senzala* (1933) – Freyre was also an extremely lucid reader of Euclides – Sérgio Buarque de Holanda's *Raízes do Brasil* (1936), Caio Prado Júnior's *Formação do Brasil Contemporâneo* (1942), and even the much more contemporary *O povo brasileiro* (1995), by Darcy Ribeiro. Other examples could of course be added to this ensemble.

[8] Robert Levine affirms that "[Canudos'] population of 25,000 (at its height in 1895 probably closer to 35,000) made it the largest urban site in Bahia after Salvador, the capital". Levine, Robert. *Vale of Tears*. Revisiting the Canudos Massacre in Northeastern Brazil, 1893 – 1897 (Berkeley: University of California Press, 1992), 185. Marco Antonio Villa, after considering different elements about the population and economic life of the region at that time, insists that this was impossible. He concludes that "everything indicates that Canudos not only was not the largest city in the hinterlands of Baia state, but that it never reached 25 thousand inhabitants, having 10 thousand dwellers at the most" ["tudo indica que Canudos não só não era a maior cidade do interior baiano, como também nunca se aproximou de 25 mil habitantes, possuindo no máximo 10 mil pessoas"]. Villa, Marco Antonio. *Canudos*. O povo da terra. (São Paulo: Ática, 1995), 220. Unless otherwise stated, all translations are mine.

[9] As a matter of fact, the conflict began when a small group of *sertanejos* destroyed a sign describing new taxes owed to the government. See Euclides da Cunha, *Rebellion in the Backlands*, 141-2. *Os sertões*, 286. It would be interesting to study the link between taxation and war in the context of the modern state. And, particularly, I wonder which was the specific relationship between these two elements in turn-of-the-century Latin America. How can taxes make war

possible? To which extent do they explain the state's desire to control and visualize its population? How can this will to impose control through taxation lead to war? I shall go back to the state's operations of legibility and simplification, as discussed by James C. Scott in *Seeing Like a State. How Certain Schemes to Improve the Human Condition Have Failed.* (Yale University Press: New Haven and London, 1998).

[10] James C. Scott. *Seeing Like a State*, 23. Charles Tilly also refers to the role of taxation in the case of the European states: "War making, extraction, and capital accumulation interacted to shape European state making". Tilly, "War making and state making", 38. Tilly's idea is particularly interesting to my perspective because it relates taxation to war and the capitalist system. This is especially pertinent to read the political process in late 19th century Latin America.

[11] See chapter 1, "States Projects of Legibility and Simplification", in Scott, *Seeing Like a State*, 10-84. However, Scott does not discuss war as an element that can modify spaces. In his book, war can be an opportunity for the state to intervene by imposing its strategies of legibility and simplification, but is *not* a legibilising or simplifying element in itself. Scott, *Seeing Like a State*, 5.

[12] The Portuguese "sertão" means originally "desert". Levine, *Vale of Tears*, 16.

[13] Deleuze, Gilles and Félix Guattari. *A Thousand Plateaus. Capitalism and Schizophrenia*. Transl. and Foreword by Brian Massumi. (Minneapolis and London: University of Minnesota Press, 1987), 368.

[14] Dabove, Juan Pablo. *Nightmares of the Lettered City. Banditry and Literature in Latin America. 1816-1929.* (Pittsburgh: University of Pittsburgh Press, 2007), 223.

[15] "propongo examinar el quedarse como un constructo epistemológico en relación con el movimiento, como una forma de cuestionar la identificación de la movilidad con la libertad, y del viajero con el sujeto cognoscente". Pratt, Mary Louise, "Los que se quedan". In: Barnabé, Jean-Philippe; Cordery, Lindsey; and Vegh, Beatriz. (Coord). *Los viajeros y el Río de la Plata. Un siglo de escritura.* (Montevideo: Universidad de la República; Lindari y Risso, 2010), 365. For a critique of the association of movement and freedom through the ideas of nomadism and the desert, see Caren Kaplan's second chapter, "Becoming Nomad" in Kaplan, Caren; *Questions of Travel: Postmodern Discourses of Displacement.* (Durham and London: Duke University Press, 1996), 65-100.

[16] Pratt, "Los que se quedan", 365-372.

[17] Levine, *Vale of Tears,* Chapter 3, "New Jerusalem", *passim.*

[18] Dabove, Nightmares of the Lettered City, 222.

[19] This description is in fact one of *Os sertões'* most frequently cited passages: "This monstrous *urbs,* this aggregation of clay huts, was a good indication of the sinister *civitas* of the erring ones who built it. The new town arose within a few days, a city of ruins to begin with. It was born old. Viewed from afar [...] it had the precise appearance of a city that has been rudely shaken and tumbled by an earthquake". Cunha, *Rebellion in the Backlands,* 144, empasis in original. "A *urbs* monstruosa, de barro, definia bem a *civitas* sinistra do erro O povoado novo surgia, dentro de algumas semanas, já feito ruínas. Nascia velho. Visto de longe [...] tinha o aspecto perfeito de uma cidade cuyo solo houvesse sido sacudido e brutalmente dobrado por um terremoto". Cunha, *Os sertões,* 291-2, emphasis in original.

[20] The following passage beautifully describes the movement of a state's militia composed of *sertanejos,* in the moment in which they attack Canudos. The narrator's disorientation seems complete: "The advance of this backlands battalion was not marked by the steady, cadenced

rhythm of the usual military quickstep when troops are marching to an attack. Instead, what was to be seen was a long, swiftly moving, swaying line of bayonets which suddenly burst into luminous flame, unfurling a brightly gleaming ribbon of steel from the riverbank all the way to the walls of the church. It was a quick, bewildering movement, characteristic of the jagunços, with nothing of the customary rectilinear formation, but in place of it an indescribable serpentine motion". Cunha, *Rebellion in the Backlands,* 461-2. "O batalhão de sertanejos avançou. Não foi a investida militar, cadente, derivando a marche-marche, num ritmo seguro. Viu-se um como serpear rapidíssimo de baionetas ondulantes, desdobradas, de chofre, numa deflagração luminosa, traçando em segundos uma listra de lampejos desde o leito do rio até os muros da igreja... O mesmo avançar dos jagunços, célere, estonteador, escapante à trajetória retilínea, num colear indescritível". Cunha, *Os sertões,* 762.

[21] "Investido no papel de etnógrafo e do pesquisador do solo, o olhar deslumbrado do autor faz-nos recordar os momentos decisivos vividos por Léry, Saint-Hilaire, Spix, Martius e outros. Trata-se de um novo descobrimento por um *viajor* audaz, que no fim se descobre a si mesmo" (51, emphasis in the original).

[22] Schwarz, Roberto. "As idéias fora do lugar". In: Schwarz, Roberto. *Ao vencedor as batatas.* Forma literária e processo social nos inícios do romance brasileiro. (São Paulo: Duas Cidades, 1992), 13-28. The essay was translated as "Misplaced Ideas", and included in Schwarz's *Misplaced Ideas. Essays on Brazilian Culture* (London: Verso, 1992), 19-32.

[23] Even though the writer always expressed interest in his country's hinterlands, and felt something like an outsider in his social context, there is no question that he belonged to the select lettered circles. The publication of *Os sertões* was decisive in this sense: in 1903 he was appointed for the Brazilian Academy of Letters [Acadêmia Brasileira de Letras] and he took up office at the Brazilian Institute of History and Geography [Instituto Histórico e Geográfico Brasileiro]. It is nonetheless important for my argument to bear in mind what Brito Broca beautifully called Euclides' "*hantisse* do sertão", since this attraction would propel him to reach the Amazonian regions of Brazil without ever setting foot in Europe. Broca, Brito. *A vida literária no Brasil: 1900* (Rio de Janeiro: José Olympio, 1960), 100.

[24] Mario Vargas Llosa's novel *La Guerra del fin del mundo* (1981), which constitutes a re-writing of *Os sertões,* chooses at one point to narrate the combat through the eyes of a momentarily blind character. This nameless character, who would represent Euclides da Cunha, loses his eyeglasses in the middle of the battle (in which he does not participate, however), and cannot distinguish anything but blots, shadows, foggy figures. This is in my opinion one of the moments in which Vargas Llosa's novel – otherwise problematic – reaches its highest narrative vigor.

[25] Cunha, *Rebellion in the Backlands (Os sertões).* "Aquela campanha lembra um refluxo para o passado. E foi, na significação literal da palavra, um crime. Denunciemo-lo". Cunha, Eculides da. *Os sertões (Campanha de Canudos).* (Ed.) Leopoldo M. Bernucci. (São Paulo: Ateliê Editorial, 2001), 67.

[26] The first Republic's intense militarism and repressive character ended up causing a strong feeling of deception in the intellectual circles, and in the public opinion in general. The early enthusiasm and support for the new regime faded around the turn of the century. In this respect, see Sevcenko, *Literatura como missão,* 121. *Os sertões* contributed fundamentally to the denunciation of the system's abuses; its immediate and extraordinary success with the public can be explained to a certain extent by this wave of discontent to which it responded and at the same time helped expand.

[27] In his analysis of the relationships between images and text in *Os sertões*, Roberto Vecchi discusses – from a biopolitical theoretical perspective – the operation of desertification to which Canudos was subjected: "the mechanism of modernity transforms thus the geographic space into an absolute biopolitical space" ["L'ingranaggio della modernità converte insomma lo spazio geografico in spazio biopolitico assoluto". Vecchi, Roberto. "Intermittenti presenze: la traccia, l'immagine, il subalterno" Silvia Albertazzi and Fernando Amigoni (Ed.) (Roma, Meltemi, 2008, 195-213), 210.

[28] Leopoldo M. Bernucci. "Prefácio" to Cunha, *Os sertões*, 17. Adriana Campos Johnson refers also to the presence of "a panoramic geological view of Brazil under the authority of a Foucauldian 'Speaking Gaze': surveying, classifying, *representing*". Campos Johnson, *Sentencing Canudos*, 120, emphasis in original).

[29] Van den Abbeele, Georges. *Travel as Metaphor: from Montaigne to Rousseau* (Minneapolis: University of Minnesota Press, 1992), xviii.

[30] Andermann, Jens. *The Optic of the State. Visuality and Power in Argentina and Brazil*. (Pittsburgh: University of Pittsburgh Press, 2007), 203. Andermann also insists on the importance of this war in the process of state consolidation, expressing that Euclides sees the conflict "as the event that is fundamental, yet impossible to assimilate, in the constitution of the state". Andermann, *The Optic of the State*, 203.

[31] The Portuguese equivalents are "avançar", "abrir", "linhas de penetração", "atravessar", "percorrer".

[32] Cunha, *Rebellion in the Backlands*, 7. Emphasis added. "É a paragem formosíssima dos *campos gerais*, expandida em chapadões ondulantes – grandes tablados onde campeia a sociedade rude dos vaqueiros... **Atravessemo-la**". Cunha, *Os sertões*, 78. (Emphasis in original, bold are mine).

[33] Cunha, *Rebellion in the Backlands*, 12. "Nas cercanias de Quirinquinquá, porém, começa a movimentar-se o solo". Cunha, *Os sertões*, 86. The translation does not say that the earth *moves*, which is the literal meaning of the Portuguese text. It thus eliminates the menacing connotations that this land adopts during war. For example, "The character of the soil made walking difficult, as the shifting sand slipped beneath their feet". Cunha, *Rebellion in the Backlands*, 246. "O terreno inconsistente e móvel fugia sob os passos aos caminhantes". Cunha, *Os sertões*, 446. This translation seeks again to explain the meaning by simplifying the language. The idea that the land would escape when being treaded upon by the army is fascinating because it adds to the idea of the enemy soil which identifies with the *sertanejo*.

[34] The uses of this image, from Humboldt to the British travelers to Domingo Faustino Sarmiento, among others, can be traced in Prieto (1996).

[35] Cunha, *Rebellion in the Backlands*, 42. "a fantasia se insurgia contra a gravidade da ciência, e [os sertões surgiram], geologicamente modernos, de um vasto mar terciário". Cunha, *Os sertões*,138.

[36] Cunha, *Rebellion in the Backlands*, 10. "não a alteraram nunca. Não a variou, mais tarde, a civilização, justapondo aos rastros do bandeirante os trilhos de uma via férrea". Cunha, *Os sertões*, 83.

[37] Cunha, *Rebellion in the Backlands*, 10. "[...] contorneavam sempre, evitando-a sempre, a paragem sinistra e desolada, subtraindo-se a uma travessía torturante". Cunha, *Os sertões*, 83.

[38] Cunha, *Rebellion in the Backlands*, 11. "[...] as lindes de um deserto". Cunha, *Os sertões*, 84.

[39] Cunha, *Rebellion in the Backlands*, 12. "E avançando célere, sobretudo nos trechos em que se sucedem pequenas ondulações todas da mesma forma y do mesmo modo dispostas, o viajante

[40] mais rápido tem a sensação da imobilidade. Patenteiam-se-lhe, uniformes, os mesmos quadros, num horizonte invariável que se afasta à medida que ele avança". Cunha, *Os sertões,* 86.

[40] The English translation uses the word "knoll", while "undulations" – the literal English word for "ondulações" – connotes a certain movable quality related to the land.

[41] Cunha, *Rebellion in the Backlands,* 48. The real martyrdom represented in the text will be a different one, and will come later one, but it can be read in this suffering quality of the land.

[42] Cunha, *Rebellion in the Backlands,* 35. "[...] a imagem singular de cabeças decepadas e sanguinolentas jogadas por ali, a esmo, numa desordem trágica". Cunha, *Os sertões,* 124.

[43] At its arrival at the Canudos region, the fourth and last expedition found the heads of the soldiers of the previous expedition, displayed next to the road as a macabre exhibition: "the jagunços then collected all the corpses that were lying here and there, decapitated them, and burned the bodies; after which they lined the heads up along both sides of the highway, at regular intervals, with the faces turned toward the road". Cunha, *Rebellion in the Backlands,* 275. "[...] os jagunços reuniram os cadáveres que jaziam esparos em varios pontos. Decapitaram-nos. Queimaram os corpos. Alinharam depois, nas duas bordas da estrada, as cabeças, regularmente espaçadas, fronteando-se, faces volvidas para o caminho". Cunha, *Os sertões,* 492. The very leader of the third expedition, General Moreira César, was known as "heads chopper" ["corta-cabeças"]. However, the strongest event to which this anticipation alludes is the systematic beheading of all the Candudos prisoners by the army at the end of the war.

[44] The adjective "aberrant" becomes particularly meaningful in this context, since it denotes "erring" and thus signifies movement. As a matter of fact, the first meaning that the Merriam-Webster dictionary gives for "aberrant" is "straying from the right or normal way". It comes from the Latin ab (away) + errare (to wander).

[45] Cunha, *Rebellion in the Backlands,* 48-49. "Abarreirados os vales, inteligentemente escolhidos, em pontos pouco intervalados, por toda a extensão do território sertanejo, três consequências inevitáveis decorreriam: atenuar-se-iam de modo considerável a drenagem violenta do solo e as suas conseqüências lastimáveis; formar-se-lhes-iam à ourela, inscritas na rede das derivações, fecundas áreas de cultura; e fixar-se-ia uma situação de equilíbrio para a instabilidade do clima, porque os numerosos e pequenos açudes uniformemente distribuídos e constituindo una dilatada superfície de evaporação, teríam, naturalmente, no correr dos tempos, a influência moderadora de um mar interior". Cunha, *Os sertões,* 137.

[46] Deleuze and Guattari, *A Thousand Plateaus,* 363.

[47] Scott, Seeing Like a State, 2.

[48] Scott, Seeing Like a State, 13.

Javier Uriarte is Visiting Assistant Professor at State University of New York, Stony Brook. He holds a PhD from New York University and a BA from the Universidad de la República, Uruguay. In his dissertation, he works on travel writing, war, and the state in 19th century Latin America. In 2010-2011 he was awarded a one-year Erasmus Mundus Fellowship at the Università di Bologna, Italy. He is the co-editor of a special issue of *Cahiers de Li.Ri.Co.* dedicated to Uruguayan literature and titled *Raros uruguayos: nuevas miradas* (Université Paris 8, 2011). He has published articles in Brazil, France, the UK, the US, and Uruguay.

Collective Traumas and Common Memories: the Colonial War of Portugal in Africa and European violence of the Twentieth Century

Roberto Vecchi

There are some apparent paradoxes in proposing that Portugal be included in the European violence of the twentieth century, especially when such an approach attempts to define as a common memory something problematically shared, such as the experience of trauma. Everything that should be rethought, starting from the particularities – of the trauma, the violence, Portuguese colonialism, etc. – is here in fact declined as an aspect that, perhaps in a surprising way, inclines us to rethink from another perspective a colonial war inscribed in the wars and immeasurable violence that swept through the twentieth century. This initial consideration serves as an attempt to formulate a more complex reflection regarding Portugal, but especially Europe – in a very critical phase, on the "abandonment" of a certain idea of Europe and what was, in the twentieth century, the tragic character that led to a surprising convergence of the multiple histories of the small countries and great nations of Europe. In a way, we might think of a unifying icon that perhaps better than any other failed attempt at a definition may express the catastrophe that overwhelmed the continent: that of ruins, that is to say, of the remains that have completely lost any reference to a definitively shattered whole.

On the other hand, the history of the "tragic" century that was the twentieth can be thought not through a "ruinous" image of incompleteness and fracture, like that of rubble, but as the domination of a "new evil", of a determined and unforeseen political regime, as Tzvetan Todorov suggests; that is, the twentieth century as the century of "totalitarianisms", where the plural indicates the impossibility of any reduction to a homogeneity or an identity what was multiple and polymorphous.

In the attempt to establish some features of a complex whole, what most characterizes this fragmented history is perhaps the impressive death toll produced by violence: eight and a half million on the fronts of the Great War, ten million civilians, six million disabled; the contemporary genocide of the Armenians (one and half million, carried out by the Turkish regime); Soviet Russia, with five million dead in the civil wars and of want in 1922, four million dead in the repression, six million dead in the famine of 1932-33; the Second World War, with 35 million dead in Europe, with six million dead in the extermination of Jews, gypsies, and mentally deficient. And all this is added to the hundreds of thousands of dead in the wars of the European countries in their colonies, such as France in Madagascar, Indochina, and Algiers, or, to the present purpose, Portugal in Africa.[1]

At this point, it may be pointed out that in the century dominated by the techniques of mass death, the "beginnings", the origins, are precisely related to the period of European empires in Africa, the space for the basic experiments in the techniques of destruction (suffice it to say that the concentration camp – which might be regarded as one of the paradigms of this frightful century – arose in a colonial context, such as the Anglo-Boer War of 1899-1902, or in Cuba by the Spaniards in 1895). In fact, the principal massacres that inaugurated the century are all of a colonial nature, as seen in the massacre of Onduruman (Sudan) of 1898, where eleven thousand Dervishes were machine-gunned by Lord Kitchner's men, or in the Herero genocide promoted by General Lothar von Trotha of 1904-1907.[2]

Without a common model of violence, the European countries, in any case, lay the foundations for the century by unanimously permitting the use of violence in their projects of conquest, which combined racism and social Darwinism in the name of the affirmation of progress and of the values said or proclaimed to be civilizing. This largely generic historical picture serves nevertheless to introduce our query: whether or not the Oversea and colonial war in Portugal make up the frame of reference and thought, as we are attempting to sketch out here, that is not outside the history of the continent but an organic, functional part of that history, albeit with its own dynamics and periods?

The tragic century rises therefore under a double sign that is in a certain way, "common": on one hand, violence as the material of colonial projects (which, as Foucault concluded, are the form by which racism is modernized and disseminated as a specific bio-political mode),[3] whether they are called war or genocide – two enormous forms of violence, sometimes interrelated, which may be indiscernible outside the legal context that explains them. On the other hand, and correlated with the former, violence is always not only individual or of the group, but violence of the state (of the government that programs it, even if it seems to be of its own making and action) as a specific feature of the immoderate violence that paradoxically, by proliferating, nevertheless "structures" the twentieth century globally, but also in a particular, one might say, European way.

With this background, the question that there exists a memory that can calculate the century's violent abuses is a relevant one – a memory of the European violence that right away shows its specific relation to a collective dimension of traumatic experience. When one speaks, as I have attempted to do here, of a combination of collective traumas and common memories, there is a kind of double *aporia* that must be confronted. One might say at once schematically that the problem goes back to the possibility of admitting collective memory itself, which is always the object of different views, even more so when the communal horizon in play is that of Europe, that is, a complex whole, we may say, that is doubtless complex, anomalous, not immediately understood, if thought of as outside a narrative that in fact has been rewritten and brought up to date after the war. On the other hand, may an already slippery terrain such as the collective European memory be considered, starting from the fractured and not easily symbolized condition of trauma, for its part extended to a plural, collective dimension, and therefore beyond its individual dimension? It is as if we have found ourselves within at least a double labyrinth.

The *Shoah* in a way contributes to deepen and rethink this question within other schemes, even because, as Jeffrey Alexander has shown, its complex construction as a paradigm of horror able to symbolize other horrors of the century has to have a definition of the field of collective and cultural trauma, going therefore quite beyond the scope of war crimes.[4]

In this sense, if one can say, combining the two aporias mentioned above, that a cultural trauma occurs[5] when the members of a community feel affected by a terrible event that leaves an indelible mark – making up a shared situation, remembered in common, that therefore becomes a "collective" memory – on the consciousness of the group, altering its identity in a radical way. For this purpose, there are dates that establish cultural "traumas" like the "9/11" of the twin towers in New York or, that of another September, the September 2, 1939, when Hitler invaded Poland, dates that become fixed as "foundational".

One thing to be considered, however, is that the limits that characterize the idea of collective memory (if one thinks of the restrictions of Susan Sontag and Rheinhart Koselleck on the irreducible nature of individual recollection) and refer to the impossibility of an individual recollection becoming that of a group unless it does not become part of a group "limited in time and space", as the functionalism of Maurice Hallbwachs would have it,[6] encounter, in the combination with another, mostly individual dimension, the possibility of being linked together and thought of as a whole.

In fact, before the question relevant to the acceptability or not of the collective memory as a complex social construction, what Aleida Assmann points out is that the physical, bodily inscription of memory made by wounds and scars is much more faithful than mental memory.[7] What therefore allows the foundation of a shared memory starting from the individual impression of pain is a relevant passage "from the physical to the metaphysical", which corresponds to a metaphorization of pain – partial, but significant – that grants a paradigmatic value to individual experience.[8] Trauma, as Jeffrey Alexander emphasizes, more than a fact in itself, is an event that by searching for a representation is founded upon multiple elements (discursive, figural, formal, etc.) that make it a cultural and symbolically dense object.[9] They are in fact (as Paolo Virno shows, referring to Adorno on the deep insistence of the materialists) the impressions of pain and pleasure that trivially but concretely relocate, in a constant but polemical way, the image of the body that feels pain or pleasure, in relation to logic or metaphysics, privileging in a way the *aesthesis* over the *logos*, sensation over discourse, the body over reason.[10]

Trauma would in this way be characterized by a constitutive dualism: on one hand, it is an obstacle that is opposed to recollection; on the other, the corporeal memory of wounds and scars is more faithful than the mental, metaphysical memory; therefore, trauma can be seen as a lasting bodily inscription of something that is not remembered but is incarnated.[11] This duality of the trauma as obstacle but also as communication is paradoxical, with the experience of the pain that leads us to rethink memory and trauma within a space that is not single but, on the contrary, collective, public or even political.

Is the European memory therefore widely constituted upon traumas that for their part have become its common links? If thinking of the relation between memory and "post-memory" of the colonial war – we wish here to refer to the controversial category of the personal memory, not of the witnesses but of their families, of the second and third generations, those that did not undergo the traumatic facts but who have borne them through inter-generational transmission[12] – we perceive that the constellation between individual and collective memory, between individual and collective trauma, is approached by starting from its first "narrative" circle, the instant at which the singular opens up, by contact, by metonym, within the family context, to a problematic shared allotment, but is, at the same time, singular-plural, therefore already "in common".[13]

In fact, a primary definition of post-traumatic stress is that, in essence, it is a matter of disturbance of the memory,[14] which is to say that it implies the impossibility that an isolated event exists that is not inserted in some narrative framework, being incomparable with any other past, present and future fact.

This emerging tip of trauma, of the effect of violence, illumines to some extent something at least evident about the century broadly constructed on the enormous violence that was unloaded on its history. It is a question of a violence that changed status, that lost any reference to the presupposed ethics of relation between ends and means (as Benjamin had already perceived in 1921, in his famous essay *"Zur Kritik der Gewalt"*).[15] For this reason, it is impossible to think of violence only in terms a pure materiality, of means without ends, because, as Balibar points out, in contemporary violence "there always exists a non-convertible remainder or a material residue of idealism, unprovided with the 'feeling' that frequently emerges, even if not only in the form of cruelty" and – even for convinced materialists – leads us to undertake, even unwillingly, a discourse on "evil".[16]

The *Gewalt* would thus be marked by a dialectical incompleteness. This would make it necessary, therefore, to find another viable concept: Balibar, on reviewing a few possibilities – "terror", but that would be historically marked; "barbarism", which would suggest an undesirable ethnocentrism – proposes the term "cruelty",[17] then, the phenomenology of violence, together with its intrinsic relation – in the even lexical *Gewalt* – with power, would also always imply another relation with cruelty. If a "spiritual" dialectic between power and counter-power is necessary, the presence of an intrinsic heterogeneity may be seen in cruelty as another reality.

This picture of historical and conceptual generalities may perhaps contribute to better illustrate the central problem established between the Portuguese War in Africa from 1961 to 1974 and European violence. The issue, in fact, shows how a mythology of the uniqueness of Portugal in the European context can contribute to the idea that Portuguese history of the twentieth century is ruled by a kind of "exceptionalism" that is ideologically constituted and different from the idea of exception,[18] even internal to the Old World and, on the contrary, is not all inscribed within the history of violence of contemporary Europe. This is not the place to analyze the political and historical trajectory of Portugal in the twentieth century as a significantly "long" century, or better, one set off by a gap that made it begin traumatically with the Ultimatum of 1890 and end even more traumatically with the colonial war in Africa. What is important to emphasize is how European history is also reflected, by its differences, in the "case" of Portugal.

A process that occurs in the twentieth century throughout Europe, within the strengthening of the modern state and the modernization of power relations, is the "naturalization" of political identities,[19] which takes over as the basis of a collective ontology, the affirmation of which will result in many of the century's massacres. In the distinction that may be formulated between a cultural community that is built around the past and the political community that is defined from an idea of a future, a project, an ideology either racial or political (the end of social classes), the west in the twentieth century attempts to make the political community and the cultural community coincide as far as possible, reducing the countries to the "identity" or "ideal model of the hegemonic elites against other groups".[20]

As it is easy to grasp in the "case" of Portugal, what occurs is an "integral" assumption (in the ideological sense of the imperial nation) on the part of the political community of the cultural community –of the past that is reflected in the future project – which can be detected in the mythicizing of Portugal's Atlantic destiny: it is, if we take note, the increase of a feature that, in different measures, connotes nevertheless the processes of a nationalist modernization of the tragic century that is a geographical deterioration of Europe's tragic endowment, although along largely common lines.

It is worth remembering that when we speak of collective traumas, they do not have geographical or cultural limitations,[21] unless within narratives of closed nations. They are not rigidly separable by groups or spaces, although groups and spaces may contribute to define their possibility of reconstruction.

If, in the Second World War, alongside the immense slaughter that took place, it was mass extermination that would stand out as paradigmatic of a violence always associated with cruelty, of a horror-terror that was mixed and confounded, that is, the *Shoah*, as a collective trauma of cultural value that, in a certain way, became fixed as a powerful, unifying "bridge metaphor", building a history fractured by horror.

In a text on Benjamin's essay mentioned above, which aims at a critique of violence, Derrida, on going deeper into the theme of the radicalization of evil by Nazism, connected to the deterioration of language, communication, the representation of information,[22] understands the "final solution" not only in the recitation of the unspeakable horror of the *Shoah*, of the catastrophe (without witness), but understands that it was not only a question of the extermination of millions of human lives, but also that the order of representation succeeded in destroying names as well, "above all the possibility of giving, inscribing, calling, and recalling the name, of the name as memory. The genocide would therefore be not only an enormous "mnemocide", but, above all, an efficient "onomasticide" that prevented its apprehension.

And recontextualizing this tragic margin of the history of Europe, we remember how there is a kind of nominalist paradox that characterizes the War of Portugal in Africa. On one hand, the lack of shared name that designates the occurrence (dominating a plurality of forms that give way to different ideological constructs: the Oversea War, Colonial War, War in Africa). On the other hand, a specificity of the event seems to gain almost an "absolute name", beyond its "own name", which distinguishes it from other conflicts that marked the history of the end of the European empires of the twentieth century: an excess and a lack, at the same time.

The lack of inscription – the non-inscription of which José Gil speaks[23] -lack of a proper name for the event, as well as the lack of a proper name of the Oversea, the Atlantic, of the empire. or the presence of names that varied enough in accordance with changes in the historical circumstances, problematize the construction of a memory of which the name is the sign that identifies and preserves and makes recognizable, in the community and in the space where it is imagined.

The colonial war has still not found its inscription, its name, just as many of the events of immeasurable violence of the twentieth century have not received their own names. They can be defined by dramatic but always "common" names (within the lexicon of mass violence) or names detached from others (Portugal's colonial war begins when another colonial war ends, that of France in Algiers, showing the strands of a common epilogue of different, apparently irreducible and unique, colonial histories).

Does it then make sense to think of the post-memory of the colonial war when memory is still in search of the names? The problematic dimension of the subject is not only related to the colonial war but covers others events of the century's violence, within the specific aspect of the violence that always joins it, even in the readings that make an effort to be the most inherent possible, to the presence of a "moral" component such as cruelty or evil.

In fact, the problem of the memory of the colonial war belongs to the same aporia as the witness that crosses the organized, directed explosions of twentieth century violence. A certain form of violence, that which always maintains a non-material but "moral" residue, harms or even undermines at the base any linear possibility of representing the violent scene. We might say that in a general way the communication of experience in modernity is at total risk because uniqueness no longer offers any guarantee of truth in the face of the violence, for example in Africa, as well as in other fields of battle inside and out of Europe; the possibility of a totalizing understanding of the facts are beyond the grasp of any individual. How therefore can one inscribe this experience that does not go beyond the personal horizon and is not shared in symbolic terms, of the immediate unspeakable nature of pain and trauma? Is it possible to locate elements that allow us to denominate them through a name of their own and not someone else's?

Even if it belongs to another irreducible historical context such as the South American dictatorship of Argentina, I would like to cite a passage from the memoirs of a victim of repression, Jacobo Timmerman, titled, significantly, *Prisoner without a name, cell without a number*: "I have many eyes on me...those eyes that I found in the clandestine jails of Argentina and that I preserved one by one have been the culminating moment, the purest moment of my tragedy. Today they are with me, and although I desire to do so, I cannot and do not know how to share them with you".[24]

The quote is interesting because it immediately brings up the question of post-memory. From my viewpoint, post-memory – which to some seems to be an undue transposition of the "real" (if this were possible) of the "experience" to the field of literariness or the imagination – represents, in fact, the first, not the primary, circle, where the disturbance of memory, the impossibility of symbolization finds a minimum viability for escape, thereby breaking what was an "aporia", ineluctably imprisoned in a closed space. It is the moment in which through countless mediations and obstacles the inscription of pain becomes, in a certain and complexly public way, like an exposed scar: it can find its own name and remove itself from its own destruction as a possibility of naming the past.

Through the indirect, mediated memory of the second generation, in fact, a deeper analytical reflection is developed, especially when it is occluded by the experience of trauma. The post-memory not only shows us that the witness more than a fact is an act, and that therefore his/her possible use in historical terms, as more of a cultural than a documentary object, is inscribed in the complex but not impossible dialectic that Pierre Nora creates between memory and history.[25]

The post-memory especially prepares us – or alerts us – to what memory will soon become after the "last witness"?[26] Everything will be the memory of a generation that did not have the experience but, at the same time, that kept itself in contact with the experiential generation in our case of the colonial war, but the problem is analogous to the *Shoah* (where the third generation is studied) or to the Italian resistance or to other cases of the "memory of violence".

It is a decisive passage for several reasons. The first, in my view, regards the idea of "patrimony": what took place in Africa, or on other contexts of problematic or disturbed "witnessability", can be part of a *patrimony* that is immaterial but nevertheless greatly contributes to the re-foundation of a communal pact. It is always the case of remembering that patrimony and community have a link – even before the theoretical or logical-etymological one that unites them. In fact, patrimony has a suffix, alongside *pater*: the term *munus*, an ambivalent term that means gift (donation) and obligation, benefit and debt, union and threat.[27] The donation of the father would be literal. It is the same term that composes the word *communitas* (abstract of the adjective *communis*), that is, a gift or donation that obliges an exchange, a relation. From this element of being "in-common" of the reciprocity that relates patrimony and community, one may think of the community not, however, from the idea of works or identity (the cultural community that I mentioned above) but reformulating the "proper name" of the community that becomes an incomplete, imperfect, unfinished community. But a Community (with a name).

One might think that the "with" is not only a prefix of *com*-munity but also goes back to a fundamental political "emotion", which is *com*-passion. As Martha Nussbaum analyzes it in her work, compassion, even though it does not represent the totality of public rationality (in a liberalism based on "consensus by intersection"),[28] but has a significant role in molding collective understanding in the face of socially relevant traumas,[29] the "traumatic patrimony" that reshapes public space. Traumas are therefore collective and public.

There is another dimension – not less problematic – that I would also like to point out, which regards the sometimes crushing weight of the past upon today, when the past manifests itself as a phantom bringing about a kind of short-circuit to the present time. It is a question of the loss of the past, of forgetfulness as an active element, despite everything, in the political construction of memory. Forgetfulness, as well as memory, can be contracted to cure scars: it is the case of the "*amnestia*" ("the non-memory") that Thrasibulus, although a victim, imposes after the banning of the thirty tyrants in Athens, so that the city can continue to live without the enormous weight, or in the prison, of the past.[30] In any case, it is important to point out how public memory is constructed by articulated processes that intersect the duty of memory with the politics of (based, however, on the idea of "just") forgetfulness.

But, alongside this traumatic memory, there are countless other disputed memories articulated problematically wherever there is still lacking compassion as a intergenerational pact, which impedes its full social contractualization, which would the presupposition for articulating a possible "history" of the war in Africa. That is because such complicated and fragile public memories as those that do not have their own name, like those of the colonial war, gain considerably, in terms of comprehension, if they are re-read, without any immediate and banal comparisons, within the enlarged areas of violence that set upon Europe as a whole, and not only in the century of tragedies, and that feed the search for a shared development in which the continent itself can be rethought, not starting from abstract or fictional identities, but from the accumulation of the ruins of its recent history, whose wounds are still open.

Perhaps this war can be seen a little like "a minor history" of European history. I use here the term "minor" not negatively, but in the sense that Delueze and Guattari read the literature of Kafka as a precisely minor literature. A minor literature is not a literature in a minor language, but the literature of a minority within a greater language (for example, German for Kafka). This literature, or this history is thus always political, because it permanently connects the minor with the greater, the individual with the collective, forming the community in the facts.[31]

As in the minor literature for Kafka (who used German, but as a "minor language"), the writer is in the language as a foreigner. In this way, by the common dimension of a European memory, constituted by the collective traumas of many small countries, the continental opening allows them to be in their own history like a foreigner. It is therefore to rethink it within a larger mold, outside the limitations of uniqueness or pseudo-exception.

Thus, in the European dimension of histories that are only apparently of one or the other nation, all of us would act in the condition of foreigners, be able in any way to be in this history or in other histories, and understand how much it is a part of the others or how much of it can be used for the construction of a possible memory – and therefore open and able to be shared – which no longer belongs only to one or another country, but much more to all of them. In this perspective, to think and articulate the Colonial War of Africa to find a proper, definitive name confers its full inscription in the portrait of a history "in common", of Portugal but also of Europe.

---

[1] Todorov, Tzvetan. *Memoria del bene, tenazione del male.* Inchiesta sul secolo tragico. (Milano: Garzanti, 2000), 15.

[2] Flores, Marcello. *Tutta la violenza di un secolo.* (Milano: Feltrini, 2005), 31.

[3] Foucault, Michel. "*Bisogna difendere la società*". Ewarld E. and Fontana A. (Ed.) Tr. It. (Milano: Feltrinelli, 1998).

[4] Alexander, Jeffrey C. *La costruzione del male.* Dall'Olocausto all'11 settembre. (Bologna: Il Mulino, 2003), 62-66.

[5] Alexander, La costruzione del male, 129.

[6] Assmann, Aleida. *Ricordare.* Forme e mutamenti della memoria culturale. (Bologna: Il Mulino, 2002), 147.

[7] Assmann, *Ricordare*, 275.

[8] Maj, Barnaba. "Lendas, lembranças e memória". In: Vecchi, Roberto and Rojo, Sara. *Transliterando o real.* Diálogos sobre as representações culturais entre pesquisadores de Belo Horizonte e Bolgna. (Belo Horizonte: FALE, 2004), 21-33.

[9] Alexander, *La costruzione del male*, 138-140.

[10] Virno, Paolo. "I rompicapo del materialista". In: AA.VV., *Il filosofo in borghese.* (Roma: Manifestolibri, 1992), 57-66.

[11] Assmann, *Ricordare*, 275.

[12] Hirsch, Marianne. *Family Frames:* Photography, Narrative, and Postmemory. (Cambridge & London: Harvard University Press, 2002), 22.

[13] Nancy, Jean-Luc. *Essere singolare plurale.* Tr. It. (Torino: Einaudi, 2001), 43.

[14] Cruz, Manuel. *I brutti scherzi del passato.* Identità, resonsabilità, storia. (Torino: Bollati Boringhieri, 2003), 139.

[15] Benjamin, Walter. *Angelus novus.* Saggi e frammenti. (Torino: Einaudi, 1962).

[16] Balibar, Étienne. "Violenza, idealità e crudeltà". In: Françoise, Hériter. (Ed.) *Sulla violenza.* (Roma: Meltemi, 1996), 44-65.

[17] Balibar, "Violenza, idealità e crudeltà", 51.

[18] Vecchi, Roberto. Excepção Atlântica: pensar a literatura da guerra colonial. (Porto: Afrontamento, 2010), 183-184.

[19] Flores, Tutta la violenza di un secolo, 32.

[20] Flores, Tutta la violenza di un secolo, 33.

[21] Alexander, La costruzione del male, 163.

[22] Derrida, Jaques. *Forza di legge.* Il fondamento mistico dell'"auatorità". (Torino: Bollati Boringhieri, 2003).

[23] Gil, José. *Portugal hoje.* O Medo de Existir. (Lisboa: Relógio d'Àgua, 2004).

[24] Timmerman, Jacobo. *Prigioniero senza nome, cella senza numero.* Tr. It. (Milano: Mondadori, 1981), 40.

[25] Nora, Pierre. "Entre Mémoire et histoire". In: *Les lieux de mémoire.* Paris: Gallimard. V.I. XVII-XLII, 1984.

[26] Bidussa, David. *Dopo l'ultimo testimone.* (Torino: Einaudi, 2009).

[27] Esposito, Roberto. *Communitas.* Origine e destino della comunità. (Torino: Einaudi, 1998).

[28] Nussbaum, Marha C. *L'intelligenza delle emozioni.* (Bologna: Il Mulino, 2004), 479.

[29] Nussbaum, L'intelligenza delle emozioni, 539.
[30] Flores, Tutta la violenza di un secolo, 108.
[31] Deleuze, Gilles e Guatarri, Felix. *Kafka. Por uma literatura menor.* (Rio de Janeiro: Imago, 1979).

(Translated from portuguese to english by Tom Burns)

Roberto Vecchi is Associate Professor of Portuguese and Brazilian Literature, and of History of Portuguese Language Cultures at the Università di Bologna, where he works at the Iberian Studies PhD program, in addition to being Scientific Coordinator of the Center of Post-Colonial Studies (CLOPEE) and Coordinator of the Eduardo Lourenço Cathedra. Vecchi studied Letters and Philosophy at the Università di Bologna, obtaining his PhD in 1993 with the dissertation entitled *La traduzione della memoria, la memoria della traduzione. Memorialismo e picaresca nell'opera di Aquilino Ribeiro*. In Portugal, he is Associate Researcher of the Universidade de Coimbra's Center of Social Studies, carrying out research on the representation of the colonial war. In Brazil, he participated in the thematic research project on "Violence Writings", with the Universidade de São Paulo and the Universidade Estadual de Campinas. Vecchi has published extensively on theory and culture of the Portuguese language, as well as on colonial war, trauma and violence.

Hunters turned into Prey:
Predation in Twentieth-Century War Literature

Luiz Gustavo Leitão Vieira

Violence is a common and inherent feature of the animal world. Carnivores are always hunting, killing, and eating other animals. Violence, and combat for that matter, must be viewed as essential for the survival of countless species – both predator and prey must resort to it in order to eat and to avoid being eaten. On the other hand, war, herein understood as collective and organized combat, is a human institution. The only creature other than man that wages war against its own species is the ant. However, ants make war because it is in their genes to do so[1] and, unlike man's, their way of war has never changed, it has never been subjected to technological progress and cultural adaptations. Man is the only being that has turned war into a cultural institution. It is therefore obvious that violence as it encountered in the natural world differs from the kind of violence that humans display at war. Nevertheless, it is possible to find some similarities between these two forms of combat and to reach some revealing conclusions by comparing the features men and animals share when it comes to fighting and killing.

The main purpose of this paper is to analyze some examples of war literature, chiefly twentieth-century literature, by applying to them the observations and remarks on the nature of combat as they are forwarded by American analyst Robert O'Connell in his study *Of Arms and Men – a history of war, weapons, and aggression* (1989). In order to do so, we shall begin by discussing O'Connell's work and his comments on combat as it is carried out by both animals and men. Next, war literature, other than twentieth-century works, shall be mentioned for comparative reasons to highlight the changes that have occurred in armed conflicts with the advent of modern technological war. Finally, works representing three conflicts of the twentieth-century, namely the First World War, the Second World War, and the Vietnam War, are to be approached and subjected to O'Connell's dual categories of predatory and intraspecific combat.

Robert L. O'Connell, a senior analyst at the US Army Intelligence Agency's Foreign Science and Technology Center with a Ph.D. in History, wrote *Of Arms and Men – a history of war, weapons, and aggression* in 1989. Resorting to research from several fields of knowledge, such as psychology, history, and anthropology, to name a few, the book traces the development of war and of weapons from the second millennium B.C. to our days, from the first application of any object for deadly purposes to the invention of nuclear weapons. O'Connell also analyses the advent of war, from its birth as a somewhat organized theft, as nomads started raiding agricultural cultures, and as farmers in turn started organizing themselves for protection against these nomad groups,[2] to the bloodshed engineered by industrialized nations in the twentieth-century. However, the point I would like to draw attention to and highlight in O'Connell's instigating work is the parallel he draws between the types of violent encounters we find in the natural world - what is called predatory and intraspecific combat - and the practices men adopt at war.

As O'Connell's chief interest lies in weapons, their evolution and their application, the author first attempts to define what a weapon is and how it is used. In order to make it clear that weapons are not an exclusively human tool, he begins by analyzing how predator and prey deploy their own natural weapons: claws, fangs, horns, poison, and the like. For him, "the mouth of a shark, the branch grasped by a frightened chimp, the bow of the hunter, and an F-16"[3] are all functionally linked together: their essence is the ability to damage or prevent damage from another organism. It is during this argumentation that he forwards the dual categories of predatory and intraspecifc combat and their respective features.

Intraspecific aggression may be defined as strife among members of the same species. First of all, and utterly relevant for our purposes of drawing parallels between war and natural combat, is the fact that intraspecific aggression displays effective restraints on combatants, its purpose being dominance rather than killing. It is also "characteristically ritualized, with the instruments of combat often being specialized to serve the ends of these ceremonial confrontations".[4] Animals of the same species seldom engage in mortal combat, and the weapons they choose for facing their likes are different from those they choose for fighting against their prey and predators. Hence, rattlesnakes do not bite each other and determine dominance through wrestling matches; deer use antlers only in social combat and their hooves against predators; piranha fish never bite other piranhas, choosing instead to use their tail fins; and while "northern elephant seals do attack conspecifics with their tusks", they try to take blows on shoulders and chest, "areas protected with heavy layers of skin".[5] Furthermore, these confrontations are "overwhelmingly individualized",[6] aiming to settle individual disputes. Finally, intraspecific combat is marked by symmetry and complexity: the same weapon is deployed by both contenders and the variety of such weapons in nature is astonishing, in terms of size, shape, and function. Some animals have even developed weapons which are in fact bordering on the bizarre as they are simply out of proportion with the rest of the body: the horn of the Hercules beetle or the horns of a bighorn sheep, for instance. Many of these developments make sense when we realize that much of nonpredatory combat moves towards bluff and ritualization, not killing. In intraspecific aggression, looking bigger or more menacing counts as much as being actually able to kill. Predation, on the other hand, is about killing and nothing else. Its characteristics are therefore very different.

Predation, in marked contrast with intraspecific combat, shows no restraints: the sole purpose is killing in the fastest and easiest way possible with "any means of offense or defense being employed without hesitation".[7] Predation is about survival and thus displays none of the limitations usually found in struggles among members of the same species - in predation there is no ritual. Predators, moreover, if given a chance, will choose the youngest and most helpless as victims. Secondly, predators, especially mammals, frequently hunt in groups – increasing the level of lethality. Also in contrast with conspecific struggle, predation is usually asymmetric: prey do not counter claws and teeth with their own, choosing rather to flee or to defend themselves with natural shells and armor. The variety of methods for killing in predation seems poor when compared to the diversity and complexity of intraspecific weapons: predators may display spectacular physiques but the killing instruments are seldom out of proportion and rely basically on penetration and poison – tools of such proven efficiency that evolution has not bothered to alter them. The shark, "evolutionarily stabilized for hundreds of millions of years",[8] remains one of the world's most efficient and feared predators with its submarine design and set of powerful teeth. Quadrupeds such as lions, tigers, and wolves, make use of tearing teeth and claws – and, in terms of design and weapon of choice, a tiger and a domestic cat only differ in size. O'Connell, however, points out to certain exceptions to the trends of "conservatism and uniformity"[9]: birds of prey that attack from above and legless serpents are alternatives to submarine and quadruped models. They nevertheless rely on penetration and poison as almost all other predators do.

In short, one may then separate both kinds of violence in the natural world as follows: predation is unrestrained, matter-of-fact killing, asymmetric, conservative in weapons, collective or individualized; whereas intraspecific combat is restrained, ritualized for dominance, symmetric, innovative in weapons, and individualized. As we now move on to our primary topic, that is, war literature, it will become clear that man is the only being to apply the characteristics, or if we dare say, the rules, of predatory combat against members of his own species.

Intraspecific combat

Perhaps the finest example to illustrate the nature of combat and of war before the advent of the gun, and of other more deadly weapons, is Homer's epic *The Iliad*, which stands as not only an archetype of war narrative, but as an archetype of intraspecific combat as well. Dubbed "the world's greatest war story"[10] and "the bible of land warfare",[11] it narrates approximately 50 days of the ten-year siege imposed by an assembly of Greek armies against the walled city of Troy. Explicitly centered on the leaders of the opposing armies - the heroes - the epic at times reads as if the whole Trojan War were a duel, to be settled by individual combat: either between Hector and Ajax, or between Diomedes and Aeneas, Patroclus and Hector, or mainly between Hector and Achilles. Few scenes depict engagements between masses of men. The *Iliad* is not about the armies, which stand in the background of the narrative and are irrelevant for the outcome of the conflict. Instead, it is about the few outstanding warriors who strive for glory – *kleos* – on the plain of Troy, and who ultimately settle the outcome of the war.

Although the text provides gruesome passages that reveal the violent nature of the fight, combat in the *Iliad* is highly ritualized. As two warriors approach each other, they often tell their names and their lineage and then engage in an exchange of threats and boasting. At times, as in the encounter between Diomedes and Glaukos, combat is even set aside once a common ground is established.[12] Combat begins by throwing spears and if this does not settle the winner they resort to swords; both contenders usually carry shields for protection. Chariots are used for arriving at and leaving the battlefield – it is a means of transportation not a weapon. Once an opponent is killed, it is acceptable to strip him of his armor as a trophy but his body should be left for proper burial. This standardized form of combat reads like a ritual, and every hero is expected to abide by the rules of the so-called warrior code. A breach of the code is met with scorn and surprise, sometimes causing anger on the opposing side. After killing Hector, Achilles refuses to leave the body for burial and instead abuses it for twelve days – an action the gods themselves reproach.[13] Diomedes scorns Paris when the Trojan wounds him with an arrow: the bow is "the blank weapon of a useless man, no fighter".[14] At times, death is not even required. In the beginning of the epic, Hector and Ajax fight a duel which is fully ritualized both pledge to return the body of the defeated, gifts are exchanged after the duel and neither combatant is killed.[15]

Though the previous remarks furnish a mere overview of the epic, it becomes clear that the most important features previously associated with intraspecific combat are notable. In consonance with the ritualized nature of combat and with non-predatory violence, symmetry is valued in the *Iliad*: spear against spear, sword against sword, scorn for the bow, an inherently asymmetric weapon. Warriors engage in individualized duels, aiming at establishing superiority, as in the case between Hector and Ajax. It should be noted, however, that as the war drags on, combat eventually acquires more somber and cruel tones, tending towards predation, principally after the death of Patroclus and the return of Achilles. Nevertheless, though unrestrained after these events, most of the basic rules of intraspecific aggression still prevail in the epic, even when the warriors strive to kill wantonly: symmetry, ritual, and individualized combat. In short, as Connell says, "the Homeric conception of warfare seems fundamentally in consonance with the characteristics of intraspecific combat".[16] And this conception has had lasting influence.

Homer, in fact, "told men how to act when they fought one another"[17] and this pattern was destined to be ingrained in people's minds, teaching them to value the search for glory in single combat – deemed fair because it was symmetric and heroic because it was "at the closest possible range".[18] The sequence of combat of the Roman army, for example, duplicates exactly what is found in the *Iliad*. Stretching well into medieval times, the Homeric *ethos* can be found in the duels between knights – another distinguishable form of intraspecific combat: ritualized, symmetric, individualized and reserved for a few nobles, aiming at dominance or superiority with a view to achieving glory. As we reach this point, however, another work of literature offers insight into the changes in warfare and the move towards predatory forms.

In Shakespeare's play "Henry V",[19] the battle of Agincourt (1415), a landmark in the Hundred Years War between France and England, shows what happens when the two kinds of aggression face each other. The French knights, whose very identity rested upon one way of combat marked by contact with the opponent in a display of courage, charged against the English bowmen. The 9,000 English, heavily outnumbered against 30,000 enemies, created an actual killing zone as the French kept on charging, like lemmings, against the arrows of the longbows. As we have seen, since Homer, the bow was viewed as a coward's weapon for it allows killing from afar, without promoting tests of courage. The French knighthood could never conceive of adopting such faceless type of combat and were thus massacred: 6,000 dead. Asymmetry (bow and arrow against charging troops), collective combat, lack of restraints and of ritual, matter-of-fact killing had definitely entered war – predation started being adopted and was to become the rule. The bow itself provides a very illustrative example when it comes to analyzing weapons and types of combat. When it first became widespread in Europe as the crossbow, it was met with such outrage for its inherent asymmetric nature that the Church, in 1139, outlawed its use against Christians.[20] Be it noted that the Church never discouraged its being used against Muslims. As the Muslims were viewed as pertaining to another, and inferior, species, there was no need for restraining combat against them – predation, after all, is by definition against another species. By applying the dual categories of predation and intraspecific combat, it is easier to understand why nations and religions use propaganda to belittle and deprecate their enemies, portraying them as the inferior other: a soldier will be more willing to kill another man if he is not perceived as such, if he is viewed as belonging to another species. The fight then is turned into predation, when killing is accepted, and moves away from intraspecific combat, when killing is not natural.

Predatory combat

However, Agincourt and medieval battles are just minor engagements when compared to the slaughter that the twentieth-century had in store once predatory features became the rule in warfare. In 1914, as many a young man welcomed the outbreak of war, eager to prove themselves in a rite of passage into adulthood and a test of manhood,[21] little did they know that they would not make war – war would be made upon them.[22] The First World War inaugurated a new kind of war and deprived men of their power. After 1914, "death at war was no longer a fate you chose",[23] war no longer the business of nobles or professional soldiers. In intraspecific combat, opponents choose to engage in combat; in predation, the prey chooses nothing – it only tries to survive. These young men who had welcomed the conflict thought they would take part in an intraspecific struggle. They found predation instead, and, what is worse, were placed in the role of the prey. A soldier's skill, training, courage and prudence, or any other quality once valuable to assure survival, were rendered useless by the machine gun, one-ton shells, and gas – survival became a matter of chance.[24]

One of the greatest classics of the First World War literature, Erich Maria Remarque's *All Quiet on the Western Front*, is a combat novel centered on the experiences of a small group of Germans in the Western Front. In the novel, the reader does not find the tests of courage or the ground for achieving glory that were present in the literature of previous wars. We are instead repeatedly reminded of men's utter helplessness before the technology of modern war. Instead of individualized duels between warriors of prowess, in this work there are masses of countless and faceless soldiers being maimed and killed by weapons they often do not even see. The First World War "made a mockery of the warrior ethic"[25] in pointless bloody battles such as Verdun, the Somme, and Passchendaele. In *All Quiet on the Western Front*, symmetry, ritual, and individualized combats do not exist: men can do nothing but flee and hide against shells and machine guns; the enemy is seldom seen; and engagements involve tens or hundreds of thousands of soldiers – the collective feature of predatory combat.

Paul Baumer, Remarque's first person narrator, stresses the fact that there is nothing he can do as he watches one after another of his colleagues die: "Kemmerich is dead, Haie Westhus is dying, they will have a job with Hans Kramer's body at the Judgment Day, piecing it together after a direct hit; Martens has no legs anymore, Meyer is dead, Max is dead, Beyer is dead, Hammerling is dead".[26] As the war drags on, another comrade, Muller, dies and then Kat. After listing the men who died, Baumer bluntly states that "[b]ut our comrades are dead, we cannot help them".[27] The list of the men who died and this statement that they cannot be helped are made soon after he thinks about the terror of the war and about how soldiers must behave in order to survive: he describes a sense of narcosis, or numbness: "terror can be endured so long as a man simply ducks;- but it kills, if a man thinks about it".[28] Baumer acknowledges his own powerlessness in relation to his dead comrades and how he cannot mourn them lest he becomes more vulnerable. This is completely different from the *Iliad*: Achilles not only mourns Patroclus but also takes revenge for his death. The death of a comrade in arms, someone you know and cherish, cannot go unnoticed and, more important, unavenged in the epic. Baumer, on the other hand, must helplessly watch all his comrades die before his eyes. Actually, "once the idea of heroic action is denied, the whole conception of the hero, and of narratives that shape the actions of such figures, is called into question",[29] that is, narratives of intraspecific combat are rendered meaningless once war only offers predatory practices.

Samuel Hynes argues that "[a]gainst the weight of [the First World] war, the individual has no power of action; he can only suffer".[30] However, even suffering, in the example of the dead comrades, must be put in relative terms. Baumer cannot suffer, i.e. grieve, for the deaths he sees – he affirms that suffering and feeling the losses would only make him more vulnerable. Baumer has the feeling of those who are preyed upon: survival is the only thing that matters and, like a herd of wildebeests when hunted by lions, a soldier must strive to live on as others are brought down. However, not even Baumer is spared: in the final lines, the novel shifts to a third person narration to tell of Baumer's death, only one month before the end of the conflict.[31]

For reasons of scope and length, *All Quiet on the Western Front* shall stand as an example for the pattern of predatory features also predominant in other works of literature written by men who witnessed the First World War, novels such as Ernest Hemingway's *A Farewell to Arms*, Henri Barbusse's *Under Fire*, Humphrey Cobb's *Paths of Glory*, William March's *Company K*,[32] not to mention the poetry of Wilfred Owen and Siegfried Sassoon. However, the representation of the conflict with an emphasis on its predatory nature is also to be found in what Petra Rau has called "post-memorial war writing",[33] that is, literature produced by those who did not live through the conflict they narrate. Pat Barker's highly acclaimed trilogy Regeneration – *Regeneration*, *The Eye in the Door* and *The Ghost Room*, written in the 1990's, depicted the trauma of those who served on the Western Front, the trauma of those who survived being hunted.

Another work written decades after the war is the Canadian Timothy Findley's *The Wars*. *The Wars* is explicitly narrated as a post-memorial work since it reads like a reconstruction of the life of the main character Robert Ross. There are, for instance, descriptions of photos and transcriptions of interviews in Findley's attempt at telling what happened to Robert Ross. It is one passage, however, that best serves the purposes of the present discussion. Ross and a group of Canadian soldiers are ordered to place guns in forward positions. Once they venture into No Man's Land, gas is released by the Germans.[34] The gas spreads over their heads and the men are forced to jump into a flooded crater. Against a gas attack there is nothing to do but run and hide. They are without their masks and to avoid the gas they must urinate into pieces of cloth and breathe through these. Utterly defenseless, they know that "if the

Germans came, their only hope was to play dead and pray".[35] How can one expect to fight gas? Gas cannot be fought against. One can defend oneself against gas, but not oppose it. Other weapons may be countered in symmetric or asymmetric ways. Planes can be fought with other planes or with anti-aircraft guns; tanks are countered by other tanks or anti tank guns; swords by swords or shields. During First World War, sixty-six million gas shells were fired, inflicting 1.3 million casualties, but with little or irrelevant tactical or strategic success.[36] Notwithstanding its inefficiency as an offensive weapon, gas cannot be stopped by gas and has always been viewed as cruel and repugnant. Like the bow in 1139, there were attempts at banning its use in warfare: it was made illegal in the 1925 Geneva Convention. Even Adolf Hitler, perhaps remembering his being gassed on the Western Front or acknowledging it would bring little advantage, refrained from deploying it in the battlefield. It would be preposterous, however, to assign this to humanitarian reasons: the Fuehrer would unfortunately find another place to gas other human beings – during the next, and more predatory, world war.

Barely thirty years after the naively called "war to end all wars", another global conflict broke out and the features of predatory combat would be more clear – and claim a higher toll in human lives. The Second World War, in the frozen steppes of Russia, the beaches of Normandy, in the islands of the Pacific and the jungles of Burma and China, and in the extermination camps of Central and Eastern Europe, became the most murderous and cruel engagement in history, for "it is hard to point a conflict more brutally fought than World War II, or to combatants more driven by the sheer urge to kill".[37] It was utterly and completely predatory. As soon as they were at war, Germans, Russians, Japanese, Americans, Englishmen, and others strove to kill the enemy in round-ups of civilians, in indiscriminate bombing of cities, in gas chambers, in sinking any type of vessel, and the like. The enemy, with a view to making predatory practices easier and more acceptable, was often portrayed as belonging to another, inferior species.

In Russian journalist Konstantin Simonov's novel *Days and Nights* and in German veteran Heinrich Gerlach's *The Forsaken Army*,[38] the Battle of Stalingrad is depicted as a merciless combat, corroborating O'Connell's assessment that against the Nazis "the Russians fought with the desperation of those preyed upon".[39] Soviet Ambassador to Berlin, Vladimir Dekanozov, seemed to know what was to come. As soon as he was informed of the Nazi invasion, he declared it was "insulting, provocative and thoroughly predatory".[40] Future events and the way the battle progressed proved him right. The clash between Nazi Germany and Communist Soviet Union showed "no compromise. The end could only come in the total obliteration of one of the two opponents".[41] German General Hermann Hoth, commander of the Fourth Panzer Army in Stalingrad, made it very clear when he said that the annihilation of Jews, who supported Bolshevism and its organization for murder, the partisans, was a "measure of self-preservation".[42] The army had already issued orders, before the beginning of hostilities, depriving Russian civilians "of any right of appeal" and exonerating German soldiers from crimes against them, whether "murder, rape or looting".[43] Hitler stated it would be a "battle of annihilation", a "race war", thus lending the campaign an unprecedented character and successfully dehumanizing the soviet enemy so that the Wehrmacht became "morally anaesthetized".[44] According to the Fuehrer, the rules of engagement and conventions such as Geneva's, did not apply there – as the rules of intraspecific combat do not apply to predation. In both *Days and Nights* and *Forsaken Army*, characters of the two armies know they will hardly be taken prisoner: their fate, if defeated, is death. Soldiers of the two sides feel, and indeed know, their roles are either predator or prey – no other choice is left.

Another common feature of predatory combat, asymmetry, is repeatedly found in representations of the Second World War. In Stefan Heym's *Crusaders* as well as in James Jones' *The Thin Red Line*,[45] although men do fight other men who are also armed with machine guns and the like, they more often are up against tanks and airplanes. And even though the novels are set in different theaters – *Crusaders* in Europe and *The Thin Red Line* in the Pacific – the experience narrated is the same: a struggle to the death against machines, faceless enemies bent on killing.

The authors of the books mentioned above, as in the first examples of the First World War, were all contemporaries of the conflict they represent: Heym took part in the American war effort; Jones fought in Guadacanal; Simonov was a war correspondent; Gerlach fought in Stalingrad. And, as in the remarks regarding the First World War, the post-memorial war writing of the Second World War provides examples of its predatory features as well. One such work is Ian McEwan's best-selling novel *Atonement*, which has a long passage on the ordeal of the British Expeditionary Force as its protagonist, Robbie Turner, tries to reach Dunkirk and escape the onslaught of the German army. The fact that there is not a single German soldier in the novel, and that the advancing Panzers are never seen already hints at predatory features: predators are not supposed to be seen by their prey until the very last moment – predation relies on surprise. Robbie Turner and the British soldiers, like a herd of deer, know that they are being chased, hunted, they just do not know where and when the enemy will actually strike.

Eventually, the threat and the danger are materialized in the form of the Luftwaffe and its planes. Turner knows, since the beginning of his walk to reach the channel, that "if he was going to survive, he had to keep a watch on the sky"[46] because even before any attack he sees "a formation of about fifty Heinkels, heading the same way to the coast".[47] Shortly after his acknowledgement of where the danger is, a single fighter strafes the column of soldiers, vehicles, and refugees that cluster on the road bringing havoc but not causing much destruction. The worst is yet to come. Later on, a formation of "at least fifteen of them"[48] not only strafes but also drops bombs on the slow-moving column. This time, there is widespread panic and people rush for cover. Turner tries to help a woman who is carrying a child. He grabs the boy and runs, a bomb falls, the ground shakes, they duck for cover. After the bombs, Turner knows the planes are going to turn around and strafe. He resumes running but the woman refuses to move. He leaves the woman and child behind. More bombs fall and when Turner looks back at the spot where he left the woman and child, there is only a crater. He thinks "that was why he had to leave them. His business was to survive".[49]

Armies had been destroyed and routed before in history, soldiers have had to flee before – but they had never been chased from above. This passage in *Atonement* serves to show the asymmetry of combat in twentieth-century wars as planes attack from above, targeting soldiers and equipment the same way birds of prey strike against rabbits and other small mammals. Besides, and more importantly, this passage is illustrative of another change in war which displays predatory features and moves away from intraspecific combat as well: the targeting of the most helpless, the civilians. According to Simon Chesterman, in the First World War, 95% of the casualties were soldiers, whereas in the Second World War, civilians answered for 50% of the casualties – in the 1990's the number of civilian casualties at war had reached 90%,[50] virtually reverting the rates in less than a century. The planes in McEwan's novel hit anything that is below them and make no distinction between combatants and otherwise. The fate of the civilians in the novel was shared by the population of London, Tokyo, Warsaw, Berlin, Hamburg, Cologne, Dresden and others. The people of St. Petersburg, then Leningrad starved to death in three years of siege. Millions of non-combatants were taken to camps where they were gassed, shot at or simply left to die by starvation. In fact, the global nature of the Second

World War and its all-encompassing brutality meant there was no front. The war was everywhere, in the battle scene and in the rear, in towns and in the countryside; once a country capitulated, there might be resistance and the beginning of executions and reprisals; cities far from the front line might be, and indeed were, relentlessly bombarded. No person or location was deemed safe, free from the war. Therefore, the elderly, the women, and children, being unarmed, untrained, weaker and slower, were likely to be killed first – something that did not happen so constantly in other wars. In intraspecific combat, opponents choose their like, they aim at dominance and superiority. A lion will not fight against a cub for leadership in a group – it chooses the current leader and challenges it in combat. The specificity and difference of the two kinds of violence are rather reiterated when it comes to lions: males do not engage in hunting, lionesses are the ones supposed to collect food for the pack. Lions fight intraspecific combat and lionesses fight predatory combat. And lionesses, like tigers, crocodiles, and all other predators, kill what is in their way, preferably selecting old animals, the young, or those left alone by the herd – easier targets. Predators do not hunt the strongest, they search for the weakest.

There is, however, a body of literature stemming out of the Second World War whose nature seems to evade the two categories herein discussed: the literature of the Holocaust. It would be preposterous, to say the least, to call such literature an example of intraspecific combat. First of all, the peoples exterminated in the gas chambers were not viewed by their executioners as equal, they had no weapons to fight symmetrically, the numbers and methods rule out individualized encounters and ritual. But would it be predation? Could we even call it combat? Hardly. O'Connell's categories apply to violent encounters in nature and have been used for human conflict in order to highlight the ways men fight and the changes in warfare. In the literature of the Holocaust there is no fighting, no struggle in the literal sense of the term. In Elie Wiesel's *Night*, Jorge Semprun's *The Long Voyage* and *Literature or Life*, in Primo Levi's *Is this a man?*,[51] the only struggle seems to be the urge to live on, to stay alive in spite of the hardships and then tell the world what has happened. Moreover, predation in nature serves a purpose: survival by means of eating the prey. One may argue that the previous examples of predation in warfare did serve a purpose as well: winning the war. However, even if we discard such reasoning by claiming that winning a war is no justification for bombing thousands of people or sending tens of thousands across no man's lands to be mowed down by machine guns, we cannot equate Auschwitz to Verdun; the Battle of Stalingrad was not like

Treblinka. Extermination camps and the system devised by Nazi Germany cannot even be compared to a slaughterhouse. Cattle are slaughtered so that they may be eaten and thus guarantee the survival of people – the killing serves a practical purpose, it is a means to an end. Treblinka, Auschwitz-Birkenau, Dachau, and many other infamous places served no practical purpose; the killing was an end in itself. The Holocaust's unprecedented nature defies our understanding: how can one deal with, and categorize, the scene Elie Wiesel witnessed as he entered Auschwitz, the image of babies being tossed into flames?[52] Primo Levi explains: "War is always a terrible fact, to be deprecated, but it is in us, it has rationality, we 'understand' it", "but Auschwitz has nothing to do with war; it is neither an episode in it nor an extreme form of it".[53] Extermination on an industrial scale is neither predation nor intraspecific combat. It is not war.

The literature of the Vietnam War displays some of the features previously discussed such as asymmetry and collective engagement. However, the most conspicuous aspect of the Vietnam, found in several works of literature but made even more familiar through the cinematic representations of the conflict is the enemy's invisibility. In Tim O'Brien's *The Things They Carried* and *Going After Cacciato*, Ron Kovic's *Born on the Fourth of July* and Larry Heinemann's *Paco's Story*,[54] American soldiers patrol a jungle full of hidden menace, searching but seldom finding the so-called Vietcong, who strikes anytime from anywhere, generally in deadly fashion. The soldiers of the NVA (North Vietnamese Army) are conspicuously absent from narratives, a way to reinforce their way of fighting American forces. In *The Things they Carried*, it is repeatedly said that Ted Lavender "was shot", in the passive voice, without an agent of the killing. O'Brien thus explains the feeling of fighting in Vietnam: "it was ghost country, and Charlie Cong was the main ghost. The way he came out at night. How you never really saw him...He could blend with the land, changing form, becoming tress and grass".[55] Ron Kovic claims that the enemy "just sort of popped up on us and started firing".[56] Tigers are stripped; lions have the color of the savanna bush. Predators have evolved to blend with their surroundings, pop up at their prey, many hunt at night, and the prey are not supposed to see them until it is too late.

Although warfare had already become faceless since the First World War, there were still fronts and everybody knew where the enemy was. One might be killed by shells fired miles away but one did know it came from the enemy's position – no soldier was killed from behind except in the cases of "friendly fire". This is what I am calling the enemy's facelessness. In Vietnam we are provided with the enemy's invisibility, and it is utterly predatory. Predators such as tigers and leopards hunt their victims by stealth; crocodiles and sharks rely on unexpected attacks, on ambush tactics. American soldiers in Vietnam ambushed and were ambushed: O'Brien and his team "move into ambush site",[57] Kovic's men leave to set up an ambush, think they have found the Vietcong but end up killing "a bunch of kids", instead.[58] The routine of the war was made of "ordinary ambushes, sniper fire, claymore mines...booby-trapped bombs"[59] – all predatory practices, and illegal: "booby-traps are clearly illegal and expressly forbidden according to the Geneva Convention Rules of War, and to use them is a war crime, the same as slave labor, the torture and execution of prisoners, the use of chemical-biological weapons, snipers, and such as that", "but everybody used them".[60] Both sides were engaged in hunting each other. The North Vietnamese Army and the Vietcong, instead of offering the traditional pitched battle the American command so eagerly wanted, insisted on a guerrilla war. Intraspecific combat is marked by the two opponents approaching each other and colliding face to face – there was no such a thing in Vietnam. Be it noted that as the previous remarks are overtly one-sided, for they only discuss examples from writers of the USA, they become thus incomplete. The nature of the conflict in Vietnam is most likely to be different when told from the Vietnamese point of view.

Due to the limitations of scope and length in a work of this nature, the present essay must stand as an overview only. The primary purpose is to apply O'Connell's observations, originally meant for an analysis of war and weapons, for the study of war literature, chiefly the one on the wars of the twentieth-century. Therefore, more attention has been devoted to the author's dual categories than to a lengthy discussion of any work of literature in particular. Examples from the above mentioned conflicts have been chosen for their position as classics, for their presence in the so-called canon of war literature. Other conflicts and other literary works could have been approached and they would surely provide fertile ground for analysis. Nevertheless, in spite of the reduced *corpus* and the somewhat brief remarks, it becomes clear that we are the only beings that have adapted ourselves, researched, and toiled to turn combat between members of the same species into merciless, predatory bloodshed.

---

[1] O'Connell, Robert. *Ride of the Second Horsemen – The Birth and Death of War*. (New York: Oxford UP, 1995), 15-21.

[2] O'Connell, Robert L. *Of Arms and Men – A History of War, Weapons, and Agression*. (New York: Oxford UP, 1989), 31.

[3] O'Connell, *Of Arms and Men*, 14.
[4] O'Connell, *Of Arms and Men*, 16.
[5] O'Connell, *Of Arms and Men*, 16-17.
[6] O'Connell, *Of Arms and Men*, 17.
[7] O'Connell, *Of Arms and Men*, 17.
[8] O'Connell, *Of Arms and Men*, 15.
[9] O'Connell, *Of Arms and Men*, 16.
[10] Goulart, Audemaro Taranto. "*Ilíada*, um poema de fundação". In: Marques, Haroldo. (Ed.) *Os gregos*. (Belo Horizonte: Autêntica, 2002), 47.
[11] O'Connell, *Of Arms and Men*, 54.
[12] Lattimore, Richmond, trans. *The Iliad of Homer*. (Chicago: U of Chicago P, 1951), VI.119-236.
[13] Lattimore, *The Iliad of Homer*, XXIV.31-54.
[14] Lattimore, *The Iliad of Homer*, XI.390.
[15] Lattimore, *The Iliad of Homer*, VII.84-302.
[16] O'Connell, *Of Arms and Men*, 46.
[17] O'Connell, *Of Arms and Men*, 46.
[18] O'Connell, *Of Arms and Men*, 70.
[19] Shakespeare, William. *The complete works*. (Oxford: Oxford UP, 1998).
[20] O'Connell, *Of Arms and Men*, 95-96.
[21] See Horne, Alistair. *The Price of Glory: Verdun 1916*. (London: Penguin, 1993); Keegan, John. *The First World War*. (New York: Vintage Books, 1998); and Tuchman, Barbara. *The Guns of August*. (New York: Ballantine, 1994).
[22] Cooperman, Stanley. *World War I and the American Novel*. (Baltimore: The Johns Hopkins UP, 1970), 193.
[23] Hynes, Samuel. *The soldiers' tale: Bearing witness to modern war*. (New York: Penguin, 1997), 70.
[24] Audoin-Rouzeau, Stéphane, and Annette Becker. *14-18, Retrouver la guerre*. (Paris: Gallimard, 2000), 46-47.
[25] O'Connell, *Of Arms and Men*, 210.
[26] Remarque, Erich Maria. *All Quiet on the Western Front*. Trans. A.W. Wheen. (New York: Fawcett Crest, 1958), 139.
[27] Remarque, All Quiet on the Western Front, 139.
[28] Remarque, All Quiet on the Western Front, 138.
[29] Hynes, Samuel. A War Imagined: The First World War and English Culture. (New York: Atheneum, 1991), 306.
[30] Hynes, *A War Imagined*, 306.
[31] Remarque, All Quiet on the Western Front, 296.
[32] Barbusse, Henri. *Under Fire: The Story of a Squad*. Trans. W. Fitzwater Wray. (London: J.M. Dent & Sons, 1926); March, William. *Company K*. (Tuscaloosa: U of Alabama P,1989); Cobb, Humphrey. *Paths of Glory*. (Athens: U of Georgia P, 1987). Hemingway, Ernest. *A Farewell to Arms*. (Middlesex: Penguin, 1966).
[33] MacKay, Marina. (Ed.) *The Cambridge Companion to the Literature of World War II*. (Cambridge: Cambridge University Press, 2009), 216.
[34] Findley, Timothy. *The Wars*. (New York: Delacorte Press, 1977), 140.
[35] Findley, *The Wars*, 144.

[36] O'Connell, *Of Arms and Men*, 253.

[37] O'Connell, *Of Arms and Men*, 280.

[38] Gerlach, Heinrich. *The Forsaken Army*. Trans. Richard Graves. (London: Cassell, 2000); Simonov, Konstantin. *Days and Nights*. Trans. Joseph Barnes. (New York: Simon and Schuster, 1945).

[39] O'Connell, *Of Arms and Men*, 286.

[40] Beevor, Antony. *Stalingrad*. (London: Viking, 1998), 8.

[41] O'Connell, *Of Arms and Men*, 290.

[42] Beevor, *Stalingrad*, 16.

[43] Beevor, *Stalingrad*, 14.

[44] Beevor, *Stalingrad*, 15.

[45] Heym, Stefan. *Crusaders*. (Boston: Little, Brown, and Company, 1948); Jones, James. *The Thin Red Line*. (New York: Delta Book, 1998).

[46] McEwan, Ian. *Atonement*. (New York: Anchor Books, 2003), 206.

[47] McEwan, *Atonement*, 201.

[48] McEwan, *Atonement*, 221.

[49] McEwan, *Atonement*, 224.

[50] Chesterman, Simon. (Ed.) *Civilians in War*. (Boulder: Lynne Rienner, 2001), 2.

[51] Levi, Primo. "Afterword: The Author's Answers to his Readers' Questions" In: Levi, Primo. *Is this a man?/ The Truce*. Trans. Stuart Woolf. (London: Abacus, 1987); Semprun, Jorge. *Literature or Life*. Trans Linda Coverdale. (New York: Viking, 1997); Semprun, Jorge. *The Long Voyage*. Trans. Richard Seaver. (Woodstock, NY: Overlook Press, 2005). Wiesel, Elie. *Night*. (New York: Hill and Wang, 2006).

[52] Wiesel, *Night*, 32.

[53] Levi, "Afterword", 395.

[54] Heinemann, Larry. *Paco's Story*. (New York: Vintage Contemporaries, 2005); Kovic, Ron. *Born on the Fourth of July*. (New York: Pocket Books, 1977); O'Brien, Tim. *Going After Cacciato*. (New York: Delacorte Press, 1978); O'Brien, Tim. *The things they carried*. (Nova York: Broadway Books, 1990).

[55] O'Brien, The things they Carried, 229.

[56] Kovic, Born on the Fourth of July, 191.

[57] O'Brien, The things they Carried, 147.

[58] Kovic, Born on the Fourth of July, 200-205.

[59] Heinemann, *Paco's Story*, 20.

[60] Heinemann, *Paco's Story*, 192-193.

Luiz Gustavo Leitão Vieira is a Brazilian scholar long devoted to the study of the literary representation of warfare. One of the founders of NEGUE, Vieira holds a Master's Degree in the field of war literature, entitled *From the Gates of Troy to the Trenches of the Western Front*, and his PhD dissertation, entitled *The Writing of War*, is planned for completion in late 2012, both degrees for UFMG. Some of his most relevant publications are "The truth the Muses carry: The issue of memory and truth-telling in Ancient Greek Poetry and in Tim O'Brien's *The Things They Carried*" ; "Ares becomes a monster: depictions of the Great War of 1914-18 as a monster"; and "The anonimity of the hero: Achilles and the Unknown Soldier in war narrative".

Die finstere Seite des Herzens. Zur Migration von Bildern der religiösen Profanation

Vicente Sánchez Biosca

Das Martyrium der Sachen

Das 25. Kapitel einer der angesehensten Studien zur religiösen Verfolgung in Spanien während des Spanischen Bügerkriegs, die *Historia de la persecución religiosa en España* 1936-1939 von Antonio Montero Moreno, trägt den Titel „Das Martyrium der Sachen".[1] Es handelt sich um eine überraschende Personifizierung eines deutlicheren Phänomens, das die Verbrechen, Folterungen und die von Geistlichen erlittenen Erniedrigungen auflistet, die während der antiklerikalen Welle nach dem Aufstand im Juli 1936 erfolgten. Auf zwei Besonderheiten weist Montero hin: dass diese Attacken ausschließlich gegen Objekte in der „roten Zone" erfolgten, da die Gewalt in der nationalen Zone sich vornehmlich gegen Personen richtete und, dass „die Aufzählung der materiellen Zerstörungen gerade die spirituellste Seite der religiösen Verfolgung enthülle".[2]

Und das - fügt er seinerseits hinzu - aus zwei Gründen: „weil die Sachen immer 'unschuldiger' sind als die Personen und weil ihre Vernichtung - immer wenn es sich dabei um in irgendeiner Hinsicht heilige Objekte handelt - einen Zorn gegen die religiöse Welt enthüllt, der wesentlich bedeutsamer ist, als wenn es sich um die Vernichtung von Menschen aus Fleisch und Blut handeln würde".[3]

Angesichts dieses offensichtlichen Paradoxons verlagert Montero den Focus seiner Aufmerksamkeit auf die Absicht der Profanation: statt sich auf Tatsachen zu beschränken, gibt er nachfolgend eine ausgearbeitete Typologie, die es erlaubt in psychologische Feinheiten einzudringen; andererseits bereitet er das Terrain vor, um die Handlung in ihrer beunruhigenden Einzigartigkeit zu verstehen, ihre Unnützigkeit in der Praxis und ihre Erscheinung mit immens symbolischer Bedeutung. Es ist genau dieser energische, symbolische Ausdruck von Zorn, der das lange Überleben der kriminellen Handlungen gegen die Dinge, vor allem gegen die sakralen Objekte, in der Erinnerung garantiert hat. Außerdem ist es diese Art von Handlungen, die an eine lange Tradition von Antiklerikalismus anknüpft und den unmittelbaren Mimetismus enthüllt, der den Urheber der Handlung mit seinem Feind verbindet, denn um Freude an der Zerstörung von sakralen Gegenständen zu haben, ist es für andere notwendig, wenigstens für einen Augenblick diese Psychologie zu übernehmen und flüchtig an den sakralen Wert zu glauben. Profanation ist demzufolge keine Säkularisation der Bilder, sondern eine Erniedrigung unter der Voraussetzung ihrer sakralen Bedeutung, die während der Ausübung der Profanation fortbesteht und die Aktion mit einer zusätzlichen Befriedigung versieht. Nichts davon geschieht im Falle einer reinen und einfachen Zerstörung.[4]

Eine immense Bibliographie hat sich dem Ikonoklasmus und seinen Beziehungen zum Antilerikalismus, mit den historischen Gründen für die Konfrontation von liberalen bzw. republikanischen Bewegungen und Arbeiterbewegungen mit der Kirche und ihren Symbolen im modernen Spanien beschäftigt. Weit davon entfernt, dieses bewegte Gebiet zu untersuchen, stellen wir uns damit zufrieden aufzuzeigen, dass im Aufwind der Verbreitung von Bildern von 1936, die praktische Sinnlosigkeit der Profanationshandlung ihren Ursprung in der weltweiten Zirkulation der Bilder hat, die der angestrebten Reputation einer Ordnung gebietenden Republik sehr teuer zu stehen kam. Diese Bilder wurden von der Presse, illustrierten Zeitschriften, Nachrichtensendungen und Dokumentarfilmen sinnentstellt auf internationaler Ebene von den Feinden der Republik wiedergegeben: allen voran Nazideutschland, die faschistischen Bewegungen in Europa, aber auch die Medien der demokratischen Länder, die sich von solch unehrerbietigen Bildern, von der gegen die Ikonen der religiösen Tradition ausgeübten Gewalt angegriffen fühlten.

Zwei Bilder

Unter den Bildern, die am meisten verbreitet waren, sind zwei Sequenzen hervorzuheben, die zu denjenigen zählen, die für das Ansehen der Republik am vernichtendsten waren: die erste zeigt die Zurschaustellung der mumifizierten Leichen von Nonnen in den geöffneten Särgen im Innenhof einer Kirche der Salesianer in Barcelona, deren Aufnahme auf die Tage unmittelbar nach dem Aufstand vom Juli 1936 zu datieren ist; die zweite Sequenz bezieht sich auf die symbolische Erschießung der Christusstatue *Sagrado Corazón de Jesús* auf dem Cerro de los Ángeles, die von einigen Milizionären Anfang August gleichen Jahres durchgeführt wurde. Die Aktionen, die in den beiden Bildfolgen dargestellt werden und die Fotos, die sie festhielten, wurden von Milizionären gemacht, mit ihrem Einverständnis und sogar ihrer stolzen Billigung. In anderen Worten ausgedrückt: es handelt sich in beiden Fällen um einen symbolischen Akt, der ohne Umschweife vor den Augen der Anwesenden zur Schau gestellt wird, aber vor allem vor den Kameras. Weder gefälscht noch nachgestellt entsprach diese dokumentarische Verfilmung ebenso wie das szenographische Umfeld den Gruppierungen, die auf der Seite der loyal zur Republik stehenden Truppen kämpften. Wenn das Rohmaterial auch aus diesem Blickwinkel entstanden ist, so sind die diskursiven Zusammenhänge, in die sich die Fotos und Filmszenen einreihten, die Montage, der es unterworfen wurde und die Kommentare die es begleiteten, Faktoren, die einen unauslöschlichen Eindruck bei seiner Wahrnehmung hinterließen. Die Verbreitung dieser Bilder hat etwas von einer symbolischen Schlacht, von Besetzung, Anklage und Verherrlichung.

Eine Erklärung des Kontextes ist unabdingbar. Der Spanische Bürgerkrieg brach aus, mitten in der von Propaganda erschütterten Zwischenkriegszeit, die mit der Wahrheit und Wahrscheinlichkeit der Informationen brach. Dieser Umstand geht einher mit einer Perspektivlosigkeit hinsichtlich der Informationen: die Erfordernis der Unmittelbarkeit des Fotojornalismus und der illustrierten Zeitschriften fiel zusammen mit der Propaganda. Diese Bilder sind der Beginn einer unaufhaltsamen Zirkulation und sie hinterlassen immer wieder ihren Eindruck in den Medienketten, sowohl in den eigenen am Ursprung der Information, wie auch in denen der Schockpropaganda des Gegners. Ihre Dimension hat die Zeitgeschichte in einer Form durchdrungen, dass sie sich im Gedächtnis von Generationen jenseits ihrer Offensivfunktion oder ihres unmittelbaren Überraschungseffektes verankert haben. Sie haben sich lexikalisiert. Wenn sie auch während langer Jahre des Franquismus immer wieder wach gerufen wurden, um die Schreckenstaten der Republik anzuklagen, so haben ebenso Dokumentarfilme, die sich als unparteiisch ausgaben, sie immer wieders in Gedächtnis gerufen, um andere allgemeine Fakten zu verdeutlichen, für die sie mutmaßlich stehen. Diese Bilder repräsentierten bald nicht mehr nur Einzeltaten, verloren ihre Verankerung und ihren spezifischen Informationsgehalt, um eine abstrakte Idee zu verkörpern, wie es gewöhnlich mit allen verweltlichten Ikonen unseres Jahrhunderts passiert.[5]

Diese beiden ikonenhaften Sequenzen sprechen vom Krieg, aber auch, mit der anachronischen Macht, die ihnen die Erinnerung verleiht, bedienen sie sich folgender Elemente, wenn sie sich auf die Gegenwart beziehen: im Moment der Desaktualisierung verlieren sie ihren Indizienwert und werden zu Ikonen. Wenn die Dokumentarfilme mit großer Leichtigkeit auf sie zurückgreifen konnten, liegt das daran, dass sie im Depot der Tradition lagerten und ihre Aktivierung einzig darin bestand, einen bereits kodifizierten Affekt zu mobilisieren.

Die Mumien der Salesianerinnen in Barcelona

Die Protagonismus der Anarchisten bei der Niederschlagung des Militäraufstandes in Barcelona war die Lunte, die die soziale Revolution entfachte, wie Franz Borkenau, H.E. Kaminski und sogar George Orwell, der in der katalanischen Hauptstadt im Dezember 1936 angekommen war, berichten.[6] Mitten in dieser Euphorie und mitten im frohlockenden Chaos, setzte sich eine wütende Dialektik der Zerstörung und des Aufbaus *ex nihilo* durch, die Jaume Miravilles durch das Mitwirken von Sektoren des Lumpenproletariats gekennzeichnet sieht.[7] Die Fotoapparate und die Filmkameras, die im Marasmus verfallen waren, registrierten die Tatsachen, in die sie verwickelt waren. Sicherlich gab es professionelle Fotografen wie Agustí Centelles oder Pérez Rozas, die unvergängliche Augenblicke des Klimas jenes Momentes einfingen, aber auch improvisierende Kameraleute tauchten ein in den faszinierenden Wirbel der Revolution während sie an ihrem Geist teil hatten. Einige anarchosyndikalistische Kameraleute widmeten sich der Aufgabe, die Euphorie jener Wochen aufzunehmen. Mit seinen Totaleinstellungen,[8] machte Mateo Santos einen Film mit dem Titel „Reportage von der revolutionären Bewegung in Barcelona" Das Prekäre des gefilmten Materials und die Überstürzung bei seiner Montage verleihen dem Film Dokumentarwert, da die Improvisation und das fehlende Kalkül es erlaubten, ein Klima der emotionalen Spontanität der Bewegung festzuhalten. Der euphorische Ton in der Berichterstimme überträgt einen Aufruf zur Zerstörung des Gegners, nach der man vom Triumph der neuen sozial-libertären Überzeugung ausgeht. Daher entspricht die Aggressivität des gesprochenen Textes den Bildern von Bränden von aufgeheizten Massen und frischen Ruinen.

Im Mittelteil dieses heterogenen und zusammenhanglosen Kurzfilms erscheint eine einfache Serie von Einstellungen, die in die Geschichte eingegangen ist. Es ist die folgende: Diese sechs Einstellungen folgen auf andere mit zerstörten Klöstern und Kirchen und scheinen ein orgiastisches Klima nachzuempfinden, das in der Kirche und ihren Repräsentanten ihr Zerstörungsobjekt findet. Die begleitende Erzählung lässt keinen Zweifel aufkommen:

> Das Maschinengewehr und das Gewehr hinter den Altären und hinter den von Liturgie und Weihrauch gesättigten Bildern, später durchdrungen von Pulvergeruch und Blasphemie. Die Maristen, die Piaristen, die Krippe von Bethlehem, der Orden der Mercedarier, der heilige Jakob und alle Redukte des Jesuitentums und Pfaffentums (...) *fielen unter dem Druck der vom Mut entfachten Massen und erleuchteten mit ihren Flammen die Morgenröte, mit der sich der spanische Horizont färbte.* (...) Das Attentat gegen das Volk

(...) *wurde vergolten mit der Zerstörung durch die Flammen des Feuers*, von allen Bastionen des Faschismus, verborgen in der Militäruniform, im pfäffischen Wams, in der Mönchskutte, in der priesterlichen Sotane und in Raubvogelgebärden der Industrie- und Bankmagnaten (kursiv vom Autor).[9]

Die Verbreitung dieses Films hat ihre dunklen Seiten[10] - wie von dem Historiker Fernández Cuenca überliefert ist - aber mit einigen von Gubern und Sala vorgenommenen Berichtigungen, habe der Industrielle José Arquer die Verbreitung des Filmmaterials in Frankreich versucht bzw. gemäß einer anderen Version über Berlin, wo es bereits im August in die Hände der Naziorganisationen fiel, die es als Negativ kopierten und wiederbenutzten. Diese Tatsache, die Joaquin Reig zugeschrieben wird, der von Falange Española zu Beginn des Krieges nach Berlin entsandt worden war, kann der Grund dafür sein, dass einige Versionen dieser Einstellungen von Hand zu Hand gingen.[11] Angesichts der Tatsache, dass die Negativkopie in jener Zeit sehr häufig war, lassen sich der Augenblick und der Anlass nicht mit Sicherheit feststellen.[12] Es scheint hingegen logisch, dass wer sich dieser Sprache der Zerstörung der alten Gesellschaftsordnung bediente, nicht ihre Verbreitung fürchtete, sondern diese ersehnte. Miquel Mir machte das erschaudernde Tagebuch des Anarchisten José E. bekannt, eines herausragenden Mitgliedes der die Stadt in den ersten Tagen kontrollierenden Milizpatrouillen, und in diesem wird nicht der libertären Verantwortung an der Profanation von Schädelstätten, Gräbern ausgewichen, darunter eben die des Klosters der Salesianerinnen vom Paseo de San Juan „um sie vor der Eingangstür im zwischen den Ruinen im vollen Tageslicht zu lassen". Weit entfernt davon die Autorschaft zurückzuweisen, ist die Tat ein Motiv stolz zu sein.[13]

Es ist eine unzweifelhafte Tatsache, dass dieses Fragment zu einem Geschenk für den Feind wurde, der die Gelegenheit nicht ungenutzt ließ, es gegen seine Autoren zu verwenden und es zu einer offenkundigen Anklage umformte, die die Besonderheit besaß, dass sie sich praktisch als eine Selbstanklage erwies.

Internationalistischer Antikommunismus

Die erste internationale Verbreitung dieser Bilder kam zustande unter dem Vorzeichen der Wiederaneignung, aufgeladen mit einem gewissen „Voyeurismus". In vielen Sequenzen, in denen sie erschienen, handelte es sich nicht um den spanischen Krieg, sondern um eine Bedrohung, die über den Verteidigern der westlichen

Zivilisation schwebte. Dieser Prototyp des Feindes und Urhebers der haarsträubenden Verbrechen wurde vom antiklerikalen Anarchosyndikalismus, verantwortlich für diese Handlungen, die filmische Dokumentation und die Montage (vor allem der Salesianerinnen in Barcelona), verlagert auf den Feind, den die Faschisten am meisten fürchteten: den Kommunismus. In vier Filmen wurde die Sequenz fast getreu wiedergegeben: der Nazifilm *Geißel der Welt* (Hans Weidemann, 1937) von Hispano-Film-Produktion, die zum ersten Male in Spanien ihre propagandistischen Waffen gegen die asiatischen Horden übte,[14] *España, una, grande, libre* (Spanien, eins, groß und frei), von der INCOM produziert unter der Regie von Giorgio Ferroni 1939, der den Konflikt aus der Perspektive des faschistischen Italien in Angriff nimmt; *La peste Rouge*/ Die rote Pest (Jean–Marie Musy, 1938), ein der Anklage der zerstörerischen Macht des Kommunismus gewidmeter Film des Schweizer Nationalkommites gegen den Kommunismus,[15] und schließlich *La división azul* (Die blaue Division von Joaquín Reig und Víctor de la Serna, 1942), ein spanischer Film, der die spanische Teilnahme am antikommunistischen Krieg sowohl in Spanien, als auch an der Ostfront des Zweiten Weltkrieges lobt. Jeder dieser Filme umfasst ein Spektrum des internationalen Einflusses des Faschismus und Antikommunismus, aber die Unterschiede im Pathos zwischen ihnen sind relevant.

Geißel der Welt klagt an, wie die kommunistische Geißel Spanien mit ihrem Netz in den Griff nimmt. Die kurze Sequenz der Einstellungen von den Salesianerinnen reiht sich ein in ein diskursives Umfeld von Chaos und Zerstörung, wobei eine deutliche Parallelschaltung der Szenen von Zerstörung und Mord mit dem unerbittlichen Voranschreiten der sowjetischen Truppen bei einer Parade erfolgt. In der Folge verbindet man die Gitter der Salesianer mit einem Gittertor, das die Ankunft des sowjetischen Botschafters in Spanien, Marcel Rosenberg, zeigt. Diese Assoziation wurde in der Folge Einstellung/Gegeneinstellung konstruiert und legt einen ursächlichen Zusammenhang trotz des fehlenden räumlichen Zusammenhangs als Referenz nahe. Auf diese Weise würde der sowjetische Botschafter zum Aufhetzer zur Profanation der Mumien.

España, una, grande, libre weist in eine ähnliche Richtung und betont die religiöse Bedeutung der Zerstörung von Kirchen und die Missachtung gegenüber den heiligen Ikonen, stellt die „Plünderung", „die ausgelöste Raserei", die „Verwüstung" dar, die sogar vor der „Feierlichkeit des Todes" keinen Halt macht, und die Ausdruck der Gemeinheit des Feindes ist. *La peste rouge* ihrerseits widmet der spanischen Episodie sehr wenige Filmmeter in einem Gesamtwerk, das sich der Denunziation der kommunistischen Infiltrations- und Agitationstaktiken verschrieben hat. Diese Marginalität hebt noch mehr die Wahl der Episodie der barceloneser Mumien hervor. Der zentrale Gegenstand von *La división azul* liegt in der Festigkeit der westlichen Zivilisation, die von Deutschland angeführt wird, seit es im Juni 1941 den neuen antisowjetischen Kreuzzug begann; einen Kreuzzug, der seine erste Schlacht bereits auf spanischem Boden nur wenige Jahre zuvor geführt hatte. Dieses Argument beruht auf Alfred Rosenberg und seinem *Der Mythos des 20. Jahrhunderts*. Daher drückt sich im Zuge einer größeren Annäherung der faschistischen Propaganda Spaniens mit dem Dritten Reich die Anschuldigung gegen den atheistischen und asiatischen Kommunismus mit Vehemenz in den Bildern aus, die Zerstörung und Profanation der Salesianerinnen beinhalten. Die begleitende Erzählung setzt das Profil des Kommunisten mit dem des Juden gleich und folgt damit klar der von den Nationalsozialisten inspirierten Vorstellung, in der offensichtlich die anarchistische Präsenz nicht einmal eine indirekte Erwähnung verdient:

Wenn diese vier Filme eindeutig die Auswirkung und Einträglichkeit zeigen, die die Episodie der Salesianerinnen im internationalen Kontext mit sich brachte und vor allem die spektakulären Bedingungen, die sie zu Idealbeispielen von Bewusstseinsschaffung machte, so ist es der Film *España heroica* (Helden in Spanien, Otto Lins-Morstadt und Joaquín Reig Gozalbes, 1938), der mit seiner Effizienz und Nachhaltigkeit im Schnitt besticht. *España heroica*: dieses gelungenste Propagandawerk des Franquismus während des Krieges geht von der Überzeugung aus, dass die cinematographische Sequenz in der *Reportaje del movimiento revolucionario en Barcelona (Reportage der revolutionären Bewegung in Barcelona)* eine Selbstanklage darstellt und es daher konsequenterweise keines Kommentars des Vergehens bedarf, sondern die Bilder bei Unterdrückung des Originaltons für sich sprechen.[16] Die Dramatik der Musik, die sich bis zum Höhepunkt steigert, und die ebenso spannungsgeladene Kette der Zerstörung auf den Bildern betonen den vermeintlich apolitischen Charakter der Anklage. Dieser Film nutzt die ikonographische Verbindung der beiden Gitter sowie die ursächliche Verbindung des Schemas Einstellung/Gegeneinstellung von *Geißel der Welt*, aber verdichtet bis zur furchterregenden Angst das Klima von Chaos, das dieses Fragment beherrscht, mittels einer Anhäufung von Einstellungen, die übervoll sind von angewandter Gewalt (Brände, Rauch, Ruinen, aufgehetzte Massen); dies alles herbeigeführt durch den unerbittlichen Rhythmus des Filmschnitts. Die Stimme von Reig ist nüchtern und dramatisch, um keinen Eindruck auf die Bilder zu hinterlassen: „Russland entsendet als seinen Botschafter nach Spanien Moisés Rosenberg". Es scheint kein Zufall zu sein, der mittels eines Versprechers den jüdischen Namen Moisés demjenigen zuschreibt, der in Wirklichkeit auf den Namen Marcel hörte, vor allem wenn man die Gleichsetzung von Judentum und Kommunismus in Betracht zieht.

Die Montage der Profanationsbilder endet mit einer Art *Unterschrift* der kommunistischen Partei, die der Schnitt bestätigt und die nicht einer dramatischen Ironie entbehrt. Gleich darauf beschleunigt sich der dramatische Rhythmus, um die Bilder von den Salesianerinnen mit der anderen dokumentarischen Serie in Verbindung zu setzen, deren frevelhafte Proportionen noch schaudernerregender waren: die Erschießung des Monuments des Heiligen Herzens Jesu. Diese „Attraktion", wenn man uns die Nutzung dieses eisensteinschen Ausdrucks erlaubt, war entscheidend, da sie für die Nachwelt die beiden schrecklichsten Motive für das „Martyrium der Dinge" gleichsetzte: eines wegen Fälschung und Unerfahrenheit des Feindes (die Salesianerinnen); das andere wegen eines Exzesses an Theatralik, eine Posse (die Erschießung), die von einer Unehrerbietigkeit zu einem Gottesmord wurde. Und die Verbindung von beiden wird, wie wir sehen werden, zu einem Explosivstoff für das Gewissen und unvergänglich in der Zeitgeschichte.[17]

Der erschossene Christus

Beide gotteslästerlichen Szenen waren bereits 1936 (wahrscheinlich seit dem Monat Oktober) zusammen in einem Dokumentarfilm aufgetaucht, den die französische Nachrichtensendung *Éclair Journal* dem Krieg in Spanien unter dem Titel *La gran angustia española* (Die große spanische Furcht) widmete. Ihre erklärte Quelle war nicht der Film, sondern die Fotografie. Einführend zeigte man zwei Plakate, die auf die vorherige Veröffentlichung in der illustrierten französischen Presse anspielten, um dann zwei Momente jedes Ereignisses zu zeigen, die nur zum Teil mit der genannten cinematographischen Sequenz übereinstimmten. Sie waren nicht in konsekutiver Abfolge, sondern es gab einen Schnitt zwischen ihnen.

Tatsächlich hatte *La petite Gironde* in Bordeaux am 29. Juli 1936 ein Foto von der Inbesitznahme des Klosters der Salesianerinnen als Aufmacher einer Reportage mit dem Titel „Die Spanische Revolution" veröffentlicht und die auflagenstarke Wochenzeitschrift *L'Illustration* hatte ein Album *Hors série* im August desselben Jahres mit Fotos von der Erschießung des Monuments vom Heiligen Herzen publiziert. Es handelte sich dabei nicht um die einzigen, aber die Assoziierung schien sich auf natürliche Weise durchzusetzen.[18]

Die durch die Erschießung repräsentierte Handlung hatte den Anschein eines Gottesmordes und schien sehr bewegend zu sein, auch wenn man noch nicht genau wusste, wo sie sich ereignet hatte und auch von der Possenhaftigkeit seiner Inszenierung keine Ahnung hatte. Wie zuvor schon mit dem Fragment der Salesianerinnen geschehen, wurde die sehr kurze cinematographische Sequenz von drei Einstellungen von den bekanntesten internationalen Nachrichtensendungen verbreitet, soweit sie im Besitz der Information waren. Wie dem auch sei, die Verbreitung implizierte notwendigerweise auch unterschiedliche Neumontagen, die in sehr verschiedenen Medien zirkulierten (*British Paramount News*, am 17. August 1936, *Universal Talking News*, am 24. August, *Pathé Journal*, am 13. August und im November 1936 wurden sie sogar von den *Fox Moviestone News* gezeigt. Im Unterschied zu anderen Inszenierungen von Antiklerikalismus und Profanation, zielte diese Sequenz auf das Mark des christlichen Glaubens ab und tat dies unter Einsatz eines anachronischen Elementes (des Gewehrs), dass in jenen Tagen von der überschäumenden ikonographischen Vergeudung der Kreuzigung nicht wenige Opfer gefordert hatte. Die nicht sehr militärischen Sandalen der Beteiligten, die Unordnung in der Aufstellung des Erschießungskommandos, die Unterschiedlichkeit der Waffen und die nicht weniger geringe Verschiedenheit in der Kleidung verleihen dem Bild etwas gewissermaßen Theatralisches, wie es öfter bei antiklerikalem Spott passiert, aber der verletzende Effekt des hingerichteten Monuments des Heiligen Herzens schließt die Komödie und eröffnet das Drama. Die symbolische Gewalt, die diese Handlung auf den ersten Blick ausübte, verbarg andere Bedeutungen dieses Bildnisses in der Liturgie und der ihm zugedachten Rolle als Denkmal in Spanien. Was war dann der Sinn dieses imponierenden Bildes, vom Himmel abgesetzt, das das improvisierte Erschießungskommando sich vorbereitete zu füsilieren.[19]

Das Herz Jesu besitzt eine äußerst komplexe Bedeutung in der christlichen Liturgie, und von ihr ergriffen die Jesuiten Besitz und übertrugen sie wie es scheint in zwei Richtungen: die Danksagung für den unergründlichen Reichtum der Gnade Christi (dessen Ursprung sich bei den Ephesern 3,8 findet) und die wiederherstellende Betrachtung des durchbohrten Christusherzens (Ursprung bei Johannes 19,37). Diese zweite Referenz impliziert eine Wiederherstellung der verletzten Liebe und seit der Zeit der Jesuitenpater, stellte es die Kirche als aus der offenen Seite des gekreuzigten Jesu geboren dar, so wie Eva im Alten Testament aus der Rippe des schlafenden Adams entstammte; wie ebenfalls das Vergießen von Blut und Wasser die Taufe und die Eucharistie symbolisierte.[20] Wenige Male hat die Dialektik zwischen symbolischer Abstraktion und obszöne Gegenständlichkeit (Blut, das aus dem Herzen rinnt, offene Brust, Dornenkrone, ...) einen solchen Aufwind gehabt. Daher kommt auch die immense Vielfalt der Ikonographie.

Diese liturgische Bedeutung wird durch eine andere Spanien betreffende angereichert: einer offensichtlich dem Jesuiten Francisco Bernardo de Hoyos im Jahre 1733 gemachten Voraussagung zufolge, erwies sich Spanien als der privilegierte Ort für die Ankunft des Königreichs Christi. Genau das beinhaltet die Devise: „Ich werde in Spanien regieren mit mehr Verehrung als an anderen Orten". Die „große Versprechung", wie seit damals diese profetische Botschaft bezeichnet wurde, war seither die Grundlage für die Verehrung des Heiligen Herzens. Die Prophezeiung wurde am 30. Mai 1919 an einem besonderen Ort umgesetzt: Der Cerro de los Ángeles, in der geographischen Mitte der Iberischen Halbinsel gelegen, wo Alfons der XIII. ein Monument einweihte, das die offizielle Widmung des katholischen Landes dem Kult des Heiligen Herzens sanktionierte und so die solide Allianz zwischen Kirche und Monarchie bestätigte. Die Gedenkfeiern des zweihundertsten Jahrestages dieser Prophezeiung im Jahre 1933 nahmen eine besonders einfordernde Gestalt gegenüber dem Laizismus der Zweiten Republik ein und der Cerro de los Ángeles wurde „Alter der Nation" getauft.

Gemäß dem hier Dargelegten erlangt die Gebärde der Erschießung, die die Milizionäre vor den Kameras der Presse und der internationalen Nachrichtensendungen am 7. August 1936 simulierten, eine vielfältige Dimension (gotteslästerlich, politisch, gesellschaftlich, teatralisch...) Die Akte der Genugtuung, mit denen die nationale Seite reagierte, ließen nicht auf sich warten, und Burgos, Salamanca und andere Städte wurden zu geeigneten Szenarien, *in absentia*, seit der Verbreitung der Nachricht.[21] Hilari Raguer berichtet von der Feierlichkeit, die am 20. August im nationalen *Sancta Sanctorum* in Salamanca abgehalten wurde zur Wiedergutmachung des Heiligen Herzens:

> Bekleidet mit dem erzbischöflichen Gewand zelebrierte Dr. Pla y Daniel die feierliche Ausstellung des Allerheiligsten Sakramentes. Danach gab es eine feierliche Ansprache des Domkapitulars Castro Albarrán, der unter anderem folgendes sagte: „Wie viele Märtyrer in diesen Tagen in Spanien! Welch eindrucksvolle Prozession von Bischöfen, Priestern, Mönchen, von Jungfrauen, von Kämpfern im Kreuzzug! Ja, ganz Spanien ist heute ein Märtyrer!" Die Zelebration, die eine Stunde dauerte, endete mit lauten Hochrufen auf das Heilige Herz, auf die Jungfrau Pilar, auf Christkönig und auf Spanien.[22]

Auslassung und Anspielungen

Als 1937 die iberoamerikanische Sektion der Abteilung für Presse und Propaganda der *Falange Española Tradicional y de las JONS* sich vornahm, in einem Dokumentarfilm den Verlauf des Krieges in Spanien (*La guerra en España*, Antonio Solano, 1937) zusammenzufassen, zögerte sie nicht, diesem *satanischen Akt* einen gewissen Protagonismus zu verleihen, wie die Erzählung verdeutlicht:

> El Cerro de los Angeles. Jenes Monument, das als Ausdruck des Glaubens des spanischen Volkes genau im Zentrum Spaniens dem Heiligen Herzen Jesu errichtet wurde, wurde ebenfalls von den Feinden Gottes und des Vaterlandes zerstört (im Hintergrund erklingt die faschistische Hymne *Cara al sol*). Hier ist der offensichtliche Beweis für den Respekt vor der katholischen Religion, den die Gefolgsleute Moskaus zu haben vorgeben, die Gottlosen und Vaterlandslosen. Ein Erschießungskommando von Gewissenlosen erschoss den Stein, der das heilige Bildnis symbolisierte.[23]

Das Bedeutsame dieser Montagem, die nach der Rückeroberung des Cerro de los Ángeles durch die nationalen Truppen am 7. November 1937 gemacht wurde, ist, dass nicht die drei Einstellungen der Sequenz der Gotteslästerung reproduziert wurden, sondern, dass man sich auf die verbale Evozierung beschränkt mit dem unvermeidlichen Verlust des visuellen Eindrucks. Eine Nichtverfügbarkeit der frevelhaften Bilder? Auch der Dokumentarfilm *¡Madrid! Cerco y bombardeamiento de la capital de España* (Madrid! Einkesselung und Bombardierung der spanischen Hauptstadt) von der Lissabonner Films Patria 1936 gedreht, (zweite portugiesische Version im Jahre 1938)[24] enthält nicht die erwarteten Einstellungen (nicht einmal die Fotos) von der Hinrichtung. Das Fragment wurde im November 1936 nach der Einnahme der Stellungen gedreht und sein Anliegen ist militärischer Natur im Zusammenhang mit dem Vormarsch auf Madrid. Vielleicht befanden sich die gotteslästerlichen Bilder zu diesem Zeitpunkt bereits in den internationalen Nachrichtensendungen in Umlauf, waren aber noch nicht in die Hände der nationalen Seite gelangt. Das Ereignis, das ursächlich für die Bilder war, fehlte jedoch nicht in der begleitenden Erzählung. Dieses Fehlen in beiden Fällen steht der Vielfalt von Einstellungen und Fotos gegenüber, die sich auf den Hügel beziehen, der ein umkämpfter militärischer Schauplatz war. Die Milizionäre, die das Monument sprengten und zuvor seine Erschießung inszenierten, verloren diese Stellung an die Legionäre Francos am 7. November. Dem republikanischen General Lister, der sich mit seinen Truppen in Perales del Rio gesammelt hatte, gelang es, den Ort am 19. und 20. Januar 1937 vorübergehend wieder in Besitz zu nehmen, um ihn dann wenig später endgültig zu verlieren. Das Kuriose dieser Verwandlungen wurzelt darin, dass es die relative Unabhängigkeit der Bilder des symbolischen Aktes von den kriegerischen Ereignissen offenbart.

Die spanische illustrierte Zeitschrift *Fotos* widmete eine umfangreiche Reportage, verfasst von Pablo Sigüenza, in ihrer zweiten Ausgabe (6. März 1937) dem Thema „Jesus in Trümmern". Der Bericht spart nicht mit morbiden Komponenten: „Schon am Haupt Christi sah man keine Geste von Erbarmen und Verzeihung, mit der er uns anschaute; es handelt sich um einen von einem Monster bearbeiteten Totenkopf, das nach seiner Entfleischung die Knochen seines Hauptes kaut".[25]

Der dreiseitige Text wird von sechs Fotografien begleitet, die den Zustand des Monuments nach seiner Sprengung zeigen, d.h. nach seiner Rückeroberung durch die nationalen Truppen.[26]

All das zuvor Gesagte lässt den Schluss zu, dass die Bilder von der Profanation, die vor den internationalen Medien von den Milizionären simuliert wurden, in den Nachrichtensendungen der Welt weite Verbreitung hatten, aber es dauerte, bis die nationale Kinematographie sie in Besitz und verfügbar hatte, was der Fall ist bei *Geißel der Welt*, deren Schnitt von Ende 1936 datiert und in Berlin durchgeführt wurde.

Wenn die eine Seite keinen Zugang zu diesem Material hatte, das ihr so nützlich hätte sein können und sich dazu gezwungen sah, es durch eine weniger attraktive verbale Erzählung zu ersetzen, so sollte die andere Seite – die republikanische – es vermeiden zu zeigen, sobald sie seinen fatalen Einfluss auf die öffentliche Meinung bemerkte. Die *Reportaje de la Causa de los* prisioneros *del Cerro Rojo* (Reportage von der Angelegenheit der Gefangenen des Cerro Rojo) ist ein unvollständiges filmisches Fragment, das sich mit dem Prozess in Madrid gegen 83 angeklagte nationale Gefangene nach der Einnahme des Hügels durch die Division von Lister beschäftigt. Die Reportage an sich besitzt sehr wenig Wert, und die Bilder beschränken sich darauf, die Zugänge und Gänge des Ortes der Verhandlung zu zeigen; demgegenüber erscheint die überlegte Auslassung der gotteslästerlichen Aktion und die Forderung nach Umbenennung in Roter Hügel in Anerkennung der sowjetischen Hilfe, die die umkämpfte Front vor Madrid aufrechterhielt. Ein Lob auf die republikanische Justiz, die in der Tat den symbolischen Kampf um die Umbenennung des Erinnerungsortes der spanischen monarchisch-religiösen Tradition beendet.

Entschädigung, Zeremonien und Topoi

Am 18. Juli 1939, Jahr des Sieges, wird der Cerro de los Ángeles zum Schauplatz eines Festes zur Wiedergutmachung des Heiligen Herzens in den Ruinen dessen, was vorher das Monument war. Dieser Anlass setzte sich für lange Jahre des Franquismus fest, wie verschiedene Reportagen enthüllen, die die offizielle und exklusive Wochenschau ab 1943 (NO-DO) herausbrachte. Die erste dieser Reportagen datiert von 1933 (n° 76, Ausgabe A) und die zweite vom folgenden Jahr (n°120, Ausgabe A). Das wirklich Überraschende dieses Erinnerungsortes ist, dass das zerstörte Monument im Ruinenzustand bewahrt wurde als eine Form um die Erinnerung an die Kirchenschändung durch den Gegner wachzuhalten und beschlossen wurde, ihm gegenüber, gewissermaßen als Spiegelbild, ein neues und moderneres Monument zu bauen, das Jahre später von demselben Bildhauer, dem schon greisen Aniceto Marinas, entworfen wurde.[27]

Das Motiv der religiösen Verfolgung in Spanien mutierte zu einem unzerstörbaren Topos, eine relativ eigenständige Gattung innerhalb der franquistischen Interpretation des Bürgerkrieges. Es wandelte sich in dem Maße, wie die kirchlichen Würdenträger den Aufstand gegen die Republik zu einem „Kreuzzug" stilisierten und die emblematischen Bilder die Schrecken und Entrüstung hervorrufen sollten nicht die von Exekutionen, Folter und Leichen waren, sondern diese zwei Sequenzen in verschiedenen Varianten. Die von der *Causa General* veröffentlichte Zusammenfassung widmete einen Absatz der „Religiösen Verfolgung", und es fehlte nicht an Beweisen für Verbrechen und Schikanen, materielle Zerstörungen und Profanationen, die sowohl auf Dokumenten wie auf Zeugenaussagen beruhten.[28]

Ein Fotoband wurde 1939 veröffentlicht: *Via Crucis del Señor en las tierras de España* (Der Kreuzweg des Herrn in spanischen Landen); der ihn begleitende Text war Werk des Poeten Manuel Augusto (Garcia Viñclas).[29] Ein Dutzendmensch wie dieser fragliche Dichter war zu jener Zeit eine der Schlüsselfiguren der kinematographischen Propaganda. Das unter der Regie von José Luis Saenz de Heredia entstandene Werk kannte nur ein Ziel auf dem Bildschirm. Aufgebaut wie ein Kreuzweg mit seinen Stationen und der Allegorie auf den Leidensweg Christi dient es als Palimpsest, der Krieg wird als eine Folgeerscheinung der ununterbrochenen Verfolgung der Christen präsentiert. Die elfte Station wurde mit dem Foto von der Füsilierung eröffnet und sofort darauf platzten die Fotos von den Salesianerinnen herein, wenn es sich auch nicht um dieselben handelt, die wir von den kinematographischen Montagen kennen. Dem Standbild wurde Vorzug gegeben, so dass diese assoziative Montage, in der Ikonen des Spotts auf das Sakrale angehäuft sind, noch durch die empathische Stimme des Erzählers verstärkt wurde. Die religiöse Verfolgung hatte ihr Eigenleben gewonnen; der spanische Krieg wandelte sich so zum Meilenstein einer ewigen Pein.

Inbesitznahme und Typisierung

Trotz der spektakulären Kraft seines visuellen Inhalts, des emotionalen Schocks, den die Bilder provozierten, verloren sie die Konkretheit der Verkörperung von Ideen. Sie verwandelten sich in sklerotische Symbole, die sich im Gedächtnis von Generationen als ein unverständlicher und verwilderter Aspekt der spanischen Revolution festsetzten. Sie wären somit die Antithese der glorreichen (wenn auch ungeschliffenen) Bilder vom Alcázar von Toledo oder auf der Gegenseite von der heroischen Verteidigung des neuen Numancia: Madrid. Dies war so festgefügt, dass 20 Jahre später, als das Francoregime etwas die Spannung seines Diskurses zum Krieg abbaute, sich mit dem Geiste der Verführung an die nachfolgenden Generationen richtete und seine Verdienste zur Erlangung und Erhaltung des Friedens herausstellte, es seinen beleidigenden Sprachgebrauch mäßigte und eine Hand (aber nur eine) den Gegnern ausstreckte und die früheren Bilder hinsichtlich ihres traumatischen Anscheins filterte, sich aber treu gegenüber der durch diese beiden ikonischen Serien ausgeübten Macht zeigte. Zwei Momente definieren gut die Überlieferung dieser Bilder im Kontext eines Umbruchs: 1959 zum zwanzigsten Jahrestages des Sieges und 1964 zur Jubelfeier des Regimes aus Anlass der Kampagne der 25 Jahre des Friedens.

El camino de la paz (Der Weg des Friedens) (Rafael Garzón, 1959) stellte eine erste Anstrengung auf dem Gebiet der Kinematographie dar, um eine teilweise Entspannung einzuführen und eine Mäßigung der vorherigen Dramatik zu bewirken. Ausgehend von dem in den Archiven der Nationalen Filmothek verfügbaren Material, zielte diese Produktion von NO-DO, begleitet von der Stimme von Matías Prats, auf die Idee des Friedens als Ersatz des „Sieges". In Wahrheit wechselte sich die Terminologie ab und die Ersetzung war eher eine Überlagerung, wenn auch die Worte wechselten, so blieben die Bilder intakt wie Funken mitten in einer entdramatisierten Lektüre des Krieges: das berühmte Foto von Alfonso von den im Patio der Madrider Kaserne *Cuartel de la Montaña* verstreuten Leichen, die

Einstellungen von Mumien der Salesianerinnen: Der Kommentar war kurz und bündig:

> Der Brandstiftung, die Profanation und die von den Massen durchgeführten Plünderungen fanden sie gerechtfertigt. Um die niedrigsten Instinkte des Sektierertums zu befriedigen war die Kirche wie so oft Ziel eines brutalen Angriffs der Barbarei, zuerst der Beleidigung und der Verleumdung, danach der Kette von Brandstiftung. Und nicht einmal vor der Heiligkeit eines Grabes machten sie Halt, die gebleichten Knochen und die mumifizierten Kadaver ermutigten sie noch.[30]

Die ersten drei Standfotos entstammen den Einstellungen, die in *España heroica* die Schändung der Mumien einleiteten; in der Folge wird die Sequenz derselben auf drei Einstellungen reduziert; Der Überfall auf die Kaserne *Cuartel de la Montaña* in Madrid wird durch ein berühmtes Bild repräsentiert; zuletzt: eine Kamerabewegung reiht drei Photogramme vom Cerro de los Ángeles aneinander, die nicht von der Sequenz der Erschießung entstammen, sondern aus dem Film *¡Madrid! Cerco y bombardeamiento de la capital de España*, der zuvor bereits analysiert wurde.

Bedeutsamer jedoch ist die Einfügung dieser Fragmente in den Film *Franco ese hombre* (J.L. Sáenz de Heredia, 1964), eine Hagiographie des Diktators und Rückrat der Feierlichkeiten zu dem, was die „XXV Jahre des Friedens" genannt wurden. Dieser Film wollte sich an erster Stelle nicht mit dem Bürgerkrieg beschäftigen, sondern sich auf die Biographie Francos konzentrieren; angesichts der Bedeutung des Krieges für das Schicksal des „Caudillo", beschränkte sich *Franco ese hombre* jedenfalls darauf, seine Aufmerksamkeit den strategischen Erfolgen des Jahres 1936 zu widmen.[31]

Außerdem entschied der Regisseur, den Krieg in einer Form „auszulassen", die zugleich verdrehend und ungenau wirkt. Er greift die Unordnung des Jahres 1936, den Aufstand und die ersten Schritte des Konfliktes bis zur Ernennung Francos als Staatschef Ende September desselben Jahres auf. An diesem Punkt unterbricht er abrupt einen Bericht, den der Zuschauer von 1964 erwartet und, neben den Filmrollen sitzend, verleiht er seiner Überzeugung Ausdruck, diesen Krieg zum Zweck der Überwindung des Zwistes zwischen den Spaniern nicht zeigen zu wollen. Diese Erklärung ist von fundamentaler Bedeutung, um den hinzugefügten Wert, den die vom Selbstverbot nicht betroffenen Bilder von den Salesianerinnen und vom Cerro de los Ángeles aufweisen, richtig beurteilen zu können. Man sprach also schon nicht mehr in diesem Zusammenhang vom Ausdruck des Krieges zwischen den Spaniern, sondern von einer schaudernerregenden Episode des revolutionären Zorns, deren Protagonist die zügellose Masse war:

> Madrid ist in den Händen der Masse und die Wildheit gipfelt ohne die geringste Einschränkung durch die Regierung; Es ereignen sich Brandstiftungen, Profanationen, Morde und das sanftmütige Wort des Spaziergangs wird für immer durch eine tragische Bedeutung angereichert.[32]

Die fragliche Sequenz beginnt in Madrid mit dem Sturm auf die Kaserne *Cuartel de la Montaña*. Das ikonische Foto von Alfonso drückt dies aus. Wenn sich also das erzählerische Motiv in Madrid befindet, wie soll man dann also einen so aufsehenerregenden Ausrutscher, wie den, der zu den Salesianerinnen in Barcelona führt, verstehen, ohne dass die begleitende Rede, sich in der Pflicht sieht, dies zu erläutern. Es ist nicht einmal logisch, den Cerro de los Ángeles einzuführen, ohne seine Lage zu erklären. In beiden Fällen haben die Bilder ihre Verankerung verloren und repräsentieren eine Idee zu Ungunsten der konkreten Fakten, die sie beinhalten. Sie sind Ikonen der zerstörerischen Revolution und der von den Massen verübten Profanation und bringen die notwendige visuelle Brisanz im Dienste der verbalen Erzählung.

Kommen wir nun auf den Entwicklungsprozess unserer Sequenzen zurück. Gegenpropaganda, eine unbemerkte Gabe für die feindliche Sache. Später, mit dem Abstand der Jahre, Verkapselung. Unter dieser Bedeutung hat es sich der Franquismus der siebziger Jahre bequem gemacht, der die Exzesse einer Regierung – der republikanischen – dämonisierte, die nicht im Stande war, die Kontrolle über ihre Bürger auszuüben und mit dem Chaos identifiziert wurde.

Zwischen die beiden franquistischen Filmen, die die Aneignung durch Typifizierung bestätigen, reiht sich jedoch die überraschende Benutzung desselben Materials durch den Film *Mourir à Madrid* (Frédéric Rossif, 1962) ein, der eine flammende Anklage des europäischen (und insbesondere des französischen) Einverständnisses mit dem Regime der Erben des 1945 besiegten Faschismus. Ein erschütternder Film gegen den Franquismus, als dieser sich im Frieden und Wohlstand wähnte und an die Pforten Europas klopfte. *Mourir à Madrid* mobilisierte machte sich auf die Suche nach Archivbildern und griff einen Teil der Sequenz der Salesianerinnen auf und gab ihr eine historische falsche Situationslage: unmittelbar nach den Parlamentswahlen im Februar 1936 und im Rahmen von gewalttätigen Auseinandersetzungen, die in der Ermordung von Calvo Sotelo gipfelten und somit vor dem Militäraufstand und dem Ausbruch des Krieges. Dieser Mangel an Genauigkeit zeigt, dass die Ikonen bereits ihren historischen Kontext verloren hatten und in einem Raum permanenter Verfügbarkeit ruhten. Dies unterstreicht auch die Tatsache, dass die Migration dieser Bilder sich von einer indirekten Quelle aus vollzog, vermutlich von *La peste rouge*, einem Film, der eine ähnliche chronologische Verwirrung stiftete. Selbstverständlich können wir nicht ausschließen, dass es zwischen dem einen und dem anderen Film einen Zwischenschritt gegeben hat, aber die Vermischung von zwei Werken so gegensätzlicher ideologischer Tendenz spricht für sich. Die Tatsache, dass solche Ikonen sich ein Stelldichein von unterschiedlichen Quellen aus geben können, beweist, dass Rossif keine Notwendigkeit sah, seine Archivquellen historisch zu situieren.

Dies ist nicht das einzige Rätsel, das jenes Jahrzehnt für uns mit sich bringt. Die Serie *Imágenes*, monographische Dokumentarfilme, von NO-DO editiert, publizierte eine symptomatische Ausgabe mit dem Titel „La Gran Respuesta, Cristo fusilado II" (Die große Antwort. Christus erschossen II) (n° 988, 1963), die sich um das Leitmotiv „Saulus, warum verfolgst Du mich" drehte. Dieser von José María Font-Espina und Jorge Feliu gedrehte Film schreibt die Bilder von der Füsilierung des Heiligen Herzens ein in eine Kaskade von konzeptuellen Schnitten, die den internationalen Kommunismus anklagen und ihn der religiösen Verfolgung bezichtigen. Unter der Ästhetik des modernen Schnitts lauert das Echo der *Via crucis del señor en las tierras de España*. Etwas änderte sich im offiziellen Diskurs des Regimes oder war zumindest zögerlich geworden, da „Altar de España" (Altar von Spanien) (NO-DO n° 1174, Ausgabe A, 1965), dessen Thema die Einweihung des neuen Monuments des Heiligen Herzens auf dem Cerro de los Ángeles ist, die Geschehnisse auf dem Jahre 1936 peinlich vermeidet und dagegen die Wiederaufnahme des Geistes von 1919 feiert, als das Monument von König Alfons XIII. eingeweiht wurde, der in seiner Festrede die Nation dem Kult des Heiligen Herzens verpflichtete. Die Bilder von damals bilden einen Portikus, es wird in einem trockenen, telegraphischen Stil berichtet, der weit entfernt ist von der blumenreichen Rhetorik, die bis zu diesem Zeitpunkt im Franquismus üblich war:

> Im Juli 1936 füsilierter rote Milizionäre das Bild des Heiligen Herzens Christi auf dem Cerro de los Ángeles. Dies ist der Zustand, in dem die Bilder des Monuments verblieben, das von König Alfons XIII. im Jahre 1919 eingeweiht worden war.

In der neuen Skulptur mit einem anderen Stil und anderer Kompostion, werden die Gruppen, die die kämpfende und triumphierende Kirche repräsentieren, dargestellt und dazu kommt jetzt das missionierende und den Glauben verteidigende Spanien... Das neue Monument erhebt sich gegenüber den Ruinen des alten Werkes...[33]

Ein weiteres Mal steht *España heroica* am Ausgangspunkt der Montage, aber der neue kinematographische Stil basiert auf dem *Zoom*, auf den Luftbildeinstellungen, und die kurze Schnittfolge verleiht eine neue Spektakularität, die im Einklang zu stehen scheint mit der Verlagerung vom Kern der Nachricht auf die von Franco verlesene Formel der Einweihung.

Ikonen eines universellen Repertoires

Wenn *Mourir à Madrid* auf ideologisch wenig mit den eigenen Intentionen verwandte Quellen zurückgriff, so zweifelte der Regisseur von *La vieja memoria* (Jaime Camino, 1976) nicht daran, an entscheidender Stelle auf die Füsilierung des Heiligen Herzens zurückzugreifen. Ein Dokumentarfilm, der während der *Transición* gedreht wurde und vom Zeugnis zahlreicher Protagonisten des Krieges handelt, hatte sehr begrenzten Zugriff auf das Archivmaterial. Der Mangel und die Bescheidenheit an Mitteln werden durch die ganze Relevanz der Fotos vom Cerro de los Ángeles wiederbelebt, die wiederum mitten in den erdrückenden Bericht von Jaume Miravitles einbrechen, der von den Turbulenzen in Barcelona in den auf den Militärputsch folgenden Tagen und insbesondere von der Exekution der putschenden Militärs im August 1936 nach ihrer Verurteilung handelt. Der ehemalige Komissar für Propaganda der *Generalitat de Cataluña* beschreibt die pathetische Szene, deren Augenzeuge er auf ausdrückliches Bitten eines der Verurteilten wurde: Fernando Lizcano de la Rosa. In dem Moment, in dem die Schüsse auf die Verurteilten fielen, zogen einige Milizionäre, die sich unter den Zuschauern befanden ihre eigenen Pistolen und Gewehre und feuerten diese gegen die Verurteilten ab. In diesem entscheidenden Moment des Berichts, baut Camino das berühmte Foto von der Erschießung des Heiligen Herzens ein und provoziert so eine zumindest merkwürdige Assoziation. So greift Camino auf ein schon ausgebeutetes Arsenal zurück und scheint dieses Bild als eine Verdichtung der heiklen Atmosphäre der ersten Kriegswochen zu betrachten. Es ist klar, dass das Foto in Getafe und nicht im revolutionären Barcelona, von dem Miravitles spricht, aufgenommen wurde; offensichtlich ist auch, dass die symbolische Füsilierung und die von Menschen schwerlich verglichen werden können; mehr noch: das Heilige Herz wird hier nicht in seiner Funktion als Akt der Profanation, den es beendet, genannt, sondern von seiner religiösen Bedeutung befreit, nimmt es die Bedeutung von zügelloser Gewalt an. *La vieja memoria* ging einen Schritt weiter als *Mourir à Madrid*, von einem Diskurs ausgehend, der weder mit der Propaganda noch der Gegenpropaganda etwas zu tun hatte; es handelte sich um den Ausdruck eines analytischen Geistes, der die spanische *Transición*, den Übergang zur Demokratie, charakterisierte.

The Spanish Civil War, eine historische Serie, die von *Granada Televisión* unter Regie von David Hart und der Beratung von Ronald Fraser, Hugh Thomas und Javier Fusell produziert wurde, enthält einen etwas schärferen Grad an Analyse. Es handelt sich um einen Dokumentarfilm, der riguros im Einklang mit dem umfassenden Dokumentarmaterial aufgebaut wurde, inklusive dem aus den Archiven, das sich auf eine Illustrationsfunktion beschränkt. Sein zweites Kapitel (Revolution, Gegenrevolution und Terror) versuchte, den sozialen Kampf zu entwirren und den Ausbruch des revolutionären Zorns, der - ohne es zu wollen - den Putsch provozierte. Ein besonderer Platz gebührte der einzigartigen barcelonesischen Erfahrung und den Bildern von den Salesianerinnen, die mitten in einer vom Berichterstatter unwiderruflich verfolgten Logik erscheinen; „Die Industrie war kollektiviert worden. Barcelona feierte seine Revolution. Die Revolution war nicht nur Jubel, sondern auch Blut, das Blut der Feinde". Unmittelbar darauf folgt eine Variante der bekannten Sequenz begleitet vom folgenden Text:

> Die erste auf der Liste war die Kirche, das Symbol der Starrheit, die Feindin der Freiheit. Dreizehn Bischöfe und mehr als sechstausend Priester und Nonnen fielen ermordet von der totalen revolutionären Raserei. Diese Verbrechen dienten dazu, die Verteidiger der Kirche noch mehr anzustachen und um noch mehr das Bild von einer atheistischen Republik zu verstärken. Angezündete Kirchen und geplünderte Gräber.[34]

Die Illustrationen, die diesen Text begleiten, sind nicht kinematographischer Natur, sondern fotografischer. Trotz allem lässt das Assoziationssystem der Einstellungen, die es umgeben, erneut *España heroica* erkennen, wenn auch nicht ausschließlich. Die Genauigkeit des Archivs ist unzweifelhaft: das Dargestellte gehört zum Barcelona vom Juli 1936 und vom thematischen Standpunkt aus gesehen, bezieht es sich auf die Auswirkungen der sozialen Revolution und den anarchistischen Protagonismus. Wie dem auch sei, die Bilder sprechen gemäß der Überzeugung des Diskurses, der sie begleitet: sie repräsentieren eine allgemeine Idee, tun dies aber nicht mit Gleichgültigkeit gegenüber dem Inhalt des Materials. Es hat eine Reflexion bei der Auswahl der Quellen, eine Beurteilung der Dokumentarbilder eingesetzt.[35]

Dieselbe Logik macht sich *Roig i negre*, der Dokumentarfilm, den Dolors Genovés im Jahr 2006 der Geschichte des Anarchismus in Katalonien widmet, zueigen. Der Teil, in dem die Bilder von den Salesianerinnen gezeigt werden, bildet eine thematische Einheit, die von den Erklärungen des Historikers Julián Casanova gelenkt werden, der über den Zustand der religiösen Opfer spricht. So übersetzt die Regisseurin das Bild vom Martyrium der Dinge als einen Ausdruck des Martyriums oder Mordes an den Nonnen; gleichzeitig wird der Historiker zum Garanten der Transformation eines spezifischen in einen allmeinen Inhalt gemacht. Zu dieser Erlaubnis, die im übrigen die Chronologie der Tatsachen mit Füßen tritt, wird die Option hinzugefügt, die fotographische Dokumentation, neu bearbeitet und mit dem zweifelhaften Effekt der Einfärbung versehen, zu präsentieren. Die Tatsachen als Fotographien zu präsentieren kommt der Umformung in eine Epiphanie gleich: ewige fotographische Melancholie.

Verlegenheiten der Erinnerung und Rückkehr zur Vergangenheit

In der jüngsten Zeit und parallel zum Gebrauch, von dem wir gerade berichtet haben, hat sich ein Wandel in der Behandlung der religiösen Verfolgung vollzogen. Der Auslöser dafür war die Gesamtheit der Vorbereitungen für die Seeligsprechung von 498 spanischen Märtyrern, die am 28. Oktober 2007 erfolgte. Der Stoff verließ den Bereich der historischen Forschung und erlangte Protagonismus im heutigen sozialen und religiösen Lebensbereich. Wenn sich auch der Ursprung des Phänomens weit zurückverfolgen lässt (Der Antrag auf die Kanonisierung datiert vom 21. Januar 1986 und im März 1987 gab es bereits eine erste Welle von Kanonisierungen), so kam es zu einem richtigen Aufwind im Zuge des *Kampfes um die Erinnerung*. Die Bewegungen zur sogenannten Wiedererlangung der historischen Erinnerung, der vorübergehende „Krieg der Todesanzeigen" im Sommer 2006 und die Debatte über das im Volk als *Ley de Memoria Histórica* (Gesetz der Historischen Erinnerung) bekannte Gesetz, die Exhumierung von Leichen der franquistischen Repression, der neofranquistische Revisionismus einer anderen historischen Erinnerung haben eine Reihe von Handlungen und symbolischen Gesten veranlasst, in denen sich eine Rückkehr zum Scheinbild der beiden Spanien vollzogen hat. Man sah ein Wiederauferstehen von rhetorischen Formen, Ausdrücken und Diskursen, die seit vielen Jahrzehnten als obsolet erschienen.[36] Und wie es ist, wenn ein Diskurs wiederkommt, steigt er in den Ring zusammen mit den Worten einer schon begrabenen Sprache, die effiziente Vision der Bilder von damals. Wenn dies schon so ist bei alten Bildern, wie wird es dann erst sein mit anderen, die man niemals wirklich begraben konnte? Kein gewissenhafter Historiker hat jemals die Welle von Verbrechen gegen den Klerus angezweifelt und die Quantifizierung hatte eine fast definitive Genauigkeit und Präzision erreicht, während die Qualität der Verbrechen bereits eindrucksvoll von der franquistischen Literatur seit der *Causa General* bis zum zitierten Buch von Antonio Montero hervorgehoben wurde. Was jetzt jedoch auf dem Spiel steht, ist eine andere Sache, die vom Blickpunkt der faktischen Geschichte wenig aufsehenerregend, aber für die Auswirkungen der Sozialisierung der Erinnerung an die Vergangenheit entscheidend ist: Der Anachronismus, die Assimilation der religiösen Konflikte der 30er Jahre mit ihren Vereinbarungen und Unstimmigkeiten zwischen Kirche und Staat, die sich in den sozialistischen Verwaltungen vollzogen. Die Unordnung in einem *totum revolutum*, zwischen der gewalttätigen Periode der ersten Monate des Krieges und dem Beginn der Republik schien durch die Historiographie bereits überwunden gewesen zu sein, ist aber wieder in einem von der wissenschaftlichen Geschichtsschreibung entfernten Feld aufgetreten, das aber im gesellschaftlichen Leben um so effizienter ist: in den Kommunikationsmitteln.

In Übereinstimmung mit dem zuvor Dargelegten werden die beiden hier analysierten Bilderserien weniger dazu benutzt, um das Verständnis, die Sympathie und die Humanität zu suchen, als vielmehr um den Horror vor der Zerstörungswut, die ihnen zugeschrieben wird, zu erwecken und zwar nicht vor dem Anarchosyndikalismus oder der kommunistischen Internationale, sondern vor der II. Republik selbst in ihrer Integrität und seit ihrer Gründung im Jahre 1931. Es handelt sich um eine verhängnisvolle Rückkehr zur Propaganda. Ihre Handlanger sind mit den Kirchenkreisen und mit den radikalsten Sektoren der Rechten verbunden, außerdem vermindern ihre geringe ästhetische Qualität und die argumentative Armut nicht ihren symptomatischen Charakter. Es ist der Wunsch, eine Stimme hörbar zu machen, die man in einem modernen Land, das nach Meinung einiger von den Mythen der politisch korrekten Linken dominiert wird, totschweigt. Unsere emblematischen Bilder tauchen wieder auf, diesmal vom dokumentarischen und intellektuellen Diskurs losgelöst, auf den sie sich seit der *Transición* gestützt hatten

Konsequenterweise werden sie auch nicht präsentiert, um einzigartige Ereignisse zu bezeichnen, die sich in einem bestimmten Kontext ereigneten. Sie wollen Attraktionen sein, die als sehr intensive emotionale oder perzeptive Entladungen organisiert, den Zuschauer zu einer ideologischen Positionsnahme bringen. Aber hier hat die Lexikalisierung nicht vergeblich operiert und die schon so oft gebrauchten Bilder sind abgenutzt und entbehren der Kraft, die sie ursprünglich und während Jahrzehnten besaßen.

Zwei Beispiele genügen: *Mártires por la fe* (Märtyrer für den Glauben) (J. M. Albelda, 2007) und *La Cruz, el perdón y la gloria. La persecución religiosa en España durante la II República y la Guerra Civil* (Das Kreuz, die Verzeihung und die Glorie. Die religiöse Verfolgung in Spanien während der II. Republik und dem Bürgerkrieg) (Diego Urbán, Círculo Hispanoamericano Isabel la Católica 2007). Beide erklären ihren Wunsch, nicht die Asche des Krieges beseite räumen zu wollen, sondern, dass sie angespornt sind durch den reinen Willen, das Gedenken an die ermordeten Katholiken (Geistliche in ihrer Mehrzahl) wiederaufleben zu lassen und die zum Zeitpunkt des Entstehens dieser Filmproduktionen vor den Toren der Seligsprechung stehen. *Mártires por la fe* widmet ein signifikantes Fragment der Analysierung des Martyriums der Dinge und beruft sich zu diesem Zweck auf die größte intellektuelle Autorität, auf Monseñor Antonio Montero, den ehemaligen Erzbischof von Mérida - Badajoz. Die didaktische Darstellung wird nicht mit der Aufstellung von Fakten unterstützt; wieder einmal werden Nonnen der Salesianer in Barcelona in den Dienst einer Idee genommen, wenn diese auch präzise ist ("das Martyrium der Dinge"). Mehr noch, es handelt sich um ein Konzept, aber Unsicherheit und Wagheit tauchen auf, wenn man eine historische Situierung versucht: wann fand ein solches Martyrium statt? Die Antwort des Films ist unbeirrbar: es hörte zwischen 1931 und 1939 nie auf, was der Behauptung entspricht, dass es sich um ein programmatisches Projekt der II. Republik gehandelt habe.

La Cruz, el perdón y la gloria. La persecución religiosa en España durante la II República y la Guerra Civil seinerseits führt die Bilder von den Salesianerinnen ein, denen die Funktion verliehen wird, den ungezügelten Hass gegen die Kirche zu verkörpern. Aber die Frage drängt sich unmittelbar auf: Wer ist Autor und Verantwortlicher für diese Verfolgung? Die Salesianerinnen repräsentieren hier auch die religiöse Verfolgung zur Zeit der Republik und des Bürgerkrieges während acht langer Jahre. Kurz darauf zwei Fotos von der Füsilierung des Heiligen Herzens werden mit anderen gegen religiöse Kultobjekte begangene Grausamkeiten in

Verbindung gebracht. Die These des Dokumentarfilms besteht in der Unterscheidung zwischen Kriegsopfern und Märtyrern des Glaubens. Die ersteren finden sich auf beiden Bürgerkriegsseiten und sind nicht Gegenstand des Filmes (auch wenn die unbewusste sprachliche Ungenauigkeit der Autoren sich als verräterisch erweist); die Märtyrer ihrerseits bilden eine spezifische Gruppe, alle gehören der nationalen Seite an und wurden Ziel der Verfolgung durch die Republik und zwar seit deren Ausrufung. Aber die Bemühung, eine Ausgewogenheit im Dokumentarfilm beizubehalten, fällt in sich zusammen, wenn wir das Beiheft durchsehen, das seine Verlagsverbreitung mit gleichem Titel und Deckblatt, unterschrieben von Ángel David Martón Rubio, begleitet:

> Wie bei so vielen anderen Gelegenheiten kam der Frieden nach dem Krieg. Das Ende der religiösen Verfolgung kam in dem Maße, in dem jeder Winkel Spaniens durch die Truppen Francos befreit wurde und endete definitiv mit dem Sieg am 1. April 1939. Dies zu verschweigen kann eine neue Geiselnahme der Erinnerung der Märtyrer sein, da man versucht zu verbergen, dass viele andere ihr Leben in den Schützengräben gaben, um dieser Situation ein Ende zu bereiten und dass man an den Fronten auch *für Gott und Spanien* starb (kursiv vom Autor).[37]

Das Bild und die Geschichte

Es hat keinen Sinn, eine Aufzählung von Beispielen einer Nachforschung fortzusetzen, die immer noch vielfach unstimmig ist. Es ist vielmehr an der Zeit, einige Teilschlussfolgerungen zu ziehen.

a) Der Umlauf dieser beiden Bilderserien (zusammen oder getrennt) ist so verschieden und ungleich im Laufe der Jahre, dass es eine nahezu unmögliche Aufgabe ist, mit Genauigkeit die Herkunft des jeweiligen Gebrauchs zu bestimmen, vor allem dann, wenn seine Entdeckung tatsächlich die Zirkulationskanäle der fotografischen und kinematographischen Bilder wie auch den Zugang zu den Archiven und Bildsammlungen enthüllte.

b) Die Bilder, die diese beiden Motive repräsentieren, stammen aus unterschiedlichen Einstellungen und in einigen Fällen wurden sie an verschiedenen Tagen gemacht; konsequenterweise sind auch ihre Autoren heterogen. Im Falle des Cerro de los Ángeles ist die Herkunft sehr unterschiedlich und zusammen mit der Simulation der Erschießung vor den ausländischen Kameras finden wir andere, die von verschiedenen kriegerischen Ereignissen auf dem Cerro herrühren (Demolierung, Besetzung durch die Legionäre Francos, vorübergehende Rückeroberung durch die

Truppen von Enrique Lister und definitive Einnahme durch das nationale Heer). Im Falle der Salesianerinnen ist der Handlungsmoment kürzer, aber wir entdecken leicht unterschiedliche Bildgenerationen (Einstellungen mit Gittern, andere Fotographien ohne). Außerdem bestätigt dies alles die Unsinnigkeit der Unterscheidung zwischen professionellen Aufnahmen und den spontanen oder Amateurbildern.

c) Die Lexikalisierung der Bilder bedeutet nicht, dass dadurch ihre Evolution aufgehalten würde oder dass ihre Bedeutung definitiv festgeschrieben würde. Dies setzt eine Verlangsamung des Wandels voraus, der parallel zu ihrer Macht der Eindringlichkeit verläuft. Sie perpetuieren sich, schläfern ein, modellieren andere nachfolgende Bilder, aber sie werden nicht für immer eingefroren.

d) Sie bilden Topoi des Bürgerkriegs, deren Bedeutung verabredet, abgeleitet oder umgeleitet, aber nicht ignoriert werden kann. Ihre Verfügbarkeit ist die Kehrseite ihrer impositiven Kraft.

Schließen wir also die begonnene Reise ab. Wir haben versucht, eine bisher wenig genutzte Form der Untersuchung der Genealogie der Bilder darzustellen, in ihrem Prozess der Zirkulation und Verfestigung und in dem Sinne, den jede dieser Anwendungen impliziert. Im engeren Sinne wäre es ein Beitrag zur Funktion der Bilder bei der Gestaltung der kollektiven Erinnerung, der gesellschaftlichen Erinnerung oder des sozialisierten Bildes der Geschichte. Diese Untersuchung kann nicht von einer einzigen Person realisiert werden. Sie verlangt die Mitarbeit von Archäologen, Filmrestaurateuren, Bildsemiotikern, Kommunikationshistorikern und allgemeinen Geschichtswissenschaftlern. Eine Gemeinschaftsarbeit, die viel Versuchs- und Experimentiercharakter hat und ihre Kompetenz in so unterschiedlichen Gebieten wie Kino, Fotographie, illustrierter Presse und Plakatkunst unter Beweis stellt und sich auf Museen, bildende Kunst, Erinnerungsarchitektur, Schulbücher, Fernsehen, Internet, also auf die Ikonographie insgesamt ausdehnen sollte.

Wenn heute die Fachleute der Geschichte die unanfechtbare Notwendigkeit fühlen, sich auf Bilder zu berufen, wenn die Kommunikationsmedien die Sozialisierung der Geschichte und anderer Räume besetzen, dann wird es dringlich, Genauigkeit bei der Nutzung der Archive durchzusetzen, die auf strenger Quellenkritik beruht. Die Schwierigkeit ist besonders groß aufgrund der prekären Materiallage, der unaufhörlichen Zirkulation des Materials in den weltweiten Medien, der Erstellung von Negativkopien und in der Gegenwart durch die Verbreitung und die fast völlige Vermischung, die das digitale Bild im Internet erfährt, dank der neuen Virtualität der

Fälschung. Nur eine strenge Betrachtung des Bildes wird dasselbe in eine Dokumentarquelle der Geschichte und nicht in eine banale Form historischen Unverständnisses umformen.

---

[1] Moreno, Antonio Montero. „El martirio de las cosas". In: Moreno, Antonio Montero: *Historia de la persecución religiosa en España 1936-1939*, (Madrid: B.A.C., 1961).

[2] „el recuento de las destrucciones materiales descubre exactamente el costado más espiritual de la persecución religiosa". Moreno, „El martirio de las cosas", 627.

[3] „porque las cosas son siempre más´inocentes`que las personas y porque, cuando esos obejtos son de algún modo sagrados, su aniquilamiento descubre una saña contra el mundo religioso mucho más significativa que si los aniquilados son hombres de carne y hueso". Moreno, „El martirio de las cosas", 627.

[4] Der eschatologische, sexuelle und Folterungscharakter, der über die Bilder der religiösen Ikonen vermittelt wird, bestätigt die Koexistenz von zwei Bedeutungen – der verehrenden und der schänderischen während der Handlung. Ohne diese Koexistenz geht die symbolische Funktion verloren.

[5] Diese Funktion des Bildes kann man auf den bedeutenden Fotos des 20. Jahrhunderts finden, die ihre Koordenaten verlieren, sich universell machen und sich so in der Imagination verankern, dass sie ihrem eigentlichen Gebrauch widersprechen. Siehe dazu eine Analyse der Veränderungen des berühmten Fotos des Jungen von Warschau mit erhobenen Armen bei Rousseau, Frédéric. *L´enfant juif de Varsovie*. Histoire d´une photographie (Paris: Seuil, 2009) oder das Zigeunerkind, das in dem Nazifilm zu Westerbork erscheint und sich zu einer Ikone der jüdischen Deportation gewandelt hat, Lindeperg, Sylvie. *Nuit et brouillard. Un film dans l´histoire*. (Paris, Odile Jacob, 2007), 63.

[6] Borkenau, Franz. *El reñidero Español*. (Paris: Ruedo Ibérico, 1971); Orwell, George. „Homenaje a Cataluña". In: Orwell, George. *Orwell en España. Homenaje a Cataluña y otros escritos sobre la guerra civil española*. (Barcelona: Tusquets, 2003); Kaminski, H. E. *Ceux de Barcelone*. (Paris: Alia, 1986).

[7] Miravitlles, Jaume. *Episodis de la guerra civil espanyola*. (Barcelona: Pòrtic, 1972), 8.

[8] Gubern, Román. *1936-1939: La guerra de España en la pantalla*. (Madrid: Filmoteca Española, 1986), 14, erwähnt der Kameramann Ricardo Alonso unter den Verantwortlichen für die Einstellungen.

[9] „La ametralladora y el fusil, tras los altares, tras las imágenes saturadas de liturgia y de incienso, impregnadas después de pólvora y de blasfemias. Los Maristas, los Escolapios, Belén, La Merced, San Jaime, todos los reductos del jesuitismo y de la clerigalla (…) cayeron bajo el empuje de las masas encendidas de coraje y alumbraron con sus llamas el alba roja de que está tiñéndose el horizonte español (…). El atentado contra el pueblo (…) se ha pagado con la destrucción, unificada con las llamas del incendio, de todos los reductos del fascismo, enmascarado tras el uniforme militar, el sayal frailuno, el hábito monjil, la sotana clerical y el gesto de rapiña de los capitanes de la industria y de la banca". [cursiva nuestra]. Santos, Mateo. Reportaje del movimiento revolucionario en Barcelona. Spain, Spanien, schwarzweiss, 22 Min. 1936.

[10] Wie del Amo, Alfonso. *Catálogo General del Cine de la Guerra civil*. (Madrid: Cátedra/ Filmoteca Española, 1996), 791 darstellt, ist die *Reportage...* eine Restaurierung der Filmoteca Española, die auf neun verschiedenen Materialien beruht.

[11] Und dies nicht nur bezüglich der Einstellungen bei den Salesianerinnen, sondern auf den ganzen Film bezogen. Gubern, *1936-1939: La guerra de España en la pantalla,* 14. Noguer, Ramón Sala. *El cine en la España republicana durante la guerra civil.* (Bilbao: Mensajero, 1993), 66 ff. Und ursprünglich Cuenca, Carlos Fernández. *La guerra de España y el cine.* (Madrid: Editora Nacional, 1972), 34 ff.

[12] Diesen Verdacht hat mir Alfonso del Amo freundlicherweise anvertraut.

[13] Mir, Miquel. *Diario de un pistolero anarquista.* (Barcelona: Destino, 2006), 60.

[14] Siehe Meseguer, Manuel Nicolás. *Las relaciones cinematográficas hispano-alemanas durante la guerra civil española y los inicios del franquismo (1936-1945),* (Murcia: Universidad de Murcia, 2008), Dissertation.

[15] Borloz, Valérie. „*La peste rouge* (1938). Un film suisse au service de l´´Antikomintern". In: Haver, Gianni. (Hrsg.), *Le cinéma au pas. Les productions des pays autoritaires et leur impact en Suisse.* (Lausanne: Antipodes, 2004), 111-128.

[16] Eine Analyse der Funktion dieses Filmes in der faschistischen spanischen Propaganda und als Verbindung mit den Motiven des Dritten Reiches kann man bei Tranche, Rafael R. und Sánchez-Biosca, Vicente. *El pasado es el destino. Propaganda y cine del bando nacional en la guerra civil.* (Madrid: Cátedra/ Filmoteca Española, 2011) im zweiten Kapitel finden.

[17] *Helden in Spanien* nutzt jedoch den Schnitt in anderer Form und führt Dolores Ibárruri ein, die ihrerseits eine in der ganzen Welt bekannte Ikone ist.

[18] Fontane, François. *La guerra d´Espagne. Un déluge de feu et d´images.* (Paris: Berg International, 2003).

[19] di Febo, Giuliana. „Reinaré en España". In: di Febo, Giuliana. *Ritos de guerra y de victoria en la España franquista.* (Bilbao: Desclée, 2002), 57-66. Von derselben Autorin: di Febo, Giuliana. *La Santa de la Raza: un culto barroco en la España franquista (1937-1962),* (Barcelona: Icaria, 1988), italienisches Original von 1987.

[20] Mortimort, A. G. *La Iglesia en oración. Introducción a la liturgia.* (Barcelona: Herder, 1992), 997-998.

[21] *Diario de Burgos* vom 18 August 1936; *El Adelanto* vom 19. August 1936; die erste skandalöse Nachricht wurde durch Radio Castilla verbreitet.

[22] „Revestido de pontifical, el Dr. Pla y Deniel ofició la exposición solemne del Santísimo Sacramento. Vino después una alocución del canónigo Castro Albarrán, quien, entre otras cosas, dijo: '¡Cuántos mártires, estos días, en España! ¡Qué hermoso cortejo de obispos, de sacerdotes, de religiosos, de vírgenes, de cruzados! ¡Sí, España entera es hoy una mártir!'. Terminó la función, que duró una hora, dándose estruendosos vivas al Sagrado Corazón, a la Virgen del Pilar, a Cristo Rey y a España" Die wörtlichen Zitate entstammen *El Adelanto* vom 21. August 1936 und wurden dem Buch von Raguer, Hilari. La pólvora y el incienso. *La Iglesia católica y la Guerra Civil española (1936-1939).* (Barcelona: Península, 2001), 106 entnommen.

[23] „El Cerro de los Ángeles. Aquel monumento que como expresión de fe del pueblo español fue erigido en el mismo centro de España al Sagrado Corazón de Jesús fue destruido también por los enemigos de Dios y de la patria. [Fondo sonoro del Cara al sol] He aquí una prueba evidente del respeto que dicen sentir por la religión católica los secuaces de Moscú, los sin Dios y sin patria. Un pelotón de desalmados fusiló la piedra que simbolizaba la sagrada imagen". Solano, Antonio. *La guerra en España.* Spain, Spanien, schwarzweiss, 40 Min. 1937.

[24] Es handelt sich um eine Serie mit dem Titel ¡Arriba España! La Reconquista de la Partia. (Vorwärts Spanien! Die Rückeroberung des Vaterlandes).

²⁵ „Jesús en los escombros" (Jesus in Trümmern), *Fotos* n° 2, 6 de marzo de 1937 ohne Seitenzahlen.

²⁶ Die folgende Nummer derselben Zeitschrift beklagt am Rande eines Fotos „Im Hintergrund der Cerro de los Ángeles in Getafe. Ohne Jesus auf der Anhöhe, den die Horden in Trümmer verwandelt haben. Unsere Soldaten bewachen die Straßen mit Maschinengewehren in den Händen" (*Fotos* n°3, 13. März 1937, ohne Seitenzahlen).

²⁷ Von der Einweihung des neuen Monuments im Jahre 1965 berichtet eine Nachrichtensendung des NO-DO (1174 A) mit dem Titel „Altar von Spanien". Siehe unten.

²⁸ *La dominación roja en España*. Causa General (Madrid, Publicaciones Españolas, 3a edición, 1953) erwähnt genau die Simulation der Erschießung (S. 192) und zeigt Fotos von der Aktion. Es fehlt ebenfalls nicht die Erwähnung der Mumien des Konvents der Salesianerinnen in Barcelona (S. 191) und die dazugehörigen Fotos.

²⁹ Augusto, Manuel. *Via Crucis del Señor en las tierras de España*. (Madrid: Editora Nacional, 1939).

³⁰ „El incendio, la profanación y el saqueo realizadas [sic] por la masa lo encontraban justificado. Para aplacar los más bajos instintos del sectarismo, la Iglesia, como tantas veces, sufrió la brutal acometida de la barbarie, primero, el insulto y la calumnia; la tea incendiaria después. Y ni ante lo sagrado de una sepultura se detendrán, alentando sus huesos resecos y sus cadáveres momificados".Garzón, Rafael. *El camino de la paz*. Spanien, schwarzweiss, 64 Min. 1959.

³¹ So zum Beispiel ist eine der am meisten gefeierten Siege im Film die Verschlagenheit Francos, mit der er Spaniens Eintritt in den Zweiten Weltkrieg verhindert und gegen immensen Druck Hitlers widersteht. Franco erscheint so als ein Stratege des Friedens ebenso wie des Krieges.

³² „Madrid está en poder de la masa y el salvajismo culmina sin el menor freno del gobierno. Se reproducen los incendios, las profanaciones, los asesinatos y la apacible palabra paseo se enriquece ya para siempre con una acepción trágica".Heredia, José Luis Sáenz de. *Franco ese hombre*. Spanien, farbig, 103 Min. 1964.

³³ „En julio de 1936, las milicias rojas fusilaban la imagen del Sagrado Corazón de Jesús en el Cerro de los Ángeles. Este es el estado en que quedaron las imágenes del monumento, que había sido inaugurado por Alfonso XIII el año 1919.
En la nueva obra escultórica, de diferente estilo y composición, se repiten los grupos que representaban a la Iglesia Militante y Triunfante a los cuales se han añadido ahora los de la España Misionera y Defensora de la Fe… El nuevo monumento se alza frente a las ruinas del antiguo…" (NO-DO n° 1174 A, 1965)

³⁴ „Primera en la lista era la Iglesia, el símbolo del inmovilismo, la enemiga de la libertad. Trece obispos y más de seis mil sacerdotes y monjas cayeron asesinados en pleno frenesí revolucionario. Estos crímenes sirvieron para enardecer aún más a los defensores de la Iglesia, para reforzar aún más la imagen de una República atea. Iglesias incendiadas, tumbas saqueadas".Hart, David. *The Spanish Civil War*, Granada Televisión. 1982.

³⁵ Im Jahre 1981 brachte Carlos Saura seine jugendlichen Delinquenten in *Deprisa, deprisa* zum Cerro de los Ángeles und filmte sie, während sie den Weg gingen, der vom neuen zum alten Monument führt. Die historisch schwerwiegende Bedeutung ihrer Umgebung war ihnen völlig unbekannt, und sie teilten sich lachend ihre ersten Erfahrungen in der kriminellen Welt mit. Kein einziges historisches Bild wird in den Film eingefügt, der realistisch sein sollte, aber für viele der Zuschauer war es schwierig, das Gespenst von der gotteslästerlichen Sequenz aus ihrer Imagination auszulöschen.

[36] Das letzte Kapitel unseres Buches *Cine y guerra civil española. Del mito a la memoria.* (Madrid, Alianza, 2006), enthält einige Reflexionen dazu.

[37] „Como en tantas otras ocasiones, la paz vino después de la guerra. El fin de la persecución religiosa tenía lugar a medida que cada rincón de España era liberado por los ejércitos de Franco y no acabó definitivamente hasta la Victoria del 1 de abril de 1939. Silenciar esto puede ser un nuevo secuestro de la memoria de los mártires, ya que se pretende ocultar que otros muchos dieron su vida en las trincheras para poner fin a aquella situación, y que también en los frentes se luchaba y se moría por Dios y por España" [cursiva del autor]. Rubio, Ánel David Martín. *La Cruz, el perdón y la gloria.* La persecución religiosa en España durante la II República y la Guerra Civil. (Madrid: Ciudadela, 2007), 92.

(Deutsche Übersetzung aus dem Spanischen von Volker Jaeckel)

Vicente Sánchez-Biosca ist Professor für Filmgeschichte an der Universität Valencia und Herausgeber der Zeitschrift *Archivos de la Filmoteca*. Er war 1991 Postdoc Fulbright Fellow und Gastprofessor an den Universitäten Paris III, Montreal, São Paulo, Buenos Aires, Havanna, Paris I, Princeton u.a. Seine letzten Buchveröffentlichungen sind *NO-DO. El tiempo y la memoria* (NO-DO. Die Zeit und die Erinnerung, 2000), *El pasado es el destino. Propaganda y cine del bando nacional en la Guerra Civil* (Die Vergangenheit ist das Ziel. Propaganda und Kino des nationalen Lagers im Bürgerkrieg, 2011), beide zusammen mit Rafael Tranche, *Cine de historia, cine de memoria* (Historisches Kino, Kino der Erinnerung, 2006), *Cine y guerra civil española* (Kino und spanischer Bürgerkrieg, 2006). Gegenwärtig leitet er ein Forschungsprojekt zu Bildern von Bürgerkriegsopfern, das vom Präsidenten der spanischen Regierung finanziert wird.

Das Eigene und das Fremde im Balkan-Film über den Krieg im ehemaligen Jugoslawien

Elcio Cornelsen

Einleitung: Filmische Bilder eines Bürgerkrieges

Unser Beitrag widmet sich einer Analyse der Beziehung zwischen dem Eigenen und dem Frenden in der Darstellung des Krieges im ehemaligen Jugoslawien durch den Balkanischen Balkan-Film, besonders in Bezug auf die Filme *Dörfer in Flammen* (*Lepa sela lepo gore*; 1996) von Srdan Dragojević,[1] *No Man's Land* (*Ničija zemlja*; 2001) von Danis Tanović,[2] und *Das Leben ist ein Wunder* (*Život je čudo*; 2004) von Emir Kusturica.[3] Der geopolitische Zusammenbruch des Landes gab Anlass zur filmischen Behandlung der Erinnerung an einevergangene Zeit vor dem Krieg, sozusagen, an eine „befriedete" Zeit, wie auch an einen Moment extremer Gewalt nach dem Kriegsausbruch, als das Eigene und das Fremde durch den Konflikt neu definiert wurden.

Außer den Filmen, die für die Analyse ausgewählt wurden, ist die balkanische Filmproduktion über die Bildung bzw. den Zusammenbruch Jugoslawiens sehr breit: dazu zählen auch andere bedeutende Filme, wie etwa *Der perfekte Kreis* (*Savrseni krug*; 1997) von Ademir Kenović, *Outsider* (1997) von Andrej Kosac, der Kurzfilm *Mein Land* (*Moja domovina*, 1997) von Miloš Radovic, *Vor dem Regen* (*Before the Rain*; 1994) von Milcho Manchevsky, der die Goldene Palme in Cannes bekam, und *Savior – Soldat der Hölle* (*Savior*; 1997) von Peter Antonijevic. Alle diese Filme haben etwas gemeinsam: das Thema de Krieges ist von den Begriffen des Eigenen und des Fremden untrennbar, indem ein Anfangszustand scheinbarer Harmonie einfach durch einen Prozess der Verschärfung der Animosität zwischen den kriegerischen Gruppen zerstört wird, die sowohl ein positives Bild von sich, als auch ein negatives Bild der Anderen zu bauen trachten.

Es soll zunächst darauf hingewiesen werden, dass die Sozialistische Föderative Republik Jugoslawien durch den Premierminister Josip Broz Tito (1892-1980), den ehemaligen Oberbefehlshaber der jugoslawischen Widerstandsbewegung gegen die deutschen Besatzungstruppen,am 29. November 1945 ausgerufen wurde, übrigens der größten Widerstandsgruppe in Europa im Zweiten Weltkrieg. Als charismatische Figur gelang es Tito, die kleinen, historisch befeindeten Republiken, zusammenzubringen – Bosnien-Herzegowina, Kroatien, Makedonien, Montenegro, Serbien und Slowenien, wie auch die Provinzen Kosovo und Vojvodina.[4] Jedoch begann nach dem Tod des Diktators 1980 der Prozess des Zusammenbruchs der sozialistischen Republik als Teil der geopolitschen und wirtschaftlichen Wandlungen in Osteuropa. Wie Andréa França darauf hinweist, "schienen die ethnischen, kulturellen und religiösen Unterschiede bis in den 1980er Jahren unter Kontrolle zu sein".[5]

Dörfer in Flammen (1996) und die Greueltaten

Der Film *Dörfer in Flammen* (im Original: *Lepa sera lepo gore*; 1996) vom serbischen Filmmacher Srdan Dragojević, der das Drehbuch zusammen mit Vanja Bulic e Nikola Pejaković schrieb, in einer serbisch-kroatischen Produktion, präsentiert die Brutalität des Krieges in Jugoslawien. Preisträger auf dem20. Internationalen Filmfestival von São Paulo, zeigt der Film die Spaltung des Landes anhand der Beziehung zwischen dem serbisch-orthodoxen Milan (Dragan Bjelogrlic) und dem bosnisch-moslemischen Halil (Nikola Pejaković, Schauspieler und Drehbuchautor). Es geht ohne Zweifel um einen polemischen Film, denn er wurde zuerst von dem serbischen Führer Radovan Karadzic finanziert, der jedoch die finanzielle Unterstützung einstellte, als er den ironischen und kritischen Ton der Handlung gegenüber dem Bosnischen Krieg merkte. Der Filmhistoriker Luiz Nazario betrachtet den Film kritisch als eine „Propaganda für ‚ethnische Säuberung'" im Dienste von Karadzic, verantwortlich für den Genozid an der Bevölkerung in Bosnien 1995, wie bpsw. der in Srebreniza: „Dragojevic begründet den Spaß seiner Landsleute daran, Dörfer in Brand zu setzen, moslemische Bürger auszuplündern und zu ermorden, indem er die Sicht der Täter annimmt, die sich jedoch als die größten Opfer des Krieges vorstellen".[6]

Der Film *Dörfer in Flammen* beginnt mit einer Tagesschau, in der von der Einweihung des Tunnels der sozialistischen „Union und Brüderlichkeit" in Bosnien am 17. Juni 1971 berichtet wird. Der Tunnel sollte Belgrad, die Hauptstadt Serbiens, mit Zagreb, der Hauptstadt Kroatiens, verbinden, um sowohl symbolisch als auch konkret die Regionen und ihre entsprechenden Bevölkerungen zu vereinigen. Beim Durchschneiden des Einweihungsbandes schneidet ein Politiker in den eigenen Finger. Das Blut fließt gleichsam als eine Vorahnung davor, dass der Tunnel später ein Ort von Greueltaten sein würde. In der nächsten Folge, also nach einem

Zeitsprung bis 1980 in Bosnien, schauen zwei Knaben, Milan und Halil, den nicht zu Ende gebauten, ruinenartigen Tunnel, ohne zu wagen, in ihn zu gehen. Sie meinten, dass der Tunnel gespenstisch wäre, denn ein Oger sollte drinnen leben. Nochmals gibt es einen Zeitsprung, und jetzt befindet sich Milan in einem Lazarett in Belgrad, der Hauptstadt Serbiens, und erholt sich von schweren, durch den Krieg verursachten Verletzungen. Als unterbrochener Durchgangsraum deutet der ruinenartige Tunnel die tragische Zukunft an und wird daher zur Alegorie der Spaltung sowohl der Beziehung der Freunde als auch des eigenen Landes.

In der nächsten Folge gibt es einen ersten Flashback, in dem Milan und Halil, schon als Erwachsene, Basketball gegeneinander 1992 in einem kleinen Dorf in Bosnien spielen, genau am Tag des Kriegsausbruchs. Nochmals gibt es einen Zeitsprung in Richtung Zukunft, und Milan nimmt an Aktionen der serbischen Miliz gegen sein eigenes Dorf teil, die Soldaten plündern es aus und setzen es in Brand. Gleich danach gibt es nochmals einen Flashback zum Tag des Kriegsausbruchs, an dem Halil und Milan ein Schild mit der Inschrift „Werkstatt" an die Fassade einer Garage hängen, die nahe an Halils Haus und an Slobas Kneipe liegt, dem Lieblingsort der beiden Freude, die eine Werkstatt gemeinsam eröffnen wollen. Plötzlich kommt die Handlung in die Zukunft, als Milan die Plünderer der eigenen serbischen Miliz, zu der er gehört, erschießt. Also entwickelt sich die Filmhandlung in einer komplexen Art und Weise, in einem ununterbrochenen Hin und Her, in dem verschiedene Bilder die Gewalt sichtbar machen, die im Krieg von beiden Seiten begangen wird, vor allem gegen Dörfer und deren Einwohner, und somit werden nach Andréa França „die größten Greueltaten, die barbarischsten Kriegsverbrechen" offenbart.[7] Übrigens ordnet Milans Standpunkt die Handlung in einer kontinuierlichen Flut von Erinnerungen.

Zum Anderen stellt man fest, dass Milan sein Verhalten in Bezug auf den Krieg ändert, als er durch Sloba erfährt, dass die bosnischen Soldaten das Dorf angriffen und seine Mutter töteten. Dies scheint der Moment zu sein, in dem Milan vom Haß gegen die Bosnier beherrscht wird, also vom Haß, den er auch im Lazarett in Belgrad zu spürt, als er sich im Krankensaal zusammen mit dem „Lehrer", seinem Kameraden von der serbischen Miliz, und mit einem bosnischen Soldaten befindet. Milan hat ein einziges Ziel: den „Türken" zu töten, so wie die bosnischen Moslems von den Serben im Film genannt werden.

Jedoch findet die zentrale Filmszene im verlassenen Tunnel statt. Nach Andréa França symbolisiert der nicht zu Ende gebaute Tunnel in Dragojevićs Film einen Ort der Kindheitsgespenster und zugleich der Greueltaten der Erwachsenen.[8] Nach schwerem Angriff sucht eine Einheit der serbischen Miliz, zu der Milan gehört, Zuflucht in den Tunnel. Milan, jetzt ohne den Freund Halil, schaut in den verlassenen Tunnel, bevor er hineingeht, und damit wiederholt er dasselbe Verhalten seiner Kindheit, als die beiden Freunde sich vor dem „Oger" fürchteten und nicht wagten, darin einzutreten. Der Tunnel wird durch bosnische Soldaten belagert, so dass ein langer und gewaltsamer Prozess von Einsperrung beginnt, markiert durch Beleidigungen von beiden Seiten.Um Hunger und Durst zu bezwingen, beginnen die serbischen Soldaten, Geschichten zu erzählen und über verschiedene Angelegenheiten zu diskutieren, u.a. über das Leben im Kommunismus und über die nicht verwirklichten Träume der Jugendzeit. Und die bosnischen Soldaten, praktisch unsichtbar, halten die Belagerung um den Tunnel aufrecht und versuchen, die Serben durch Beschimpfungen zu provozieren. Per *Walkie-Talkie* schreien die Bosnier: „Wir werden eure Mütter ficken" und „Serben, Ihr Hurensöhne!"[9] Eine nordamerikanische Journalistin schließt sich der Gruppe im Tunnel an. Sie wurde von einem serbischen Soldaten dorthin gebracht, der die Belagerung durchbricht und in den Tunnel mit einem Lastwagen hineinfährt. In einer anderen Szene nimmt ein serbischer Soldat den *Walkie-Talkie* und erzählt den Bosniern einen Witz: „Kennt ihr den Witz der moslemischen Blondine, die unter einer Kuh aufwacht? Sie schaut die Euter der Kuh und sagt: Hallo, Serben!"[10] In einer anderen Szene schreien die Bosnier: „Serben! Wir werden ein leckeres Gericht von euch zubereiten: geräucherter Serbe mit Käse".[11] Schließlich erkennt Milan die Stimme von Halil und sie wetten, wie in alten Zeiten, als sie noch Freunde waren. Aber diesmal wird mit Handgranaten gespielt und nicht mit Geld. Nachdem fast alle schon tot waren, inklusive die Journalistin, versuchen Milan und der „Lehrer", den verwundeten „Schnellen" zuzusammenzutragen und den Tunnel zu verlassen. Draußen steht Halil dem Tunnel und spricht Milan an:

Halil: „Bist du schließlich in den Tunnel eingegangen?"

Milan: „Ja, ich bin hineingegangen".

Halil: „Warum hast du unsere Werkstatt in Brand gesetzt?"

Milan: „Weil du meine Mutter getötet hast".

Halil: „Ich habe niemanden getötet".

Milan: „Und ich habe unsere Werkstatt nicht in Brand gesetzt".

Halil: „Wer war es dann? [Pause] War vielleicht der Oger im Tunnel? War der Oger, Milan?"[12]

In diesem Moment wird Halil von der Explosion einer Granate betroffen und fällt vom Dach des Tunnels vor die Füße Milans, tot. Dann kommt ein Flash-Forward, in dem Milan sich in einem Lazarett neben dem Bett des bosnischen Soldaten befindet und bereit ist, ihn mit einer Gabel zu töten. Jedoch ist er so erschöpft, dass er blutend von seinem Bett bis dahin kriechen musste, so dass er sich zu Boden fallen lässt und sagt: „Oger, du Hurensohn!"[13] Danach folgt die Fahrt der Kamera, die unzählige Leichen fokussiert: Leichen von alten Menschen, Frauen, Jugendlichen und Kindern bedecken den Boden im Tunnel, und am Schluss der Fahrt der Kamera stehen Halil und Milan als Kinder; sie laufen nach draußen. Ein plötzlicher Schnitt, für den Film als ganzen bezeichnend, markiert den Beginn einer Szene, in der Halil und Milan in der Kneipe von Sloba sind und trinken, und Halil stellt dieselbe Frage wie in den ersten Filmszenen: „Komm her, du, sag mal. Wird es jenen Krieg geben?" Und Milan antwortet darauf anders als am Anfang: „Es wird nicht".[14] Gleich danach gibt es eine Tagesschau, in der von der Einweihung des Tunnels berichtet wird: „Wer hat gesagt, dass die Schäden, die vom Krieg verursacht wurden, nicht schnell beseitigt werden könnten? Es gibt kein besseres Geschenk zu Beginn des 21. Jahrhunderts als den Tunnel des Friedens, im Rekordtempo gebaut und die europäischen und weltlichen Normen beachtend".[15] So wie zu Beginn des Filmes ist der Finger desjenigen, der den Tunnel einweihen wird, auf dem Band. Dann gibt es einen Schnitt in Schwarz und einen langen Schrei im *Off*-Ton. Damit kommt der Film an seinen Anfang und übernimmt einen kreislaufartigen Charakter.

Bedeutend für den Film ist der Übergang von der Anfangsphase der Freundschaft zwischen Milan und Halil, in der Identitätsfragen überhaupt keine Rolle spielen, in den Kriegszustand zwischen Serben und Moslems, in einem Prozess, in dem man den Anderen mit gegenseitigen negativen Merkmalen brandmarken will.

No Man's Land (2001) und der unbegründete Haß

Im Film *No Man's Land* (in Original: *Ničija zemlja*; 2001), in einer gemeinsamen bosnischen, belgischen, französischen, britischen und italienischen Produktion, gelang es dem bosnischen Filmmacher Danis Tanović, eine dramatische Satire auf die Absurdität des kriegerischen Konflikts in Bosnien zu machen. Szenen von Horror und Leiden werden mit tragikomischen Momenten aneinander gereiht. Tanovićs Film erlebte eine positive Rezipierung seitens der Kritik, die mit dem Verleih des Oscar in der Kategorie "Bester ausländischer Film" 2002 gekrönt wurde, sowie im selben Jahr mit dem "golden Globe" und dem Preis in der Kategorie „Bestes Drehbuch" in Cannes.

Danis Tanović, verantwortlich fürs Filmarchiv der Bosnischen Armee während des Krieges, beschränkt seine Fabel praktisch auf einen einzigen Raum und ist auf eine Art und Weise gestaltet, dass die Dialoge zwischen den befeindeten Soldaten die Szenen vorwiegend beherrschen. Der Filmmacher führt die Eskalation des Konflikts bis an den Rand der Absurdität. Sogar wird gegenüber den Medien, den europäischen Bürokraten und der UNO nicht mit bissigem Humor gespart. Mit seinem Film entlarvt Tanović die Unfähigkeit der UNO-Truppen und den Mangel an Zielsetzung und Planung seitens der Institutionen, die im Konflikt verwickelt sind, aber er warnt: „Das Ziel meines Films ist nicht anzuklagen oder auf diejenigen zu weisen, die etwas Falsches machten, sondern einen lauten Schrei gegen jede Art von Krieg zu erheben. Dies ist mein Votum gegen jede Art von Gewalt".[16]

Die Fabel von *No Man's Land* besteht grundlegend aus den folgenden Ereignissen im Laufe eines sommerlichen Tages: eine Gruppe bosnischer Soldaten verläuft sich mitten in einem dichten Nebel an einem Abend im Jahr 1993, also während des Krieges. Als die Sonne aufgeht, werden die Soldaten zu leichten Zielscheiben für die serbische Artillerie. Alle außer Ciki (Branko Djuric) sterben dabei. Bei einer Granatexplosion wird er an der Schulter verletzt und weit in einen Schützengraben geworfen, der anscheinend verlassen ist. Plötzlich sieht er sich unbemerkt vor einem jungen Soldaten, Nino (René Bitorajac) und vor einem Veteranen (Mustafa Nadarevic), beide Soldaten der Serbischen Armee, die die Aufagbe von ihren Vorgesetzten bekamen, den Schützengraben zu überprüfen und dort Landminen zu installieren. Nachdem Ciki entdeckt wurde, tötet er den Veteranen und hält Nino, der verletzt war, im Korn seines Gewehrs. Beide beginnen einen Kampf um die Macht im Schützengraben, einem echten „Niemandsland" zwischen den befeindeten Linien. Aber die Schießerei an der Front verschärft sich, was dazu führt, dass die Stimmung beider Soldaten sich steigert. Sie füllen einen unbegründeten Haß gegeneinander, beschimpfen sich und zeigen eine gegenseitige Intoleranz, wenn auch in einer anscheinend ausweglosen Situation. Das ist ohne Zweifel das Grandiöseste des Films, denn der unbegründete Hass ist weder bei Ciki noch bei Nino deutlich, und in der Annäherung von beiden weist der Filmmacher darauf hin, dass unter anderen Umständen nicht unbedingt eine echte Freundschaft zwischen beiden entsehen würde, aber sicher eine gegenseitige Toleranz. Es ist genau in einem dieser Momente im Film, in dem die verschiedenen Blicke für sich selbst und für den Anderen hochkommen, so wie es ähnlicherweise im Film *Dörfer in Flammen* der Fall ist. Keiner von den beiden weiß genau, was der Sinn des Krieges ist. Sie diskutieren: Ciki behauptet, „ihr könnt nur Krieg führen"; und Nino widerlegt, dass „unsere Städte brennen wie eure":[17]

> Ciki: „Und Bombenminen unter die Toten legen, ausplündern, mördern, vergewaltigen, was ist das?"
>
> Nino: „Von wem sprichst du?"
>
> Ciki: „Von euch!"
>
> Nino: „Ich habe nie was gesehen, wovon du redest".
>
> Ciki: „Ich habe gesehen, wie meine Stadt in Brand gesetzt wurde".
>
> Nino: „Ich war nicht dabei".
>
> Ciki: „Aber ich war dabei!"
>
> Nino: „Man hat auch unsere Städte in Brand gesetzt! Wer hat unsere Leute ermordert!?"
>
> [...]
>
> Ciki: „Was hat uns dazu gebracht, dieses schöne Land zu zerstören?"
>
> Nino: „Wir?"
>
> Ciki: „Ihr!"
>
> Nino: „Du bist verrückt. Ihr habt die Trennung gewollt, nicht wir!"
>
> Ciki: „Weil ihr mit dem Krieg begonnen habt".
>
> Nino: „Ihr habt damit begonnen!"
>
> Ciki: „Was? Wer hat damit begonnen!? Ihr habt mit dem Krieg begonnen! Wer hat mit dem Krieg begonnen?" (Ciki droht Nino mit dem Gewehr)
>
> Nino: „Wir".
>
> Ciki: "Ihr habt damit begonnen".[18]

Als sie jedoch feststellen, dass Cera (Filip Sovagovic), Cikis Freund, der bis dahin für tot gehalten wurde, noch am Leben war und auf einer Landmine lag, die dem serbischen Veteranen unter seine mutmaßliche Leiche gelegt wurde, versuchen sie beide, die Aufmerksamkeit ihres Kameraden zu erwecken. Obwohl Cera verletzt ist, will er, dass Ciki Nino erschießt, weil der serbische Soldat nicht weiß, wie er die Landmine entschärfen kann. Cera bittet Ciki darum, ihm die Waffe zu geben, damit er Nino erschießen kann. Aber Ciki lehnt es ab, Nino zu erschießen und argumentiert: „Nein, wir sind nicht wie sie!"[19] Als Ciki sich um den verletzten, auf einer Landmine liegenden, Cera kümmern will, merkt er nicht, dass Nino die Waffe nimmt und sich damit das Machtverhältnis im Schützengraben ändert:

> Nino: „Übrigens, wer hat mit dem Krieg begonnen? Wer hat mit dem Krieg begonnen?"
>
> Ciki: „Wir".
>
> Nino: „Ihr".
>
> Cera: „Es ist egal, wer damit begonnen hat! Wir befinden uns alle in derselben Scheiße".[20]

Gleich danach, als Nino versucht, eine Zigarette für Cera anzuzünden, wird er von Ciki dominiert. In diesem Moment besteht, sozusagen, ein Verhältnis von Gleichheit, als Nino, damit Cera ihn losläßt, damit einverstanden ist, dass beide die Waffen bei sich behalten, aber sich nicht gegenseitig töten. Ciki und Nino entscheiden sich dafür, den Schützengraben zu verlassen und ihren Kameraden Zeichen zu geben. Da sie aber ihre Uniforme ausziehen, kann nicht deutlich identifiziert werden, zu welcher Armee sie gehörten. Dies ist nochmals ein sehr wichtiger Aspekt, denn mehr als sich bloß von ihrem „identitären Gegenstand" auf dem Schlachtfeld zu entkleiden – also den Uniformen –, gleichen sich die Soldaten im Unglück des Krieges.

Danach warten die drei Soldaten darauf, dass die UNPROFOR (United Nations Protection Force) – eine militärische Einheit der UNO, die für die Friedensverhandlungen zuständig war, – dazu gerufen werden würde, um sie zu retten. In diesem Moment etabliert sich einen freundlichen Dialog zwischen Ciki und Nino. Sie entdecken sogar, dass sie in der Vergangenheit ein Mädchen kennengelernt hatten, Sanja, Ex-Freundin von Ciki und Schulkameradin von Nino in Banja Luka.

Trotzdem passiert das Unvermeidbare: Die „Schlumpfe", wie die UNO-Soldaten mit ihren Blauhelmen von den Soldaten im Bosnischen Krieg genannt wurden, kommen endlich an, aber ihnen gelingt es nicht, die Landmine zu entschärfen und Cera so zu retten. Nino will mit den Blauhelmen weggehen, aber Ciki schießt auf sein Bein. Später nach einer Unachtsamkeit von Ciki versucht Nino, ihn mit einem Messer zu töten. Die UNPROFOR kommt wieder und bringt einen deutschen Soldaten, einen

Experten in Landminenentschärfung, und Ciki und Nino sind endlich aus dem Schützengraben geholt.

Zum Schluss erschießt Ciki Nino und wird sofort von einem UNO-Soldat erschossen. Beide überleben dem Konflikt nicht, ohne einen plausiblen Grund für ihren Tod zu geben. Sie hassten einfach gegeneinander, weil sie nicht zur selben Seite gehörten. Die Vernunft unterwirft sich dem Gefühl, weil sie sich als unfähig aufweist, die Überwindung des Konflikts zu ermöglichen. Man stirbt im Namen des „Vaterlandes", aber man weiß nicht, warum. Und es kann nichts für Cera gemacht werden. Um das Scheitern der Mission vor den Kameras der Journalisten nicht zu übernehmen, befiehlt der General der UNPROFOR, dass der Körper eines Soldaten in den Hubschrauber gebracht wird, als ob Cera noch am Leben wäre und dadurch gerettet würde. Aber Cera wird einfach im Schützengraben gelassen, mit der scharfen Landmine unter seinem Körper. Als ein Ganzes passen die tragischen Ereignisse am Ende des Films den Absichten von Danis Tanović:

> Ich wollte, dass dieser Film voll von verschiedenen Arten von Kontrasten und Mißklängen wäre. Aber ich wollte, dass der Mißklang und der Haß künstlich wären, also unfähig dazu wären, zu irgendwelcher Lösung zu führen.
>
> Ich habe irgendwo gelesen, dass die Liebe einem Konflikt Harmonie mit sich bringt, ohne jede Seite zu zerstören. Der Haß macht das Gegenteil. Wenn der Haß das führende Lebensprinzip wäre, gäbe es keine Opposition mehr in der Welt. Da es aber Feuer und Wasser existieren, soll die Liebe das Prinzip sein, das alles herrscht.[21]

Das Leben ist ein Wunder (2004) und die Liebe

Der Film *Das Leben ist ein Wunder* (in Original: *Život je čudo*; 2004), eine gemeinsame französisch-serbische Produktion, vom bosnischen Filmemacher Emir Kusturica, der das Drehbuch zusammen mit Ranko Bozic geschrieben hat, stellt die Erlebnisse einer Familie im Balkankrieg zu Beginn der 1990er Jahre dar, die von einer komplizierten Beziehung eines Liebespaares während des Konflikts tief betroffen wird. In einem zu Beginn des Films lustigen Ton, der sich allmählich zu einer bitteren Tragödie entwickelt, hebt Kusturica die Absurdität des Krieges hervor und nimmt zugleich eine entschiedenantinationalistische Haltung an. Die e hohe künstlerische Qualität des Films wurdedurch die Verleihung mehrerer Preise anerkannt, u.a. den „Cesar" – den Preis der Europäischen Union 2005 in der Kategorie „Bester Film" – und im selben Jahr den Preis in der Kategorie „Bester Film des Balkans" im Internationalen Filmfestival von Sofia.

Die Filmfabel hat als zentrales Thema eine Familie, die unter den Missgeschicken, die vom Krieg und vom daraus folgenden Zusammenbruch Jugoslawiens verursacht werden, tief leiden wird. Im Jahre 1992 lässt sich Luka Duric (Slavko Štimac), ein serbischer Ingenieur, in einem kleinen Dorf in Bosnien nieder, das fern der großen Städten liegt, zusammen mit seiner Ehefrau Jadranka (Vesna Trvalić), einer gescheiterten Opernsängerin und mit seinem Sohn Miloš (Vuc Kostic). Luka bekam den Auftrag, die Eisenbahnschienen wiederaufzubauen, damit der Tourismus in der Region, reich an herrlichen Landschaften, belebt werden sollte. Der Sohn Miloš, der Fußball liebt, träumt von einer Karriere als Fußballspieler in einem Profiklub, dem Partisan Belgrad, aber er wird zum Wehrdienst einberufen. Nach Miloš Abschiedsparty flieht Jadranka mit einem ungarischen Musiker, da sie noch von einer erfolgreichen Karriere als Opernsängerin träumt.[22] Gleich danach bricht der Bosnienkrieg aus. Ohne in Betracht zu ziehen, dass der kriegerische Konflikt auch die Verkehrsplanungen betreffen würde, setzt Luka den Wiederaufbau der Eisenbahnschienen fort und scheint den Krieg zu ignorieren, trotz der immer näher kommenden intensiven Bombardements, bis er die Aufforderung erhält, die Eisenbahnlinie in Betrieb zu halten, auf der Waffen und geschmuggelte Waren transportiert werden. Inzwischen wird Miloš von bosnischen Soldaten gefangen genommen. Wiederum übergibt die serbische Miliz Luka die junge Sabaha (Nataša Šolak), eine moslemische Geisel, die gegen seinen Sohn getauscht werden soll, und die Luka früher im Krankenhaus, wo sie als Krankenschwester arbeitete, kennengelernt hatte, als Jadranka zum Arzt hätte gehen müssen. Jedoch verliebt sich Luka in sie und gerät im Laufe der Zeit in einen entscheidenden Konflikt: den Verlust entweder des Sohnes oder der Geliebten bitter zu büßen. Aufgrund des Vormarschs der Bosnier im Gebiet verlassen Luka und Sabaha das Dorf und schließen sich dem langen Treck von Flüchtlingen an, bis sie Zuflucht im alten Haus von Lukas Vater finden, wo sie Vujan, einen alten serbischen Bauer und eine Art Weisen, treffen. Jedoch kommt Lukas Ehefrau Jadranka plötzlich zurück, schlägt und beschimpft Sabaha und behauptet, dass sie einen "moslemischen Spuk" gegen ihren Mann gemacht hätte.[23] Zum Schluss entscheidet sich Luka für Sabaha und will sie daher dem serbischen Hauptmann Aleksic nicht übergeben, damit sie gegen seinen Sohn oder sogar gegen einen anderen serbischen Gefangenen getauscht werden sollte, da ihr Name auf der Liste der UNPROFOR stand. Stattdessen fliehen Sabaha und Luka und versuchen, den Fluss Dirna zu überqueren, der Bosnien von Serbien trennt. Sabaha wird dann von einem bosnischen Soldaten ins Bein geschossen. Sie kommen zu Aleksic zurück, aber Sabaha verblutet auf dem Weg. Während sie in einem serbischen Lazarett operiert wird, machen Luka und sie Pläne für ein künftiges Leben in Australien mit vielen Kindern. Sabaha erleidet dabei einen Herzinfarkt, wird aber wiederbelebt und zu einer Stelle der UNPROFOR gebracht, um schließlich gegen Miloš getauscht zu werden. Durch die Barrieren der Blauen Helmen an der Brücke, wo der Tausch von Häftlingen stattfindet, führen Sabaha und Luka getrennte Wege: sie wird auf einer Bahre zur anderen Seite der Brücke getragen; er kommt ins Dorf zurück, zusammen mit Miloš, Jadranka und Aleksic, und findet das Haus teilweise zerstört vor. Zum Schluss versucht Luka, Selbstmord zu begehen, indem er sich auf die Eisenbahnschienen in der Nähe des Tunnels legt, aber in letzter Sekunde von einem Esel gerettet wird – einer Art Leitmotiv im Film, der Luka bei seinem Herumirren immer begleitet –, der vor dem Zug auf den Schienen stillsteht, sodass der Lokführer den Zug sofort hält. Die letzte Szene zeigt Luka und Sabaha auf dem Esel sitzend, sie verlassen den Tunnel und reiten die Eisenbahnschienen entlang in eine ungewisse Richtung.[24]

Der Film ist sozusagen ein wunderbares Gedicht, das dem Leben, der Schönheit der Natur mit ihren herrlichen Landschaften, wie auch der Liebe gewidmet ist. Er erweist sich als eine Botschaft für Toleranz und zugleich für eine antirassistische Haltung, in der die Fragen des Eigenen und des Fremden einfach aufgehoben werden. Es gibt eine gegenseitige Akzeptanz der Verschiedenheiten zwischen Luka und Sabaha. Statt den Krieg durch Szenen von blutigen Schlachten darzustellen, wie es im Film *Dörfer in Flammen* der Fall ist, entscheidet sich Kusturica dafür, die Absurdität des Krieges durch die Lebensweg von zwei Liebenden mit verschiedenen ethnischen Wurzeln auf entgegengesetzten Seiten zu schildern. Statt den Krieg mit seiner Zerstörungskraft darzustellen, macht der Filmmacher paradoxerweise eine Mischung aus scharfem Humor, mit lustigen und lyrischen Szenen und einer bevorstehenden Tragödie vor der brutalen Realität, und zeigt damit, dass das Leben, im Grunde genommen, „ein Wunder" ist.

Schlussbetrachtungen: die Greueltaten, der Hass und die Liebe

In den Filmen, die hier analysiert wurden, kann man feststellen, dass das Verhältnis vom Eigenen und vom Fremden Bestandteil der Darstellung des Krieges im Balkan ist. Im Film *Das Leben ist ein Wunder* kommt die Liebe als Element vor, das dazu fähig ist, die ethnischen Verschiedenheiten zu überwinden. Luka und Sabaha lernen sich während des Konflikts kennen, so wie Ciki und Nino im Film *No Man's Land*. Jedoch versuchen die Figuren Kusturicas den Konflikt gemeinsam zu überwinden, während die Figuren Tanovićs auf unversöhnliche Stellungen beharren und vor den Augen – und der Nachlässigkeit – der Welt, durch die Friedenstruppe UNPROFOR dargestellt, der Tragödie nicht überleben. Milan und Halil, im Film *Dörfer in Flammen*, enge Kindheitsfreunde, werden sich als solche nicht mehr erkennen, sie kämpfen gegeneinander an verschiedenen Fronten und sind in Greueltaten während des Krieges verwickelt. Der Unterschied zwischen den Filmen von Dragojević bzw. von Tanović scheint darin zu liegen, dass im Film *Dörfer in Flammen* der Hass ein unüberwindbares Gefühl ist, so dass es kein Zeichen von Toleranz zwischen den Befeindeten geben kann, während *No Man's Land*, unabhängig vom tragischen Ende, zeigt, dass der unbegründete Hass zwischen Ciki und Nino unter anderen Umständen zu einer Versöhnung führen könnte.

Es lohnt sich noch eine letzte Betrachtung zur Frage des Raums, verbunden mit den Begriffen des Eigenen und des Fremden. Die analysierten Filme zeigen grundlegend drei bedeutende Räume: der nicht zu Ende gebaute Tunnel im Film *Dörfer in Flammen*; der Schützengraben im Film *No Man's Land*; die Eisenbahnschienen im Bau und verschiedene Tunnels im Film *Das Leben ist ein Wunder*. Solche Räume sind mehr als bloße Passagen oder Barrieren der Bewegung zwischen den Menschen, denn sie sind auch Passagen oder Barrieren für die Verschiedenheiten. Während der Tunnel die eigene Alegorie der Unmöglichkeit von einer Verbindung zwischen zwei unterschiedlichen Räumen darstellt, symbolisiert der Schützengraben die Trennung zwischen diesen beiden Räumen, und die Eisenbahnschienen und die Tunnels scheinen die eigene Metapher des Lebensflusses und des Herumirrens des Menschen zu sein. Wie "ein Wunder", ohne der Kontinuität der Handlung zu entsprechen, gehen Luka und Sabaha ihren Weg, zusammen auf einem Esel reitend, auf der Suche nach einem "Happy End",[25] während Ciki und Nino den Schützengraben unversöhnlich verlassen und sterben. Und für die Kindheitsfreunde Milan und Halil gibt es überhaupt keinen Ausweg. Jeder auf seine Weise, haben die drei Filmmacher versucht, die Umstände im Balkankrieg darzustellen, von einer relativierten Sicht – und zugleich revisionistischen Sicht, wie Luiz Nazario richtig darauf hinweist – des Konflikts, wo man die gegenseitige Intoleranz verschärft, die in Greueltaten gipfelt, über eine pessimistische Sicht vor der Sinnlosigkeit des Krieges, bis zu einer Sicht, die auf ihre Weise auf eine versöhnungsorientierte Sicht eines „Panslavismus" abzielt, und auch eine optimistische Sicht in Bezug auf die Überwindung der Verschiedenheiten, wenn auch für einen alten, schon abgenutzten Slogan plädiert: *make love, no war*.

---

[1] Dragojević, Srdan. *Dörfer in Flammen* (*Lepa sela lepo gore*). Serbien / Kroatien, farbig, 115 Min. 1996.

[2] Tanović, Danis. *No Man's Land* (*Ničija zemlja*). Bosnien / Belgien / Frankreich / Großbritannien / Italien, farbig, 93 Min., 2001.

[3] Kusturica, Emir. *Das Leben ist ein Wunder* (*Život je čudo*). Frankreich / Serbien, farbig, 156 Min., 2004.

[4] Calic, Marie-Janine. *Das Ende Jugoslawiens*. Informationen zur politischen Bildung. (Bonn: Bundeszentrale für politische Bildung, 1996), 1-16, hier 5.

[5] França, Andréa. „Imagens do subterrâneo". In: Ramos, Fernão Pessoa (Hrsg.). *Estudos de Cinema – Socine*, vol. II und III (São Paulo: Annablume, 2000), 13-20, hier 14. Alle Übersetzungen ins Deutsche sind von unserer Authorschaft.

[6] Nazario, Luiz. „As chamas que consomem as belas aldeias não são belas (Notas sobre uma premiada propaganda de limpeza étnica)". In: *O estado da sociedade*, Nr. 4, Jg. 11, S. 1-4, 1996, S. 1.

[7] França, Imagens do subterrâneo, 14.

[8] França, Imagens do subterrâneo, 14.

[9] Dragojević, Dörfer in Flammen.

[10] Dragojević, Dörfer in Flammen.

[11] Dragojević, Dörfer in Flammen.

[12] Dragojević, Dörfer in Flammen.

[13] Dragojević, Dörfer in Flammen.

[14] Dragojević, Dörfer in Flammen.

[15] Dragojević, Dörfer in Flammen.

[16] Tanović, Danis. „Noten zur Produktion". In: Tanović, *No Man's Land*.

[17] Tanović, No Man's Land.

[18] Tanović, No Man's Land.

[19] Tanović, No Man's Land.

[20] Tanović, No Man's Land.

[21] Tanović, „Noten zur Produktion".

[22] Kusturica, Das Leben ist ein Wunder.

[23] Kusturica, Das Leben ist ein Wunder.

[24] Kusturica, Das Leben ist ein Wunder.

[25] Kusturica, Das Leben ist ein Wunder.

Elcio Loureiro Cornelsen ist seit 2001 Dozent für Deutsche Sprache, Literatur und Kultur (Graduierung) und für Literaturtheorie und Komparatistik (Postgraduierung) an der Universidade Federal de Minas Gerais. Studium der Germanistik an der Universidade de São Paulo und 1999 Promotion mit einer Dissertation zum Thema *Gott oder Natur? "Metaphysische Unterströmung" im Werk Alfred Döblins* an der Freien Universität Berlin. Seit 2011 Forschungsstipendiat des CNPq. Zahlreiche Veröffentlichungen zur Darstellung von Gewalt in der Literatur und im Film, sowie zur Zeugnis-Literatur und zum Verhältnis von Literatur und Autoritarismus, u.a. als Herausgeber des Buchs *Literatura e Guerra* (Belo Horizonte: Ed. UFMG, 2010) zusammen mit Tom Burns. Zurzeit arbeitet er an einem Projekt zum Verhältnis von Fußball und Literatur in Brasilien.

Kampf um Authentizität
Autobiographische Berichte und Sachbücher über den Krieg in Afghanistan

Helmut P. E. Galle

1 Deutschland und der Krieg des 21. Jahrhunderts

Seit 1990 werden deutsche Soldaten wieder verstärkt im Ausland eingesetzt.[1] Es handelt sich meist um sogenannte humanitäre Interventionen, die von UNO-Mandaten gedeckt sind, aber in einigen Fällen sind deutsche Soldaten auch in Auseinandersetzungen verwickelt die zumindest als kriegsähnlich bezeichnet werden müssen – wie im Falle des Afghanistan-Einsatzes –, selbst wenn sie nach offizieller Definition die staatliche Infrastruktur stärken sollen.[2] Immerhin starben während solcher Einsätze bisher 95 Soldaten,[3] nicht nur durch Unfälle oder Suizid,[4] sondern seit 2005 vor allem bei Attentaten, mehr als die Hälfte davon in Afghanistan.[5] Die dort stationierten deutschen Soldaten, im Juni 2011 ca. 5300, gehören zum größten Teil der ISAF-Truppe an (International Security Assistance Force), die – anders als bei Blauhelm-Einsätzen – alle (Gewalt-) Mittel anwenden darf, um der Autorität der gewählten Regierung Geltung zu verschaffen und Insurgenten zu bekämpfen, was sie in die Nähe der alliierten Streitkräfte der Operation Enduring Freedom (OEF) bringt, die seit 2001 in Afghanistan gegen Taliban und Al Quaida kämpfen. Eventuelle Straftaten, die deutsche Soldaten dort begehen, werden nicht aufgrund des Straf- sondern des Völkerstrafgesetzbuchs geahndet, da der Konflikt als Bürgerkrieg gewertet wird.[6] Die Deutschen stehen in Afghanistan nicht unbedingt in vorderster Front wie ihre US-Kollegen, sind aber involviert in einen gewaltsamen Konflikt, der an Schärfe zunimmt und auf den weder die Charakteristika des „klassischen Krieges" zwischen zwei Staaten, noch die des Guerrilla-Krieges zutreffen,[7] sondern eher die Merkmale der von Herfried Münkler als „neue Kriege" bezeichneten Konflikte.[8] Das „Neue" besteht nach Münkler vor allem in 1) „Entstaatlichung" (Privatisierung und Kommerzialisierung der Gewalt), 2) „Asymmetrisierung" (die Gegner sind ungleichartig) und 3) „Autonomisierung" (Gewaltakte sind nicht mehr militärisch eingebunden). (Münkler, Neue Kriege, 10 f.) Zur Asymmetrie gehört einerseits, dass die überlegene Partei bemüht ist, mittels technologischer Präzisionswaffen das Leben ihrer Soldaten maximal zu schützen, aber auch Verluste unter der Zivilbevölkerung gering zu halten. Andererseits bedeutet Asymmetrie auch, dass die technisch und militärisch unterlegene Partei Terror als Propaganda einsetzt, um den nach kriegsrechtlichen Prinzipien operierenden Gegner zu demoralisieren und ihn seinerseits zu Gewaltmaßnahmen zu provozieren, die seine Legitimität untergraben. Reguläre Soldaten der Bundesrepublik und der USA sehen sich hier einem Gegner und Gewaltformen gegenüber, die zwangsläufig ihr Verständnis vom Krieg und von sich selbst verändern.

Die demokratische Legitimation des Einsatzes ist umstritten (er wird nur von etwa einem Viertel der Deutschen befürwortet) und sein Sinn ist fragwürdig, gemessen an den offenbaren Schwierigkeiten, demokratische und rechtsstaatliche Einrichtungen im Land durchzusetzen, gegen die kulturellen Prägungen der Bevölkerung und den hartnäckigen Widerstand der Taliban. Anders als in den beiden Weltkriegen, rekrutiert sich die Armee nicht mehr aus Wehrpflichtigen, sondern aus Berufssoldaten, die diese Karriere aus privaten Motiven anderen vorgezogen haben und damit freiwillig das Risiko eines Kriegseinsatzes eingegangen sind. Insofern sind die Bedingungen, unter denen gekämpft wird, weniger ein gesamtgesellschaftliches Anliegen, als dies in den Weltkriegen der Fall war bzw. in Kriegen, in denen es um das Wesen der „politischen Existenz" geht, was – nach Carl Schmitt – überhaupt nur einem Staat die „ungeheure Befugnis" gibt, „von Angehörigen des eigenen Volkes Todesbereitschaft und Tötungsbereitschaft zu verlangen".[9] Da die Auseinandersetzungen in Afghanistan nur auf sehr indirekte Weise Einfluss auf die Integrität der Bundesrepublik (und auch der USA) haben, gibt es für den Einsatz der Berufssoldaten letztlich keine so fundamentalen Motive, dass diese das Opfer des eigenen Lebens rechtfertigen würden. Die Berufsentscheidung für die Bundeswehr mag für den einzelnen auch mit einer Abenteuerlust einhergehen, aber prinzipiell kann der Staat kaum von einem auf 10 oder 20 Jahre verpflichteten jungen Mann verlangen, sein Leben dafür zu geben, dass in Afghanistan – vielleicht – rechtsstaatliche Strukturen geschaffen werden.

Man muss also einerseits davon ausgehen, dass Soldaten in einer „postheroischen Gesellschaft"[10] ihre Aufgabe nicht prinzipiell anders angehen als andere: als einen von vielen möglichen „Jobs". Andererseits ist die Relevanz dieses Einsatzes in der öffentlichen Meinung vielen politischen und wirtschaftlichen Problemen nachgeordnet: er wird kontrovers diskutiert wie alle politischen Entscheidungen der Regierung, ohne dass eine stärkere Identifikation mit „unseren Jungs" oder „unserer

Sache" im Spiel wäre. Das bedeutet, dass die existentiellen Erfahrungen, die möglicherweise von den Soldaten dort in Afghanistan gemacht werden, von vornherein einen anderen Stellenwert einnehmen, als jene Bücher, in denen einst Ernst Jünger und E. M. Remarque ihre Kriegserlebnisse formulierten. War es damals die ganze Gesellschaft, die zivile und die von der Front zurückgekehrte, die „ihren Krieg" anhand dieser Bücher zu verstehen versuchte, so sind es heute eher einzelne, die sich mit der Berichterstattung der Massenmedien nicht zufrieden geben und nach Darstellungen suchen, die direkt von den Beteiligten produziert wurden, auf einem Schauplatz, wo es um Leben und Tod geht.

Der „Krieg in Afghanistan" stößt, gemessen daran, bei den Deutschen auf starkes Interesse und Publikationen zum Thema finden sich immer wieder auf den Bestsellerlisten. Einige davon berichten aus der Perspektive des Augenzeugen von den mehr oder weniger direkten Erfahrungen der Gewalt. Das bedeutet nicht unbedingt, dass es sich bei den Autoren um Mitglieder der „kämpfenden Truppe" handelt. Eines der ersten Bücher stammt von Achim Wohlgethan,[11] der im deutsch-niederländischen „Vorauskommando" 2002 sechs Monate lang zur Infrastruktur für die nachfolgenden Soldaten beitragen sollte; das mit dem Ex-Presseoffizier Dirk Schulze verfasste Buch erschien unter dem Titel *Endstation Kabul* (2008). *Ein schöner Tag zum Sterben* stammt von der Oberstabsärztin Heike Groos, die ihre Erlebnisse vor allem bei den Afghanistan-Einsätzen in den Jahren 2003 und 2004 schildert.[12] Oberst Artur Schwitalla[13] erinnert und reflektiert in seinem Band von 2010 die vier Jahre zurückliegende Aufbauarbeit in der Nordostprovinz Badakhshan.

Neben solchen Arbeiten von deutschen Autoren,[14] liegen angloamerikanische Bücher in Übersetzung vor, darunter die von Jon Krakauer: *Auf den Feldern der Ehre*[15] und Sebastian Junger: *War. Ein Jahr im Krieg*[16] als Bestseller und zugleich literarisch ambitionierteste Texte hervorragen. Diese Bücher bilden das Korpus, auf das sich die folgenden Überlegungen stützen.

2 Schwierige Genrebestimmung

Auf den ersten Blick scheint es sich um eine einheitliche Gattung zu handeln, da die Bücher in ähnlicher Aufmachung auf den aktuellen Tischen der Buchhandlungen liegen: Titelbilder mit den Autoren in Uniform vor einer Wüstenlandschaft bei Wohlgethan und Groos oder auf der Rückseite wie bei Schwitalla; bei Krakauer ein einsamer Soldat von hinten vor der horizontweiten Wüste; und auch der Zivilist

Junger erscheint in uniformähnlicher Kleidung auf dem inneren Schutzumschlag, während vorn eine übergroße, detailscharfe Gesichtshälfte mit einer Läsion um das Auge zu sehen ist, dessen insistierender Blick den Betrachter trifft.

Bei genauerem Hinsehen sind diese Berichte über den Krieg am Hindukusch jedoch durchaus heterogen und gar nicht eindeutig zu klassifizieren. Die Gattungsangaben der Paratexte sind schillernd; Bezeichnungen wie „Insiderbericht" (Wohlgethan), „Erlebnisbericht" (Schwitalla), „Mitschnitt" (Junger), „Reportage" (Krakauer) stellen Konnotationen her zum Augenzeugen mit Zugang zu geheimem Wissen, zur journalistischen Recherche und sogar zur technischen Aufzeichnung faktischen Geschehens (Mitschnitt), was im Fall Jungers mehr als nur eine marktgängige Metapher ist, da der Autor seinen Text anhand des umfangreichen Kameramaterials seines Kollegen Tim Hetherington erstellt und überprüft hat.

Obwohl sich aber alle Texte im Bereich der „Wirklichkeitserzählung"[17] bewegen, handelt es sich um je unterschiedliche Genres. Wohlgethan berichtet chronologisch seine diversen Erlebnisse in Kabul und Umgebung nicht zuletzt, um seine Konflikte mit Vorgesetzten ins rechte Licht zu rücken. Das Buch der Ärztin Heike Groos erzählt auf mehreren Zeitebenen von ihrem Afghanistan-Einsatz und dem traumatischen Anschlag auf einen Bus, vor allem aber von der langwierigen psychischen Verarbeitung dieser Ereignisse, wodurch der Text einen autobiographischen Charakter erhält. Schwitalla integriert mehr Beobachtungen über sein Einsatzland, und legt Rechenschaft ebenso von den konstruktiven Bemühungen seiner Einheit sowie von den auf ihn und seine Leute gezielten Gewaltakte ab, sein Bericht ist sachhaltiger, interessierter, weniger subjektiv und emotional. Krakauer rekonstruiert eigentlich die Biographie eines amerikanischen Football-Stars, der sich freiwillig zum Einsatz im „Krieg gegen den Terror" gemeldet hatte. Jungers Buch wirkt mit den Kapitelüberschriften „Angst", „Töten" und „Liebe" wie ein Essay, in den szenischen Beschreibungen wie ein Roman und im bibliographischen Apparat wie eine wissenschaftliche Studie: in seiner Hybridität steht es mit den vorangegangenen Sachbüchern des Autors in der Tradition des Dokumentarromans Truman Capotes und des *new journalism*.

Krakauer, Wohlgetan und Groos verstehen ihre Bücher auch als politische Interventionen: sie wollen auf bestehende Missstände aufmerksam machen, die in erster Linie die Beziehung zwischen Soldaten und militärischer Führung betreffen (Wohlgetan), die problematische Behandlung der traumatisierten Soldaten durch den psychologischen Dienst der Bundeswehr (Groos) oder die offizielle

Informationspolitik über den Krieg durch Armeeführung und Bush-Administration (Krakauer). Bei Schwitalla ist die Kritik nicht Hauptzweck, sondern nur ein Nebeneffekt der Beobachtungen. Bei Junger ist die kritische Tendenz ebenfalls eher implizit zu spüren, sofern der Autor versucht, sich radikal in die Wahrnehmungsperspektive der Soldaten zu versetzen, womit er in allen konfliktträchtigen Fragen praktisch auch Partei ergreift.

Gemeinsam ist aber allen fünf Texten die Positionierung im Feld des Faktualen, zwischen Memoiren, Biographie, Journalismus und (Zeit-) Geschichtsschreibung. Diese Gattungen stehen bekanntlich seit einiger Zeit in dem Verdacht, lediglich „eine fiktive Realität" herstellen zu können.[18] Dagegen halten Autoren wie Matías Martínez an der grundsätzlichen Unterscheidung von journalistischem und fiktional-literarischem Erzählen fest, da Reportagen zwar durchaus Realitäten ‚konstruieren', diese aber „auf eine intersubjektiv gegebene Wirklichkeit bezogen" bleiben.[19] Reportage, historiographischer Text und Autobiographie teilen den referentiellen Anspruch, unterscheiden sich aber durch die Leitdifferenzen (Luhmann), welche die Kommunikation in den diversen sozialen Systemen steuern und Hinweise zur funktionalen Gattungsbestimmung geben, wie dies im Band von Klein und Martínez aufgezeigt wird. Ohne eine solche Bestimmung hier im Einzelnen durchführen zu wollen, werden im Folgenden einige Aspekte der Kriegsdarstellung in den fünf Büchern unter sachlichen und formalen Gesichtspunkten herausgehoben. Dabei wird das Hauptaugenmerk auf das Buch von Junger fallen, das in jeder Hinsicht das ambitiöseste, aber auch problematischste ist.

3 Die Darstellung der Soldaten und des Krieges

Wer von den Büchern in erster Linie die Schilderung von Kämpfen erhofft, wird – mit Ausnahme von Junger – weitgehend enttäuscht. Es kennzeichnet gerade die deutschen Texte, dass ihre Autoren relativ selten in Gefechte verwickelt werden. Gleichwohl möchte Wohlgethan offenbar Leser mit solchen Erwartungen befriedigen, wenn er in Überschriften „echten Raketenbeschuss" und ein „Selbstmordkommando am Kabul-Stadion" ankündigt. Das Kapitel „Auge in Auge mit afghanischen Kämpfern" freilich handelt zum großen Teil von den Vorbereitungen zu einer „Ladies Night" Party, um dann doch noch von einer Begegnung mit acht bewaffneten Männern in den Bergen zu berichten, die aber nach einigen angespannten Minuten dem Autor einen Hisefladen anbieten.[20] Abgesehen davon, dass der Autor in dieser Situation wohl zunächst tatsächlich Todesangst ausgestanden hat, registriert der Text vor allem die Krämpfe in den Beinen und eine psychische Lähmung, während sich die beiden Gruppen abwartend gegenüberstehen. Der „Kampf" findet zwar nicht eigentlich statt, aber der Text vermerkt die zugehörigen Schmerzen und wird damit der Erwartung gerecht. – Später kommt es während der Massoud-Gedenktage zu einem Bombenattentat auf einem Marktplatz, das Wohlgethan von einem Versteck aus beobachtet. Als er mit den Kameraden hinauseilt, um den Verletzten zu helfen, beschreibt er die Situation:

> Blutüberströmte Menschen oder nur noch Teile von ihnen lagen überall verstreut herum. Diese Bombe hatte ganze Arbeit geleistet. Das Geschrei der Verwundeten steigerte sich von Sekunde zu Sekunde immer mehr und wurde fast unerträglich. Bis zu den Knöcheln im Blut watend, arbeiteten wir uns bis an die Stelle der Detonation vor. [...] Ich war vollkommen überfordert, schaltete mein Gehirn ab.[21]

Wie er später erfährt, wurden bei dem Attentat 26 Menschen getötet und mehr als 150 verletzt. Was die Soldaten belastet, sind nicht Kämpfe, sondern die plötzlichen, nach langer Untätigkeit aus dem Nichts hereinbrechenden Gewaltakte und das Miterleben von sinnlosen Gemetzeln, die sich gegen die internationalen Soldaten, aber eben auch gezielt gegen die Zivilbevölkerung richten.

Im Buch von Heike Groos steht der Anschlag auf einen Bus im Zentrum, bei dem vier Soldaten umkommen und 29 verwundet werden. Als sie mit ihrem Sanitätsteam vermeintlich zu einem Verkehrsunfall gerufen wird, erleidet einen Schock, als sie feststellt, dass es nicht um einen afghanischen, sondern einen Bus der Bundeswehr handelt.

> Was ich fühlte, kann ich nicht beschreiben. Ich glaube, eigentlich gar nichts. Die Wahrnehmung aller dieser Eindrücke [eine zwei Seiten lange Beschreibung, H.G.] hatte nur einige Sekunden in Anspruch genommen. Lange Jahre und über fünfzehntausend Einsätze als Notärztin in Deutschland hatten mich darauf trainiert, zunächst, sofort und zügig, der Situation Genüge zu tun und alles Denken, Fühlen und Bewerten der Ereignisse auf später zu verschieben.[22]

Was auf den ersten Blick wie eine geradezu rassistische Selektion der Gefühle erscheint, klärt sich auf, wenn die Autorin aus einem Bericht zitiert, den sie später für holländische Militärmediziner verfasste:

> Sanitätspersonal ist ja den Umgang und die Auseinandersetzung mit Tod und Sterben gewöhnt. Hier aber fanden wir Verletzte und Tote in der gleichen Uniform, die wir selbst getragen. Kameraden, die wir kannten, Freunde, mit denen wir am Tag zuvor noch

Abschied gefeiert hatten. Welche von uns. Der Tod kam auf einmal trotz aller Professionalität ganz nah an uns heran.[23]

Die Traumatisierung erfolgt (wie schon im Ersten Weltkrieg) nicht unbedingt darüber, dass man selbst verwundet wird, sondern darüber, dass Personen des Nahverhältnisses getötet oder verletzt werden und so das Grundvertrauen in die Sicherheit des eigenen Lebens untergraben wird. Hinzu kommt, dass gerade die Bundeswehrsoldaten ihre Präsenz im Land ja keineswegs als feindlich auffassen: sie unterstützen die Einheimischen beim Aufbau von Infrastruktur und der Ausbildung von Personal. Um so schwerer fällt es ihnen, den Angriffen auf ihr Leben einen Sinn zuzuordnen, wie z.B dem Hauptfeldwebel, der den Tod eines Freundes nicht verarbeiten kann:

> […] er blickte nur vor sich auf den Boden und sagte leise: ‚Ich frage mich immer wieder, warum das passiert ist.' Er hob den Blick, sah mich an und wiederholte: ‚Warum? Warum nur?' Er dachte einen Moment nach und fügte hinzu: ‚Warum er, warum überhaupt jemand und wofür eigentlich?' Er hatte Tränen in den Augen und konnte nicht mehr weitersprechen.[24]

Für Groos und ihre Kameraden besteht das Hauptproblem allerdings nicht darin, dass dieser Einsatz ohne ausreichende politische Motive erfolgt wäre und daher die Opfer in keinem rechten Verhältnis zu den damit verfolgten Zielen stünden. Vielmehr hält sie die institutionellen Strukturen, welche die permanent traumatisierten Soldaten unterstützen müssten, für unzureichend und kontraproduktiv, da sie die Menschen psychiatrisierten, anstatt sie in ihrer Trauer zu unterstützen und zu begleiten.[25] Für Groos stellt auch der Einsatz „an der Front" eine pragmatisch zu lösende Aufgabe dar, die unter den entsprechenden Bedingungen zu bewältigen ist. Als sie aber 2007, kurz vor der Entlassung, gebeten wird, sich ein zweites Mal freiwillig nach Afghanistan zu melden, um einen krank gewordenen Kollegen zu ersetzen, antwortet sie:

> Herr Oberstarzt, Sie können nicht erwarten, dass wir uns freiwillig melden und dann vielleicht für den Rest unseres Lebens mit einem Arm oder einem Bein herumlaufen und damit leben müssen, dass wir auch noch selbst dran schuld sind. Dafür muss schon irgendjemand anderes die Verantwortung übernehmen.[26]

Die Weigerung führt dann dazu, dass sie abkommandiert wird, glücklicherweise ohne dass es tatsächlich zu Angriffen auf ihre körperliche Unversehrtheit kommt.

Auch bei Artur Schwitalla ist spürbar, dass die Bedrohung durch die Terrorakte des „Feindes" eigentlich als unzumutbar verstanden wird, wenn er im Nachwort eine Bilanz der während seines Einsatzes miterlebten Terrordrohungen, Anschläge (mit Verletzten und einem Toten) und auch Erdbeben zieht und diese mit der offiziellen Lageeinschätzung der Sicherheitslage durch das deutsche Militär kontrastiert: „'Die Lage ist ruhig, aber nicht stabil'. Jeder möge es selbst bewerten!"[27] Gerade im Hinblick auf die von seiner Einheit geleistete Hilfe und Aufbauarbeit für die Bevölkerung dieser ärmsten Provinz in Afghanistan ist es demoralisierend, dass er und seine Leute permanent mit dem Leben bedroht werden, denn die klare Unterscheidung zwischen Zivilisten und Terroristen wird in der afghanischen Situation praktisch unmöglich. Die Mentalität der Einwohner bleibt weitgehend unverstanden, trotz aller ernsthaften Versuche, sich ihr anzunähern.

In seinem wie in den beiden anderen deutschen Afghanistan-Büchern ist der eigentliche Krieg eher ein Phantom, das sich in einer permanenten Bedrohung und gelegentlichen Terrorakten äußert. Diese Struktur zeigt sich prinzipiell auch bei den Texten von Krakauer und Junger, allerdings sind ihre Protagonisten gemäß dem Auftrag der *Operation Enduring Freedom* deutlich häufiger in Kampfhandlungen verwickelt.

Diese beschränken sich allerdings in *Auf den Felder der Ehre* auf das letzte Drittel des Buches. Krakauers Protagonist Pat Tillman, der ein Millionenangebot der American Football League ausgeschlagen hatte, um sich – trotz starker Zweifel an der Glaubwürdigkeit der offiziellen Propaganda[28] – mit seinem jüngeren Bruder zur Armee zu melden. Es war wohl kein expliziter Akt von Patriotismus, aber auch keine bloße Abenteuerlust. Krakauer zitiert aus einem persönlichen „Dokument" Tillmans, das die Entscheidung begründet:

> Ich bin mit dem Weg, den ich bisher gegangen bin, nicht mehr zufrieden ... Er ist nicht mehr wichtig. / Ich weiß nicht genau, wohin diese neue Richtung mein Leben führen wird, aber ich bin sicher, dass sie auch Opfer und Schwierigkeiten mit sich bringen wird [...]. Trotzdem bin ich mir ebenso sicher, dass diese neue Richtung unser Leben am Ende voller, reicher und bedeutsamer machen wird.[29]

Mit seiner eher reflektiven Haltung ist Tillman nach Krakauers Ansicht in der Eliteeinheit die Ausnahme:

> Die meisten Ranger in Tillmans Zug [...] wollten Angehörige einer exklusiven Kriegerkultur werden. Deshalb wollten sie Gefechten auf Leben und Tod keineswegs

ausweichen. [...] Sie wollten unbedingt dem Feind Auge in Auge gegenübertreten und sich selbst unter Feuer beweisen.[30]

Die entscheidenden Ereignisse um Tillmans Todsind allerdings alles andere als ein unerbittlicher Kampf mit dem Feind, in dem es um die eigene Existenz geht. In Krakauers Darstellung handelt es sich zum einen um die inkompetente Führung, die den eigenen Soldaten unnötige Risiken zumutet, und zum anderen um die „schießwütigen" Kameraden,[31] die in der Stresssituation eines Überfalls auf alles feuern, was sich bewegt, selbst wenn es die eigenen Leute sind. Der eigentliche Feind bleibt nahezu unsichtbar, identifizierbar lediglich in „vier feindlichen Kämpfer[n] auf dem nördlichen Canyonrand", in „grauen Männergewändern",[32] die vielleicht aus dem mehrheitlich freundlichen Dorf stammen, das die Gruppe wenige Minuten zuvor passiert hat.[33]

Es entspricht der Logik von Krakauers politischer Botschaft, dass der Leser den Eindruck bekommt, die wahre Ursache für den Tod der Amerikaner in Afghanistan sei die eigene politische und militärische Führung sowie die psychische Disposition der Kämpfer. Die Afghanen sind hier insgesamt präsenter als in den anderen vier Büchern – der im selben *friendly fire* wie Tillman getötete Milizsoldat trägt sogar einen Namen – doch auch hier erscheinen die für Amerikaner fremdartigen, geschlechtlich ambiguen, Sitten der Männer (Blumen im Haar, Lidstrich, Händchenhalten etc. S. 316) nur unverständlich, nicht als Merkmale eines zu erkennenden und zu bekämpfenden Feindes.

Bei Junger wird dies noch deutlicher. Obwohl sich die Soldaten im Einsatz sicher sind, dass bestimmte von ihnen beobachtete Zivilisten identisch sind mit den „Unsichtbaren", von denen sie kurz zuvor oder danach beschossen werden, dürfen sie die Männer aus politischen und kriegsrechtlichen Gründen nicht angreifen, solange sie den Anschein von Zivilisten erwecken.

> Nach einer Weile sehen wir Lichter, die sich über die Hänge des Abas Ghar bewegen: Aller Wahrscheinlichkeit nach sind es Taliban-Kämpfer, die ihre Verwundeten und Toten bergen. Ein Soldat gibt die Information über Funk weiter und schlägt vor, mit Artilleriebeschuss einzugreifen. Das Battalion befürchtet, dass es sich auch um Schafhirten auf hohen Weidegründen handeln könnte, und lehnt das Ansinnen ab. / ‚Immer drauf auf die mit dem .50 cal [Maschinengewehr], wir hatten gerade ein verdammtes TIC [Gefecht], scheiß auf die Typen', sagt jemand".[34]

Obwohl mit den besten denkbaren technischen Möglichkeiten ausgerüstet, um Tag und Nacht ständig alle möglichen Informationen über ihr Operationsgebiet und die

Planungen des Feindes zu erhalten, befinden sich die amerikanischen Soldaten in einer gespenstischen Situation, in der sie nie sicher sein können, ob die Dorfbewohner, mit denen sie gerade friedlich verhandeln, nicht identisch sind mit den „Aufständischen", „einheimischen Kämpfern", „Taliban", die ihnen auf dem Rückweg im nächsten Hinterhalt auflauern. Wo aber die Identifikation des Feindes durch institutionelle Zeichen wie die Uniform unmöglich wird, verfällt die Psyche auf prämoderne Hilfsmittel wie die Physiognomik: „die Bewohner sind Taliban vom harten Kern – die Männer sagen, dass man es an ihrem Blick erkennt".[35]

Junger stellt die einheimische Bevölkerung in den (populär-)wissenschaftlichen Exkursen seines Buches durchaus differenziert und unparteiisch dar. Da es aber sein Ziel ist, die Situation dezidiert aus der Sicht des von ihm begleiteten *Platoons* (Zug, Truppeneinheit von ca. 30 Mann) zu schildern, gehen in der eigentlichen Darstellung die „unsichtbaren" Feinde eine Verbindung mit der Topographie, dem Klima, der Flora und Fauna des Korengal-Tales ein, das er mit paronomastischer Intensivierung als „Afghanistan von Afghanistan" bezeichnet:[36] den Amerikanern erscheint diese extreme Realität ebenso widrig und undurchdringlich wie ihr menschlicher Gegner, der seit Jahrtausenden an sie gewöhnt ist: „Es war, als ob sämtliche Lebewesen im Tal, selbst die wilden Tiere, die Eindringlinge verscheuchen wollten".[37] Die Erfahrung dieser feindlichen Realität resultiert für die Amerikaner, die sich ihr aussetzen, in einer radikalen Veränderung: „das Korengal-Tal erwarb sich allmählich den Ruf eines Orts, der den Geisteszustand eines Mannes auf schaurige Weise unwiderruflich verändern konnte".[38]

Die jungen Männer, die als Freiwillige in Afghanistan kämpfen, gehören von vornherein einer spezifischen Bevölkerungsschicht an. Viele sind aus den unterschiedlichsten Gründen mit dem Gesetz in Konflikt gekommen,[39] Brendan O'Byrne, einer von Jungers wichtigsten Protagonisten, hatte einen alkoholkranken und gewalttätigen Vater,[40] und wie die meisten seiner Kameraden hatte er im zivilen Leben Probleme sich einzuordnen, neigt zu Alkoholexzessen und unmotivierter Gewalt und diese Tendenzen steigern sich noch, wenn er nach einem monatelangen Einsatz unter Extrembedingungen zurück in die Zivilgesellschaft kommt, an deren Regeln er sich nicht mehr halten kann und deren normalisierte „Unterhaltungsangebote" seine Bedürfnisse nicht mehr befriedigen.

Junger begleitet diese Männer mit Sympathie und lässt sich auf ihre Perspektive auch hinsichtlich der Gesamtkonstellation des Krieges ein. Wie sich selbst im Falle eines kritischen Kopfes wie Pat Tillman zeigt, sind die politischen Zweifel in der

„Frontsituation" irrelevant. Ob es sich um einen gerechten Krieg handelt, wie ihnen die Regierung versichertoder nicht, ändert nichts daran, dass die Soldaten in einem eng umgrenzten Handlungsfeld ihren „Job" machen müssen und das bedeutet einerseits Befehle befolgen – selbst wenn diese sich mit ihren Erfahrungen nicht in Einklang bringen lassen – und andererseits in der Kampfsituation die „Feinde" als das behandeln, was sie für die Soldaten sind: Leute, die sie mit allen Mitteln auslöschen wollen und sich dabei an keinerlei humanitäre oder kriegsrechtliche Regeln halten. Anders als zu Zeiten des Vietnamkrieges wird die hierarchische Ordnung und der Sinn des Einsatzes nicht prinzipiell in Frage gestellt, und Journalisten, die eine solche Strategie verfolgen, werden von den Soldaten isoliert, da sie eine solche Haltung nur als Parteinahme gegen sie und für den Feind verstehen können.[41]

Junger bemüht sich, auch mithilfe seiner wissenschaftlichen Exkurse, die psychische Realität dieser Männer weder als Heldentum zu glorifizieren, noch von vornherein als menschliche Deformation zu denunzieren. Ihre extremen Reaktionsweisen erscheinen letztlich als konsequente Folge der extremen Belastung, der sie ausgesetzt sind und die auch einer anthropologischen Grundsituation entspricht. Keiner der Männer ist – im Unterschied zu ihren Gegnern – ein Selbstmörder, alle wollen eigentlich zurück in eine sichere bürgerliche Existenz, aber die Anpassung an das Leben in der kleinen Gruppe unter konstanter Todesdrohung, die Möglichkeit, ihren Stress von Zeit zu Zeit in den Gewaltorgien des Gefechts auszuagieren, die intime Nähe von Personen, denen sie in jedem Moment bedingungslos vertrauen können, dies alles hat sie „süchtig" nach dieser Art von Leben gemacht und auch die „intensive psychiatrische Betreuung" kann diese Konditionierungen nicht einfach auflösen und bleibt letzlich hilflos.[42]

Da der Autor die Gefahren mit den Soldaten teilt – er entgeht nur knapp einem Bombenattentat auf einen Jeep – bleibt sein Bemühen um Empathie keine abstrakte Übung. Die Nähe zum Attentäter, der wenige Meter entfernt hinter dem Felsen saß und die Zünddrähte in Kontakt brachte, rückt jede Reflexion über dessen politische oder religiöse Motive in den Hintergrund. Trotzdem kann Junger die Dinge nach wie vor von einer ethischen Warte beurteilen, der bestimmte Reaktionen der Soldaten unverständlich bleiben; so ist es ihm z.B. unmöglich, den spontanen Applaus „seiner Leute" nachzuvollziehen, als sie über Funk verfolgen, wie ein Mann – wahrscheinlich ein Feind – mit nur noch einem Bein auf einem „Hang umherkriecht" und schließlich stirbt. Angesichts der Leiden eines nunmehr wehrlosen Gegners ist Jungers

Empathievermögen intakt, das der Kämpfer jedoch hat sich ins Gegenteil verkehrt. Die Reaktion lässt ihm keine Ruhe und er lässt sich erklären: „Man stellt sich vor, dass dieser Typ den eigenen Freund ermordet haben könnte [...]. Der Beifall kommt von der Gewissheit, dass es sich um jemanden handelt, gegen den wir nie wieder kämpfen müssen".[43]

Für den Autor stellt sich hier die prinzipielle Frage: steht diese unvermeidliche psychische Veränderung der in Afghanistan eingesetzten jungen Amerikaner in angemessenem Verhältnis zu dem erzielten Gewinn, der sich – auf der Mikroebene – nur in den je hundert Metern bemessen lässt, für die ein Soldat sein Leben lässt, für die aber auch alle Überlebenden den Preis zahlen, „gelernt zu haben, den Tod eines Menschen zu beklatschen".[44]

Auch die amerikanischen Soldaten in Jungers Buch passen nicht mehr in das Profil heroischer Gesellschaften, das in Europa von der Französischen Revolution bis zum Beginn des Ersten Weltkrieges dominierte. Anders als ihre muslimischen Gegner, sind sie nicht bereit, ihre Gesundheit für eine höherwertige Sache auf das Spiel zu setzen und tun prinzipiell alles, um ihre körperliche und seelische Integrität zu erhalten. Lediglich in der konkreten Kampfsituation riskieren sie – zum Schutz der Kameraden – ihr Leben und scheinen dadurch einer anderen, archaischeren Sphäre anzugehören. Aber selbst wenn die Gesellschaft der USA eine stärkere religiöse und patriotische Grundierung aufweisen mag als die deutsche, wäre diese nicht ausreichend, um ihren Bürgern (und sei es auch nur einem geringen Teil) zuzumuten, sich für die Ideale der Demokratie am Hindukusch aufzuopfern. Auch die GIs sind als Gefallene und als psycho-physisch Beschädigte eher Opfer (*victima*) als opferbereite Helden (*offerendum*), obgleich die offizielle Propaganda (wie im Fall Tillman) sie zuweilen dazu machen möchte.[45]

4 Der Referenzanspruch der Bücher

Alle fünf Bücher untermauern ihren faktualen Anspruch mit einem großen Aufwand an textuellen und paratextuellen Elementen. Dadurch stehen sie in deutlichem Kontrast zu Werken der zwanziger und fünfziger Jahre, die zwar ebenfalls nicht ohne die Kriegserfahrung ihrer Autoren auskamen, diese aber in unterschiedlichem Maße fiktionalisierten.[46]

Die deutschen Bücher stützen sich explizit auf Tagebuchaufzeichnungen, sind weitgehend im Stil des Berichts bzw. der Reflexion über das vergangene Geschehen gehalten. Sie enthalten Vor- und Nachworte, die das Zustandekommen der Texte kommentieren. Neben Landkarten und Begriffserklärungen werden Fotos und Dokumente hinzugefügt, welche die persönliche Anwesenheit in Afghanistan belegen. Der burschikose Stil bei Wohlgethan, die leicht lebensmystisch angehauchte Note von Groos und die umsichtige, sachliche Schreibweise Schwitallas bringen zwar ein subjektives Element hinhein, das freilich den Authentizitätseindruck der Texte noch erhöht.

Bei Krakauer und Junger finden sich statt der Dokumente umfangreiche Anmerkungsapparate und Bibliographien, die auch für eine wissenschaftliche Studie ausreichend wären. Beide unterstreichen die Recherchen vor Ort und die zusätzlichen Informationen sowohl von Experten wie aus der Sekundärliteratur. Krakauer schmückt seine Kapitel zusätzlich durch Epigraphen aus der Weltliteratur.

Interessant an Jungers Buch ist vor allem der ständige Wechsel von Bericht zu Interview, szenischer Darstellung, wissenschaftlichem Exkurs und Reflexion. Einerseits betont er in einer einführenden „Anmerkung",[47] als eingebetteter Reporter keinerlei Zensur erfahren zu haben, aber andererseits ist er so auf seine Kampfeinheit angewiesen, dass – wie er später im Text anmerkt – „reine Objektivität [...] im Krieg nicht einmal ansatzweise möglich" ist.[48] Dennoch insistiert der Autor nicht nur auf der Faktizität seiner Erinnerungen und Notizen, er verweist auch auf die hundertfünfzig Stunden Videomaterial seines Kollegen Hetherington, und die Tatsache, dass er

> wann immer es möglich war [...] das Material benutzt [habe], um die Korrektheit [s]einer Berichterstattung zu überprüfen. Dialoge oder Zitate, die in doppelter Anführung wiedergegeben sind, wurden direkt mit der Kamera aufgezeichnet oder in mein Notizbuch übertragen. [...] Ich habe einen unabhängigen Faktenkontrolleur beschäftigt, mit dessen Hilfe ich mich der unvermeidlichen Irrtümer journalistischer Arbeit erwehren wollte [...]. In manchen Fällen habe ich Zitate aus Interviews und Texten gekürzt, um den Leser zu schonen.[49]

Trotz dieser Absicherung nähert sich gerade Jungers Text am deutlichsten fiktionalen Schreibweisen, insbesondere in den dramatischen Kampfszenen, die – wie der überwiegende Teil des Buches – im Präsens gehalten sind. Durch die intensive, fast visuelle Beschreibung des Geschehens, wird die Faktenreihe zur Szene:

> Die Soldaten gehen im Gänsemarsch auf dem Grat des Gebirgsausläufers, jeweils zehn bis fünfzehn Meter voneinander entfernt, das Gelände fällt nach beiden Seiten in Stechpalmenwälder und Schiefergeröll steil ab. Der Mond scheint so hell, dass sie nicht

einmal ihre Nachtsichtgeräte benutzen. Ohne dass Winn und seine Männer es ahnen, haben sich drei feindliche Kämpfer jenseits des Kamms unter ihnen mit ihren AK-47 aufgestellt.[50]

Auch wenn dieser Hinterhalt zum Teil aus nachträglichen Informationen und den Aussagen der Überlebenden rekonstruiert wurde, gibt Junger in allen verfügbaren Details an, welcher dieser namentlich benannten Männer zuerst stürzt, wo er getroffen wird, und wie die nachfolgenden reagieren. Um den Kameraden aus den Händen der Taliban zu retten, wagen einige Soldaten blitzschnell und quasi instinktiv ihr eigenes Leben, indem sie sich direkt in den Kugelhagel stürzen.

> Er wirft seine letzte Granate und sprintet dann über das letzte Stück an den Ort, wo sich Brennan befinden sollte. Der Gatigal-Gebirgsausläufer ist in Mondlicht getaucht, und in den silbrigen Schatten der Stechpalmen sieht er zwei feindliche Kämpfer, die Josh Brennan den Berghang hinunterschleifen. Er leert sein M4-Magazin auf sie und läuft los zu seinem Freund.[51]

An dieser Stelle – dem Spannungshöhepunkt – unterbricht Junger die Erzählung mit einem sechsseitigen Exkurs über militärische Forschungen zu dieser Art von „altruistischem" Verhalten im Krieg. Wenn er den Handlungsfaden wieder aufnimmt, schildert er die „Rettung" Brennans, die sofortigen Versuche seine Verletzungen zu versorgen, an denen er gleichwohl bald darauf stirbt. Obwohl alle Elemente der Darstellung durch das verfügbare Material gedeckt sein mögen, wird ein Grad an Vergegenwärtigung und emotionaler Beteiligung des Lesers hergestellt, der einer Filmsequenz gleichkommt – und es ist durchaus denkbar, dass der Autor den Ehrgeiz hatte, in dieser Hinsicht mit der filmischen Arbeit seines Kollegen Hetherington zu „konkurrieren".

Man kann das verstehen als Tribut an die Sensationslust der Leser, die dieser Bestseller zweifellos auch bedienen möchte. Sofern man aber das Bemühen Jungers ernst nimmt, der Wahrnehmungsrealität der OEF-Kämpfer möglichst gerecht zu werden, dann muss man ihm zugestehen, bei seinen Lesern zumindest einen gewissen Anteil des Adrenalins zu provozieren, das in ihm und den Protagonisten der beschriebenen Szenen wirksam ist. Faktentreue und lebendige Darstellung müssen sich offenbar nicht ausschließen.

Kann man von einer Logik sprechen, der diese Wechselbeziehung von faktengestützter Kontrolle und vergegenwärtigender Darstellung folgt? Wenigstens scheint deutlich zu werden, dass das Erzählen vom Krieg unter Verdacht steht und dass dieser Verdacht um jeden Preis ausgeräumt werden soll. Anstelle der künstlerischen Imagination, die noch vor achtzig bzw. fünfzig Jahren problemlos zu

Hilfe genommen wurde, um extreme Lebenserfahrungen zu „verdichten", bedient sich Junger Mischung aus Bericht, Referieren und logischem Schließen, um eine möglichst lückenlose und intensive Erzählung zu liefern, in der es nicht eigentlich um „historische" Fakten geht, sondern um die Authentizität der Beschreibung von extremen Erfahrungen amerikanischer Elitesoldaten im Afghanistan-Einsatz.

[1] Seit 1960 gabe bereits eine Vielzahl von humanitären Hilfsaktionen im Ausland, bei denen Bundeswehrsoldaten zum Einsatz kamen. Neu ist, dass seit der Vereinigung auch Einsätze in (Bürger-) Kriegen hinzukommen, bei denen von der Waffe Gebrauch gemacht werden kann.

[2] Kurioserweise kann das Wort „Krieg" von politischer Seite nicht offiziell verwendet werden, da die Risiken der Soldaten in diesem Fall von den Versicherungen nicht gedeckt wären. Vgl. Werber, Niels. „Soldaten und Söldner. Krieg, Risiko und Versicherung in der ‚postheroischen' Epoche". In: *Merkur* 724/725, 2009, 793-802, 794.

[3] Vgl. die offiziellen Informationen im Internetportal der Bundeswehr: Todesfälle im Auslandseinsatz seit 1992. Verfügbar unter: http://www.bundeswehr.de/portal/a/bwde/!ut/p/c4/DcjBDYAgDAXQWVyA3r25hXohRT7YgMUE1ITpJe_2aKdB-ZXITYpyppW2Q2b3Gfd5mAgPTVDT-cxQ-6i3gVMb04pHDYycYeWyEK3cOt1pmX5GIQYT/#par6.

[4] Seit 1990 kam es zu insgesamt 19 Selbstmorden während Auslandeinsätzen. Siehe Fußnote 3.

[5] Zum Afghanistan-Einsatz vgl. den Fortschrittsbericht Afghanistan zur Unterrichtung des Deutschen Bundestags von Dezember 2010. Verfügbar unter: http://www.bundesregierung.de/Content/DE/__Anlagen/2010/2010-12-13-fort schrittsbericht-afghanistan,property=publicationFile.pdf.

[6] Entscheidung der Bundesanwaltschaft vom 19. 3. 2010.

[7] Wenngleich einige Aspekte des Krieges in Afghanistan an Partisanenkriege erinnern, handelt es sich weniger um die Befreiung eines Landes von einer Okkupation mit Hilfe der einheimischen Bevölkerung, sondern um einen jahrzehntelangen Bürgerkrieg, in dem vor allem die Interessen von einzelnen Warlords und der Einsatz von Terror auch gegen die eigene Bevölkerung eine zentrale Rolle spielen.

[8] Münkler, Herfried. *Die neuen Kriege*. (Reinbek bei Hamburg: Rowohlt, 2002).

[9] In: Der Begriff des Politischen (1963), zitiert nach (Werber, Soldaten und Söldner, 794)

[10] Münkler, Herfried. „Heroische und postheroische Gesellschaften". In: *Merkur* 700, 2007, 742-52.

[11] Wohlgethan, Achim und Dirk Schulze. *Endstation Kabul*. Als deutscher Soldat in Afghanistan - ein Insiderbericht (Berlin: Ullstein, 2009). Wohlgethan, der nicht mehr der Bundeswehr angehört, veröffentlichte 2009 noch ein zweites Buch mit dem Titel *Operation Kunduz*, über einen weiteren, dreimonatigen Einsatz im Jahr 2003.

[12] Groos, Heike. *Ein schöner Tag zum Sterben*. Als Bundeswehrärztin in Afghanistan (Frankfurt a. M.: Fischer, 2009).

[13] Schwitalla, Artur. *Afghanistan, jetzt weiß ich erst...* Gedanken aus meiner Zeit als Kommandeur des Provincial Reconstruction Team Feyzabad (Berlin: Miles, 2010).

[14] Weitere deutsche Erfahrungsberichte finden sich in den Sammlungen: Heike, Groos. *Das ist auch euer Krieg:* Deutsche Soldaten berichten von ihren Einsätzen. (Frankfurt: Krüger, 2010) und: Brinkmann, Sascha und Hoppe, Joachim. *Generation Einsatz:* Fallschirmjäger berichten ihre Erfahrungen aus Afghanistan (Frankfurt: Krüger 2010).

[15] Krakauer, Jon. *Auf den Feldern der Ehre*. Die Tragödie des Soldaten Pat Tillman (München: Piper, 2011).
[16] Junger, Sebastian: *War. Ein Jahr im Krieg*. Übers. T. Schwaner. (München: Karl Bleßing, 2010). OA: Junger, Sebastian. *War* (London: Fourth Estate, 2010).
[17] Klein, Christian und Martinez, Matias. *Wirklichkeitserzählungen*. Felder, Formen und Funktionen nichtliterarischen Erzählens (Stuttgart, Weimar: Metzler, 2009).
[18] Schulz, Winfried H. zit. nach Matías Martínez. „Erzählen im Journalismus". In: Klein/Martínez, *Wirklichkeitserzählungen*, 184.
[19] Schulz, Erzählen im Journalismus, 184.
[20] Wohlgethan, *Endstation Kabul*, 184
[21] Wohlgethan, *Endstation Kabul*, 209 f.
[22] Groos, Ein schöner Tag zum Sterben, 19.
[23] Groos, Ein schöner Tag zum Sterben, 128.
[24] Groos, Ein schöner Tag zum Sterben, 211.
[25] Neben dieser Hauptkritik beschreibt sie auch den vielfach unsensiblen oder sogar würdelosen Umgang der Bürokratie und der Generalität den toten Soldaten und den Gefühlen der überlebenden Kameraden. Z. B. (Groos, *Ein schöner Tag*, 64 ff.)
[26] Groos, Ein schöner Tag zum Sterben, 205.
[27] Schwitalla, Afghanistan, jetzt weiß ich erst..., 264.
[28] Laut Krakauer war Tillman ständig mit einem Buch unterwegs und las R. W. Emerson ebenso wie N. Chomskys polititische Interventionen.
[29] Krakauer, Auf den Feldern der Ehre, 186.
[30] Krakauer, Auf den Feldern der Ehre, 304.
[31] Krakauer, Auf den Feldern der Ehre, 323.
[32] Krakauer, Auf den Feldern der Ehre, 325.
[33] Krakauer, Auf den Feldern der Ehre, 314.
[34] Junger, *Im Krieg*, 44. „After a while we see lights moving on the slopes of the Abas Ghar, almost certainly Taliban fighters gathering up their wounded and dead. A soldier radios that in and suggests dropping artillery on them. Battalion is worried the lights might be shepherds up in the high pastures and denies the request. / ‚Put the .50 over it, we just had a fucking TIC [troops in contact], fuck those people', someone says". Junger, *War*, 30.
[35] Junger, *Im Krieg*, 218. „[…] the inhabitants are hard-core Taliban – the guys say they can tell by the looks in their eyes". Junger, *War*, 181.
[36] Junger, *Im Krieg*, 27.
[37] Junger, *Im Krieg*, 22. „It was as if every living thing in the valley, even the wildlife, wanted them gone". Junger, *War*, 12.
[38] Junger, *Im Krieg*, 21. „[…] the Korengal Valley was starting to acquire a reputation as a place that could alter your mind in terrible and irreversible ways". Junger, *War*, 10.
[39] Junger, *Im Krieg*, 54.
[40] Junger, *Im Krieg*, 23.
[41] Junger, *Im Krieg*, 163.
[42] Einem Soldaten, der nach ein paar Monaten Afghanistan seinen Betreuer um Rat bittet, wird empfohlen „mit dem Rauchen anzufangen". Junger, *War*, 40.

[43] Junger, *Im Krieg*, 186. „You're thinking that this guy could have murdered your friend [...]. The cheering comes from knowing that that's someone we'll never have to fight again". Junger, *War*, 153.

[44] Junger, *Im Krieg*, 187.

[45] Zu Soldaten in „postheroischen Gesellschaften" siehe die oben zitierten Texte von N. Werber und Münkler sowie: Speckmann, Thomas. „Wie unheroisch ist der Westen? Eine historische Rückschau". In: *Merkur* 745, 2011, 528-36.

[46] Das gilt für die Romane von E. M. Remarque, A. Zweig, E. Köppen, L. Renn ebenso wie für das „Tagebuch" von E. Jünger und noch für die Bücher zum Zweiten Weltkrieg von H. Böll, Th. Plievier und A. Kluge.

[47] Junger, *Im Krieg*, 8.

[48] Junger, *Im Krieg*, 39.

[49] Junger, *Im Krieg*, 8 f..

[50] Junger, *Im Krieg*, 145 f.

[51] Junger, *Im Krieg*, 146.

Helmut Galle ist seit 2001 Professor für Deutsche Literatur an der Universidade de São Paulo. Studium der Älteren und Neueren Deutschen Literatur an der Freien Universität Berlin und 1989 Promotion mit einer Dissertation zum Thema *Deutsche Psalmendichtung vom 16. bis zum 20. Jahrhundert*. Im August 2011 Habilitation (*Livre-docência*) an der Universidade de São Paulo mit einer Arbeit über *Possibilidade(s) da autobiografia*. DAAD-Lektor in Portugal, Brasilien und Argentinien. Zahlreiche Veröffentlichungen zur Autobiographie, zum Kollektiven Gedächtnis, zur Darstellung von Gewalt und zu verschiedenen deutschsprachigen Autoren. Zur Zeit Arbeit an einem Projekt zum Verhältnis von Fakt und Fiktion in Werken der deutschen Gegenwartsliteratur.

Le vrai problème n'est pas de raconter –
Jorge Semprún und das 20. Jahrhundert

Ursula Hennigfeld

Jorge Semprún gilt als „europäischer Autor par excellence", als Vermittler zwischen den Sprachen und Kulturen, als „Zeuge des Jahrhunderts" oder als „ein wahrhaft mit dem Jahrhundert verbundener Reisender, Held und Zeitzeuge der Geschichte" ("auténtico viajero comprometido con el siglo y protagonista y testigo de la historia". Nicolas Sarkozy nennt ihn in einem Nachruf eine „Leuchtgestalt der engagierten Literatur des 20. Jahrhunderts".[1] Das 20. Jahrhundert, von dem Semprúns Werke zeugen, ist vor allem das Jahrhundert der Katastrophen, geprägt von militärischen Konflikten und dem ungeheuerlichen Verbrechen der Shoah. In der Biographie des republikanischen Anti-Franquisten, Buchenwald-Überlebenden, Ex-Kommunisten und überzeugten Europäers Jorge Semprún kreuzen sich individuelle und kollektive Geschichte; in seinem literarischen Werk sind individuelle Erinnerung und kollektives Gedächtnis auf das Engste miteinander verbunden.

Die maßgeblichen Stationen seines Lebens korrespondieren mit den wichtigsten Ereignissen des 20. Jahrhunderts.[2] Jorge Semprún wird am 10.12.1923 in Madrid als Sohn einer großbürgerlichen, republikanischen Familie geboren. Als der Spanische Bürgerkrieg ausbricht, flüchtet die Familie zunächst nach Den Haag, später nach Paris. Dort besucht Semprún das berühmte Gymnasium Henri IV. und studiert Philosophie an der Sorbonne. 1941 schließt er sich der Résistance an, genauer der Organisation *Francs-Tireurs et Partisans*. Zwei Jahre später wird er von der Gestapo arretiert, gefoltert und nach Buchenwald deportiert. Dort arbeitet er in der sogenannten „Arbeitsstatistik", in der er auf Karteikarten Neuankömmlinge sowie verstorbene Häftlinge ein- bzw. austrägt. Diese Arbeit verdankt er dem lagerinternen Widerstand der KPD, der er als politischer Häftling („Rotspanier") angehört.

Nach der Befreiung des Lagers kehrt er nach Paris zurück und arbeitet zunächst als Übersetzer für die UNESCO. Später koordiniert er unter dem Decknamen Federico Sánchez den kommunistischen Widerstand gegen Franco. Aufgrund von kritischen Äußerungen und mangelnder Linientreue wird Semprún jedoch – kurz nach dem Erscheinen seines ersten Romans *Le grand voyage* im Jahr 1963 – aus der KP ausgeschlossen. Nach Francos Tod wird Semprún von 1988-1991 spanischer

Kulturminister unter der Regierung von Felipe González. Als Minister eher glücklos, kehrt er jedoch bald nach Paris zurück.

Jorge Semprún hat sowohl autofiktionale Romane über seine Lagererfahrung als auch über seine Kindheit, seinen Widerstand gegen Franco, die Erinnerung an den Spanischen Bürgerkrieg und die Aufarbeitung des Franquismus verfasst. Außerdem ist er Autor einiger Dramen und zahlreicher Filmdrehbücher.[3] Neben Literaturpreisen wie dem Prix Formentor (1963), Prix Fémina (1969), Premio Planeta (1977) und dem Literaturpreis für Menschenrechte (1995) ist Semprún u.a. mit dem Friedenspreis des Deutschen Buchhandels (1994), dem Weimar-Preis (1995) und der Goethe-Medaille (2003) der Stadt Weimar, dem Staatspreis für Europäische Literatur (2006) und der Medalla de Oro de Bellas Artes (2008) ausgezeichnet worden. Seit 1996 war er Mitglied der Académie Goncourt; eine Berufung in die Académie Française hat Semprún abgelehnt, da er dafür seine spanische Staatsbürgerschaft hätte aufgeben müssen.

In der Sekundärliteratur wird vielfach die Bedeutung von Sempruns Werk für die Historiographie des 20. Jahrhunderts oder die Identitätsproblematik und intertextuelle Dimension seiner Texte untersucht, dafür stehen in jüngster Zeit stellvertretend die Dissertationen von Ulrike Vordermark und Monika Neuhofer.[4] Beide gehen – im Anschluss an Philippe Lejeune – von einem autobiographischen Pakt aus, den Semprún mit dem Leser schließt und ordnen Semprún dem *autobiographischen* Schreiben zu. Anders als autobiographische Texte dies in der Regel suggerieren, schreibt er jedoch gezielt gegen die Konzeption eines einheitlichen Subjekts im Schreibprozess an. Daher halte ich es für angemessener, seine Werke im Anschluss an Serge Doubrovsky als *autofiktionale* Texte zu bezeichnen. Denn der Ich-Erzähler jener Texte, die um Buchenwald kreisen, rekurriert immer wieder auf den Schreibprozess, weist das eigene Schreiben als fiktional aus und dekonstruiert durch Metakommentare jeglichen Authentizitätsanspruch seiner Texte.[5]

Semprún spricht sich auch im Kontext der Shoah klar dafür aus, dass das Zeugnis der literarischen Fiktion bedürfe. Keine historische Rekonstruktion, sondern nur die Literatur könne das mitteilen, was er als Essenz der eigenen Erfahrung (*la vérité essentielle de l'expérience*) bezeichnet.[6] Erinnerung und Vergessen werden zum Strukturprinzip der Darstellung selbst.

Im Folgenden werde ich Sempruns eigenständige Position in der Debatte über die Unsagbarkeit und Undarstellbarkeit der Shoah resümieren (1.), um dann auf seine Konzeption einer *mémoire charnelle* einzugehen (2.). Das spezifische

Leistungsvermögen der Literatur und die Art und Weise, wie Semprún Erinnerung literarisch inszeniert, werde ich anhand der Figuren des „Muselmanns" (3.) und des Wiedergängers (4.) erläutern.

1. Der Topos der Unsagbarkeit und Undarstellbarkeit der Shoah

Jorge Semprún folgt – anders als beispielsweise Robert Antelme, David Rousset oder Claude Lanzmann – keinem dokumentarischen Ansatz.[7] Stattdessen wählt er die literarische Inszenierung von Erinnerung, da das Vermögen der Literatur für ihn vor allem darin besteht, die Erinnerung in all ihren Facetten und ihrer synästhetischen Qualität an die folgenden Generationen weiterzugeben. Seine literarischen Vorbilder in Bezug auf diese Entscheidung für eine fiktionale Bearbeitung der Shoah sind vor allem Primo Levi, den er explizit in seinen Werken erwähnt, und implizit – so meine These – auch Jean Cayrol. Semprún und Cayrol eint zum Beispiel die Konzeption des Überlebenden als Wiedergänger. Cayrol nennt diesen Wiedergänger ‚Lazarus', Semprún spricht vom ‚revenant'. Darauf werde ich im 4. Abschnitt zurückkommen.

Maurice Blanchot hatte die Shoah als *Ereignis ohne Zeugen* bezeichnet. Im Grunde könne nur die Unmöglichkeit des Zeugnisses bezeugt werden. Giorgio Agamben nennt die Shoah sogar ein *Ereignis ohne Zeugen im doppelten Sinne*.[8] Jean-François Lyotard hat in seinen Überlegungen zum *différend* (Widerstreit) dargelegt, dass das grundlegende Problem darin bestehe, dass man als Toter nicht den eigenen Tod in der Gaskammer bezeugen kann. Das Opfer der Shoah kann nicht nachweisen, dass es Unrecht erlitten hat, da nicht nur die zur Beweisführung nötigen Dokumente, sondern auch der Kläger selbst vernichtet wurden.[9] Nur die Kunst könne auf das Undarstellbare verweisen. Geoffrey Hartman hingegen sieht im „Reden-über" eine der wichtigsten Aufgaben von Erinnerungskulturen, die sich nicht hinter das Nicht-Verstehbare der Shoah zurückziehen sollten.[10]

In seinem gesamten Werk setzt sich Semprún mit der Frage auseinander, ob die Shoah darstellbar, mitteilbar ist.[11] Ausgangspunkt seiner Überlegungen ist Wittgensteins Diktum „Wovon man nicht sprechen kann, darüber muß man schweigen".[12] Semprún ist jedoch der Ansicht, dass die Literatur es sich gerade zur Aufgabe machen muss, das zu behandeln, worüber man (scheinbar) nicht sprechen kann:

> Ist die Literatur nicht eben der Versuch, die Lust, sogar die Leidenschaft, über das Verschwiegene, das Verdrängte, das Unsagbare zu reden und zu schreiben?

Wovon man nicht sprechen kann, weil es verboten oder verdrängt ist, weil es nicht zur Rede kommt, nicht in Rede steht, darüber muß man schreiben.

Darüber darf man keinesfalls schweigen.[13]

Es gibt also nichts, was *per se* unsagbar wäre, sondern nur Dinge, die der offizielle Diskurs, die Sprache der Macht, verbietet oder verdrängt. Wie Ulrike Vordermark zu Recht hervorhebt, wendet sich Semprún dezidiert gegen den Topos der Undarstellbarkeit und zeigt vielmehr, dass die Grenzen – sowohl des Darstellbaren als auch die Grenze zwischen Fiktion und historischer Wahrheit – nicht für immer festgeschrieben sind, sondern von der Kunst verschoben werden können.[14]

Semprún betont, dass das Erlebte keinesfalls unsagbar (*indicible*), sondern vielmehr unlebbar (*invivable*) war. Es gehe nicht so sehr um die Frage nach der *Form* eines möglichen Zeugnisses, sondern um seine *Substanz*. Der Topos der Unsagbarkeit sei nur ein Vorwand oder Faulheit.[15] Entscheidend sei vielmehr, ob man als Zuhörer alles anhören, sich alles vorstellen könne. Wie man das Erlebte später – falls man überlebt – mitteilen könne, diskutieren in *L'écriture ou la vie* die Häftlinge schon im KZ:

> Das wirkliche Problem ist nicht das Erzählen, wie schwierig es auch sein mag... Sondern das Zuhören... Wird man unseren Geschichten zuhören, auch wenn sie gut erzählt sind ? [...] Gut erzählt heißt: daß man gehört wird. Das gelingt nicht ohne ein paar Kunstgriffe. Genügend, daß es Kunst wird.[16]

Der Zuhörer bzw. Leser muss Geduld (patience), Leidenschaft (passion), Mitleid (compassion) und Unerbittlichkeit (rigueur) aufbringen, um dem Zeugnis folgen zu können. Um die Aufmerksamkeit des Lesers nicht zu verlieren, braucht das Zeugnis des Überlebenden die literarische Fiktion. Nur wenn das Zeugnis des Überlebenden von einem gemeinsamen kulturellen, mythischen und literarischen Erfahrungsschatz ausgeht, kann und will der Zuhörer bzw. Leser dem Überlebenden folgen.

2. *Mémoire charnelle*

Semprún hebt in seinen Romanen mehrfach hervor, dass die Erinnerung des Augenzeugen eine ganz spezifische Qualität hat, da sie alle Sinne umfasst und eine körperliche Dimension hat, die mit seinem Tod unwiederbringlich verloren geht. Diese besondere Qualität der Erinnerung nennt er *mémoire immédiate* oder *mémoire charnelle*:[17]

> Der Tag würde kommen, relativ bald, an dem es keine Überlebenden von Buchenwald mehr gäbe. Es würde kein unmittelbares Gedächtnis von Buchenwald mehr geben: niemand mehr könnte mit Wörtern der körperlichen Erinnerung sprechen, nicht nur mit den Worten einer theoretischen Rekonstruktion sagen, wie der Hunger, der Schlaf, die Angst gewesen war, die gleißende Gegenwart des absoluten Bösen – in dem Maße absolut, wie es in jedem von uns nistet, als mögliche Freiheit. Niemand mehr hätte in seiner Seele und in seinem Gehirn unauslöschlich den Geruch von verbranntem Fleisch der Verbrennungsöfen.[18]

Die Literatur kann also nur die Erinnerung dieser Erinnerung bergen. Aber dass nur die Augenzeugen das Recht haben, von der Shoah und anderen traumatischen Erlebnissen zu berichten, dass nur sie die nötige Glaubwürdigkeit besitzen, hält er für einen Irrtum. Anders als etwa Claude Lanzmann begrüßt Semprún daher Bücher wie *Le non de Klara* von Soazig Aaron oder *Les bienveillantes* von Jonathan Littell, die als Nachgeborene und mit fiktionalen Mitteln das Thema der Shoah aus Opfersicht (Aaron) bzw. sogar aus der Täterperspektive (Littell) behandeln.[19] Nach dem Tod der Augenzeugen werde die Shoah kein Erlebnis mehr sein, sondern eine historische Gegebenheit. Nur die Literatur könne die Erinnerung an die Vernichtung durch die Nazis lebendig halten und sie so der „objektiven Kälte der Wissenschaft" entreißen.[20] Diese Einschätzungen legt Semprún nicht in theoretischen Manifesten, sondern als Metakommentar seiner eigenen Gedächtnistheorie und Poetik in autofiktionalen Romanen dar.

Semprún erzählt in seinen Romanen auch mehrere, voneinander abweichende Varianten einer Geschichte, z.B. vom Tod seines Lehrers Maurice Halbwachs, vom Tod eines deutschen Soldaten und von der Goethe-Eiche im KZ Buchenwald. Damit weist er darauf hin, dass Erinnerung nicht nur von Individuum zu Individuum unterschiedlich ist, sondern auch für jeden Einzelnen einem ständigen Prozess der Veränderung unterworfen ist. Schreiben und Erinnern sind unabschließbare Prozesse, die bei jedem neuen Mal das zuvor Geschriebene oder Erinnerte überschreiben bzw. umschreiben

Die Erinnerung des Augenzeugen ist vor allem körperlich oder auch ‚ver-körpert'. Am Beginn der Transmission von Erinnerung steht der Blick. So heißt folgerichtig das erste Kapitel seines Romans *L'écriture ou la vie*, den man als Summe seines gesamten Werkes bezeichnen kann, *Le regard*. Der Roman beginnt mit dem Überlebenden, der aus dem KZ tritt und dessen Blick den von drei Offizieren kreuzt. In ihrem Blick sieht der Erzähler sein Spiegelbild, seinen eigenen, vom Horror des Erlebten getränkten Blick: „Es ist das Grauen meines Blicks, das der ihre offenbart, von Grauen erfüllt. Wenn ihre Blicke ein Spiegel sind, dann muß ich einen irren, verwüsteten Blick haben".[21] Wie Perseus den Blick der Medusa nur durch die mediale Spiegelung seines Schildes ohne Gefahr für sein Leben aushalten kann, ist auch ein unmittelbarer Zugang zum Grauen der Konzentrationslager unmöglich. Der Blick des Überlebenden muss gespiegelt werden, damit das Grauen nicht tötet: Für ihn selbst bilden die Offiziere den Spiegel, für den Leser ist die Literatur der mediale Schutzschild, der es ermöglicht, dem Blick der Medusa zu begegnen.

Zu den erinnerten Blicken gehören aber auch die „brüderlichen Blicke" der Mithäftlinge oder seines sterbenden Lehrers Maurice Halbwachs („Er lächelte, sterbend, sein Blick ruhte auf mir, brüderlich".), die leeren Blicke der unzähligen Leichen („Die weit geöffneten, über dem Grauen der Welt aufgerissenen Augen mit ihren undurchdringlichen, anklagenden Blicken") sowie der hasserfüllte Blick der SS („Der Blick des SS-Mannes dagegen, voll von beunruhigtem, tödlichem Haß").[22]

Neben dem Blick ist die Stimme ein wichtiges Element der Erinnerung, das im zweiten Kapitel, *Le kaddish*, im Vordergrund steht. Auf der Suche nach Überlebenden hört der Erzähler auf einmal eine Stimme – menschlich oder unmenschlich? – die das jüdische Totengebet singt: „Eine Stimme? Eher eine unmenschliche Wehklage. Das unartikulierte Stöhnen eines verwundeten Tiers. Ein schauriger Singsang, der das Blut gefrieren läßt".[23] Diese Stimme löst beim Erzähler nun die Erinnerung an andere Stimmen aus, z.B. an den *La Paloma* singenden deutschen Soldaten, der kurz darauf erschossen wird und an das Lied von der Lorelei, das ebenfalls auf den Tod verweist. Die Erinnerung an Stimmen umfasst sowohl Gespräche mit anderen Häftlingen, als auch die Befehle der SS („Krematorium ausmachen!", „Schnell!", „Weg", „Los!" usw.). Ebenso wie der Blick ist auch die Stimme ambivalent, kann Leben wie Tod bedeuten.

Sprache gerät bei Semprún im Sinne der derridianischen Platon-Analyse zum *phármakon*, kann Gift wie Heilmittel sein.[24] Für Semprún ist die deutsche Sprache so ambivalent wie die Erinnerung: Sie oszilliert zwischen Weimar als paradigmatischem Ort der Klassik und einer kritischen Vernunft einerseits und Buchenwald als Ort der Vernichtung und des radikal Bösen (als Teil menschlicher Willensfreiheit) andererseits. Sie ist sowohl Sprache der Macht als auch Sprache des Widerstands gegen die Macht.[25] Die Erinnerung aber ist immer literarisch überformt, z.B. wenn den Alpträumen vom KZ das zweimalige Singen einer Nachtigall vorausgeht. Selbst die Abwesenheit von Stimmen – z.B. von Vogelstimmen auf dem Ettersberg – wird bedeutsam und illustriert die allgegenwärtige Präsenz des Todes, der zum Verstummen bringt. Schreiben wird so bei Semprún nicht nur zur Erinnerung an

Stimme als Präsenz eines Lebendigen, sondern außerdem als Abwesenheit von Stimme zur Todeserfahrung.

Geruchssinn und Tastsinn bilden ebenfalls eine Dimension der *mémoire charnelle*, die in den Leitmetaphern von Rauch (bzw. dem Geruch nach verbranntem Menschenfleisch) und Schnee literarisch überformt wird. Sie leiten die unbewusste, im Wachzustand oder in Träumen wieder ausgelöste Erinnerung an das KZ ein, machen aber gleichzeitig deutlich, dass ein direkter, klarer, unverstellter Zugang zu Vergangenheit und den eigenen Erlebnissen unmöglich ist. Sie sind sowohl konkrete Lebenswirklichkeit im KZ als auch Metaphern für die Körperlichkeit der Erinnerung und Symbole des Todes. Nur im Medium literarischer Fiktion kann die synästhetische, körperliche Dimension der Erinnerung, zu der notwendigerweise auch das Vergessen gehört, kommuniziert werden. Damit illustriert Semprún ein Paradox der Shoah-Literatur: Einerseits soll sie die Erinnerung an die Opfer bewahren und den Tod überwinden, andererseits wird sie selbst zur Spur der Abwesenheit und der Macht des Todes.[26] Schreiben erweist sich in diesem Sinne als unabschließbarer Prozess, als *tâche interminable* im Kampf gegen Macht, Vergessen und Tod.

3. Der „Muselmann"

In vielen Romanen über das KZ werden die sogenannten „Muselmänner" behandelt. Als „Muselmänner" werden im KZ-Jargon diejenigen Häftlinge bezeichnet, die den Überlebenskampf aufgegeben haben und nur noch dahinvegetieren.[27] Sie verweigern die Zwangsarbeit und warten – scheinbar seelenlosen Tieren gleich – nur noch auf ihren baldigen Tod. Dabei taucht die Frage auf, ob diese vom Tode Gezeichneten noch als menschliche Wesen bezeichnet werden können:

> Der Muselmann ist der zerstörte Mensch zwischen Leben und Tod. Er ist das Opfer einer schrittweisen Vernichtung des Menschen. Bevor absolute Macht mit unmittelbarer Körpergewalt tötet, betreibt sie eine gezielte Politik der Verelendung, der Transformation der Conditio humana.[28]

Wolfgang Sofsky, der das Phänomen des „Muselmanns" auch aus medizinischer Sicht beleuchtet, bezweifelt, dass der „Muselmann" in Kategorien der Nosologie überhaupt angemessen zu verstehen ist. Die „materielle und soziale Situation der absoluten Ohnmacht" entziehe sich eigentlich der Benennung mit Hilfe von medizinischen Fachtermini. Die mentale Agonie des „Muselmanns" erreiche eine Grenze, die man kaum erklären könne.[29] Insofern scheint er ein Produkt des Lagers und ein ethisches Grenzphänomen zu sein, dem der medizinische oder wissenschaftliche Diskurs nicht gerecht werden kann.

In den meisten Überlebendenberichten werden die „Muselmänner" jedoch eindeutig abwertend und negativ beschrieben, u.a. auch bei Jean Améry und Primo Levi.[30] Agamben weist darauf hin, dass die „Muselmänner" zwar von den Überlebenden als zentrales Element der Konzentrationslager beschrieben werden, in historischen Untersuchungen jedoch selten vorkommen. Er glaubt jedoch, dass der „Muselmann" entscheidender Schlüssel zum Verständnis von Auschwitz sei. Agamben betont, dass ihr Anblick für die KZ-Häftlinge schwerer zu ertragen ist als der von Leichen, denn sie sind gleichsam eine Ankündigung des eigenen Schicksals, verweisen auf den (in den meisten Fällen) baldigen Tod im KZ.[31]

Wie Sofsky darüber hinaus betont, stirbt der „Muselmann" nicht nur den physischen Tod totaler Erschöpfung, sondern zuvor schon den sozialen Tod. In dem Maße, wie er sich von der Außenwelt abwendet, wenden sich die anderen Häftlinge von ihm ab. Er wird verlacht, erniedrigt und grausam behandelt, wird zum Sündenbock der Häftlingsgemeinschaft. Da er für Befehle und selbst rohe Gewalt unempfänglich ist, beleidigt er die Macht. Er wird zum doppelt Ausgegrenzten, SS wie Häftlinge hassen ihn. Er ist auch deswegen bei den Mithäftlingen so unbeliebt, weil er deutlich macht, dass die Demarkationslinie zwischen Leben und Tod im Lager aufgehoben ist. Der Tod ist nicht mehr Eintritt von einem klar definierten Zustand in einen anderen, der von Übergangsritualen begleitet wird. Der Tod des Einzelnen fällt im Lager nicht auf, jeder Tote wird sofort ersetzt. Da die Demarkationslinie zwischen Leben und Tod verschwommen ist, versuchen die Häftlinge, eine neue Grenze zu ziehen, indem sie die Muselmänner isolieren.[32]

Agamben weist auf die sowohl in Berichten wie in literarischen Texten über Konzentrationslager rekurrente Metapher der Gorgo Medusa hin. Primo Levi etwa beschreibt in *Se questo è un uomo* (*Ist das ein Mensch?*) den „Muselmann" mit Hilfe dieser Metapher: Er ist der, der ‚die Gorgo erblickt hat'. Auch hier scheint die normale Sprache zu versagen, das Erlebte nur mit Hilfe von literarischen Mythen und Metaphern kommunizierbar zu sein. Agamben fragt nun, was „die Gorgo erblicken" im Kontext des Lagers bedeuten soll und kommt zu der Schlussfolgerung, dass es „die Unmöglichkeit des Sehens zu erblicken" bedeutet. Der „Muselmann" könne nichts mehr sehen und erkennen außer der Unmöglichkeit zu sehen und zu erkennen.[33]

Diese grauenhafte Erfahrung schildert auch Semprún in seinen Romanen, kleidet sie aber in eine poetische Sprache, die den Kontrast zum Beschriebenen umso augenfälliger macht:

> Seit bald zwei Jahren lebte ich umringt von brüderlichen Blicken. Sofern es Blicke gab: die meisten Deportierten hatten keinen Blick mehr. Er war erloschen, umnebelt, blind geworden vom grellen Licht des Todes. Die meisten von ihnen lebten nur noch dahin: mattes Licht eines toten Sterns, ihr Auge.[34]

Anders als bei Améry und Levi werden die Muselmänner bei Semprún jedoch nicht negativ bewertet. In *Le mort qu'il faut* (*Der Tote mit meinem Namen*) steht ein sog. „Muselmann" im Zentrum des Romans, mit dem der Ich-Erzähler die Identität tauschen wird. Der autofiktionale Erzähler überlegt, was die kommunistischen Widerstandskämpfer im Lager eigentlich an den sog. Muselmännern stört:

> Die Muselmänner stören ihn [= den kommunistischen Mithäftling Kaminsky], das ist es. Sie verwirren durch ihre schiere Existenz das Bild, das er sich von der Welt der Konzentrationslager gemacht hat. Sie widersprechen dem Verhalten, verneinen es sogar, das ihm für das Überleben unabdingbar zu sein scheint. Die Muselmänner führen in sein ideologisches Weltbild ein ungreifbares Element der Unsicherheit ein, weil sie sich gerade aufgrund ihrer Natur, ihrer unproduktiven Marginalität, ihrer Ataraxie über die manichäische Logik des Widerstands, des Kampfs ums Dasein, ums Überleben hinwegsetzen.[35]

Während der „normale" Häftling verzweifelt versucht, die Gesetze des Lagers zu verstehen und Eindeutigkeit herzustellen, um seine Überlebenschancen zu erhöhen, bedeuten die Muselmänner gerade das Gegenteil, nämlich Ambivalenz („Sie verwirren [...] das Bild", „Sie widersprechen [...] verneinen", „führen [...] ein ungreifbares Element der Unsicherheit ein", „weil sie sich [...] über die manichäische Logik [...] hinwegsetzen"). Die Muselmänner irritieren also die bestehende Ordnung und den Ablauf im Lager, weil sie eben nicht kooperieren, nicht nützlich sind.

Der Ich-Erzähler verdankt jedoch einem „Muselmann" sein Überleben: Als die kommunistischen Gefangenen, die den heimlichen Widerstand in Buchenwald organisieren und die wichtigsten Posten besetzen, erfahren, dass die Lagerleitung sich nach dem Häftling Semprún erkundigt, interpretieren sie dieses Schreiben als große Gefahr. Denn wen man sucht, so die traurige Erfahrung, der soll exekutiert werden. Um Semprún zu retten, suchen die Kommunisten einen „Muselmann", mit dem er die Identität tauschen kann. Der künftige Tote soll unter Sempruns Namen sterben, Semprún mit dem Namen des anderen weiterleben. In François L., einem jungen

Pariser Studenten, der mit demselben Transport in Buchenwald eingetroffen ist, finden sie „le mort qu'il faut". Dieser junge Franzose ist von seinem eigenen Vater denunziert worden und wird innerhalb kürzester Zeit an Hunger und Erschöpfung sterben. Der Ich-Erzähler soll den Franzosen in der Krankenbaracke besuchen und die Identität mit ihm tauschen.

Als der Erzähler schließlich François L. in der Krankenbaracke kennenlernt, verschwimmen ihre Identitäten zunehmend. Dies schlägt sich auch auf sprachlicher Ebene nieder: Ist François L. zu Beginn des Treffens noch eine eigenständige Person, den der Erzähler beim Namen nennt, wird er später nur noch „er", „dieses Wesen", „mein Muselmann" oder sogar „das da" genannt. Der Erzähler verleibt sich den „Muselmann" also auch gleichsam auf sprachlicher Ebene in dem Maße ein, wie er sich seiner Identität bemächtigt:

> Er – falls es zulässig oder angemessen war, ein Personalpronomen zu verwenden; vielleicht wäre es richtiger, berechtigter gewesen, ‚es' zu sagen – , er jedenfalls war lediglich ein Haufen ekler Lumpen. Ein unförmiges Bündel, zusammengesackt an der Außenwand des Latrinengebäudes.[36]

Zunächst vollzieht der Erzähler die Geste der anderen Häftlinge nach, die sich von den Muselmännern abgrenzen. Auch er bezeichnet François L. als Lumpenhaufen („amoncellement de hardes") und unförmige Masse („tas informe"). Die Schwierigkeit der Benennung wird im Adjektiv „innommables" ausgedrückt (in der deutschen Übersetzung des Romans leider anders und etwas preziös mit „ein Haufen *ekler* Lumpen" widergegeben). Doch trotz der Abgrenzung von diesem abstoßenden und unbeschreiblichen Wesen wird deutlich: Indem der Erzähler mit ihm die Identität tauscht, wird auch er zum „Muselmann", das scheinbar Inhumane wird Teil von ihm, und er wird das Lager zwar überleben, trotzdem aber nie mehr verlassen können. Im Unterschied zu den anderen Gefangenen, die sich von den Muselmännern mit aller Gewalt abgrenzen wollen, stellt der Erzähler gerade die Gemeinsamkeiten zwischen sich und dem jungen Pariser Studenten fest:

> Dieser lebende Tote war ein junger Bruder, vielleicht mein *Doppelgänger*: ein anderes Ich oder ich selbst als ein anderer. Es war die erkannte Andersheit, die existentielle Identität, wahrgenommen als Möglichkeit, ein anderer zu sein, die uns einander so nahebrachte.[37]

Indem sich der Erzähler des „Muselmanns" bemächtigt, verleibt er sich auch das „élément d'incertitude" ein, das er nicht mehr loswerden kann und das seine Identität dauerhaft gefährden wird. Im Gegensatz zur von Agamben vertretenen These trifft den semprunianischen Erzähler jedoch keineswegs die Unmöglichkeit des Sehens. Sondern der Roman *Le mort qu'il faut* wie auch die anderen Buchenwald-Romane Semprúns heben gerade das Motiv des Sehens und des Blicks besonders stark hervor: Im Blick und der Beschreibung des Blickes werden alle menschlichen Beziehungen gestiftet, sei es der eigene Blick des Erzählers, der die amerikanischen Offiziere fürchterlich erschreckt, da sich in ihm das ganze Grauen des Erlebten spiegelt (hier wird der Überlebende selbst zu Medusa); sei es der brüderliche Blick des sterbenden Halbwachs und der solidarische Blick der kommunistischen Mithäftlinge, der hasserfüllte Blick der SS usw. Der Augenzeuge ist der, der mit eigenen Augen angesehen hat, was die Shoah bedeutet, er ist aber auch der, in dessen Blick das Grauen aufscheint. Nur im Blickkontakt, d.h. durch den furchterfüllten, brüderlichen, solidarischen oder hasserfüllten Blick der Anderen kann er zu sich selbst kommen. Damit ist er ein zutiefst relationales Subjekt, das nur durch die Bindung an andere zu einer – freilich immer nur vorübergehend fixierbarer – Identität gelangen kann.

4. Der revenant

Der Wiedergänger ist ein literarischer Topos, der beispielsweise aus Shakespeares *Hamlet* oder Ibsens *Die Gespenster* bekannt. Dem Wiedergänger begegnet man aber auch in Baudelaires *Fleurs du Mal*, genauer im *Spleen et idéal* betitelten Teil, dem das folgende Sonett angehört:

Der Wiederkehrende

Wie die Engel, deren Blicke sich verklären,

will ich an dein Lager wiederkehren,

mit dem Schattenwurf der Nächte gleite

lautlos ich an deine Seite.

Küsse sollst du von mir haben,

die kalt sind wie die Mondesstrahlen

und die den Schlangen gleichen,

die zärtlich um die Gräber schleichen.

224 Le vrai problème n'est pas de raconter

> Wenn bleich die Morgensonne gleißt,
>
> ist meine Bettstatt dann verwaist,
>
> und kalt bis in die Nacht hinein.
>
> Während andere dir Zärtlichkeiten geben,
>
> deiner Jugend, deinem Leben,
>
> soll meine Macht das Grauen sein.[38]

Das „je reviendrai" ist in Baudelaires Sonett kein Versprechen, sondern eine Drohung. Der nächtliche Besuch kommt lautlos („sans bruit"), kündigt kalte Küsse („baisers froids") und Schlangenliebkosungen an, deren Bisse bekanntlich töten („caresses de serpent"). Diese Schlange kriecht um eine „fosse" herum, hier assoziiert man sofort die „fosse commune", das Massengrab. Der unheimliche Wiedergänger steht im Zeichen der Abwesenheit („tu trouveras ma place vide"), der Stille („sans bruit"), der Kälte („il fera froid"), der Nacht („Avec les ombres de la nuit") und des Schreckens („effroi"). Sein erklärtes Ziel ist, über Leben und Jugend zu herrschen („Sur ta vie et sur ta jeunesse,/…je veux régner"). Zwar muss er dem Tag weichen, aber auch dieser ist schon leichenblass („matin livide"), ist also schon von der Vorahnung der Nacht und des Todes gezeichnet.

In diesem Sonett wird kein erotisches nächtliches Stelldichein geschildert, sondern eine *danse macabre*. Der geheimnisvolle Wiedergänger ist der Tod selbst. Stille, Schatten, Nacht, Kälte, Grab und Schrecken sind die Schlüsselwörter des Sonetts. Wie dieses Sonett exemplarisch deutlich macht, stellt das literarische Motiv des Wiedergängers eine Sprache bereit, in der das Grauen, auch das der Konzentrationslager, kommuniziert werden kann.

Baudelaire ist in diesem Zusammenhang bedeutsam, weil Semprúns Werk von Baudelaire-Intertexten durchzogen. Der Roman *Adieu, vive clarté…* (1998) verdankt sogar seinen Titel dem zweiten Vers aus Baudelaires *Chant d'Automne*.[39] Die Lyrik von Baudelaire stellt im Werk Semprúns eine Gemeinsamkeit zwischen Leser und Erzähler her, von der aus die Schilderung des Grauens ihren Anfang nimmt. Gleich im ersten Kapitel von *L'écriture ou la vie* zitiert Semprún das Gedicht *Le Voyage* aus dem sechsten und letzten, *La Mort* betitelten Teil der *Fleurs du Mal*:

> O Tod, alter Kapitän, es ist Zeit! laß uns die Anker lichten...
>
> [...]
>
> ...unsere Herzen, die du kennst, sind voller Strahlen.[40]

Der Intertext wird eingefügt, als der Erzähler den Tod seines Lehrers Maurice Halbwachs beschreibt. Über den baudelaireschen Intertext wird das Motiv der Reise mit dem Tod und dem Bösen verbunden. Auf diese Weise gelingt es dem Ich-Erzähler, Worte für das traumatische und hochemotionale Erlebnis zu finden, den Tod von Halbwachs mit ansehen zu müssen:

> Und in jäher Panik, da ich nicht weiß, welchen Gott ich anrufen könnte, damit er Maurice Halbwachs begleite, doch im Bewußtsein, daß ein Gebet notwendig ist, spreche ich mit zugeschnürter Kehle und lauter Stimme, wobei ich versuche, sie zu beherrschen, ihr die nötige Klangfarbe zu geben, einige Verse von Baudelaire. Das ist das einzige, was mir einfällt.[41]

In der geschilderten Situation äußerster Bedrängnis, Panik und Verzweiflung („dans une panique soudaine", „la gorge serrée"), in der jeder Glaube an eine richtende, rettende höhere Instanz verloren ist („ignorant si je puis invoquer quelque Dieu"), bietet dem Erzähler nur die Literatur Zuflucht. Sie ermöglicht es dem Erzähler selbst im Lager, in dem die Grenze zwischen Leben und Tod unkenntlich geworden ist, noch einen Rest von Würde zu bewahren und erfüllt die Funktion eines Übergangsrituals. Dies wird im Bild des Todes als Fährmann evoziert, der die Toten über den Fluss des Vergessens in die Unterwelt bringt.

Die sogenannte *littérature des camps* hat vielfach die Figur des Wiedergängers (*revenant*) gewählt, um die Erinnerungen an das KZ literarisch zu gestalten. Der Überlebende ist ein *revenant* im doppelten Sinne: einerseits kehrt er (in den meisten Fällen) in das Land zurück, aus dem er deportiert wurde, andererseits ist er ein Wiedergänger, der aus der Welt des Todes in die Welt der Lebenden zurückkehrt. Er hat aber nicht vergessen, was er in der Welt des Todes erlebt hat und bringt diese Erfahrung in die Welt der Lebenden mit, wie Semprún in *L'écriture ou la vie* schreibt: „Die Gewißheit, daß es nicht wirklich eine Rückkehr gegeben hatte, daß ich nicht wirklich zurückgekehrt war, daß ein wesentlicher Teil von mir nie zurückkehren würde, diese Gewißheit erfüllte mich bisweilen, verkehrte mein Verhältnis zur Welt, zu meinem eigenen Leben".[42] Dass eine vollständige Rückkehr unmöglich und das Erlebte irreversibel bleibt, ist für den Erzähler eine Gewissheit

(„certitude"). Das Erlebte wirkt sich sowohl auf das Verhältnis zur Welt („mon rapport au monde") als auch zu sich selbst („à ma propre vie") aus.

Auch der Schriftsteller Jean Cayrol, der in den 1950er Jahren beschließt, in seinen Romanen eine fiktionale Annäherung an die Shoah zu versuchen, geht davon aus, dass die Erfahrung des Überlebenden nicht nur diesen für immer verändert, sondern auch die Welt, in die er zurückkehrt.[43] Die Welt wird für immer von jener Erfahrung des Todes geprägt sein. Das KZ ist kein abgeschlossener Bereich jenseits von Raum und Zeit, sondern dringt in die normale Welt ein. Auch nach dem Ende des Zweiten Weltkrieges gebe es ein „élément concentrationnaire", das bestehen bleibt.[44] Cayrol verbindet die biblische Figur des Lazarus mit der Erfahrung des KZ. Der Überlebende ist aus der Hölle des Lagers zurückgekehrt, kann aber anders als sein biblisches Vorbild in der Welt der Lebenden nicht mehr heimisch werden und hat auch keine Hoffnung auf Erlösung.[45]

Seine Thesen zum „quotidien concentrationnaire" und zum Überlebenden als Lazarus hat Cayrol 1950 in seinem Essay *Lazare parmi nous* (*Lazarus unter uns*) formuliert.[46] Seines Erachtens muss aus der Erfahrung des KZ eine neue Literatur entstehen, die er „lazarenische Kunst" nennt. Der Protagonist einer solchen Literatur ist von einer seltsamen Gleichmut gekennzeichnet, wundert sich über nichts mehr und ist durch nichts zu erschüttern. Die Welt ist für ihn ambivalent geworden, er kann sich nicht mehr zurechtfinden, seine Identität ist multipel.[47] Der aus dem Konzentrationslager Befreite stellt fest, dass es kein „draußen" für ihn mehr gibt, die ganze Welt ist ihm zum Lager geworden. Wie Cayrol in seinen Romanen zeigt, ist für den Lazarus der Lager die Welt feindlich und unbewohnbar geworden.

Auch für den semprunianischen Wiedergänger, der mit einem „Muselmann" die Identität tauscht, bleibt das Lager das alles entscheidende, identifikatorische Erlebnis.[48] Diese Identität als Wiedergänger und die Erfahrung, den Tod gleichsam durchlebt zu haben, trennt den Überlebenden für immer von seinen Mitmenschen und kann nur im Medium der Literatur kommuniziert werden. Das wird dem Erzähler aus *L'écriture ou la vie* bereits klar, als er unmittelbar nach der Befreiung Buchenwalds auf alliierte Offiziere trifft, aus deren zutiefst erschrockenem Blick er auf seine Identität als Wiedergänger zurückgeworfen wird:

> Plötzlich ist mir eine Idee gekommen – sofern man jene belebende Hitzewallung, jenen Blutandrang, jenen Stolz auf ein Wissen des Körpers eine Idee nennen kann – , jedenfalls das plötzlich sehr starke Gefühl, dem Tod nicht entronnen zu sein, sondern ihn durchquert zu haben. Vielmehr von ihm durchquert worden zu sein. Ihn gewissermaßen durchlebt zu

> haben. Zurückgekehrt zu sein, wie man von einer Reise zurückkehrt, die dich verändert, vielleicht verklärt hat.
>
> Ich habe plötzlich begriffen, daß diese Soldaten recht hatten zu erschrecken, meinem Blick auszuweichen. Denn ich hatte den Tod nicht wirklich überlebt, ich war ihm nicht ausgewichen. Ich war ihm nicht entgangen. Vielmehr hatte ich ihn durchlaufen, von einem Ende zum andern. Ich hatte seine Wege durchlaufen, hatte mich darin verloren und wiedergefunden, ungeheurer Landstrich, durch den die Abwesenheit rinnt. Kurz, ich war ein Wiedergänger.[49]

Wie anhand der mehrmaligen Wiederholung von „soudain" deutlich wird, handelt es sich – analog zur *mémoire involontaire* bei Proust – auch bei der Erkenntnis um einen plötzlichen, unwillkürlichen Prozess. Doch es wird darüber hinaus deutlich, wie schwer es ist, das Erlebte und die Erkenntnis in Worte zu fassen: immer wieder wird die Erinnerung umformuliert, ergänzt, relativiert, mit anderen Worten umschrieben („si l'on peut appeler", „plutôt", „en quelque sorte", „peut-être", „en somme"). Dem erzählenden Ich ist etwas widerfahren, was es nicht aktiv herbeigeführt hat, wie die Passivkonstruktionen im ersten Abschnitt deutlich machen („D'avoir été", „De l'avoir vécue", „D'en être revenue"). Dennoch ist dies alles einer konkreten Person widerfahren, einem menschlichen Wesen, das nur langsam wieder zu Bewusstsein kommt und handlungsfähig wird. Darauf verweisen die Sätze im zweiten Abschnitt des Zitats, die in parallelem Satzbau alle mit „Je" beginnen („J'ai compris", „je n'avais pas", „J'étais" usw.). Die Erfahrung des Konzentrationslagers kann nicht heilen, ist irreversibel; der Überlebende ist für immer von ihr geprägt und traumatisiert. Das neutralere „verändert" („transformé") wird durch „verklärt" („transfiguré") ersetzt, das dem religiösen Sprachgebrauch entstammt und ebenso wie Cayrols Lazarus-Figur wiederum auf den biblischen Kontext verweist. Das Erlebte betrifft Geist und Körper des Überlebenden („idée", „sensation"). Wie auch an anderer Stelle wird abermals die Körperlichkeit betont, die die spezifische Qualität der Erinnerung des Augenzeugen ausmacht („savoir du corps"). Die Brutalität des Erlebten, der gewaltsame Eingriff in Psyche und Physis scheint auf, wenn der Erzähler sich selbst korrigiert, dass nicht er den Tod durchquert hat, sondern vielmehr selbst vom Tod durchquert worden ist („D'avoir été, plutôt, traversé par elle").

Fazit

Das Leben Jorge Semprúns ist von den Kriegen des 20. Jahrhunderts mehrfach auf die schrecklichste Weise erschüttert und in andere Bahnen gelenkt worden. Das prägendste Erlebnis des kommunistischen, antifaschistischen Widerstandskämpfers ist sicher das KZ Buchenwald. Um die Thematik des Erinnerns, Vergessens, Verdrängens und Schreibens kreisen seine literarischen Texte, die die Prozeßhaftigkeit der Erinnerung selbst zum Darstellungs- und Strukturprinzip machen. Seiner Ansicht nach bedarf es literarischer Fiktion, um die „vérité essentielle de l'expérience" mitteilen zu können und die „capacité d'écoute" des Lesers zu behalten. Einer theoretischen Rekonstruktion von Fakten oder einem dokumentarischen Zugang setzt er seine Poetik einer *mémoire charnelle* im Medium der Literatur entgegen. Dabei bleiben Sprache wie Erinnerung immer zutiefst ambivalent (*phármakon*). Die synästhetische *mémoire charnelle* des Augenzeugen kann nur im Medium der Literatur geborgen werden. Das als relational gedachte Subjekt der Zeugenschaft kann nur durch Blick und Stimme an die ethische Verpflichtung des Zuhörers appellieren und so auch von Rauch und Schnee (als Metaphern für Geruchs- und Tastsinn) sprechen.

Der „Muselmann", medizinisch nicht fassbares, biopolitisches Produkt des Lagers, ist das doppelte Ergebnis einer Grenzaufhebung (zwischen Leben und Tod, Humanem und Inhumanem) wie einer Grenzziehung (von anderen Häftlingen isoliert). Er zeigt insofern die perfide Logik der nationalsozialistischen Biopolitik, als auch die Opfer noch gezwungen werden, schuldig zu werden, indem sie sich von ihm lossagen. Diejenigen, die selbst unmenschlich handeln und mit der Macht kollaborieren, tun dies, um Menschen zu bleiben, d.h. um zu überleben. Indem er ihn zum Protagonisten seines Romans *Le mort qu'il faut* macht, verleiht Jorge Semprún jedoch – anders als etwa Primo Levi und Jean Améry – auch dem „Muselmann" eine Stimme und zeigt gerade durch den Identitäts- und Namenstausch die Übergänglichkeit und das Verschwimmen der Grenze. Das ‚ungreifbare Element der Unsicherheit' („élément d'incertitude insaisissable") ist genau das entscheidende Charakteristikum des „Muselmanns", das sich dem wissenschaftlichen Diskurs entzieht und die ethische Frage aufwirft, die im Medium der Literatur zwar nicht beantwortet, aber doch immerhin zur Sprache gebracht werden kann.

Der Wiedergänger (*revenant*) ist einerseits ebenso wie der „Muselmann" ein Ergebnis der nationalsozialistischen Biopolitik. Er ist jedoch auch ein Produkt der Literatur, ein Phantasma, das schon vor der Erfahrung der Shoah die Grenze zwischen Tod und Leben heimsucht. Semprún nutzt diese literarische Figur des *revenant*, um den Leser in die Welt des Todes mitzunehmen und eine Sprache für das unvorstellbare Grauen zu finden, das die Erfahrung des KZ bedeuten muss. Der

Wiedergänger tritt dem Vergessen entgegen, ohne dass er Eindeutigkeit schaffen oder Sinn stiften würde. Er beweist jedoch, welch immense Aufgabe der Literatur an der Grenze zwischen Leben und Tod zukommt und bezeugt die unabschließbare Aufgabe der Erinnerung. Die Verpflichtung, uns auf diesen unendlichen Prozess der Erinnerung und der Arbeit am kollektiven Gedächtnis einzulassen, um auch den Opfern eine Stimme zu verleihen, geht nun an uns über: Jorge Semprún ist am 7.6.2011 verstummt.

---

[1] Neuhofer, Monika. „Écrire un seul livre, sans cesse renouvelé". Jorge Sempruns literarische Auseinandersetzung mit Buchenwald (Frankfurt/M.: Klostermann, 2006), 21. Schütte, Wolfram. „Brüderlichkeit". Jorge Semprun, Zeuge des Jahrhunderts, wird 75. In: Frankfurter Rundschau vom 10.12.1998, 9. Jiménez Barca, Antonio. „Un tributo de literatura y memoria". In: El país vom 9.6.2011, 48. Communiqué de presse von Nicolas Sarkozy, Verfügbar unter: http://www.elysee.fr/president/les-actualites/communiques-de-presse/2011/deces-de-jorge-semprun.11529.html?search=Semprun&xtmc=Semprun&xc=1 abgerufen am: 30.06.2011.

[2] Zur Biographie Semprúns vgl. vor allem Cortanze, Gérard de. Jorge Semprun, l'écriture de la vie (Paris: Gallimard, 2005) sowie Augstein, Franziska. Von Treue und Verrat. Jorge Semprún und sein Jahrhundert (München: Beck, 2008).

[3] Zu den Werken über Buchenwald gehören die vor allem die Romane Le grand voyage (1963, dt. Die große Reise), L'évanouissement (1967, dt. Die Ohnmacht), Quel beau dimanche! (1980, dt. Was für ein schöner Sonntag!), L'écriture ou la vie (1994 dt. Schreiben oder Leben), Le mort qu'il faut (2001, dt. Der Tote mit meinem Namen) sowie das Drama Le retour de Carola Neher (1997, dt. Bleiche Mutter, zarte Schwester). Seine Kindheit in Spanien schildert er in Adieu, vive clarté... (1998, dt. Unsre allzu kurzen Sommer), seine Agententätigkeit u.a. in La deuxième mort de Ramón Mercader (1969, dt. Der zweite Tod des Ramón Mercader), Autobiografía de Federico Sánchez (1977, dt. Federico Sánchez: Eine Autobiographie), Federico Sánchez vous salue bien (1993, dt. Federico Sánchez verabschiedet sich). Den Spanischen Bürgerkrieg behandelt sein letzter Roman Veinte años y un día (2003, Zwanzig Jahre und ein Tag). Die bekanntesten Filme, zu denen er das Drehbuch verfasste, sind La guerre est finie (1966, Der Krieg ist aus, Regie Alain Resnais), Z ou l'anatomie d'un assassinat politique (1969, Z oder die Anatomie eines politischen Mordes, Regie Constantin Costa-Gavras), Stavisky (1974, Stavisky, Regie Alain Resnais). Zusammen mit Dominique de Villepin hat er seine Vision für ein vereintes, pluralistisches Europa skizziert: L'homme européen (2005, Was es heißt, Europäer zu sein).

[4] Vgl. Neuhofer, Écrire un seul livre und Vordermark, Ulrike. Das Gedächtnis des Todes. Die Erfahrung des Konzentrationslagers Buchenwald im Werk Jorge Semprúns (Köln: Böhlau, 2008).

[5] „Autofiction" verwende ich im Anschluss an Serge Doubrovsky als Hybrid zwischen Autobiographie und Fiktion. Zur Theorie der Autofiktion vgl. Gronemann, Claudia. Postmoderne/postkoloniale Konzepte der Autobiographie in der französischen und maghrebinischen Literatur. Autofiction – nouvelle Autobiographie – double Autobiographie – aventure du texte (Hildesheim: Olms, 2002), speziell zur Autofiktion bei Semprún vgl. Molero de la Iglesia, Alicia. La autoficción en España. Jorge Semprún, Carlos Barral, Luis Goytisolo, Enriqueta Antolín y Antonio Muñoz Molina (Bern: Lang, 2000). Soto Fernández verwendet in Bezug auf Semprún den Terminus „autobiografía ficticia". Soto Fernández, Liliana. La

autobiografía ficticia en Miguel de Unamuno, Carmen Martín Gaite y Jorge Semprún. (Madrid: Pliegos, 2000).

[6] „Tout y sera vrai... sauf qu'il manquera l'essentielle vérité, à laquelle aucune reconstruction historique ne pourra jamais atteindre, pour parfaite et omnicompréhensive qu'elle soit... [...] L'autre genre de compréhension, la vérité essentielle de l'expérience, n'est pas transmissible... Ou plutôt, elle ne l'est que par l'écriture littéraire". Semprún, Jorge. *L'écriture ou la vie.* (Paris: Gallimard, 1994) 167. „Alles darin wird wahr sein... außer daß die wesentliche Wahrheit fehlen wird, an die keine historische Rekonstruktion je herankommen wird, so vollkommen und allgemeinverständlich sie auch sein mag... [...] Die andere Art des Verstehens, die grundlegende Wahrheit der Erfahrung, die läßt sich nicht wiedergeben... Oder vielmehr nur durch das literarische Schreiben..." Semprún, Jorge. *Schreiben oder Leben.* Aus dem Französischen von Eva Moldenhauer (Frankfurt/M.: Suhrkamp, 2002), 152.

[7] Diese drei Namen sollen stellvertretend für eine realistisch-dokumentarische Annäherung an die Shoah in Form von Erlebnisberichten, Sachbüchern und Dokumentarfilmen stehen. Antelme, Robert. *L'espèce humaine.* (Paris: Cité Universelle, 1947); Rousset, David. *L'univers concentrationnaire.* (Paris: Pavois, 1946); Lanzmann, Claude. *Shoah* (New Yorker Films, 1985).

[8] „Es ist ebenso unmöglich, von innen her davon Zeugnis abzulegen – denn es ist nicht möglich, aus dem Inneren des Todes Zeugnis abzulegen, es gibt keine Stimme für das Verschwinden der Stimme – wie von außen her – , denn der *outsider* ist *per definitionem* vom Ereignis ausgeschlossen". Agamben, Giorgio. *Was von Auschwitz bleibt. Das Archiv und der Zeuge (Homo sacer III).* Aus dem Italienischen von Stefan Monhardt (Frankfurt/M.: Suhrkamp, 2003), 31. – Auch Shoshana Felman nennt die Shoah das „unbezeugte Ereignis", da es ein Ereignis sei, dass in der planvollen Auslöschung seiner Zeugen besteht und die Möglichkeit einer „Gemeinschaftlichkeit des Sehens" ausschließe. Felman, Shoshana. „Im Zeitalter der Zeugenschaft: Claude Lanzmanns Shoah". In: Baer, Ulrich (Hrsg.). *Niemand zeugt für den Zeugen. Erinnerungskultur und historische Verantwortung nach der Shoah* (Frankfurt/M.: Suhrkamp, 2000), 173-193, hier 181.

[9] Lyotard, Jean-François. *Le différend.* (Paris: Minuit, 1983). Es stellt sich jedoch die Frage, ob wirklich nur als Augenzeuge der Shoah bezeichnet werden kann, wer in der Gaskammer umgekommen ist. Augenzeuge ist wohl auch derjenige, der im KZ gewesen ist und überlebt hat. Zur Kritik an Agamben vgl. auch Slavoj Žižek, der Agamben vorwirft, mit seinen Thesen den Blick für eine konkrete Analyse der historischen Singularität der Shoah zu verstellen: Žižek, Slavoj. *Welcome to the desert of the Real! Five essays on September 11 and related dates* (London: Verso, 2002), 137.

[10] Hartman, Geoffrey. *Der längste Schatten.* Erinnern und Vergessen nach dem Holocaust (Berlin: Aufbau, 1999), 17.

[11] Zur theoretischen Debatte vgl. Köppen, Manuel (Hrsg.). *Kunst und Literatur nach Auschwitz* (Berlin: Schmidt, 1993); Mertens, Pierre. *Écrire après Auschwitz? Semprun, Levi, Cayrol, Kertész* (Tournai: Renaissance du Livre, 2003); Jurgenson, Luba. *L'expérience concentrationnaire est-elle indicible?* (Paris: Rocher, 2003).

[12] Wittgenstein, Ludwig. *Tractatus logico-philosophicus. Tagebücher 1914-1916. Philosophische Untersuchungen.* Bd. 1. Text neu durchgesehen von Joachim Schulte (Franfurt/M.: Suhrkamp, 1989), Zf. 7, 85.

[13] Semprún, Jorge. „Wovon man nicht sprechen kann". In: Semprún, Jorge und Gstrein, Norbert. *Was war und was ist.* Reden zur Verleihung des Literaturpreises der Konrad-Adenauer-Stiftung

am 13. Mai 2001 in Weimar (Frankfurt/M.: Suhrkamp 2001), 10f. Vgl. auch Semprún, Jorge und Wiesel, Elie. *Se taire est impossible*. (Paris: Mille et une nuits, 1995).

[14] Vordermark, *Das Gedächtnis des Todes*, 103.

[15] „On peut toujours tout dire, en somme. L'ineffable dont on nous rebattra les oreilles n'est qu'alibi. Ou signe de paresse. On peut toujours tout dire, le langage contient tout. [...] On peut tout dire de cette expérience. Il suffit d'y penser. Et de s'y mettre. D'avoir le temps, sans doute, et le courage, d'un récit illimité, probablement interminable, illuminé – clôturé aussi, bien entendu – par cette possibilité de se poursuivre à l'infini. Quitte à tomber dans la répétition et le ressassement. Quitte à ne pas s'en sortir, à prolonger la mort, le cas échéant, à la faire revivre sans cesse dans les plis et les replis du récit, à n'être plus que le langage de cette mort, à vivre à ses dépens, mortellement". Semprún, *L'écriture ou la vie*, 26. „Man kann also immer alles sagen. Das Unsagbare, mit dem man uns ständig in den Ohren liegen wird, ist nur ein Alibi. Oder ein Zeichen von Faulheit. Man kann immer alles sagen, die Sprache enthält alles. [...] Man kann alles über diese Erfahrung sagen. Es genügt, an sie zu denken. Und sich an die Arbeit zu machen. Zeit zu haben, zweifellos, und Mut für einen unbegrenzten, wahrscheinlich unendlichen Bericht, der beleuchtet – selbstverständlich auch eingemauert – ist von der Möglichkeit, sich endlos fortzusetzen. Auf die Gefahr hin, in der Wiederholung, im Wiederkäuen zu versacken. Auf die Gefahr hin, nicht mehr herauszufinden, möglicherweise den Tod zu verlängern, ihn in den verborgenen Winkeln des Berichts unaufhörlich wieder auf eben zu lassen, nur noch die Sprache dieses Todes zu sein, auf seine Kosten zu leben, tödlich". Semprún, *Schreiben oder Leben*, 23f.

[16] Semprún, *Schreiben oder Leben*, 150. „Le vrai problème n'est pas de raconter, quelles qu'en soient les difficultés. C'est d'écouter… Voudra-t-on écouter nos histoires, même si elles sont bien racontées? [..] Raconter bien, ça veut dire: de façon à être entendus. On n'y parviendra pas sans un peu d'artifice. Suffisamment d'artifice pour que ça devienne de l'art!" Semprún, *L'écriture ou la vie*, 165.

[17] Luba Jurgenson betont ebenfalls, dass die Erfahrung des Konzentrationslagers in den Körper des Überlebenden eingeschrieben ist, er gleichsam ein „corps-mémoire" ist. Jurgenson, *L'expérience concentrationnaire est-elle indicible?*, 70.

[18] Semprún, *Schreiben oder Leben*, 344. „Un jour viendrait, relativement proche, où il ne resterait plus aucun survivant de Buchenwald. Il n'y aurait plus de mémoire immédiate de Buchenwald: plus personne ne saurait dire avec des mots venus de la mémoire charnelle, et non pas d'une reconstitution théorique, ce qu'auront été la faim, le sommeil, l'angoisse, la présence aveuglante du Mal absolu – dans la juste mesure où il est niché en chacun de nous, comme liberté possible. Plus personne n'aurait dans son âme et son cerveau, indélébile, l'odeur de chair brûlée des fours crématoires". Semprún, *L'écriture ou la vie*, 374.

[19] Aaron, Soazig. *Le non de Klara* (Paris: Nadeau, 2002); Littell, Jonathan. *Les bienveillantes* (Paris: Gallimard, 2006). Vgl. hierzu auch Sempruns Vorwort zur deutschen Ausgabe von Aarons Roman: Semprún, Jorge. „Vorwort". In: Aaron, Soazig. *Klaras Nein* (München: btb, 2005), 7.

[20] Semprún, „Vorwort", 6.

[21] Semprún, *Schreiben oder Leben*, 12. „C'est l'horreur de mon regard que révèle le leur, horrifié. Si leurs yeux sont un miroir, enfin, je dois avoir un regard fou, dévasté". Semprún, *L'écriture ou la vie*, 14.

[22] Semprún, *Schreiben oder Leben*, 28, 38, 35. „Il souriait, mourant, son regard sur moi, fraternel", „Les yeux grands ouverts écarquillés sur l'horreur du monde", „ Le regard du S.S., en revanche, chargé de haine, inquiète, mortifère". Semprún, *L'écriture ou la vie*, 31, 41, 39.

[23] Semprún, *Schreiben oder Leben*, 37. „Une voix? Plainte inhumaine, plutôt. Gémissement inarticulé de bête blessée. Mélopée funèbre, glaçant le sang". Semprún, *L'écriture ou la vie*, 40.

[24] Vgl. Derrida, Jacques. *La dissémination* (Paris: Seuil, 1972).

[25] Vgl. zu diesem Aspekt Hennigfeld, Ursula. „Wovon man nicht sprechen kann: Sprache der Macht und Macht der Sprache. Jorge Semprúns Buchenwald-Tetralogie". In: Saeverin, Peter (Hrsg.). *Europäische Geschichtsdarstellungen - Diskussionspapiere. Interdisziplinäre Arbeiten zu Historiographie, Geschichtserzählungen und -konstruktionen von der Antike bis zur Gegenwart.* Jahrgang 3/2006, Heft 4 (Verfügbar unter: http://docserv.uni-duesseldorf.de/servlets/DocumentServlet abgerufen am: 27.04.2012).

[26] Vgl. hierzu die Analyse von Thomas Klinkert: „War es bislang die Funktion der Literatur, den Tod zu überwinden, die Vergangenheit zu bewahren und zeitüberdauerndes Gedächtnis zu stiften, so fällt sie nunmehr dem Tode anheim und situiert sich im Spannungsfeld von Bewahren und Auslöschen, ja sie wird von den Spuren des Vergessens und des Todes schließlich selbst erfaßt". Klinkert, Thomas. *Bewahren und Löschen. Zur Proust-Rezeption bei Samuel Beckett, Claude Simon und Thomas Bernhard* (Tübingen: Narr, 1996), 288.

[27] „'Musulmans'. Je connaissais la réalité que ce mot désignait: la frange infime de la plèbe du camp qui végétait en marge du système de travail forcé, entre la vie et la mort". Semprún, Jorge. *Le mort qu'il faut* (Paris: Gallimard, 2001), 35. „'Muselmänner'. Ich kannte die Realität, die dieses Wort bezeichnete: den äußersten Rand des Lagerplebs, der außerhalb des Systems der Zwangsarbeit dahinvegetierte, zwischen Tod und Leben". Semprún, Jorge. *Der Tote mit meinem Namen*. Aus dem Französischen von Eva Moldenhauer (Frankfurt/M.: Suhrkamp, 2002), 30.

[28] Sofsky, Wolfgang. *Die Ordnung des Terrors*: Das Konzentrationslager. (Frankfurt/M.: Fischer, 2008), 229.

[29] Sofsky, *Die Ordnung des Terrors*, 230f.

[30] Sofsky und Agamben beziehen sich in ihren Ausführungen zum Muselmann auf die Erinnerungen von Jean Améry, Aldo Carpi, Zdzisław Ryn und Stanisław Kłodziński, Primo Levi, Hermann Langbein sowie auf die wissenschaftlichen Arbeiten von Bruno Bettelheim, Eugen Kogon und auf Definition von ‚Muselmann' in der *Encyclopedia Judaica*. Vgl. Sofsky, Wolfgang. „Der Muselmann". In: Sofsky, *Die Ordnung des Terrors*, 229-236 und Agamben, Giorgio. „Der ‚Muselmann'". In: Agamben, *Was von Auschwitz bleibt*, 36-75.

[31] „Der Muselmann verkörpert eine ausweglose Hoffnungslosigkeit, die alle betraf. Er war ein Spiegel des Elends, in dem sich die anderen wiedererkennen mußten. In ihm war der eigene Tod fortwährend gegenwärtig. Was dem Muselmann widerfuhr, konnte jedem widerfahren. Er nahm die Zukunft der anderen vorweg". Sofsky, *Die Ordnung des Terrors*, 235.

[32] „Das Schicksal des Muselmanns war ein soziales Geschehen. Er unterlag einem Prozeß der Dissoziation, an dem auch die Mithäftlinge mitwirkten. Wie er sich zusehends von der Außenwelt abwandte, so wendeten sich die anderen von ihm ab, verfolgten und isolierten ihn. [...] Der Muselmann wurde zur bevorzugten Zielscheibe roher Witze, Erniedrigungen und Grausamkeiten. [...] Da er fortwährend gegen Ordnung und Sauberkeit verstieß, erklärte man ihn zum Sündenbock. [...] Befehle richteten nichts aus, auch die Gewalt verpuffte wirkungslos. Die Passivität des Muselmanns beleidigte die Macht". Sofsky, *Die Ordnung des Terrors*, 233f.

[33] Agamben, *Was von Auschwitz bleibt*, 47.

[34] Semprún, *Schreiben oder Leben*, 27. „Depuis bientôt deux ans, je vivais entouré de regards fraternels. Quand regard il y avait: la plupart des déportés en étaient démunis. Éteint, leur regard,

obnubilé, aveugle par la lumière crue de la mort. La plupart d'entre eux ne vivaient plus que sur la lancée: lumière affaiblie d'une étoile morte, leur œil". Semprún, *L'écriture ou la vie*, 29.

[35] Semprún, *Der Tote mit meinem Namen*, 31. „Les musulmans le [= le déporté communiste Kaminsky, U.H.] dérangent, voilà. Ils troublent, par leur simple existence, la vision qu'il s'est forgée de l'univers concentrationnaire. Ils contredisent, dénient même, le comportement qui lui semble indispensable pour survivre. Les Musulmans introduisent dans son horizon idéologique un élément d'incertitude insaisissable, parce qu'ils échappent, par leur nature même, leur marginalité improductive, leur ataraxie, à la logique manichéenne de la résistance, de la lutte pour la vie, la survie". Semprún, *Le mort qu'il faut*, 35.

[36] Semprún, *Der Tote mit meinem Namen*, 37. „Lui – si tant est qu'il fût licite, ou approprié, d'employer un pronom personnel; peut-être aurait-il été plus juste, plus ajusté, de dire ‚ça' – lui, en tout cas, ce n'était que ça, un amoncellement de hardes innommables. Un tas informe, avachi contre la paroi extérieure du bâtiment des latrines". Semprúr, *Le mort qu'il faut*, 41.

[37] Semprún, *Der Tote mit meinem Namen*, 39. „Ce mort vivant était un jeune frère, mon double peut-être, mon Doppelgänger: un autre moi-même ou moi-même en tant qu'autre. C'était l'altérité reconnue, l'identité existentielle perçue comme possibilité d'être autre, précisément, qui nous rendait si proches". Semprún, *Le mort qu'il faut*, 43.

[38] Baudelaire, Charles. *Die Blumen des Bösen*. Übersetzt von M. Burkert (Essen: Die Blaue Eule, 1995), 70f. „Le revenant./Comme des anges à l'œil fauve,/Je reviendrai dans ton alcôve/Et vers toi glisserai sans bruit/Avec les ombres de la nuit;//Et je te donnerai, ma brune,/Des baisers froids comme la lune/Et des caresses de serpent/Autour d'une fosse rampant.//Quand viendra le matin livide,/Tu trouveras ma place vide,/Où jusqu'au soir il fera froid.//Comme d'autres par la tendresse,/Sur ta vie et sur ta jeunesse,/Moi, je veux régner par l'effroi". Baudelaire, Charles. „Les Fleurs du Mal". In: Baudelaire, Charles. *Œuvres complètes*. Hg. v. Y.-G. Le Dantec/Claude Pichois (Paris: Gallimard, 1961), 61f.

[39] „Bientôt nous plongerons dans les froides ténèbres;/Adieu, vive clarté de nos étés trop courts !" – Semprún erzählt in diesem Roman seine Kindheit und Jugend, die abrupt enden und „allzu kurz" sind, weil die Familie beim Ausbruch des Spanischen Bürgerkriegs ins Exil fliehen muss. Semprún, Jorge. *Adieu, vive clarté...* (Paris: Gallimard, 1998).

[40] Semprún, *Schreiben oder Leben*, 34. „Ô mort, vieux capitaine, il est temps, levons l'ancre... [...] ...nos cœurs que tu connais sont remplis de rayons" Semprún, *L'écriture ou la vie*, 37.

[41] Semprún, *Schreiben oder Leben*, 33f. „Alors, dans une panique soudaine, ignorant si je puis invoquer quelque Dieu pour accompagner Maurice Halbwachs, conscient de la nécessité d'une prière, pourtant, la gorge serrée, je dis à haute voix, essayant de maîtriser celle-ci, de la timbrer comme il faut, quelques vers de Baudelaire. C'est la seule chose qui me vienne à l'esprit". Semprún, *L'écriture ou la vie*, 37.

[42] Semprún, *Schreiben oder Leben*, 140. „La certitude qu'il n'y avait pas vraiment eu de retour, que je n'en étais pas vraiment revenu, qu'une part de moi, essentielle, ne reviendrait jamais, cette certitude m'habitais parfois, renversant mon rapport au monde, à ma propre vie". Semprún, *L'écriture ou la vie*, 154.

[43] Zu Cayrols Konzeption einer lazarenischen Literatur und seiner fiktionalen Annäherung an die Shoah vgl. Hennigfeld, Ursula. Nachwort zu Cayrol, Jean. *Im Bereich einer Nacht*. Aus dem Französischen von Paul Celan (Frankfurt/M.: Schöffling, 2011), 237-255.

[44] Giorgio Agamben argumentiert in eine ähnliche Richtung, wenn er vom Lager als Paradigma oder Nómos der Moderne spricht: „Das Lager und nicht der Staat ist das biopolitische Paradigma

des Abendlandes". Agamben, Giorgio. *Homo sacer. Die souveräne Macht und das nackte Leben.* (Frankfurt/M.: Suhrkamp, 2002), 190.

[45] „On remarque que dans ce monde que je tente de décrire, le visage du Christ n'apparaît pas; le lazaréen n'a que le mal du Camp, ce mal qui garde autour de lui un voile d'ambiguïté et pose une équivoque". Cayrol, Jean. Pour un romanesque lazaréen. In: Cayrol, Jean. *Œuvre lazaréenne* (Paris: Seuil, 2007), 801-823, hier 817. „Man merkt, dass in dieser Welt, die ich zu beschreiben versuche, das Gesicht von Christus nicht aufscheint; der Lazarener hat nur Heimweh nach dem Lager, dieser Schmerz umgibt ihn mit einem Schleier der Mehrdeutigkeit und bringt Täuschungen hervor" (meine Übersetzung).

[46] Cayrol, „Jean. Lazare parmi nous". In: Cayrol, Jean. *Œuvre lazaréenne*, 757-823.

[47] Seine theoretischen Überlegungen zur lazarenischen Literatur setzt Cayrol beispielsweise mit dem Roman *L'espace d'une nuit* (*Im Bereich einer Nacht*) und seinem Protagonisten François um. Vgl. Cayrol, Jean. *L'espace d'une nuit* (Paris: Seuil, 1954).

[48] „Manchmal, wenn man mich fragt, wer ich wirklich bin, Franzose oder Spanier, Schriftsteller oder Politiker, gebe ich zur Antwort – und das erste Mal geschah dies mit kategorischer Spontaneität: mit einem Aufschrei des Herzens –, daß ich zunächst und vor allem, oder vor allem anderen, ehemaliger Häftling von Buchenwald bin. Das ist das Erste, Ursprünglichste, das, was am meisten in die Tiefe reicht und meine Identität am meisten prägt". Semprún, Jorge. *Blick auf Deutschlands Zukunft.* Rede zur Entgegennahme des Weimar-Preises der Stadt Weimar am Tag der Deutschen Einheit 3. Oktober 1995 (Frankfurt/M.: Suhrkamp, 1995), 17.

[49] Semprún, *Schreiben oder Leben*, 24f. „Une idée m'est venue, soudain – si l'on peut appeler idée cette bouffée de chaleur, tonique, cet afflux de sang, cet orgueil d'un savoir du corps, pertinent – , la sensation, en tout cas, très forte, de ne pas avoir échappé à la mort, mais de l'avoir traversée. D'avoir été, plutôt, traversé par elle. De l'avoir vécue, en quelque sorte. D'en être revenu comme on revient d'un voyage qui vous a transformé: transfiguré, peut-être. J'ai compris soudain qu'ils avaient raison de s'effrayer, ces militaires, d'éviter mon regard. Car je n'avais pas vraiment survécu à la mort, je ne l'avais pas évitée. Je n'y avais pas échappé. Je l'avais parcourue, plutôt, d'un bout à l'autre. J'en avais parcouru les chemins, m'y étais perdu et retrouvé, contrée immense où ruisselle l'absence. J'étais un revenant, en somme". Semprún, *L'écriture ou la vie*, 27.

Ursula Hennigfeld ist Juniorprofessorin für Romanische Philologie an der Universität Freiburg im Breisgau. Zu ihren Forschungsschwerpunkten zählen die romanische Lyrik des 16./17. Jahrhunderts, KZ-Literatur, Terror-Diskurse im 21. Jahrhundert sowie romanistische Kultur- und Medienwissenschaft. Publikationen u.a.: *Nicht nur Paris. Metropolitane und urbane Räume in der französischsprachigen Literatur der Gegenwart* (2012), *Der ruinierte Körper. Petrarkistische Sonette in transkultureller Perspektive* (2008), *Literarische Gendertheorie: Eros und Gesellschaft bei Proust und Colette* (2006, zus. mit Ursula Link-Heer und Fernand Hörner). Ihr aktuelles Forschungsprojekt trägt den Titel *Terror und Roman – 9/11-Diskurse in Frankreich und Spanien* (gefördert vom Ministerium des Landes Baden-Württemberg).

La Gran Guerra Europea: Germanophobie und Schrecken des Krieges in Romanen von Blasco Ibañez und ihren Verfilmungen

Volker Jaeckel

Das umfangreiche Werk des spanischen Naturalisten Vicente Blasco Ibañez kann in verschiedene Zyklen gegliedert werden. Während er sich im ersten den lokalen und pittoresken Motiven seiner Region Valencia widmet, geht er im zweiten Zyklus auf drängende soziale Fragen, wie bspw. die prekäre Lage der andalusischen Landarbeiter und einen anarchistischen Aufstand (*La bodega* 1905), ein. Der folgende Zyklus (1916-1919) hat eindeutig den Ersten Weltkrieg und durch ihn verursachte Angst und Entsetzen zum Thema, ein Konflikt, in dem er, trotz erheblicher Anfeindungen in seiner Heimat Spanien, offen für sein Gastland Frankreich Partei ergreift, in dessen Auftrag er seine Texte verfasst, die u.a. aus zahlreichen journalistischen Reportagen, Erzählungen und einer neunbändigen *Historia de la Guerra europea de 1914* bestehen.

Bekannt wurde seine Kriegsliteratur aber vor allem durch die beiden Romane *Los cuatro jinetes del apocalipsis* (1916) und *Mare Nostrum* (1918), die erhebliche Beachtung fanden bei der zeitgenössischen Kritik und in großer Auflage verkauft wurden. In den zwanziger Jahren erfolgten die ersten Verfilmungen mit Rex Ingram als Regisseur und dann erneut 1948 bzw. 1962 in Spanien und den USA. Im vorliegendem Beitrag soll uns vor allem das Erleben der Kriegsschrecken durch die Romanfiguren und das Bild von den Deutschen in den Originaltexten und in den späteren filmischen Versionen, die nicht nur als Transpositionen in ein anderes Medium, sondern als Neulektüren des Krieges unter anderen politischen Vorzeichen zu verstehen sind, beschäftigen.

Einige biographische Anmerkungen zum Autor

Vicente Blasco Ibañez wurde 1867 in Valencia geboren und gehörte zur 98er Generation, einer Gruppe spanischer Autoren, die zwischen 1890 und 1900 zu schreiben begann und sich auch mit Fragen der hispanischen Identität und ihren Wurzeln auseinandersetzte.

Zwischen 1894 und 1902 verfasste der Autor die Romane seines valencianischen Zyklus, die als naturalistische bzw. costumbristische Werke etikettiert wurden, obwohl sie deutlich soziale Veränderungen einforderten und sich mit so vielfältigen Themen wie dem Großgrundbesitzertum, der Agraroligarchie, der durch Börsenspekulation verursachten Ungerechtigkeit, dem Kazikentum u.a. kritisch befasste. Diese literarische Produktionsphase verläuft simultan und in Einklang mit seinem politischen Engagement, was dann auch auf den Romanzyklus des Ersten Weltkrieges zutrifft.

Seit 1889 war er Mitarbeiter verschiedener Tageszeitungen und Zeitschriften in Valencia und gründete *La Bandera Federal* als Organ der Meinungsartikulation der lokalen Sektion der *Unión Republicana*, der er angehörte. Im Jahr 1894 wurde die Zeitung *El Pueblo* gegründet, die er viele Jahre leitete. Seit seiner Jugend war er politisch aktiv und kandidierte als Abgeordneter zu den spanischen Parlamentswahlen in den Jahren 1898, 1899, 1901, 1903, 1905. Die von ihm gegründete Partei *Fusión Republicana* erhielt bei den Wahlen zum Stadtparlament von Valencia die absolute Mehrheit im Jahre 1901.

Gleichzeitig entwickelt er auch eine bemerkenswerte Herausgebertätigkeit, in deren Verlauf er zunächst erfolglos das Projekt der Zeitschrift *La República de las Letras* verfolgte und später in Valencia mit seinem Freund Francisco Sempere den Verlag Prometeo gründete. Sein verlegerischer und ökonomischer Spürsinn führte dazu, dass der Verlag erhebliche Gewinne abwarf, vor allem mit der Veröffentlichung von gut verkäuflichen Klassikern und den für andere Autoren seiner Zeit unvorstellbaren Verkaufszahlen der Romane von Blasco Ibañez, die mit geschickter Verlagsstrategie vertrieben wurden. Im Bildungssektor setzte er sich sich für das Projekt der Laizierung der Schulen ein und schuf im Jahre 1903 in Valencia „La Universidad Popular", ein Kulturangebot für Arbeiter, wie es bereits in anderen spanischen Städten existierte.

Im Jahre 1910 versuchte er, die Idee einer Agrarkolonie zu verwirklichen, indem er valencianische Bauern in Argentinien in den Kolonien Cervantes und Nueva Valencia anzusiedeln versuchte. Dort blieb er bis 1914, als er, durch seine missglückten Unternehmungen ruiniert und unglaubwürdig geworden, aufgeben musste und sich per Schiff nach Paris begab, wo ihn der Krieg ereilte.

Bei dem hier längst nicht vollständig erwähnten politisch-sozialen Engagement von Blasco Ibañez nimmt es sicher nicht Wunder, dass er gegenüber den Ereignissen des Jahres 1914 nicht indifferent bleiben konnte. Auf Bitten des französischen

Ministerpräsidenten Raymond Poincaré bleibt er in Paris, um einen ersten Kriegsroman zu verfassen, der als literarisches Werk um Sympathie für die Sache Frankreichs werben soll.

Blasco Ibañez' Begegnung mit dem Ersten Weltkrieg

Vicente Blasco Ibañez befand sich gerade nach eigenen Aussagen völlig ruiniert und desillusioniert auf der Rückfahrt von Argentinien an Bord des deutschen Passagierschiffes *König Friedrich August*, als er erstmals von der Wahrscheinlichkeit eines bevorstehenden europäischen Konfliktes erfährt, den die Deutschen einen Präventivkrieg nennen. Der deutsche Dampfer kann dann auch nicht Le Havre anlaufen, sondern die Passagiere werden auf der Reede ausgebootet, da sich das Kaiserreich auf eine große Offensive gegen Frankreich vorbereitet.[1]

Das Wettrüsten zwischen Deutschland und England sowie die Marokko-Krise und die Balkankriege in den Jahren 1912 und 1913 hatten die Spannungen so verschärft, dass es nur eines Funken in Gestalt des Attentates vom 28. Juni 1914 auf den Thronfolger der Donaumonarchie Franz Ferdinand bedarf, um die Lage nach diplomatischen Verwicklungen in den ersten Augusttagen mit den Kriegserklärungen zur Explosion zu bringen. Der valencianische Autor entscheidet sich, in Paris zu bleiben und den Konflikt zu begleiten und, für Frankreich Partei nehmend, in seinen Zeitungsreportagen, sowie in Romanen und Erzählungen zu beschreiben. Er engagiert sich für sein Gastland und beginnt, auf einer Reise nach Valencia über die Ursachen des Konfliktes zu informieren. Seine Artikel sendet er an die Zeitschriften *La Esfera* und *Mundo Gráfico*, zu einem Zeitpunkt, als sich Spanien in germanophile und frankophile bzw. alliiertenfreundliche Anhänger aufzuteilen scheint. Es handelt sich um einen Krieg der Worte und Diskussionen in Cafés, der die Intellektuellen Spaniens in zwei unversöhnliche Lager teilt. Es gibt bereits in den ersten Kriegsmonaten keinen Schriftsteller, der sich dieser Entwicklung entziehen kann und nicht Position bezieht.

Während die alliiertenfreundlichen Intellektuellen die Werte von Freiheit, Laizismus, Rechtsstaat, Fortschritt, Zivilisation für sich ins Feld führten im Gegensatz zur vermeintlichen Barbarei, Grausamkeit, dem Militarismus, der Gewalt und dem reaktionärem Despotismus der anderen Seite taten die Germanophilen das gleiche mit den Werten Autorität, Religion, Disziplin, Gehorsam, Streben gegenüber dem Atheismus, Korruption, Verweichlichung, Dekadenz und Desorganisation,

Attributen, die sie dem lateinischen Charakter der Franzosen als Ursprung zuschrieben.

Es wurden Unterstützungsmanifeste auf beiden Seiten verfasst, die die wichtigsten Äußerungen zum Kriegsgeschehen darstellten. Am 12. Februar 1915 wurde das lateinische Manifest der Sorbonne veröffentlicht, ein frankophiler Propagandaakt, bei dem Blasco Ibañez eine herausragende Rolle spielte. Weitere Unterstützer waren Falla, Galdós, Azorín, Perez de Ayala y Palacio Valdés.

Mitten in diesem Disput betreibt Blasco Ibañez sein eifriges Engagement: er reist, schreibt, besucht die Fronten, trifft Militärs, Politiker, um seine Vision dessen zu vermitteln, was er für wünschenswert hält: einen alliierten Sieg.

Blasco bewegt sich zwar mit großer Entschlossenheit in diesem Ambiente, aber seine journalistische Arbeit und sein deutlicher Einsatz für die Sache Frankreichs bringen ihm zahlreiche Probleme auf seinen Spanienreisen ein und sorgen für Entrüstung in verschiedenen Kreisen. Trotzdem werden seine Artikel und später auch seine Romane von einem großen Publikum als ein wichtiger Beitrag zugunsten der alliierten Sache gelesen.

Der europäische Krieg im Werk von Vicente Blasco Ibañez

Chroniken und Zeitungsreportagen sowie vor allem die *neunbändige História de la Guerra Europea de 1914* stellten den Hauptgegenstand seiner Beschäftigung mit dem Krieg dar. Diese Geschichte des Ersten Weltkrieges wurde mit tausenden von Fotografien, Zeichnungen und Abbildungen illustriert. Zu Beginn seiner Einleitung unterstreicht Blasco die einzigartige Bedeutung dieses Krieges, wenn er schreibt:

> In der Geschichte der Menschheit gibt es keinen Krieg, der mit dem gegenwärtigen zu vergleichen ware. Die großen Invasionen der Barbaren, die das sogenannte Altertum beendeten; die galoppierenden Eroberungswellen der Hunnen und der mongolischen Horden; die euopäischen Konfrontationen, die wegen ihrer Dauer die Namen Hundertjähriger Krieg und Dreißigjähriger Krieg erhielten; der vernichtende Vormarsch der Türken bis vor die Tore Wiens; die Feldzüge der spanischen Könige gegen die halbe Welt; die napoleonischen Eroberungen die 15 Jahre lang den Kontinent erschütterten; all diese Tatsachen der Kriegsgeschichte der Menschheit erscheinen fahl und klein im Vergleich zum Krieg von 1914.[2]

Aber auch sein narratives Werk diente der Unterstützung seiner Argumentation mit denselben politischen Zielsetzungen. Sowohl die drei Romane als auch die Erzählungen erscheinen ab 1916, als der Konflikt bereits zwei Jahre andauerte. Der erste Roman dieses Zyklus *Los cuatro jinetes del Apocalipsis* erschien im März 1916, *Mare nostrum* im Januar 1918 und *Los enemigos de la mujer* erst im Jahr 1919, als der Krieg schon mehrere Monate beendet war. Die acht Erzählungen, die z. T. Drehbuchcharakter besitzen, sind zwischen 1916 und 1921 veröffentlicht worden. Ihre Titel sind: *El monstruo, La noche servia, El empleado del coche-cama; Las vírgenes locas; El novelista* (alle 1916), *Un beso, La loca de la casa, La vieja del "cinema"* (alle drei 1921).

Los cuatro jinetes del Apocalipsis

Dieser Roman von Vicente Blasco Ibañez, 1916 veröffentlicht, wurde zu einem Bestseller, auch in seiner englischen Übersetzung. Im Jahre 1921 bezeichnete *The Illustrated London News* das Buch als das meistgelesenste nach der Bibel und machte aus Blasco Ibañez nicht nur einen Autor von Weltruf, sondern auch einen reichen Mann. Für die erste Verfilmung im Jahre 1921 erhielt er 200.000 Dollar während ihm die Übersetzungsrechte ins Englische nur 300 Dollar einbrachten. Von diesem Roman waren allein in Spanien bis September 1924 148.000 Exemplare gedruckt, und in Lateinamerika gab es verschiedene Auflagen in spanischer Sprache ohne Lizenz des Autors.

Es handelt sich um einen Roman der offenen Parteinahme für die französische Republik und gegen die Ideologie des preußischen Militarismus. Im Roman sind die Barbarei, das Reich des Drachen, der sogenannten *Bestia*, gleichgesetzt mit dem Deutschen Kaiserreich.

Der Roman ist linear aus drei Teilen aufgebaut, im ersten werden die Grundlagen des zu entwickelnden Themas vorgegeben, die Ursachen des Krieges und die Umtriebe in dessen Vorfeld. Im zweiten Teil wird auf den Schlachtverlauf eingegangen mit seinen ideologischen, historischen und erzählerischen Elementen, im dritten kommt es zum Handlungshöhepunkt, in dem alle Beteiligten die Konsequenzen des noch andauernden Krieges am eigenen Schicksal spüren.

Tatsächlich folgt Blasco dem Aufbau des biblischen Textes von der Apokalypse und der Öffnung der sieben Siegel: Das erste Siegel enthält den Reiter auf dem weißen Pferd, der Sieg und Macht symbolisiert, das zweite Siegel ist der Reiter auf dem roten Pferd, der für den Krieg steht, das dritte Siegel bringt den Reiter auf dem schwarzen Pferd, der den Hunger repräsentiert und schließlich erscheint der vierte Reiter mit einer fahlen Rüstung und steht für den Tod und hinter ihm der Abgrund.

Von den weiteren drei Siegeln macht Blasco nur von dem fünften Gebrauch, in dem die Opfer sich versammeln, um Gerechtigkeit und Wiedergutmachung zu fordern. Die Antwort, die sie erhalten ist negativ, da die Welt ein Produkt von Zufälligkeiten, von Lügen und Trostworten sei, damit der Mensch sein Ausgeliefertsein ertrage, ohne sich zu erschrecken; so endet dann auch der Roman, den wie ein roter Faden die Macht der vier apokalyptischen Reiter über den vierten Teil der Erde durchzieht, wo sie mit Hunger, Epidemien, Krieg und Tod die Menschen heimsuchen.

Dies ist auch die grobe Struktur, die der Autor im ersten Teil verfolgt, in dem von dem Eroberungswillen des deutschen Volkes ausgegangen wird, und an dessen Ende der Tod erscheint, als eine Frau sich wegen des bevorstehenden kriegerischen Konfliktes umbringt.[3]

Als Desnoyers eingeladen wird, die Front zu besuchen, dort wo sein Sohn kämpft, spricht er am Vorabend mit dem Russen Tchernoff und in seinem Enthusiasmus glaubt er, dass die Offensive des französischen Heeres ein Auftakt für das Kriegsende sein kann, wärend der Russe weitaus pessimistischer ist, wenn er sagt:

> Nein, der Drache stirbt nicht. Es ist der ewige Begleiter des Menschen. Er versteckt sich von Blut triefend 40 Jahre lang... sechzig... ein Jahrhundert, aber dann taucht er wieder auf. Alles, was wir uns wünschen können, ist, dass seine Wunde tief genug sei, so dass er sich lange Zeit versteckt hält und die Generationen, die noch unsere Erinnerung bewahren, ihn niemals wiedersehen werden.[4]

Die Darstellungen des Krieges und seiner Resultate besitzen Elemente des Grotesken, des Ironischen und wecken beim Leser in ihrer Grausamkeit ein Gefühl des Schauderns und der Abscheu, das ihn den Konflikt als etwas Antiheroisches und Abstoßendes erkennen lässt.

Ein Beispiel finden wir an folgender Stelle, als die Franzosen in und am Schloss der Desnoyers ihre verlorene Positionen von den Deutschen zurückerobern können:

> Einer der Reiter hielt am Eingang des Parkes, das Pferd verschlang gierig einige Sträucher, während der Mann auf dem Sattel in sich versunken blieb, als wenn er schlafen würde. Desnoyers berührte ihn an einem Schenkel, wollte ihn aufwecken und unmittelbar darauf fiel er auf der anderen Seite runter. Er war tot; die Eingeweide hingen ihm aus dem Bauch. So war er auf seinem Ross vorangetrabt und mit den anderen verwechselt worden.[5]

Auch an anderer Stelle, als die Deutschen im Schloss von den Franzosen angegriffen werden, zeigt sich die kinematographisch schockierende Genauigkeit, die zugleich völlig surreal erscheint, seiner Beschreibungen des Kampfgeschehens:

Er war gerade dabei, das dritte Mal die Eimer zu füllen und beobachtete rücklings den Leutnant, als sich etwas Unwahrscheinliches, Absurdes ereignete, das ihn an die phanstastischen Mutationen des Kinos erinnerte. Der Kopf des Offiziers verschwand ganz plötzlich: zwei Blutströme entsprangen seinem Hals und der Körper fiel zusammen wie ein leerer Sack; Gleichzeitig rauschte ein Zyklon an der Wand vorbei, zwischen dieser und dem Gebäude, der Bäume entwurzelte, Kanonen umwarf und Personen in einem Strudel mit sich riss, so als wären sie trockene Blätter. Er ahnte, dass der Tod jetzt in eine andere Richtung blies.[6]

Blasco nimmt nicht am Kampfgeschehen teil, er beobachtet: die Heldentaten des Krieges werden nicht direkt berichtet sondern vom Hörensagen, die Kampfszenen sind sehr selten, und die Hauptpersonen des Buches nehmen nicht an ihnen teil, sie werden von unbekannten, namenlosen Soldaten in Uniform, von einer Gemeinschaft in Waffen, protagonisiert. Was Blasco mehr interessiert als der Kampf, sind die Geschehnisse hinter der Front, in der Etappe, wo er sehr treffend das Verhalten der Figuren und die Atmosphäre angesichts einer unmittelbaren Bedrohung nachzeichnet: dafür hat er die Familie Desnoyers ausgewählt, eine argentinische Familie, die in Frankreich lebt und deren Schicksal in den Kapiteln 1.2 und 1.3 erzählt wird.

Die Hauptperson ist Julio Desnoyers, dessen Großvater 1870 nach Argentinien ausgewandert war. Im Jahre 1914 ist Argentinien zwar neutral und die Familie sieht sich zunächst nicht vom Konflikt betroffen, doch dann fühlen sie sich wegen ihrer Herkunft mit dem Schicksal Frankreichs verbunden. Der Krieg trennt die Familien Desnoyers und von Hartrott, die miteinander verschwägert sind, da die jeweiligen Familienoberhäupter die beiden Schwestern Luisa und Elena geheiratet haben, die wiederum aus einer Verbindung von Madariaga und einer Indianerin abstammen. Für Madariaga (Zentaur), den Besitzer einer enormen Hazienda in Argentinien, hat der europäische Nationalismus keinen Platz in seinem Leben. So sagt er zu Desnoyers:

-Schau mal Franzmann -, sagte er und vertrieb mit den Rauchblasen seiner Zigarre die Mosquitos, die um ihn herschwirrten-. Ich bin Spanier, du Franzose, Karl ist Deutscher, meine Töchter sind Argentinierinnen, der Koch ist Russe, sein Helfer Grieche, der Vorarbeiter Engländer, die Chinesinnen der Küche sind zum Teil Einheimische, andere sind Galicierinnen oder Italienerinnen und die Viehknechte sind vielerlei Herkunft und Abstammung Und wir alle leben in Frieden. In Europa hätten wir uns zu dieser Zeit vielleicht schon verprügelt, aber hier sind wir alle Freunde.[7]

So erscheint Argentinien als das Einwanderungsland in Lateinamerika zu Beginn des 20. Jahrhunderts mit seiner Integrationskapazität als Gegenpol zum kriegerisch zerstrittenen, von nationalen und ethnischen Rivalitäten gebeutelten, Europa am Vorabend des Ersten Weltkrieges.

Madariaga geht noch weiter und sagt, dass der Mensch dort ein Vaterland habe, wo er reich wird und eine Familie gründet gemäß dem lateinischen Grundsatz *ubi bene, ubi patria.*

In dem Roman erscheint der Krieg als eine Extremsituation, in der man auf die Liebe oder die Geliebte, die Familie und das Klassenbewusstsein verzichten muss, das in den frühen Romanen von Blasco Ibañez noch von entscheidender Bedeutung war. Die sozialistischen Arbeiter ziehen in den Krieg und singen die Marsellaise.[8] Der Erste Weltkrieg war sicherlich die letzte kriegerische Auseinandersetzung, in dem sich die Jugend mit so viel Enthusiasmus für eine nationale Sache in verschiedenen Staaten an die Fronten begab.

In dem Roman sind wie bereits erwähnt schaudererregende Beschreibungen von Schlachtfeldern und von Eroberungsszenen zu finden. Trotzdem besitzt der Roman keinen eindeutigen Antikriegscharakter, da sich bei Blasco Ibañez die Toten in zwei Kategorien aufteilen lassen: in die von niederen Beweggründen getriebenen Angreifer und in die legitimen Verteidiger, die Franzosen.

Die Deutschen werden als blutrünstige Bestien dargestellt und die Franzosen als heldenhafte Männer. Der Autor verfällt in eine kollektive Anklage der Deutschen, die von einer inhumanen Ideologie angetrieben werden und bezeichnet sie als ein Volk von Lakaien. Im Verlauf der Handlung erweisen sich auch die vermeintlich sympathischen Teutonen wie Blumhardt als Menschen, die erschießen und vergewaltigen.

Die Deutschen treten durchweg als negative Charaktere in Erscheinung, denen der Eroberungsdrang schon im Blut liegt, wie sich selbst an den Mitgliedern der verschwägerten Familie von Hartrott erkennen lässt. An einer Vielzahl von Stellen im Text lässt Blasco Ibañez deutliche Kritik an der Überheblichkeit der Deutschen und ihrer Ideologie durchblicken, so dass es kein Wunder nimmt, dass dieses Buch als eine Vorwegnahme des nationalsozialistischen Rassenwahns gesehen wird. So sind bspw. folgende Aussagen zu finden:

> Der germanische Stolz, die Überzeugung, dass diese Rasse dazu von der Vorsehung ausgewählt ist, die Welt zu beherrschen, vereinte Protestanten, Katholiken und Juden[9]

> Nein, ich bin Deutscher. Egal wo einer von uns geboren wird, gehört er zur Mutter Deutschland (...)

> Sie waren miserable Kelten, aufgegangen in der Gemeinheit einer minderen Rasse, die sich mit den Römern gemischt hatte, was die Situation nur verschlimmert. Glücklicherweise wurden Sie von den Goten und anderen Völkern unserer Rasse erobert, die Ihnen die Menschenwürde beibrachten. Vergessen Sie nicht junger Mann, dass die Vandalen die Großväter der Preußen waren![10]

> Mit der Sicherheit eines Professors, der nicht erwartet, von seinen Zuhörern widerlegt zu werden, erklärte er die Überlegenheit der germanischen Rasse; Die Menschen lassen sich einteilen in zwei Gruppen: die Langschädeligen und die Kurzschädeligen, je nach der Form ihres Schädels. Ein anderes wissenschaftliches Unterscheidungsmerkmal teilt sie in Menschen mit blonden Haaren und mit schwarzen Haaren ein. Die Langschädeligen stehen für die Reinheit der Rasse und eine überlegene Mentalität, die Kurzschädeligen waren Mischlinge mit allen Merkmalen von Degeneration. Der Germane, der Prototyp des Langschädeligen, war der einzige Nachfolger der primitiven Arier. Alle anderen Völker, vor allem die im Süden Europas, die sogenannten lateinischen, gehörten einer degenerierten Menschheit an.[11]

> Er sprach von zukünftigen Eroberungen, als wären diese Erhabenheitserweise, mit denen sein Land die übrigen Völker auszeichnete. Diese würden politisch weiterhin wie vorher leben mit ihren eigenen Regierungen, aber unter der Führung der germanischen Rasse. Wie Kinder, die die starke Hand des Lehrers brauchen. Sie würden die Vereinigten Staaten der Welt bilden unter einer vererbbaren und allmächtigen Präsidentschaft, dem Kaiser von Deutschland. So würden ihnen die Vorzüge der germanischen Kultur zuteil und sie würden diszipliniert unter dieser arbeitsamen Leitung arbeiten... Aber die Welt ist undankbar und die menschliche Schlechtigkeit widersteht immer jedem Fortschritt.[12]

Auf der anderen Seite wird der Verteidigungscharakter des Krieges für die Franzosen mehrfach unterstrichen, wenn z.B. Roberto, ein Arbeiter und ehemaliger Antimilitarist folgende Position vertritt:

> Wir werden für unsere eigene Sicherheit kämpfen und gleichzeitig auch für die Sicherheit der Welt, für die Existenz der schwachen Völker. Wenn es ein Angriffskrieg wäre, würde unser Antimilitarismus erwachen. Aber es handelt sich um Verteidigung und die Regierenden haben keine Schuld daran. Wir sehen uns vor einem Angriff und müssen alle gemeinsam marschieren.[13]

Der Roman erweckt den Eindruck eine Überlastung an Dokumentation und Fakten zu Lasten von Dialogen oder der Weiterführung der Handlung zu besitzen. Die Handlung wird zugunsten der Darstellung zurückgestellt, der Autor interveniert als omnipräsenter Erzähler, der alle anderen gestaltenden Elemente überragt oder außer Kraft setzt. Der Roman wird über seine erzählerische Kraft zu einem weiteren Element in der Auseinandersetzung zwischen den Anhängern der beiden Blöcke, dem deutschen- und dem französenfreundlichen, die sich auf allen gesellschaftlichen

Ebenen in Spanien bekriegen. Die narrativen Elemente stehen im Dienst der politischen Ziele, so dass es dem Roman an ideologischer und rhetorischer Unabhängigkeit mangelt, was sich in der fehlenden Geschicklichkeit niederschlägt, mit der er seine Eigendynamik entwickelt, wie Navarro in ihrer Dissertation schreibt.[14]

Die Kombination von allegorischen Elementen, den vier apokalyptischen Reitern und der unmittelbaren Kriegsrealität zusammen mit den Sympathiebekundungen für die alliierte Sache stellen wahrscheinlich den Schlüssel für den Erfolg des Romans unter seinen Zeitgenossen dar, so dass das Werk seinen ursprünglichen Auftrag im Sinne Poincares erfüllt.[15]

Die Verfilmungen des Romans *Los cuatro jinetes del apocalipsis*

Von diesem Erfolgsroman sind zwei Verfilmungen erhalten geblieben,[16] eine davon ist der von Rex Ingram im Jahre 1920/21 mit Rudolfo Valentino als Julio Desnoyers in der Hauptrolle gedrehte Stummfilm. Diese Verfilmung, die dem italienischen Darsteller zum Durchbruch verhilft, folgte treu dem Buch des Valencianers und machte sowohl Regisseur als auch Hauptdarsteller berühmt. Ingram kontrastiert die auf Wolkenfetzen dahinfegenden apokalyptischen Reiter mit seinen karikaturhaften Übertreibungen bei der Darstellung der Deutschen. Dieser Film wurde am 6. März 1921 uraufgeführt und zählt – gemessen an den Einspielergebnissen – zu den erfolgreichsten Stummfilmen aller Zeiten. Er wird als früher Antikriegsfilm interpretiert, da am Ende des Filmes beide Familien, die Desnoyers und die von Hartrotts, ihre auf dem Schlachtfeld gefallenen Söhne betrauern.

1962 kommt es zu einer 153 Minuten langen Neuverfilmung des Romans unter Regie des Amerikaners Vincente Minnelli mit Glenn Ford, Ingrid Thulin, Charles Boyer, Paul Lukas, Karl Boehm und Lee J. Cobb in den Hauptrollen. Diese neue filmische Version entfernt sich nicht nur sehr weit von dem Romanstoff des spanischen Autors, indem eine Transposition der Handlung in die Zeit unmittelbar vor und während des Zweiten Weltkrieges vorgenommen wird, sondern verdreht auch die Hauptaussagen des Romans und die politische Intention von Blasco Ibañez in ihr Gegenteil. Statt einer Beschreibung der Leiden, die die vier Reiter der Apokalypse über das französische Volk in Form des Weltkrieges bringen, stehen persönliche Leidenschaften, Begierden und Intrigen im Vordergrund.

Einzig die negative Vision von den Deutschen wird beibehalten und durch die Gleichsetzung mit dem nationalsozialistischen Deutschland noch verschärft, was vor allem über die Einblendung von dokumentarischen Kampfszenen, Bombardements und Reden Hitlers auf den Reichsparteitagen erreicht wird. Julio Desnoyers erscheint als Casanova, der ein Verhältnis mit einer verheirateten Frau beginnt, deren Mann an der Front sein Leben für Frankreich einsetzt. Als beide zum Tanzen ausgehen, versucht ihm ein deutscher General, der Stadtkommandant von Paris, die Geliebte unter Einsatz seiner hoheitlichen Machtmittel auszuspannen. Sein Cousin Heinrich von Hartrott ein sehr einflussreicher SS-Oberst, kann dies aber noch verhindern. An dieser Stelle wird der Gefolgsmann von Heydrich zum Verteidiger der Ehre der französischen Geliebten seines argentinischen Cousins. Auch der weitere Verlauf des Films hat mit dem Buch des spanischen Autors eigentlich nur noch die Namen der Hauptdarsteller gemein: die Kinder von Marcelo Desnoyers schließen sich der französischen Resistance an und kommen dabei letztlich um, während die Familien von Hartrott zu den Besatzern Frankreichs zählen und die Macht ausüben, so dass Marcelo seinen Schwager Karl um Hilfe bitten muss, damit die Tochter Chichi aus den Händen der Gestapo befreit werden kann.

Im dramatischen Schluss reisst Julio Desnoyers Heinrich von Hartrott mit in den Tod, da er bei einem Besuch dessen Hauptquartier der englischen Luftwaffe über einen Peilsender preisgibt. Die Kritik an den Deutschen wird abgeschwächt, da diesem Zweig der Familie auch menschliche Gefühle wie väterliche Sorge zugeteilt werden. Auch das Verhältnis von Julio zu der verheirateten Marguerite Laurier wird stark aufgewertet und zu einem Melodrama verwandelt, da sich der später von der Gestapo zu Tode gefolterte Ehemann und der Liebhaber als Seite an Seite stehende Widerstandskämpfer begegnen.

Insgesamt erscheint der Film, der ursprünglich mit Alain Delon und Romy Schneider in den Hauptrollen hätte besetzt werden sollen, sehr dramatisch überladen und zu sehr in Gefühlen schwelgend, was der Aussage des Romans letztlich nicht gerecht wird, da der Buchautor einen klaren Appell gegen die Schrecken des modernen Krieges und die Eroberungsgelüste der Deutschen trifft.

Mare Nostrum

Im August 1917 beginnt Blasco seinen zweiten Kriegsroman zu schreiben, zu einem Zeitpunkt, als sich der Krieg an seinen verschiedenen Fronten stabilisiert hat, und die

Erschöpfung sowohl unter Kämpfenden als auch unter der Zivilbevölkerung spürbar wird. Von diesem erstmals 1918 veröffentlichten Roman wurden bis zum September 1924 allein in Spanien 104.000 Exemplare verkauft.

Auch dieser Roman besitzt zwei Ebenen der Lektüre, eine symbolische, die ihn mit mit der mediterranen Mythologie verknüpft und die unmittelbare Erzählebene, auf der die Geschichte seines Helden Ulises Ferragut im Rahmen des I. Weltkrieges erzählt wird.[17] Im Vergleich zum ersten Roman ist die Beziehung zwischen den beiden Ebenen nicht eng, sondern sie erscheinen in getrennten Kapiteln. Die Kohärenz des Romans geht zu Lasten der fehlenden Verknüpfung von mythologischen Bildern und ihren jeweiligen Entsprechungen in der Romanhandlung auf der Gegenwartsebene.

Das Mittelmeer erscheint als ein Raum, der die Menschen anzieht und ihnen die Möglichkeit verschafft, für ihren Unterhalt zu sorgen und den Kontakt zu anderen Völkern zu finden bzw. aufrecht zu erhalten. Gleichzeitig stellt es aber auch eine ständige Lebensgefahr dar für die Menschen, die an seinen Ufern leben oder es auf ihren Schiffen befahren. Diese Gefahr des Todes lauert in den Tiefen des Meeres und zeigt sich in der Seenymphe Anfitrite, die den Auftrag hat, die Männer zu verführen und auf den Grund des Meeres zu Poseidon herabzuführen.[18]

In diesem Werk des valencianischen Autors ist das Kriegsgeschehen weniger unmittelbar präsent als in dem vorausgegangenen. Hier handelt es sich um einen Roman, der auf die Spionagetätigkeit während des Krieges und ihre Folgen eingeht. Das Kampfgeschehen findet nicht mehr auf den Schlachtfeldern Frankreichs statt, sondern es handelt sich um den U-Boot-Krieg im Mittelmeer.[19] Als Blasco Ibañez den Roman niederschreibt, hat diese neue Art von Meereskrieg, die dem Angreifer erhebliche Vorteile verschafft, schon einen Höhepunkt erreicht und zum Kriegseintritt der USA entscheidend beigetragen. Die Verbindung von Krieg und Spionage stellt die thematische Basis des Romans dar, vor dessen Hintergrund sich eine Liebesgeschichte, Intrigen und zahlreiche persönliche Schicksale entwickeln.

Erzählt wird die Geschichte von dem spanischen Kapitän Ulises Ferragut, der sich in eine Spionin im Dienste des Deutschen Reiches verliebt und daher letztlich den Auftrag annimmt, Deutsche U-Boote, die im Mittelmeer operieren, mit Treibstoff zu versorgen. Als er erfährt, dass sein Sohn, der auf der Suche nach dem verschollenen Vater war, bei einem deutschen U-Bootangriff auf das Schiff *California* ums Leben kommt, befallen ihn schwerste Gewissensbisse. Fortan stellt er sich und sein Schiff in den Dienst der Alliierten, um sich an den Deutschen zu rächen. Mit der Spionin, die später von einem französichen Kriegsgericht zum Tode verurteilt wird, bricht er alle Beziehungen ab. Der Autor Blasco Ibañez lässt den historischen Moment des Romans mit dem Erscheinen der deutschen U-Boote zusammenfallen und macht damit den Protagonisten Ulises Ferragut für das Erscheinen dieser neuen Kriegswaffe im Mittelmeer und deren Folgen verantwortlich, da es bis zu diesem Zeitpunkt noch frei vom deutschen Einfluss war. Auch wenn die historischen Ereignisse des I. Weltkrieges nur den Hintergrund für die Romanhandlung abgeben, so beinhaltet der Roman doch eine Problematisierung hinsichtlich der individuellen Schuld jedes Einzelnen an den Auswirkungen und Folgen des Krieges. So steht bei Ulises Ferragut der innere Konflikt wegen des Todes seines Sohnes durch einen deutschen U-Bootangriff im Vordergrund, für den er sich verantwortlich fühlt, da er den Deutschen mit seiner Versorungsaktion Zugang zum Mittelmeer verschaffte, zu der ihn die Spionin Freya als seine Geliebte veranlasste. Freya wiederum weist verschiedene Züge der historischen Mata Hari auf.[20]

Wiederum erscheinen die Deutschen in diesem Roman als skrupellose Zeitgenossen, die die Welt um jeden Preis - und hier vor allem das Mittelmeer - in Besitz nehmen wollen, ohne dabei vor hinterhältigen Machenschaften zurückzuschrecken, wie sich z.B. in den Figuren von Kramer und der ständigen Begleiterin von Freya, die im Roman nur die „Doktorin" genannt wird, zeigt. Sie ist eine kompetente Philologin, wird als weise beschrieben, zeigt stolz ihre Kenntnisse und übt gerne Macht auf andere aus. Ihre Aufgabe ist es, den deutschen U-Booten Zugang zum Mittelmeer zu verschaffen. Um den Erfolg dieser Aktion zu garantieren, benutzt sie Ulises Ferragut. Sie vereint verschiedene negative Charaktermerkmale, die im Roman dem Feind, den Deutschen, zugeordnet werden: sie ist eine unabhängige, sehr gebildete Frau und repräsentiert die operative Fähigkeit der Deutschen zur Zerstörung, die zwangsläufig den Tod des Gegners herbeiführen. Darin unterscheidet sie sich von der Spionin Freya, die nicht aus patriotischen Motiven handelt, sondern weil sie die Spionage als ihre Arbeit ansieht, die ihr Auskommen sichert.[21]

Die Schrecken des Krieges werden im Falle der Versenkung des englischen Dampfers *Californian* deutlich, in diesem Falle die Torpedierung eines zivilen Schiffes durch ein U-Boot als Merkmal des modernen Krieges und seiner katastrophalen Auswirkungen. Es ist der Tod des Sohnes von Ferragut, der von einem anderen Passagier berichtet wird.

> Plötzlich hatte eine schwarze Linie das Meer durchschnitten, etwas wie ein Dorn mit einer Schaumkrone der rasend schnell näherkam und sich auf dem Wasser abzeichnete..... Danach ein Stoß an den Rumpf des Schiffes, der es vom Bug bis zum Heck erzittern ließ, ohne dass eine Planke oder eine Schraube dieser enormen Wucht hätten widerstehen können.... Darauf ein Vulkanausbruch, ein gigantischer Lichtkegel von Rauch und Flammen, eine gelbe Wolke, ein Gelb von Drogerie, in dem dunkle Objekte flogen: Bruchstücke aus Metall und Holz, in Stücke gerissene Körper.
>
> Ein Freund von mir, ein Landsmann – fuhr er seufzend fort, trennte sich von mir, um das Unterseebot besser sehen zu können und stand genau am Ort der Explosion....Er verschwand plötzlich, so als wäre er ausgelöscht worden
>
> Ich sah ihn und sah ihn nicht.... Er zerbarst in tausend Stücke, so als wenn eine Bombe in seinem Körper explodiert wäre.[22]

Die Unsichtbarkeit und Lautlosigkeit des Angreifers und die verheerenden Auswirkungen einer Torpedierung, ohne, dass sich die Schiffsbesatzung und die Passagiere davor hätten schützen können und die Tatsache, dass die Ziele durch Spione den Deutschen bekanntgegeben werden, lassen die Hinterhältigkeit der Kriegsführung der Mittelmächte in einem besonders negativen Licht erscheinen. Derselben Waffe, die aus dem Nichts auftaucht und tötet, fällt dann schließlich auch der Protagonist des Romans mit seinem *Mare Nostrum* zum Opfer, denn am Ende des Buches steht die Torpedierung von Ferraguts Schiffes vor der Küste von Valencia, die folgendermaßen beschrieben wird:

> Aber noch war nicht eine Sekunde vergangen, als noch etwas zu diesem Stoß hinzukam, das die Annahmen von Ferragut widerlegte. Ein bläulicher Lichtschein schrumpfte unter Donnerschlag zusammen. In der Nähe des Bugs stieg eine Rauchwolke auf, von explodierenden Gasen, von blitzendem gelbem Dampf, der von seinem Innern her in Form eines Fächers aufstieg und schwarze Objekte, kaputtes Holz, Stücke von Metallplanken, brennende Taue ausspie, die sich in Asche auflösten.[23]

Mit diesem Ende des Helden und seines Schiffes wird wiederum die Grausamkeit und Sinnlosigkeit des Krieges unterstrichen, eines Krieges der mit seinen Waffen Unglück, Gewalt und Zerstörung bringt. Spionage und U-Bootkrieg haben gemeinsam, dass es sich sozusagen um indirekte Kriegsmethoden handelt, deren Ausmaß der Zerstörung und Zahl der Opfer nicht unmittelbar sichtbar wird für ihre Vollstrecker. So hebt der spanische Autor hervor, mit welcher Kaltschnäuzigkeit die Spione handeln, wenn sie die Schiffe des Gegners dem Untergang preisgeben. Demzufolge begleitet die französische Zivilbevölkerung auch mit großer Gleichgültigkeit die Exekution von feindlichen Spionen.

Der Autor enthüllt das wahre Gesicht des Krieges und betreibt seine Entmythologisierung auch an einer anderen Stelle, als sich drei Fremdenlegionäre mit Ulises über den Konflikt unterhalten. Sie hatten einen kurzen und glorreichen Spaziergang zum Sieg erwartet und werden enttäuscht, als sie unerwartet mit den unangenehmen Seiten wie Schmutz, Hunger, Todesgefahr und blutigen Kämpfen konfrontiert werden.

> Die drei erinnerten sich an die Monate der Hölle, die sie kürzlich auf den Dardanellen durchlitten hatten, auf einem Gebiet von sechs Kilometern, das sie sich mit dem Bayonett erkämpft hatten. Ein Geschossregen ging unaufhörlich auf ihnen nieder. Man musste unter der Erde wie Maulwürfe leben und selbst so wurden sie von zerplatzenden großen Mörsergranaten erreicht (...)
>
> Sie huben Schützengräben aus auf einem Stück Erde, das den Türken als Friedhof gedient hatte. Die aufgedunsenen Bäuche zerfielen unter den Schaufeln und die Säfte der Verwesung verteilten sich.[24]

Diese drei Legionäre stehen stellvertretend für unzählige junge Menschen im Europa jener Zeit, die mit patriotischer Begeisterung in den Ersten Weltkrieg zogen und bitter enttäuscht, desillusioniert und deprimiert heimkehrten.

Die Verfilmungen von *Mare Nostrum*

Der Roman wurde zum ersten Male wiederum als Stummfilm von 102 Minuten Länge von Rex Ingram im Jahre 1926 mit Antonio Moreno und Alice Terry in den Hauptrollen verfilmt. Diese erste Version folgt wiederum dem Buch in sehr authentischer Weise, da auch die Rahmen- und Nebenhandlungen des Buches wiedergegeben werden und das Argument des U-Bootkrieges unverändert bleibt. So treten auch die Figuren der ersten einführenden Kapitel des Buches in Erscheinung, und die Episode mit seiner Frau in Barcelona wird ebenfalls in Szene gesetzt.

Ganz anders gestaltet sich hingegen die Neuverfilmung des Romans von Blasco Ibañez im Jahre 1948 in Spanien mit Rafael Gil als Regisseur und Antonio Abad Ojuel als Drehbuchautor, mit Fernando Rey, María Felix und Porfiria Sanchiz in den Hauptrollen. Auch in diesem 86 Minuten langen Film wurde eine Transposition der Handlung vom Ersten in den Zweiten Weltkrieg und verschiedene andere Veränderungen vorgenommen, so dass in der Filmversion der U-Bootkrieg keine Rolle mehr spielt, sondern der Auftrag von Ferragut sich auf die Verminung von Mittelmeerhäfen bezieht. Demzufolge fällt sein Sohn dann auch einer dieser Minen zum Opfer, und der Vater kann ihn nur noch sterbend in seinen Armen halten, was die Melodramatik des Stoffes weiter verstärkt.

Besonders interessant erscheint die Tatsache, dass in dieser Phase der Francozeit die Intention deutlich wird, die strikte Neutralität Spaniens im Zweiten Weltkrieg zu unterstreichen, die Ulises Ferragut mit seiner Aktion verletzt. Die Deutschen erscheinen als durchtriebene Spione im Einsatz für ihr Vaterland, während die amerikanischen und englischen Truppen visuell in Erscheinung treten und zusammen mit dem spanischen Kapitän einen deutschen Spion in einem Feuergefecht zur Strecke bringen.

Marseille und Barcelona spielen als Handlungsorte keine Rolle, sondern nur das Mittelmeer und Neapel. Am Ende des Romans wird das Schiff von Ferragut auch nicht durch ein U-Boot versenkt, sondern durch einen Luftangriff.

Der zentrale Strang mit der Liebesgeschichte zwischen der Spionin Freya Talberg und dem Kapitän Ulises Ferragut bleibt jedoch ziemlich getreu erhalten und dokumentiert sowohl seine Abhängigkeit von der Geliebten als auch seine späteren Gewissensbisse hinsichtlich des Todes seines Sohnes, auch wenn diese im Roman von größerer Bedeutung sind.

In der filmischen Version wird die Skrupellosigkeit von Freya noch mehr herausgestrichen, da sie ihre weiblichen Reize vielfach einsetzt, um auf jede erdenkliche Art an geheime Informationen zu kommen und sogar auch Mitkämpfer dem Tod ausliefert, wenn es oportun erscheint. Das Augenmerk verlagert sich somit von der Lebensgeschichte des Kapitäns auf die Figur der Spionin und ihre Aktionen, wobei ihre wichtigste diejenige war, den Kapitän Ferragut dazu zu bringen, dass er sich quasi in Selbstaufgabe aus Liebe zu ihr erniedrigt, Schmach auf sich nimmt und sich großer Gefahr aussetzt.

Die Verbindung zum Kriegsgeschehen wird über willkürlich eingeblendete Zeitungsmeldungen und Bilder aus Dokumentarfilmen des Zweiten Weltkrieges hergestellt, eine eindeutige Problematisierung der tatsächlichen Schrecken des modernen Krieges und der Charakterlosigkeit der Deutschen findet hingegen im Film nicht mehr statt. Diese Tatsachen scheinen einem spanischen Kinopublikum nur neun Jahre nach Beendigung des Spanischen Bürgerkrieges und angesichts der noch immer anhaltenden Guerrillaaktivitäten von Widerstandkämpfern als nicht zumutbar zu erscheinen, so dass einer als weitgehend unpolitisch erscheinenden Liebesgeschichte zwischen einem Seemann und einer schönen Spionin der Vorzug gegeben wird.

Zusammenfassung

Die Analyse dieser beiden Kriegsromane von Vicente Blasco Ibañez und der Vergleich mit den neueren Verfilmungen haben einige erstaunliche Tatsachen gezeigt: So ist der Erste Weltkrieg mit seinen Schrecken als erster moderner Krieg des 20. Jahrhunderts so sehr in Vergessenheit geraten, dass offensichtlich eine Transposition der Handlung in die Zeit des Zweiten Weltkrieges für den Erfolg der Filme unabdingbar erscheint. Die Kontextualisierung in die Zeit der jüngsten Vergangenheit scheint den jeweiligen Regisseuren auch zu Lasten einer werktreuen Verfilmung als angebracht. Selbst bei dieser Umsetzung in die Zeit des Nationalsozialismus kann das extrem negative Bild von den Deutschen, das der Autor seiner Zeit den Lesern vermitteln wollte, nicht vollständig umgesetzt werden, weder in der amerikanischen Verfilmung von *Los cuatro Jinetes del Apocalipsis* noch in der spanischen von *Mare Nostrum*. Die politischen Aussagen zugunsten der französischen Republik werden ebenso weitgehend unberücksichtigt gelassen wie die mythologischen Aspekte der beiden Romane und die Kritik an der Kriegsführung mit modernen Waffen.

Obwohl die analysierten Romane seiner Zeit Bestseller waren, finden sie heute auch im Bereich der Hispanistik wenig Beachtung innerhalb des Gesamtwerkes von Blasco Ibañez. Den beiden späteren filmischen Relektüren mit ihren stofffremden Adaptationen gelang es ebenfalls nicht, an die Erfolge der Stummfilme von Rex Ingram anzuknüpfen. Diese Tatsachen lassen die Schlussfolgerung zu, dass es sich bei den Kriegsromanen keinesfalls um zeitlose Werke handelt, auch wenn deren Lesbarkeit und Verständnis nicht an geographische und temporäre Grenzen gebunden sind. Ihre politische Brisanz mit der klaren Parteinahme zugunsten Frankreichs inmitten eines gespaltenen Spanien mindert jedoch das Interesse nachfolgender Lesergenerationen an Romanen, die nicht als erzählerische Meisterleistungen gelten.

---

[1] Diese Begebenheiten, die der spanische Autor schildert, sind nicht authentisch. Das deutsche Schiff wurde im April 1914 in Hamburg aufgelegt und verblieb dort bis zum Ende des Krieges, kann also im Juli 1914 keine Fahrt von Argentinien nach Frankreich durchgeführt haben.

[2] No hay en la historia de la humanidad guerra alguna que pueda compararse con la presente. Las grandes invasiones de los bárbaros que dieron fin a la llamada Edad Antigua; las avalanchas galopantes de los hunos y de las hordas mongólicas; los choques europeos que por su duración recibieron los títulos de Guerra de Cien Años y Guerra de Treinta Años; los avances arrolladores del turco hasta los muros de Viena; las campañas de los reyes españoles contra medio mundo; las conquistas napoleónicas que durante quince años trajeron trastornado al continente; todos los hechos de la historia belicosa de los hombres, palidecen y se achican frente a la guerra de 1914.

Vicente Blasco Ibañez: *Historia de la guerra europea de 1914: ilustrada com millares de dibujos, fotografías y laminas*. Verfügbar unter:
http://www.archive.org/stream/historiadelaguer01blas/historiadelaguer01blas_djvu.txt, abgerufen am: 03.11.2011.

[3] Navarro Mateo, María José. *Blasco Ibañez y las novelas de la Guerra Europea*. (Valencia: Facultad de Filología, Universidad de Valencia, 1991), 185. Dissertation.

[4] No; la Bestia no muere. Es la eterna compañera de los hombres, Se oculta chorreando sangre cuarenta años... sesenta años... un siglo, pero reaparece. Todo lo que podemos desear es que su herida sea larga, que se esconda por mucho tiempo y no la vean nunca las generaciones que guardarán todavía nuestro recuerdo. Ibañez, Vicente Blasco. *Los cuatro jinetes del Apocalipsis*. (Madrid: Alianza Editorial, 2008), 396.

[5] Uno de estos jinetes se detuvo junto a la entrada del parque. El caballo devoró con avidez unos hierbajos, mientras el hombre permanecía encogido en la silla, como si durmiese. Desnoyers le tocó en una cadera, quiso despertarlo, e inmediatamente rodó por el lado opuesto. Estaba muerto; las entrañas colgaban fuera de su abdomen. Así había avanzado sobre su corcel, trotando confundido con los demás. Ibañez, *Los cuatro jinetes del Apocalipsis*, 359-360.

[6] Estaba llenando por tercera vez los cubos y contemplaba de espaldas al teniente, cuando ocurrió una cosa inverosímil, absurda, algo que le hizo recordar las fantásticas mutaciones del cinematógrafo. Desapareció de pronto la cabeza del oficial; dos surtidores de sangre saltaron de su cuello y el cuerpo se desplomó como un saco vacío. Al mismo tiempo un ciclón pasaba a lo largo de la pared, entre esta y el edificio, derribando arboles, volcando cañones, llevándose las personas en remolino como si fuesen hojas secas. Ibañez, *Los cuatro jinetes del Apocalipsis*, 356-357.

[7] Fijate, gabacho – decía, espantando con los chorros de humo de su cigarro a los mosquitos que volteaban en torno de él-. Yo soy español, tú francés, Karl es alemán, mis niñas argentinas, el cocinero ruso, su ayudante griego, el peón de cuadra inglés, las chinas de la cocina unas son del país, otras gallegas o italianas, y entre los peones hay de todas castas y leyes. ¡Y todos vivemos en paz! En Europa tal vez nos habríamos golpeado a estas horas, pero aqui todos amigos. Ibañez, *Los cuatro jinetes del Apocalipsis*, 69-70.

[8] Landa, José Àngel Garcia. Los cuatro jinetes del Apocalipsis, de Vicente Blasco Ibañez. Verfügbar unter:
http://www.unizar.es/departamentos/filologia_inglesa/garciala/publicaciones/blasco.html, abgerufen am: 03.11.2011.

[9] El orgullo germánico, la convicción de que su raza está destinada providencialmente a dominar el mundo, ponía de acuerdo a protestantes, católicos y judíos. Ibañez, *Los cuatro jinetes del Apocalipsis*, 69-70.

[10] —No; yo soy alemán. Nazca donde nazca uno de nosotros, pertenece siempre a la madre Alemania.(...)
—Ustedes eran celtas miserables, sumidos en la vileza de una raza inferior y mestizados por el latinismo de Roma, lo que hacía aún más triste su situación. Afortunadamente, fueron conquistados por los godos y otros pueblos de nuestra raza, que les infundieron la dignidad de personas. No olvide usted, joven, que los vándalos fueron los abuelos de los prusianos actuales. Ibañez, *Los cuatro jinetes del Apocalipsis*, 125.

[11] Con la seguridad de un catedrático que no espera ser refutado por sus oyentes, explicó la superioridad de la raza germánica. Los hombres estaban divididos en dos grupos: dolicocéfalos y braquicéfalos, según la conformación de su cráneo. Otra distinción científica los repartía en

hombres de cabellos rubios o de cabellos negros. Los dolicocéfalos representaban pureza de raza, mentalidad superior. Los braquicéfalos eran mestizos, con todos los estigmas de la degeneración. El germano, dolicocéfalo por excelencia, era el único heredero de los primitivos arios. Todos los otros pueblos, especialmente los del Sur de Europa, llamados «latinos», pertenecían a una humanidad degenerada. Ibañez, *Los cuatro jinetes del Apocalipsis*, 126.

[12] Hablaba de las futuras conquistas como si fuesen muestras de distinción con que su país iba a favorecer a los demás pueblos. Éstos seguirían viviendo políticamente lo mismo que antes, con sus gobiernos propios, pero sometidos a la dirección de la raza germánica, como menores que necesitan la mano dura de un maestro. Formarían los Estados Unidos mundiales, con un presidente hereditario y todopoderoso, el emperador de Alemania, recibiendo los beneficios de la cultura germánica, trabajando disciplinados bajo su dirección industrial... Pero el mundo es ingrato, y la maldad humana se opone siempre a todos los progresos. Ibañez, *Los cuatro jinetes del Apocalipsis*, 130-131.

[13] Vamos a batirnos por nuestra seguridad y al mismo tiempo por la seguridad del mundo, por la vida de los pueblos débiles. Si fuese una guerra de agresión, nos acordaríamos de nuestro antimilitarismo. Pero es de defensa, y los gobernantes no tienen culpa de ella. Nos vemos atacados y todos debemos marchar. Ibañez, *Los cuatro jinetes del Apocalipsis*, 186.

[14] Navarro Mateo, *Blasco Ibañez y las novelas de la Guerra Europea*, 225.

[15] Navarro Mateo, *Blasco Ibañez y las novelas de la Guerra Europea*, 226.

[16] Auf der Homepage der Fundación del Centro de Estudios Vicente Blasco Ibáñez ist eine weitere Verfilmung aus dem Jahre 1917 unter der Regie von André Huzé verzeichnet. Doch sie gibt keine Auskunft über deren Verbleib. Verfügbar unter: http://www.blascoibanez.es/filmografia.html abgerufen am: 03.11.2011.

[17] Einen interessanten Forschungsbeitrag im deutschsprachigen Raum zu den mythischen Aspekten stellt sicherlich die Arbeit von Cornelia Moser: *„Donde Espumoso El Mar..." – Rediskursivierungen von Mythen im spanischen `realistischen´ Roman*, Aachen: Shaker Verlag, 2002, S. 107-208 dar.

[18] Weibliche Wesen, die die Seeleute auf den Grund der Meere oder der Flüsse bringen, hat es zu allen Zeiten in der Mythologie der verschiedenen Völker gegeben. Es sei hier bspw. an Iemanjá in der Ioruba-Kultur, an die Yara Amazoniens oder auch die deutsche Loreley erinnert.

[19] Im Jahre 1915 hatte Deutschland 30 U-Boote, diese Zahl stieg im Januar 1917 auf 154 und bei Kriegsende 1918 waren es 170 Unterseeboote.

[20] Margaretha Geertruida Zelle (1876-1917) war eine holländische Tänzerin, unter dem Künstlernamen Mata Hari bekannt, die von den Franzosen der Spionage für Deutschland beschuldigt wurde. Sie war als exotische Nackttänzerin und exzentrische Künstlerin bekannt. Die Doppelagentin wurde von den Deutschen unter dem Decknamen H21 geführt, arbeitete unter anderem in Frankreich und Spanien, wo sie Zugang zu einflussreichen, Politikern, Diplomaten und Militärs als deren Geliebte hatte. Sie gilt bis heute als bekannteste Spionin aller Zeiten (http://www.focus.de/wissen/bildung/mata-hari_aid_57757.html). Ihr Leben und vor allem ihr Tod durch Erschießung in Vincennes weisen sehr große Ähnlichkeiten auf. Daher kann davon ausgegangen werden, dass sich der spanische Autor bei der Figur Freya an der Meisterspionin Mata Hari inspirierte.

[21] Navarro Mateo, *Blasco Ibañez y las novelas de la Guerra Europea*, 41-42.

[22] De pronto una linea negra había cortado el mar: algo así como una espina con raspas de espuma, que avanzaba vertiginiosamente, formando relieve sobre las aguas... Luego, un golpe en el casco,

que lo había hecho estremecer de la proa a la popa, sin que ni una plancha ni un tornillo escapasen a la enorme dislocación.... Después, un estallido de volcán, un haz gigantesco de humo y llamas, una nube amarillenta, de un amarillo de droguería en la que volaban obscuros objetos: fragmentos de metal y de madera, cuerpos humanos hechos pedazo.
Un amigo mío, un muchacho de mi tierra – continuó suspirando-, acababa de apartarse de mí para ver mejor el sumergible, y se colocó precisamente en el lugar de la explosión....Desapareció de pronto, como si lo hubiesen borrado. Le vi y no le vi....Estalló en mil padazos, lo mismo que si llevase una bomba dentro de su cuerpo. Ibañez, *Mare Nostrum*, 347.

[23] Pero aún no había transcurrido un segundo, cuando algo vino a añadirse a este choque, desmintiendo las suposiciones de Ferragut. El aire azul y luminoso se arrugó bajo el zarpazo de un trueno. Cerca de la proa se produjo una columna de humo, de gases en expansión, de vapores amarillentos y fulminantes, subiendo por su centro en forma de abanico en chorro de objetos negros, maderas rotas, pedazos de plancha metalíca, cuerdas inflamadas que disolvían en ceniza. Ibañez, *Mare Nostrum*, 505.

[24] Los tres recordaron los meses de infierno sufridos recientemente en los Dardanelos, en un espacio de seis kilómetros conquistado a la bayoneta. Una lluvia de proyectiles caía incesantemente sobre ellos. Había que vivir debajo de la tierra como topos, y aun así, les alcanzaba el estallido de los grandes obuses. (...)
Estaban abriendo trincheras en un pedazo de terreno que había servido de cementerio a los turcos. Los vientres hinchados se partían bajo las palas, derramando los zumos de su putrefacción. Ibañez, *Mare Nostrum*, 380-381.

Volker Jaeckel 1963 in Fulda geboren, studierte in Berlin und Sevilla Spanisch, Germanistik, Politologie sowie Deutsch als Fremdsprache. Lehraufträge in Potsdam, Berlin (FU) und Jena, war 1997-2001 DAAD-Lektor in Belém (Brasilien), promovierte 2003 an der Friedrich-Schiller Universität in Jena in Romanischer Philologie. Seit September 2006 Professor Adjunto für Germanistik und Komparatistik an der Universidade Federal de Minas Gerais (UFMG) in Belo Horizonte. Gastprofessuren in Freiburg i. Br. 2009 und La Plata (Argentinien) 2011. Fellow des Freiburg Institute for Advanced Studies (FRIAS) 2010. Derzeit arbeitet er in Valencia (Spanien) an einem Forschungsprojekt zu Mythos und Propaganda in Dokumentarfilmen über den Spanischen Bürgerkrieg als Stipendiat der brasilianischen Regierung. Er ist einer der Leiter der Forschungsgruppe Krieg und Literatur. Letzte Buchveröffentlichung (Hrsg): *Olhares lítero-artísticos sobre a cidade moderna*, (Literarisch-künstlerische Blicke auf die moderne Stadt), München, 2011.

Schuld in Kempowskis *Echolot*

Valéria Sabrina Pereira

Das fiktionale Werk Walter Kempowskis ist vielfach wegen seiner Darstellung der Kriegsjahre kritisiert worden. Die Perspektive auf das bürgerliche Leben und seine eigene Familiengeschichte ließ wenig Raum für die Repräsentation und Diskussion der Schrecken des Krieges – Themen, die von vielen Kritikern für unerlässlich gehalten wurden. In Rahmen der *Deutschen Chronik* beschränkt sich die Präsenz des Holocaust auf die kurzen Erwähnungen in dem „Befragungsbuch" *Haben Sie davon gewußt?*, das die unterschiedlichsten Antworten von Deutschen enthält, die jene Zeit erlebten.

Erst 1993 publizierte Kempowski die ersten vier Bände des *Echolot – Ein kollektives Tagebuch* betitelten Projektes, in dem der Krieg zum Hauptthema avancierte. In insgesamt zehn Bänden wurden von 1993 bis 2004 anhand von Zitaten aus von Zeitzeugen verfassten Dokumenten entscheidende Momente des Zweiten Weltkrieges präsentiert, nämlich der Kampf um Stalingrad, die massenhafte Flucht der Deutschen aus den von russischen Truppen bedrohten Gebieten, die Invasion der UdSSR und das Kriegsende. Ausschnitte aus Tagebüchern, Briefen, Erinnerungen, Reden, Militärberichten und Radionachrichten wurden nach dem Datum angeordnet, an dem sie geschrieben wurden, bzw. auf das sie sich bezogen, um auf diese Weise eine Art von „kollektivem Tagebuch" zusammenzustellen, in dem der Krieg aus den verschiedensten gesellschaftlichen Perspektiven betrachtet werden konnte: Politiker, Militärs, Intellektuelle, deutsche Zivilisten, die von den Nazis als Juden aus der „Volksgemeinschaft" ausgeschlossenen und andere Opfer. Die benutzten Texte stammen teilweise aus bereits publizierten Büchern, aber annähernd die Hälfte des Materials wurde vom Autor über zwei Jahrzehnte hinweg durch Zeitungsanzeigen zusammengebracht, mit denen er nach Tagebüchern und Briefwechseln aus der Zeit von 1900 bis 1950 suchte, sowie durch Funde auf Flohmärkten und in Antiquariaten. Daraus entstand ein großes Archiv von unpublizierten biographischen Texten („Biografienarchiv"). Mit Ausnahme des Vorwortes ist die Stimme des Autors in den Büchern nicht vorhanden und der Leser muss seine eigenen Schlüsse aus dem so verfügbar gemachten Material ziehen.

Obwohl die Bücher diesmal exklusiv davon handeln, wie der Krieg von Zivilisten, Tätern und Opfern wahrgenommen wurde, stand auch dieses Werk im Visier der Kritik. Zitiert sei der Artikel von Klaus Köhler, der den Autor beschuldigt, dass er „die darin [im kollektiven Tagebuch] enthaltene Möglichkeit nicht [nutzt], den Mentalitätshaushalt der Volksgemeinschaft so auszuleuchten, dass in den scheinbar nebensächlichen Äußerungen des Alltags der Bogen erkennbar wird, der sich spannt von der für harmlos ausgegebenen antisemitischen Phrase bis zum Genickschuß".[1] Die Zitate in *Echolot* lassen viele deutsche Soldaten durch Texte in der ersten Person Singular zu Wort kommen, wodurch tatsächlich der Eindruck entstehen könnte, der Autor habe eine stärkere Identifizierung mit den Tätern angestrebt; aber wäre es deshalb angemessen zu behaupten, er habe keine Texte ausgewählt, in denen die Schuld der Beteiligten deutlich wird? Welche Texte von Zeitzeugen standen ihm eigentlich zur Verfügung, um die Bücher zu zusammen zu stellen?

In einem Interview mit Sven Michaelsen sagte Kempowski 2007: „Meine ganze Arbeit zielt darauf ab, unsere Schuld aufzuzeigen".[2] Diese Aussage wird vom Titel des „elften" Bandes der *Echolot*-Serie bestätigt: *Culpa*. Hier stellt Kempowski seine eigenen Tagebücher und die seiner damaligen Assistentin Simone Neteler vor, in der Absicht, die Arbeit am *Echolot* zu rekonstruieren. Der Frage, ob und in welcher Weise der Autor versucht hat, die Schuld der Deutschen sichtbar zu machen, soll nun in diesem Beitrag nachgegangen werden, indem die Auswahl der Zitate von einzelnen Personen in *Echolot – Barbarossa '41*[3] kommentiert und dabei grundsätzlich nach dem Anteil des Autors Kempowskis an der Gestalt und der Wirkung dieser literarischen Montage gefragt wird.

Barbarossa '41 ist der neunte Band in der Reihenfolge der Publikation und weist eine konzisere und entwickeltere Ordnung auf als die vorangegangenen. Aus Sicht der historischen Chronologie dagegen ist es der erste Teil[4] und handelt vom anfänglichen Ablauf des Überfalls auf die UdSSR im Juni und Juli 1941 sowie vom etwas fortgeschritteneren Zustand des Krieges zu Beginn des Winters im Dezember desselben Jahres.

Im Rahmen der Archivstudien zu meiner Dissertation,[5] die ich in der Akademie der Künste in Berlin durchführte, analysierte ich das in *Barbarossa '41* publizierte Material von 21 Personen. Schon während der Lektüre der Tagebücher der ersten von mir ausgewählten Person – Grete Dölker-Rehder – konnten bedeutsame Auslassungen festgestellt werden. Im *Echolot* wird dem Leser eine Frau mit mystischen Neigungen und Anhängerin des Nazismus vorgestellt, die wiederholt die

Großartigkeit der Taten Hitlers lobt, die aber vor allem darunter leidet, dass ihr Sohn Sigfried seit der Versenkung des Schlachtschiffes Bismarck, auf dem er Dienst tat, vermisst ist. Das wiederholte Auftauchen dieses Themas vom vermissten Sohn kennzeichnet die Texte von Grete Dölker-Rehder und macht sie leicht wiedererkennbar in dem Gewirr von Stimmen, die hier versammelt sind. Die erste Erwähnung des Sohnes erfolgt in ihrem dritten Eintrag vom 23. Juni, dem dritten „Tag" des Buches: „Von Sigfried natürlich noch nichts. Meine Trauer lässt nicht nach, aber meine Festigkeit nimmt zu. – Er lebt, und ich bete für ihn, das wird ihn schon erreichen".[6]

Dölker-Rehder feiert jeden deutschen Sieg und verfolgt den Fortgang des Krieges mit Interesse in den Radionachrichten. Sie ist überzeugt von der Größe Hitlers und von der Notwendigkeit des Krieges, was in dem Moment völlig deutlich wird, als sie enthusiastisch den japanischen Angriff auf die USA kommentiert: „Erst ging es um die Vormachtstellung u. völlige Neuordnung in Europa, jetzt wird die ganze Erdeinteilung wohl neu geordnet werden. Hoffentlich geordnet, – dann lohnt sich alles. Wenn aber die jüdisch-bolschewistischen Mächte der Finsternis siegen würden, wäre für alle ideal u. edel gesinnten Menschen ein schneller freiwilliger Tod die einzige Rettung vor Chaos u. grausamster Vernichtung".[7]

Sogar ihr Mystizismus scheint eng verknüpft mit ihrer nazistischen Einstellung, was bereits vom ersten Zitat belegt wird, in dem sie bedauert, dass „man der Sonnenwende kaum gedenkt".[8] Doch dieser Mystizismus wird noch stärker von ihrem Aberglauben bestimmt, der sie dazu treibt, auch die unbedeutendsten „Zeichen" als Nachrichten vom Überleben ihres Sohnes zu deuten, oder – viel seltener – als Hinweise auf seinen Tod. Träume, der zerbrochene Stein in einem glückbringenden Ring, sogar die Blüte einer ihr von Sigfried geschenkten Pflanze werden als "klare" Zeichen interpretiert, was sie jedoch nicht daran hindert, zwischen blindem Glauben und Verzweiflung zu schwanken. Ihre Beziehung zum Verschwinden des Sohns ist obsessiv.

In *Barbarossa '41* gibt es wenige Erwähnungen von Sigfrieds Bruder Hartwig, der ebenfalls im Kriegseinsatz ist. Im Eintrag vom 6. Juli erscheint er als Quelle der Beunruhigung: „Auch um Hartwig muss ich in Angst leben. Die entsetzliche Sorge, sollte Sigfried denn doch tot sein u. Hartwig als unser nunmehr einziger, nun womöglich auch fallen, weicht keinen Augenblick des Tages u. der Nacht von mir".[9] Er wird nur ein weiteres Mal erwähnt, als er in der Vorweihnachtszeit die Familie besucht, zur Freude der Mutter, die aber auch die Beklommenheit des Abschieds verzeichnet. Die Aufzeichnungen in den Originaltagebüchern von Grete Dölker-Rehder im Archiv der Akademie der Künste eröffnen jedoch ein ganz anderes Bild.

Dölker-Rehder hatte die Gewohnheit, sehr ausführlich Tagebuch zu führen, so dass sie zwar in *Barbarossa '41* durchaus häufig zitiert wird, aber ebenso lange Abschnitte auch ausgeschlossen wurden,[10] unter denen sich zahlreiche Erwähnungen der übrigen Kinder befinden. Im Gegensatz zu dem vom Buch vermittelten Eindruck, hatte Sigfried nämlich außer dem Bruder Hartwig auch noch eine Schwester Gude. Diese wird in *Barbarossa '41* geradezu verheimlicht – der Name Gude ist nur einer unter anderen an der Festtafel des zweiten Weihnachtsfeiertages.

Im Unterschied zur publizierten Version, wird Hartwig im Tagebuch noch vor Sigfried genannt, nämlich schon am 21. Juni (??), als die Mutter sich darüber freut, dass sie eine Postsendung erhalten hat: „ein grosses Paket, d.h. es war ein Munitionsblechkasten voll interessanter Dinge"[11] und am 22. Juni, als sie sich Sorgen macht, dass der Sohn sich in der Nähe der Zone befindet, in der sich nun die Kampfhandlungen vollziehen. Auch am 7. Dezember, nach weiteren Erwägungen über die Möglichkeit, dass Sigfried selbst so lange Zeit nach dem Schiffbruch am Leben sein könnte, erkennt Dölker-Rehder, dass sie sich über Hartwig freuen sollte: „Ja, ja, so denkt u. denkt man daran herum. Doch bin ich nicht nur froh, sondern auch fröhlich, denn Hartwig ist ja da!" Auch wenn die Freude über die Gegenwart des Sohnes beim Besuch von Hartwig Ausdruck findet, tritt diese niemals in Konkurrenz zu dem Bild Sigfrieds, in klarem Gegensatz zur Situation im Tagebuch. Hartwig wird in *Barbarossa '41* nicht einmal erwähnt bevor das Verschwinden des jüngeren Bruders angesprochen wird. Er erscheint gleichzeitig mit Sigfried lediglich als Grund zur Besorgnis und nicht als etwas, dass die Leiden der Mutter lindern könnte.

Die Tochter Gude, im *Echolot* nur Bestandteil einer Aufzählung, gibt im Tagebuch Anlass zu großer Freude, da sich eine feste Partnerschaft mit ihrem Freund herausbildet, was die Tagebuchschreiberin am 4. Juli mit den Worten feiert: „Sollte wieder ein hellerer Stern aufgegangen sein über unserm Leben? Gude ist glücklich, da sie sich mit ihrem Freund Eugen Sch. einig ist. […] Ein großer Trost in unserm Kummer ist uns die Entwicklung dieser Angelegenheit, hoffen wir doch, dass sie Gudes Glück sein wird". In diesem Abschnitt vom 4. Juli finden nur positive Dinge Ausdruck, im Unterschied zu den anderen Tagen. Sogar zu Weihnachten, als sie glücklich ist über die Ankunft der Enkelin und sich mit den Festvorbereitungen beschäftigt, ist die Erinnerung an den verschwundenen Sohn immer noch ständig präsent – durch Fotos vom ihm und vom Schlachtschiff Bismarck, die sie auf seinen

Stuhl an den Tisch gestellt hat – und die Zufriedenheit über den kürzlichen Besuch Hartwigs spiegelt die Sorgen wegen seines erneuten Abschieds. Der oben zitierte Text zeigt eine Mutter, die sich ebenso um die im Haus verbliebene Tochter kümmert und zu echter Freude über die sie umgebenden Menschen fähig ist. Da die diesbezüglichen Textbelege aus dem Echolot ausgeschlossen wurden, ist Dölker-Rehder gekennzeichnet durch ihr Leiden, als Mutter abwesender Söhne, als Mutter eines vermissten Soldaten.

Dies ist freilich kein Einzelfall; viele der analysierten Texte enthalten Hinweise auf Familienmitglieder, die in den *Echolot*-Zitaten ausgeschlossen wurden. Der Arzt Hermann Türk ist am Ufer des Bug im Einsatz, als der Angriff beginnt; auch bei ihm sind alle Hinweise auf die Familie in den Zitaten getilgt. Türk ist hier nicht nur ein Arzt, der nicht nur von seiner Aufgabe, Freunde zu retten begeistert ist, sondern auch von dem ganzen "Abenteuer" des Krieges. Er besitzt einen guten, schwungvollen Stil und beschreibt seine Kriegserlebnisse mit einer Prise Sarkasmus. Nach den Kriegsvorbereitungen ist Türk begeistert über sein unmittelbares Bevorstehen und einer der ersten, die ihn in Barbarossa'41 ankündigen: „Die Spannung wächst auf den Höhepunkt. Im Radio immer noch nichts. Diese Nacht soll es losgehen! Das Wetter ist prima. Hitlerwetter, sagen wir".[1] Wenngleich Türk diesen Ausdruck gebraucht, gibt es in seinen Texten nicht viele Hinweise auf den Nationalsozialismus. Wenn er über Goebbels oder Ribbentrop schreibt, so ausschließlich weil durch diese neue Aufgaben übermittelt werden. Türk ist eher ein enthusiastischer Soldat als ein Nazi. Er beschreibt den Krieg, seine Bewaffnung, das Personal der Truppe und die mit Vergnügen durchgeführten Maßnahmen sowie, etwas später, mit einem gewissen Zynismus die verletzten Russen: „Im Bahnhof Koden liegen schwer verwundete Russen. Keiner kümmert sich um sie. Einer hat seine ganzen Eingeweide zwischen den Knien und – raucht. Das scheint wirklich ein tolles Volk zu sein. Das kann ja gut werden".[12] Allerdings abstrahiert diese Beschreibung auch in gewissem Grad von der Tatsache, dass die Russen Feinde sind und behandelt sie wie Gegner in einem Spiel. Die Zerstörung, der Tod und die Verletzungen werden von Türk angesprochen als Teil einer Normalität, an die man sich mit der Zeit „erst gewöhnen" muss, was von seinem Fahrer erwartet, der beim Anblick von Toten ohnmächtig wird.

Türk ist ein ausgesprochen eifriger Arzt, der nur zwei Tage nach einem Unfall, bei dem er fast in Schlammmassen ums Leben gekommen wäre und sich zwei Rippen gebrochen hat, 28 Stunden lang am Operationstisch steht und die chirurgischen Maßnahmen detailliert wiedergibt, mit denen er einen Kameraden vor der

Amputation beider Beine bewahrt. Obwohl die deutsche Armee mit großem Erfolg zügig vorrückt, ist die Zahl der Toten und Verwundeten enorm, da Türk sich in einem der vordersten Frontabschnitte befindet, kann er dies beobachten. Daher findet der Arzt kaum Zeit zum Ausruhen und gelangt an einen Zustand der Erschöpfung, in dem ihm „zum Kotzen elend" ist.

Vergleicht man das Buch mit dem Tagebuch aus dem Biografienarchiv, stellt man fest, dass nur wenige Auslassungen vorgenommen wurden, die in der Mehrheit die bloße Wiederholung eines Themas betreffen. Zwei jedoch sind von größerer Tragweite: eine bezieht sich auf die gerade eintreffende Post: „Eben kommt Albrecht. Er hat Post mitgebracht. Nun aber schnell hin! – 8 Briefe! Welch ein Glück. Unbeschreiblich ist dies Gefühl Post bekommen zu haben. Es ist wie Weihnachten. – Ich werde beneidet wegen meiner vielen Briefe. 5 Briefe von Elisabeth mit einem Bild von Bübchen. Das Bild muss natürlich gleich die Runde machen. Was ist er doch für ein allerliebster Kerl!" In *Barbarossa '41* wird Türks Familie nur ein einziges Mal erwähnt, als dieser in den Schlammmassen untertaucht und sein Ende gekommen glaubt, erinnert er sich an die Frau, den Sohn und seine Eltern. Im oben zitierten Text bezieht er sich wieder mit großer Freude auf seine Familie. Türk wird nicht nur von seinen Kameraden geliebt und geachtet, wie sich aus den im Buch zitierten Stellen ablesen lässt, sondern er genießt auch außerhalb dieses Kreises große Wertschätzung. Keiner seiner Kollegen erhält acht Briefe auf einmal und nicht nur seine Frau schreibt ihm so häufig, er erhält auch drei Briefe von anderen Absendern.

Die andere Auslassung findet sich im letzten Tagebucheintrag Türks von 1941, in dem der Arzt teilweise seine Heimreise schildert. Diese wird im *Echolot* unter dem 9. Dezember dargestellt und setzt sich bis zu seiner Ankunft in Deutschland fort. Obwohl der Text nicht datiert ist, beginnen die Aufzeichnungen vom Januar 1942 mit der Information dass er sich bereits seit einem Monat im Lazarett befindet, was darauf schließen lässt, dass er bereits Mitte Dezember in Deutschland ankam. Sein Bericht ist bewegt und bewegend und steigert sich mit der Annäherung an die Heimat, der ersten Gelegenheit, sich zu rasieren, auf deutsche Frauen zu treffen und sogar ein Bier zu trinken, doch er erreicht seinen Höhepunkt, als er beschließt, einen Abstecher nach Hause zu machen, bevor er sich im Militärhospital meldet (wo er mindestens ein Jahr lang stationiert sein wird, wie das Tagebuch von 1942 bezeugt). „Die Taxe hält. Morgens 6 Uhr. Was würde jetzt Elisabeth sagen? Warum darf das nicht sein? – Nur einmal noch. – Das Herz will zerbrechen. – Mutti öffnet. Erstaunen. – Angst! Dann schallt von oben eine helle Kinderstimme: ‚Papa!' Ich drücke ihn so ganz fest an mich. Alle Schmerzen der Wunde sind vergessen. Dicke Tränen stehen in meinen Augen. / Daheim und doch nicht!"

Die Erzählung von der Heimkehr eines Soldaten, ohne deutliche Hinweise auf seine baldige Rückkehr (aufs Schlachtfeld oder, wie hier, ins Lazarett) würde dem Leser nicht nur den Eindruck einer abgeschlossenen Geschichte hervorrufen, sondern auch eine gewisse Erleichterung verschaffen, geradezu wie ein Happyend. Außerdem ist das Bild des Vaters, der seinen Sohn wiedersieht, so bewegend, es enthält soviel Pathos, dass es deutlich mehr Sympathie weckt als Türks Texte vom Kriegsgeschehen durch ihre gelungene stilistische Gestaltung bzw. seine Hingabe an die Pflege der Kameraden. Der Arzt bleibt beschränkt auf das Bild eines Kriegsbegeisterten. Seine Berichte im *Barbarossa '41* gehören ausschließlich der Sphäre des Gefechts an.

Das ähnelt in vieler Hinsicht dem Befund der Analyse des vom Leutnant Georg Kreuter geschriebenen Materials, eine der am häufigsten im ganzen Buch zitierten Stimmen. Wie Türk ist Kreuter sehr begeistert und beschreibt mit Vorliebe den Krieg und Gefechtssituationen; sein Stil ist ebenfalls ziemlich elaboriert, aber es gelingt ihm nicht, einen Sympathieeffekt hervorzurufen. Die Funktion, die beide im Krieg ausüben, dürfte einen starken Einfluß darauf haben: während Türk Leben rettete (auch wenn seine Kameraden Täter sind), beteiligt sich Kreuter an den Schlachten mit ihrem brutalen Gemetzel und beschrieb die Personen, denen er begegnete mit Arroganz und Vorurteilen. Kreuter vergleicht den Feind mit Hasen aufgrund der Art, wie sie davonrennen, um ihr Leben zu retten und macht Wortspiele von äußerst üblem Geschmack, wenn er den grauenhaften Tod beschreibt, dem die Feinde zum Opfer fallen: „Eigene Feindpanzer säubern noch das Vorfeld. Wenn sie einen Bolschewisten 'anleuchten', sieht man eine gespenstige Fackel weglaufen".[13] Am 25. Juni beschwert er sich über das Schreien einer als „irrsinnig" bezeichneten Frau, die einen Säugling bei sich hat; dies ist nicht jedoch in der Lage, sein Mitgefühl zu wecken, denn er ist befriedigt, als sie mit einigen „der schlimmsten Vagabunden" zusammen hingerichtet wird. Er beendet seinen Bericht: „Ich bin froh, als dieses Kapitel abgeschlossen ist".[14]

Wie Türk präsentiert das letzte Zitat im Buch Kreuter mit anderen Verwundeten in einem Waggon, auf dem Rückweg nach Deutschland. Zuvor gibt es eine lange Beschreibung der Schlacht, in der er verletzt wird, als eine Granate in seine Deckung geworfen wird und die Pferde an seiner Seite tot umgerissen werden. Aber dies ist nicht die einzige Gemeinsamkeit der Zitate aus den Tagebüchern von Türk und

Kreuter. Wie im Fall des Arztes bieten auch die Aufzeichnungen Kreuters eine Beschreibung der Rückkehr nach Deutschland und des Wiedersehens mit der Familie noch im Jahr 1941.

Obgleich das letzte Zitat von Kreuter auf den 21. Dezember fällt, führt der Leutnant sein Tagebuch intensiv weiter und der Text der vier folgenden Tage wurde aus dem Buch ausgeschlossen. So wird der Leser nicht informiert über seine Ankunft in Deutschland, seinen Gesundheitszustand (es handelt sich nicht um eine schwere Verletzung) oder die Zusammenkunft mit der Familie, die immerhin flüchtig erwähnt wird: „Um 10.15 kommen wir an. Werden in das Laz. aufgenommen. Nach einem nützlichen Bad erhalten wir Besuch. Peter kommt mit seiner Mutti!" Lediglich das Ausrufezeichen markiert die Wiedersehensfreude, doch die Figur des Sohns wird vorsätzlich ausgeblendet, denn eine andere Erwähnung des Jungen wurde bereits fortgelassen, als Kreuter am 11. Dezember die jüngst erhaltenen Briefe kommentierte: „Endlich kommt mal wieder Post von zuhause. Auch ein Bild ist mit dabei! – Peter staunt ganz ordentlich!!" Mit dem Ausschluss der Vaterfreude beim Empfang der Bilder von seinem Sohn oder dem persönlichen Wiedersehen wird aus dem Buch jegliche Möglichkeit der Empathie mit Kreuter eliminiert. Was interessiert, ist nicht sein privates Familienleben, sondern ausschließlich sein Verhalten auf dem Schlachtfeld und die wüsten Kommentare in seinem Kriegstagebuch.

Bekanntlich konnten die Täter, so grausam sie auch im Krieg und im Konzentrationslager agieren mochten, liebevolle Ehemänner und Väter sein, ohne größere Ähnlichkeit mit den Personen, die ihre Opfer kannten. Dieses Bild wird jedoch im *Echolot – Barbarossa '41* häufig unterlaufen. Nicht, dass es auf dem Schlachtfeld keine Väter gebe – wie etwa Franz Wieschenberg, der Briefe mit seiner Frau Hilde wechselt, die Mutter von zwei kleinen Mädchen ist, aber diese Fälle bleiben vereinzelt und dienen als Beispiel für das "große Ganze", während andere die Rolle des "reinen" Täters übernehmen müssen.

Eine Auswahl von solchen Texten kann in den Tagebüchern von Ernst-Günter Merten gesehen werden, einem jungen Mann von 20 Jahren. In seinen Aufzeichnungen erzählt Merten über Tod und Zerstörung auf eine extrem unpersönliche Weise, ohne Kommentare abzugeben, die seine Meinung oder seine Gefühle durchscheinen lassen. Merten beschreibt den Tod seiner eigenen Kameraden in sachlicher Form, ohne jedes Mitgefühl: „Der Führer des Rgt. Radfahrzeug fiel schwerverwundet in russische Hände. Daß die Russen keine Gefangenen machen, ist ja bekannt. Jung, der Melder d. 9. Kp. fiel, 19 Jahre ... Wir haben ihn nachher aus der Schlucht rausgeholt und bestattet. 6 Russen jagten ihm eine MG-Garbe in den Bauch und stachen dann noch mit dem Bajonett zu. Plünderten ihn aus. Brieftasche, Kamm, Spiegel, alles lag wüst umher".[15] Hier gibt es keine Interjektion, kein Bedauern, nur die Beschreibung des Wahrgenommenen, das wie banale Fakten wirkt.

Heftigere Reaktionen finden sich nur, wo Mertens eigenes Leben in Gefahr gerät. „Zermürbend ist der Heckenschützenkrieg. Stundenlang in glühender Sonne im Korn liegen und wenn man nur den Kopf hebt, huuih, da pfeift es von vorne aus den Bäumen. Mit einer MG-Garbe die Halunken aus dem Baum jagen, geht auch nicht, weil dahinter dt. Truppen sind. Na, schließlich sind wir doch in den Hof gekommen und haben uns die Burschen nacheinander gekrallt. Und wo sie nicht freiwillig kamen, haben wir sie ausgeräuchert. Einfach die Gehöfte angesteckt. Der Troß hat es nachher dauernd so gemacht. Mit dem Kolben zusammengeschlagen haben sie die Bengels, wenn sie sie bekamen. Geschah ihnen ganz recht! Es gibt nichts Gemeineres als diese Schüsse hinter der kämpfenden Truppe!"[16] Hier zeigt Merten wiederum, dass seine Perspektive völlig einseitig ist. Was die Feinde tun, ist „gemein", aber er selbst glaubt, dass die Vernichtung dieser Feinde gerecht ist, da sie seine eigene Existenz gefährdet haben. Für ihn sind die Russen tatsächlich die „Schurken" der Geschichte, denn er ist unfähig, sein eigenes Handeln im Krieg in Frage zu stellen.

In Mertens Kurzbiographie am Ende des Buches findet sich lediglich die Information, dass er ein Pastorensohn aus Hildesheim war. Im *Echolot* lässt sich allerdings nichts über die Art seiner Religiosität erfahren. Sein Tagebuch ist in den Dezembereinträgen voll von Aussagen über den wahren Sinn der Weihnacht und der Geburt Christi, aber in der dieser Kriegsphase entsprechenden zweiten Hälfte des Buches fehlen die Einträge von Merten völlig. Seine Betrachtungen über das Weihnachtsfest hindern ihn nicht, eine unpersönliche Einstellung dem Krieg gegenüber einzunehmen und sie stehen für ihn auch nicht im Konflikt zur nazistischen Ideologie (die Ankunft des Neuen Jahres wird im Tagebuch mit der Zeichnung einer aufgehenden Sonne unter einem Hakenkreuz begrüßt).

Dabei ist es nicht so, dass das Thema Weihnachten an sich aus *Barbarossa '41* ausgeschlossen worden wäre, wovon sich jeder Leser leicht überzeugen kann. Der ganze zweite Teil des Buches wird von Kommentaren über die Weihnacht und das Fest durchzogen, wobei es mehr um das Feiern als um den eigentlich christlichen Gehalt geht. Figuren des zweiten Teils mit deutlich religiöser Prägung sind z. B. Jochen Klepper und Wolfgang Buff. Obgleich Buff an der Belagerung von Leningrad teilnimmt, verkörpert er hier einen "guten Kerl", der ständig um seine Familie besorgt ist und seine Kurzbiographie informiert darüber, dass er beim Versuch, einem russischen Soldaten Hilfe zu leisten, umkommt. Es scheint, als würde der Autor Kempowski entscheiden, wer von Christus sprechen darf und wer nicht. Und da die Handlungen und vor allem die Reflexionen von Merten in keiner Weise die Gebote des Christentums spiegeln, kann er kein Repräsentant dieses Diskurses sein. Sogar Klepper[17] wird verkürzt wiedergegeben, weniger im Hinblick auf seine protestantisches Bekenntnis als in einer eher allgemeinen Weise. Anfangs, als er noch im Heer Dienst tut, werden die Erwähnungen seiner Familie ausgeschlossen: „Zwei Briefe von Hanni nach der Pause. Darunter der besonders erwartete Brief vom Tage der russischen Kriegserklärung".[18] In der zweiten Hälfte des Buches dagegen, als er bereits zu Hause ist und sich intensiv beschäftig mit den Weihnachtsfeiern und den Befürchtungen hinsichtlich des Schicksals seiner Stieftochter Renate, Tochter seiner jüdischen Gattin Johanna Stein, werden seine sentimentalen Erinnerungen an die Kollegen von der Front beschnitten: „Aus den Kameradenbriefen spricht eine große Wärme, sie sind eine Bestätigung für mein Leben unter den Männern, die ich nicht missen möchte".[19] Aus dem Zitat spricht die große Wertschätzung Kleppers für seine Kameraden, und auch wenn ihm das Leben im Krieg schwergefallen sein mag – er schreibt an anderer Stelle wie ihm auf dem Schlachtfeld der Gottesdienst fehlte – so wollte er doch diese Bindungen weiter aufrecht erhalten. Im Buch jedoch wird das Kriegserlebnis Kleppers klar von seinem Privatleben getrennt, es gibt eine eindeutige Zäsur zwischen der Darstellung des ersten Teils, wo Klepper nur Soldat ist und dem zweiten, in dem er bei der Familie lebt. Am Anfang werden Kleppers Familienbande wie bei allen Soldaten ausgeblendet, zumindest bis zum letzten Eintrag im Juli, der seine spezifische Situation, die "Mischehe" erwähnt: „Dabei sagt er mir, daß er mich zum Gefreiten machen möchte und es trotz der bestehenden Schwierigkeiten versuchen will. Ich nehme an, daß er dabei weniger an die Mischehe dachte, als an den auch bekannten Umstand, daß nach den neuen Verfügungen man erst nach bestimmter Zeit Obersoldat werden kann, es eine bestimmte Weile bleiben muß".[20] Die Erwähnung seiner jüdischen Ehefrau ist markiert wie eine Wende zum zweiten Teil, der just mit Klepper eröffnet wird, nämlich wie dieser den Advent begeht und damit nur noch als religiöser Dichter in Erscheinung tritt. So wird eine scharfe Kluft zwischen dem ersten und zweiten Teil eingeführt, durch die sich Klepper in zwei verschiedene Menschen aufspaltet. Seine Sorge um die gefährdete Familie und sein Christentum werden offenbar nicht in Einklang mit der Beteiligung am Krieg verstanden und werden daher auch in der Phase eliminiert, in der er als Soldat und Täter agierte.

Im Verlauf meiner Recherche am Archivmaterial zum *Echolot* konnte ich feststellen, dass der größte Teil der Täter sich auf eine beträchtlich humanere Weise darstellte, wenn man Zugang zu ihren Originaldokumenten erhielt. Türk ist mit Hingabe Arzt und liebevoller Gatte; Kreuter wird beglückt von Nachrichten von seinem kleinen Sohn; Merten schreibt seine Tagebücher, um sie einem früheren Freund zu schicken, dessen Zuneigung er wiedergewinnen möchte; Buff ist der Soldat, deren Briefe parallel in Deutschland und Russland herausgegeben werden, um die Einweihung des größten deutschen Soldatenfriedhofs in St. Petersburg / Sologubowka zu begehen;[21] und sogar der entschiedene Nazi Helmut N. erweist sich als weniger böse, wenn er kurz vor seinem Tod in einem Brief an seine Frau voller Entsetzen schreibt: „Sie haben Flugblätter abgeworfen, mit Fotos. Wie ist es möglich, daß all das geschehen konnte?"[22]

Man kann nicht behaupten, dass Kempowski absichtlich eine Auswahl von weniger belasteten Tätern getroffen habe, gerade weil viel von dem Material, was das Mitgefühl mit diesen Personen weckt, aus dem publizierten Text eliminiert wurde. Es dürfte eher so sein, dass zahlreiche von den privaten Einsendungen zu Kempowskis Biografienarchiv ebenso wie die als selbständige Publikationen erschienenen Kriegstagebücher und -briefe (etwa die Bücher von Buff und Helmut N.) von Familienangehörigen präsentiert wurden, die sich nicht unbedingt dafür schämten, was ihre Väter und Brüder im Krieg getan hatten. Diese Dokumente bieten eine gewissermaßen gemäßigte Perspektive, die auch unter heutigen Gesichtspunkten nicht prinzipiell als Schande gelten muss. Selbst im Fall Georg Kreuter, dessen Texte dem Leser wenig ersparen, war es der Sohn, der die Tagebücher an das Archiv sandte, weil er seinen Vater als eine Art von Kriegsopfer ansah, der am „31. 10. 1974 an den Spätfolgen der Gefangenschaft"[23] starb, wie er in einem Brief an Kempowski erklärte.

Briefe und Tagebücher von bekannten Kriegsverbrechern werden normalerweise nicht von den Angehörigen an ein Archiv geschickt, damit man sie für die Nachwelt aufbewahrt. Solche Dokumente würden von der Familie, eher als peinlich empfunden, nicht öffentlich ausgestellt. So lässt sich nachvollziehen, warum der Autor größere Anstrengungen unternehmen musste, um schockierende Texte zu finden. Praktisch alle Zitate mit Beschreibungen von großer Brutalität gegen Juden stammen aus dem Buch „*Schöne Zeiten" – Judenmord aus der Sicht der Täter und*

Gaffer.[24] Hier sind verschiedene Berichte über den Völkermord während des Zweiten Weltkriegs zusammengestellt, aber diese haben mehrheitlich einen anderen Charakter als die übrigen Texte des *Echolot*, denn sie stammen aus späteren Aussagen über die Kriegszeit, die vor Justizorgangen gemacht wurden; hier beteuerten alle Aussagenden stets, das größte Mitleid mit den Opfern der Vernichtungsmaßnahmen gehabt zu haben, ohne dass sich nachprüfen ließe, ob das zum Zeitpunkt der Ereignisse auch wirklich der Fall war. Nur eine Stimme hebt sich aus diese Gruppe ab: Felix Landau. In *Schöne Zeiten* wird aus dem Tagebuch Landaus zitiert, der noch während des Krieges die Morde an den Juden mit bezeichnender Grausamkeit und großem Zynismus beschrieb. Seine Texte wurden ins Echolot aufgenommen und er erscheint so als einer der Hauptrepräsentanten für die brutalen Täter jener Epoche.

Untersucht man das Material, das für die Montage des Buches zur Verfügung gestanden hat und zieht man zugleich in Betracht, dass es geplant war als Erzählung aus der Perspektive der Zeitzeugen und verfasst in der "Hitze des Gefechts", versteht man, warum Kempowski in der Tat die Schuld der Deutschen herausheben wollte. Die Mutter des vermissten Sohns war permanent mit Hitlers Reden beschäftigt und unterstützte eifrig den Krieg, der ihr den Sohn entrissen hatte. Das Bild der Täter wird ständig entkoppelt von ihrer Familie, so dass die Wirkung der von ihnen während der Kampfhandlungen begangenen Taten stärker hervortritt und auch die religiösen Betrachtungen (nicht nur die zu den Festen) werden beschränkt auf jene, die grundsätzlich fähig sind zu einer differenzierteren Reflexion über den Krieg und ihre eigene Rolle darin. Sogar Jochen Klepper wird in diesem Sinn "zensiert", dass eine klarere Darstellung der Bedingungen unterbleibt, unter denen er und so viele andere zu leben hatten. Die im Krieg so gegenwärtigen Widersprüche werden von einigen typischen Figuren repräsentiert; Wieschenberg erhält die Rolle des Vaters, Buff die des zärtlichen Sohnes etc. Dieses Vorgehen erleichtert dem Leser die Identifikation der Schuld in dem Bereich, wo sie anzutreffen sein soll, diese Auswahl leitet seinen Blick. Und schließlich ist die Suche nach brutalerem Material wie den Texten von Felix Landau Ausdruck der Sorge, die Kempowski seit dem Erscheinen der ersten Bände des *Echolots* bewegte, wie die Publikation seiner eigenen Tagebücher belegt: „Wir brauchen noch ein paar richtige Nazis".[25]

Die Konstruktion des Werks konnte den Charakter des verfügbaren Materials – sowohl aus dem Archiv wie aus den Publikationen – nicht grundsätzlich verleugnen, schon weil eine umfangreiche Einbeziehung von Historikern und Soziologen das Konstruktionsprinzip des "kollektiven Tagebuchs" zerstört hätte, aber die Auswahl bemüht sich darum, bestimmte Aspekte wie die Schuld und die Brutalität des Krieges besonders hervorzuheben, ohne das Alltägliche zu vernachlässigen. Der vom Autor vorgenommene Zuschnitt hat immer die Tendenz, die Härte der Beteiligten zu betonen, wenngleich bei den in erster Person während der Ereignisse geschriebenen Texten sicherlich viele der Autoren nicht wahrnahmen, wozu sie gebracht wurden und die Erklärungen nicht so explizit sein können, wie es heute wünschenswert wäre. Es bleibt dem Leser des *Echolots* überlassen, diese Signale angemessen zu deuten und zu erkennen, wann das Bild verzerrt ist, das die Beteiligten vom Krieg hatten. Es ist aber die Hand des Autors, die ihn dabei leitet und ihm hilft, den Blick auf die entscheidenden Passagen zu richten.

---

[1] Köhler, Klaus. „Chronik der Apologie. Walter Kempowski und die Welthöllen der Menschheit"., 77. In: Arnold, Heinz Ludwig. *Text + Kritik. Heft 169. Walter Kempowski.* (München: edition text + kritik, 2006), 72-81.

[2] Michaelsen, Sven. „Der Ärger muss raus". Interview mit Walter Kempowski. Verfügbar unter: http://www.stern.de/kultur/buecher/walter-kempowski-der-aerger-muss-raus-148204.html, abgerufen am: 03.04.2002.

[3] Kempowski, Walter. *Echolot – Barbarossa '41* (München: Albert Knaus Verlag, 2002).

[4] Kempowskis Titel für der Band lautete gemäß den in der Akademie der Künste einsehbaren Typoskripten: Echolot I.

[5] Die Dissertation wurde mithilfe von Stipendien der brasilianischen Stiftung FAPESP und des DAAD realisiert.

[6] Kempowski, Echolot – Barbarossa '41, 53.

[7] Kempowski, Echolot – Barbarossa '41, 366.

[8] Kempowski, Echolot – Barbarossa '41, 10.

[9] Kempowski, Echolot – Barbarossa '41, 252.

[10] Ich möchte darauf hinweisen, dass im Gegensatz zu dem, was im Echolot behauptet wird, nicht alle Auslassungen innerhalb von Zitaten entsprechend gekennzeichnet sind; dies ist nur die Regel bei denjenigen Texten, die vom Urheberrecht großer Verlage geschützt sind, nicht aber bei denen aus dem Biografienarchiv Kempowskis.

[11] Sämtliche Zitate ohne Quellennachweis sind in den entsprechenden handschriftlichen Dokumenten des Biografiearchivs Walter Kempowskis in der Akademie der Künste Berlin nachprüfbar. Verfügbar unter: http://www.adk.de/de/archiv/archivbestand/literatur/index.htm?ng=literatur&we_objectID=336.

[12] Kempowski, Echolot – Barbarossa '41, 58.

[13] Kempowski, Echolot – Barbarossa '41, 152-154.

[14] Kempowski, Echolot – Barbarossa '41,100.

[15] Kempowski, Echolot – Barbarossa '41,113.

[16] Kempowski, Echolot – Barbarossa '41, 120.

[17] Klepper war und ist ein bekannter Autor von religiös gefärbten Romanen und Kirchenliedern.

[18] Klepper, Jochen. *Überwindung. Taschenbücher und Aufzeichnungen aus dem Kriege 1941.* (Stuttgart: Deutsche Verlags-Anstalt, 1958), 65.

[19] Klepper, Jochen. *Unter dem Schatten deiner Flügel.* (Stuttgart: Deutsche Verlags-Anstalt, 1956), 1002.
[20] Kempowski, Echolot – Barbarossa '41, 288.
[21] Buff, Wolfgang. *Vor Leningrad.* (Kassel: Volksbund Deutsche Kriegsgräberfürsorge, 2000).
[22] N., Helmut. *Briefe des Soldaten Helmut N. 193-1945.* (Berlin, Weimar: Aufbau-Verlag, 1988), 249.
[23] Man muss darauf hinweisen, dass der Sohn den Tod des Vaters als „Spätfolgen der Gefangenschaft" bezeichnet, obwohl dieser mehr als zwanzig Jahre danach an Bluthochdruck starb.
[24] Klee, Ernst; Dressen, Willi und Riess, Volker. *„Schöne Zeiten". Judenmord aus der Sicht der Täter und Gaffer.* (Frankfurt am Main: S. Fischer, 1988).
[25] Kempowski, Walter. *Culpa.* Notizen zum „Echolot". (München: Albert Knaus Verlag, 2005), 132.

Valéria Fereira studierte deutsche und brasilianische Literatur an der Universität São Paulo. Nach Stipendienaufenthalten in Deutschland verfasste sie ihre Mestrado-Arbeit über die weiblichen Figuren im *Nibelungenlied* und der *Völsungasaga*. Im Jahr 2011 promovierte sie über Kempowskis *Echolot – Barbarossa '41*. Zurzeit arbeitet sie als Dozentin für Deutsch an der Fakultät São Francisco der Univesität São Paulo und an einem Projekt zur politischen Dystopien des 20. Jahrhunderts.

ibidem-Verlag

Melchiorstr. 15

D-70439 Stuttgart

info@ibidem-verlag.de

www.ibidem-verlag.de
www.ibidem.eu
www.edition-noema.de
www.autorenbetreuung.de